Baseball's Comeback Players

ALSO BY RICK SWAINE
AND FROM MCFARLAND

*The Integration of Major League Baseball:
A Team by Team History* (2009; paperback 2012)

*The Black Stars Who Made Baseball Whole: The Jackie Robinson
Generation in the Major Leagues, 1947–1959* (2006)

*Beating the Breaks: Major League Ballplayers
Who Overcame Disabilities* (2004)

Baseball's Comeback Players

Forty Major Leaguers Who Fell and Rose Again

Rick Swaine

McFarland & Company, Inc., Publishers
Jefferson, North Carolina

Topps baseball cards used courtesy of The Topps Company, Inc.
For more information about The Topps Company,
please see www.topps.com

LIBRARY OF CONGRESS CATALOGUING-IN-PUBLICATION DATA

Swaine, Rick, 1950–
Baseball's comeback players : forty major leaguers who fell and rose again / Rick Swaine.
    p.   cm.
Includes bibliographical references and index.

ISBN 978-0-7864-7654-1 (softcover : acid free paper) ∞
ISBN 978-1-4766-1435-9 (ebook)

1. Baseball players—United States—Biography.
2. Baseball—United States—History.   I. Title.
GV865.A1S928 2014   796.3570922—dc23   [B]   2014001665

BRITISH LIBRARY CATALOGUING DATA ARE AVAILABLE

© 2014 Rick Swaine. All rights reserved

*No part of this book may be reproduced or transmitted in any form
or by any means, electronic or mechanical, including photocopying
or recording, or by any information storage and retrieval system,
without permission in writing from the publisher.*

On the cover: Tommy John (National Baseball
Hall of Fame Library, Cooperstown, New York)

Manufactured in the United States of America

*McFarland & Company, Inc., Publishers
Box 611, Jefferson, North Carolina 28640
www.mcfarlandpub.com*

Table of Contents

Introduction 1

1. Tommy John — 5
2. Hank Greenberg — 10
3. Smoky Joe Wood — 16
4. Monty Stratton — 21
5. Bo Jackson — 25
6. Eric Davis — 30
7. Andres Galarraga — 36
8. Ted Williams — 40
9. Stan Musial — 47
10. Grover Cleveland Alexander — 54
11. Rabbit Maranville — 60
12. Willie McCovey — 65
13. Eddie Waitkus — 70
14. Tony Conigliaro — 74
15. Charley Gelbert — 79
16. Dennis Eckersley — 84
17. Red Schoendienst — 91
18. Rico Carty — 97
19. Dave Dravecky — 103
20. Jack Quinn — 108
21. John Hiller — 114
22. Steve Howe — 118
23. George McQuinn — 123
24. Luis Tiant — 128
25. Robin Roberts — 134
26. Babe Adams — 139
27. Mark Koenig — 146
28. Orlando Hernandez — 150
29. Sal Maglie — 155
30. Jimmie Wilson — 161
31. Satchel Paige — 166
32. Darryl Strawberry and Dwight "Doc" Gooden — 173
33. Dennis Martinez — 183
34. Fernando Valenzuela — 188
35. Julio Franco — 194
36. Johnny Lindell — 198
37. Fred Mitchell — 203
38. Tony Cuccinello — 208
39. Van Lingle Mungo — 213

Appendix: Comeback Player of the Year Award 221
Chapter Notes 223
Bibliography 231
Index 235

Introduction

The comeback may be the most compelling phenomenon in sports. No true fan can resist rooting for the punch-drunk ex-champion gathering his last bit of strength to regain the title, or the aging former star quarterback coming off the bench to rally his charges to victory, or the sore-armed veteran hurler coaxing one more season from his tortured wing.

The intrigue of the comeback is obvious. Everyone loves an underdog. Overcoming adversity to rise to the top is a feat admired by all yet accomplished by few. Far fewer are able to survive a fall from the heights and claw their way back to the top a second time.

According to *Webster's*, the term *comeback* was coined in 1889. It's possible that the world of sports, with its natural tendency to simplify complex ideas and concepts into a few syllables, is where the term originated. *Oxford*, in fact, even refers to sports, defining a comeback as "a return by a well-known person, especially an entertainer or sports player, to the activity in which they have formerly been successful."

For decades, sports comebacks have been the subject of numerous films and a recurring theme in sports novels. The classic sports comeback story is familiar to everyone. A faded star, staggered by age, assorted injuries, or personal problems, struggles to hang on to the remnants of a once proud career. Our hero will have already been written off by the powers that be (the front office, the press, and the fans) but will take advantage of a last slim chance to get back in the lineup. Through experience, guile, pure willpower, or fate the old warhorse rallies for one more heroic effort—exhorting one more roar from the crowd, savoring the adulation one last time.

Sound familiar? Well, every comeback covered in this book includes at least a piece of that story.

Comebacks in individual sports like tennis, boxing, or golf occur more commonly than in team sports, as athletes in these games have more control over their destiny. They can make their own schedule and pick their spots to return to competition. In team sports such as baseball, football, basketball, hockey, and soccer, the athlete is subject to the vagaries of league schedules, economics, managerial prejudices, and the needs of the team.

Of the major team sports, baseball seems to lend itself more readily to individual player comebacks than the others. This is perhaps because of baseball's unique status as an individual sport within a team sport. While teamwork is certainly critical to the success of a baseball squad, each player regularly competes unassisted within the framework of the team. It's strictly one on one when a batter steps in the box against a pitcher.

Another reason for more dramatic comebacks in baseball is that purely physical attributes, such as stamina, raw strength, and sheer speed are less critical on the diamond, while finesse talents, like hand-eye coordination and quick reflexes, are more important. One seldom hears a football coach urge his players to "loosen up," but a pitcher can actually be more effective taking something off his fastball, and a hitter can be more successful cutting down on his swing. In addition, baseball players have more career flexibility because positions are not tied to physical size. Therefore a baseball player can more readily change positions to compensate for lost or fading skills. Baseball players also enjoy longer careers, providing more opportunity to make comebacks.

Although basketball and football have recently realized the publicity value of recognizing a Comeback Player of the Year, baseball has been doing it for more than a half a century. The practice started at least as far back as 1950 when the Associated Press touted Eddie Waitkus as major league baseball's Comeback Player of the Year. Soon the AP guys were honoring a top comebacker in each league annually, although the nominations were generally buried in the back pages of *The Sporting News*. In addition, chapters of the Baseball Writers Association of America and other sports-oriented organizations would occasionally honor a Comeback Player of the Year when a local boy happened to enjoy a noteworthy resurgence.

In 1965, *The Sporting News*, which still considered itself "The Baseball Bible" back then, began selecting an official Comeback Player of the Year in each league. Unfortunately, the criteria or qualifications for consideration were never established—or at least never published—and have been at times hard to fathom.

For instance, the very first American League award recipient was 30-year-old Detroit Tigers first baseman Norm Cash, whose unremarkable 1965 campaign wasn't much better than his 1964 season. Three years later the publication chose Ken Harrelson, who did enjoy a fine 1968 campaign with the Boston Red Sox, but it was also his first above-average performance. Likewise, it was difficult to tell what that year's National League winner, Alex Johnson, was coming back to, since the 25-year-old had never established himself as a big league regular prior to winning the award.

The selection process failed to improve with age. In 1980, 24-year-old starting pitcher Matt Keough was honored for his "return to a former condition of prosperity"—as *Webster's* would have put it—that had resulted in a grand total of 11 victories from 1977 to 1979, his first three big league seasons. In 1992, Gary Sheffield was cited for an inspiring "comeback" from nagging injuries at the advanced age of 23.

After 40 years of such nonsense, Major League Baseball stepped up in 2005 to present its version of the award, but with criteria no more clearly defined. The official Major League Baseball Comeback Player of the Year Award would go to the player who has "re-emerged on the baseball field during a given season." (See the Appendix for a complete list of the winners.)

Therefore it is no surprise that Major League Baseball followed the same winding path that *The Sporting News* blazed in honoring baseball's best comebackers. In fact, the competing organizations have agreed with each other's thinking 13 of 16 times in the eight years they've simultaneously honored a top comeback player.

The majority of Comeback Player of the Year honorees have been established stars simply rebounding from a statistically subpar season or recovering from routine occupational injuries. Generally, these have been players who were expected to return to their previous level of performance. For instance, 25-year-old Buster Posey, of the San Francisco Giants, captured the award for his 2012 Most Valuable Player season after an injury put him out for most of the previous campaign. There were few knowledgeable baseball folks who doubted that Posey would pick up where he left off after winning 2010 Rookie of the Year honors. Many other award winners have been late bloomers who garnered a lot of attention with surprising breakout campaigns or average Joes who enjoyed a freakishly good season in mid-career. Since these players had never previously approached the level of performance they attained in their award-winning season, it's puzzling that they could be considered to be "coming back." A good recent example is Carlos Peña, who surprised everyone with a sensational 2007 season with the Tampa Bay Rays at age 29, performing at a level he had never approached before.

The last major group of comebackers consists of former top-notch players whose performance significantly declined, often to the extent that they were no longer considered to be valuable major league talents. Usually their age, reputation, or physical condition made it improbable that they'd ever regain their old standing, yet they managed to make it back. These are the type of players this book is about.

In this regard, the following working definition of a comeback was developed strictly for this publication: *A comeback opportunity occurs when an established major league star's value has declined significantly, and either his career appears to be over (or on the brink of ending), or he's been relegated to a much-reduced status (e.g., benchwarmer). The comeback itself has to be a return to something close to his former status or level of performance, even though it may be for a relatively brief time.*

This definition eliminates the numerous instances of stars simply rebounding from subpar campaigns or returning from routine, though often quite serious, baseball injuries, as well as the sudden success stories. Likewise, this definition eliminates the majority of players who returned from World War II military service in their prime, as well as stars who returned to the active ranks after voluntarily retiring near their peak, such as Hall of Famers Ryne Sandberg, Kid Nichols, and Home Run Baker.

Since there's no realistic or widely accepted statistical measurement to evaluate comebacks, the selection and ranking of the top 40 comeback subjects was, of necessity, a subjective process, done with the following criteria in mind:

- Historical significance—The impact of the comeback on baseball's championship races, as well as individual player record and awards.
- Uniqueness—The human interest aspect of the comeback. Physical or emotional disabilities overcome, as well as the age of the player and the length and irregularities of the road traveled back to the top.
- Dramatic content—The excitement or publicity generated by the comeback and surrounding circumstances, as well as the event's contribution to baseball lore and legends.
- Degree of difficulty—The magnitude of the obstacle(s) the player had to overcome to reestablish himself.
- Player's stature—The comeback player's overall reputation and standing in terms of fame, popularity, and career accomplishments.

Of course "artistic license" could also be added to the list to cover any undocumented, emotional, and possibly biased considerations that might have unwittingly allowed a personal favorite to slip in.

1

Tommy John

"It's an operation that's never been done before and we don't know if it will work," cautioned a grim Dr. Frank Jobe, the Los Angeles Dodgers team physician in September 1974. "The chances of him pitching again would be slim. A fair guesstimate is he'd have a one in a hundred chance. MAYBE!"[1]

More than 18 months later, on April 21, 1976, 33-year-old Tommy John took the first step on a comeback trail that would lead him to 164 more major league victories. That day he shut out the Houston Astros for seven innings, earning another start—which would lead to another—and another—and still others, before the baseball world was convinced that he was back. His wildly successful comeback would revolutionize the game.

Before the surgery, John was a very good major league hurler, though not quite among the game's elite. He broke in with the Cleveland Indians in 1963, but won only 2 of 13 decisions for the Tribe before going to the Chicago White Sox with John Romano and Tommie Agee in 1965 in a three-way deal that brought Tribe favorite Rocky Colavito back to Cleveland. With the White Sox, he was a key member of the staff of the latter day version of the "Hitless Wonders." From 1965 through 1971, he posted an impressive 2.96 ERA, twice tied for the league lead in shutouts, and was an All-Star. Yet he won only 82 games while losing 80 times in his seven-year stretch with the Sox.

He got better support after he was traded to the Dodgers for slugger Dick Allen prior to the 1972 campaign. In fact, his 16–7 won-lost record gave him the best winning percentage in the National League in 1973, but his career won-lost record was still only 111–103 at the end of that year.

Nineteen seventy-four looked like it was going to be Tommy's breakout season. At age 31, he'd overcome the control problems that put him among the league leaders in wild pitches and walks

Tommy John won 164 games with a bionic arm (1978 Topps card).

a few years earlier. He won his first five starts and sported a league-leading 13 wins against only 3 losses as he prepared to make his last start before the All-Star Game break. His ERA stood at 2.50 and he'd already thrown three shutouts. Despite his sensational record, however, National League All-Star Team manager Yogi Berra of the New York Mets had left him off the squad.

Although Tommy scoffed at the idea, he may have been trying to put a little extra mustard on his pitches to show Berra and the rest of baseball that he really belonged on the All-Star Team. At any rate, he wasn't pitching with his usual effectiveness in an otherwise ordinary game against the Montreal Expos. He gave up two hits, walked a pair, and threw a wild pitch in the first two innings, although the Expos failed to score. To start the third inning, he yielded a single to Willie Davis and walked Bob Bailey, before he blew out his arm pitching to Montreal first baseman Hal Breeden.

In his autobiography, *T.J.: My 26 Years in Baseball*, Tommy described it this way: "My first pitch to Breeden was ... strange. As I came forward and released the ball, I felt a kind of nothingness, as if my arm weren't there, then I heard a "pop" from inside my arm, and the ball just blooped up to the plate. I didn't feel soreness or pain at this point, but just the strange sensation that my arm wasn't there. It was the oddest thing I ever felt while pitching. I shook my left arm more baffled than concerned. My next pitch would be the last one I threw in a big league game for the next 21 months."[2]

He went on to describe that next pitch: "I released the ball, and this time I heard a slamming sound, like a collision coming from inside my elbow. I felt as if my arm had come off. I immediately called time and started walking off the mound."[3]

After taking X-rays, Dr. Jobe diagnosed a torn ligament, although he couldn't tell for sure without surgery. He told Tommy to rest his arm a few weeks to see what happened. After a month, he rejoined the team and tried to throw batting practice, but he couldn't even get the ball to the plate, which seemed to confirm Jobe's diagnosis. Jobe told Tommy's wife, Sally, "If there's only a slight tear, I'll surgically repair it and the rehab will be a short one.... If the ligament's torn at both ends of the bone, it's easy to simply staple the ligament to the bone, it will grow back, and he'll be pitching next year. But if it's torn in the middle," he continued, "that's the worst case scenario, because the ligament would be unrepairable. We'll have to transplant ligament from the wrist area of his right hand into the elbow or use a teflon ligament."[4]

Though similar operations had been performed on polio patients, nobody had ever tried it on the arm of a major league pitcher.

There was never a question in Tommy's mind if the worst-case scenario played out. A one-in-a-hundred chance was infinitely better than no chance at all. The operation was performed on September 25, 1974, and the extent of the damage proved even worse than expected. The ligament was torn in two with the skin and the nerve running through the joint the only thing holding the elbow together. The muscles on the inside of the arm were ripped loose also and were sitting two inches out of place, toward the wrist. One of the assisting doctors remarked, "It looked like a bunch of spaghetti in there."[5]

The surgical team extracted a six-inch-long tendon from John's right forearm and threaded it through holes drilled in the bone above and below the left elbow. In a three-hour operation, the tendon was woven back and forth across the joint and the muscles were repositioned.

After the operation, Jobe stood by his one-in-a-hundred estimate and advised Tommy to start looking for another line of work. But, he also said he'd talked to Dodgers owner Walter O'Malley and the team was willing to keep him on the payroll through next year to see what he could do.[6]

Boosted by John's sensational first half pitching, the Dodgers captured the 1974 Western Division Championship. When they returned to Los Angeles after winning the first two games of the League Championship Series, Tommy threw out the ceremonial first pitch right-handed. The Dodgers won the League Championship Series in four games but lost the World Series in five games to the Oakland Athletics.

On December 15, 1974, Tommy underwent another operation to unknot and reroute the ulnar nerve to correct a clawed left hand that had resulted from the original operation. Dr. Jobe said that the nerve would have to regenerate before John would regain full use of his left hand. A timetable for this was estimated at 18 months.[7]

Tommy spent all of 1975 doing exercises to rebuild the arm. At first he threw lightly to Sally, serving as his catcher. He still couldn't straighten his fingers so he had to shove the ball into his claw-like left hand with his right one. He reported to the Dodgers' Vero Beach complex for spring training and spent most of his time tossing the ball against a brick wall at the back of the complex. Progress was discouragingly slow, but gradually the hand improved and the arm gained strength. By August he was able to throw batting practice and after the season ended, he went to the Dodgers' instructional league for further rehabilitation.

Reporting to spring training before the 1976 season, Tommy knew he had to re-establish himself in the Dodgers' starting rotation. But fate still seemed to be working against him. In one of the first major salvos of the ever escalating labor-management dispute that's now part of the fabric of major league baseball, an owner lockout kept the players out of camp for three weeks. As a result, he did not get to pitch enough to prove he had regained his stuff.

When the 1976 season opened, Tommy was ineffective in his first start. The next day he was called into manager Walter Alston's office and informed that he would get one more shot. Dodger management had been patient and generous throughout his rehab, but there was much doubt that he could come close to regaining his form. The Dodgers were competing with the powerful Cincinnati Reds for the Western Division Championship and couldn't risk falling too far behind.

After 11 years in the major leagues, 124 victories, a radical reconstructive elbow operation followed by more surgery, and 18 long months of rehabilitation, it came down to one start. As the Dodgers lefthander prepared to face Houston in the Astrodome, he was well aware that every pitch could be his last.

Tommy's "last shot" started out shaky. He came close to being yanked early but managed to pull it together. Despite yielding eight hits and walking three batters, he held the Astros scoreless for seven innings before leaving for a pinch-hitter. He didn't get the win because the Dodgers failed to score against Houston ace J.R. Richard, but at least he'd earned a reprieve. In his next start, he pitched into the eighth inning to beat the Pittsburgh Pirates, and one of the most significant comebacks in the history of baseball was underway.

Taking his regular turn in the rotation for the rest of the season, Tommy ended the campaign with a credible 3.09 ERA for 207 innings of work. Due to lackluster support, his won-lost record was only 10–10, but he proved his arm was sound by completing six games and firing two shutouts. Not a bad effort from a 33-year-old has-been with a completely rebuilt pitching arm.

But the best was yet to come!

In 1977, Tommy astounded the experts by winning 20 games for the first time in his career. He lost only seven times and posted a 2.78 ERA, tying for third place in the league in wins and fifth in ERA. His performance boosted the Dodgers to the National League pennant, although they lost the World Series to the New York Yankees in six games. The next year was a rerun of the previous season as the Dodgers again lost the Series to the Yankees in six games. Tommy dispelled any lingering doubts that his comeback was for real by winning 17 games during the regular season, throwing a four-hit shutout against the Philadelphia Phillies in the League Championship Series, and pitching effectively in two World Series starts.

After the 1978 season, Tommy left Los Angeles to sign a lucrative three-year pact with the Yankees. He proceeded to win 20 games in each of the next two years, even leading the American League in shutouts in 1980 at the age of 37. In the strike-shortened 1981 campaign, he posted an excellent 2.64 ERA, although his won-lost record was an ordinary 9–8. When the Yankees faltered in 1982, the 39-year-old southpaw, who had a 10–10 won-lost mark in New York, was shipped to the California Angels late in the season. His four victories down the stretch helped the Angels capture the American League West flag.

Over the next three seasons, John won only 22 games against 36 losses with the Angels and Oakland Athletics. It looked like he was finished when Oakland didn't renew his contract after a horrible 4–10 won-lost mark in 1985. But at 43, he wasn't ready for retirement. He re-enlisted with the Yankees for the 1986 season and pitched effectively for them before his season ended prematurely with a torn ligament in his left thumb.

In the off-season, Tommy officially retired to accept a coaching position at the University of North Carolina. He had a change of heart, however, and returned to the Yankees for the 1987 season. At the age of 44, he astonished everyone with another improbable comeback, winning 13 games against only 6 losses. The next year he started 32 games and posted a 9–8 won-lost record. Tommy's major league career finally ended in 1989 when his record fell to two wins and seven losses.

For his career, John won 288 games and lost 231 while posting a tidy 3.34 ERA. He had the highest winning percentage in the National League in both 1973 and 1974, the year he injured his arm. He was a three-time 20-game-winner and a four-time All-Star selection, and twice he finished second in voting for the Cy Young award. When he retired, his 26-year career tied him with Deacon McGuire for the second longest of all-time behind Cap Anson's 27 years. (Nolan Ryan retired after 27 seasons a few years later.)

Yet, Tommy has never received serious support for Hall of Fame selection by the Baseball Writers and his fate now rests with the Veterans Committee. He has the most victories of any eligible hurler who has not been inducted.

But his incredible comeback may be the most important in baseball history. The phenomenally successful operation he underwent ushered in a new era in reconstructive surgery for pitchers and became forever known as "Tommy John surgery." Today it is a fairly common procedure for pitchers and other players of all ages and levels. John's legacy is a long list of major league pitchers who have successfully undergone the procedure that includes the likes of John Smoltz, Tim Hudson, Kerry Wood, Kenny Rodgers, David Wells, Billy Wagner, Matt Morris, and C.J. Wilson. Rookie phenom Stephen Strasburg had the surgery at the age of 21 in 2010 and veteran Jamie Moyer had it done in 2011 in order to come back to pitch at age 50. St. Louis Cardinals ace Chris Carpenter has successfully undergone the operation twice while long-time reliever Jason Isringhausen underwent the procedure three times. Yet, no one has come close to matching Tommy's post-operative longevity. Late in his career, when admirers marveled at his durability, he would joke that while he was well over 40, his arm hadn't even reached voting age.

"Tommy John surgery" has provided a lifeline for many pitchers whose career would otherwise be over, but it's doubtful that the technique would have gained acceptance and advanced as rapidly if "Patient Number One" hadn't engineered such a magnificent comeback.

In fact, almost 25 years later, John's comeback would place number 56 in *Baseball Weekly*'s ranking of the "Top 100 Things That Impacted Baseball in the 20th Century."[8]

Tommy John

Born: 5/22/43

Year	Team	Lg	G	IP	W	L	ERA	WHIP
1961	Dubuque	MIDW	14	88	10	4	3.17	1.51
1962	Charleston	EL	21	128	6	8	3.87	1.56
1962	Jacksonville	IL	8	34	2	2	4.76	1.32
1963	Charleston	EL	12	95	9	2	1.61	1.02
1963	Jacksonville	IL	18	102	6	8	3.53	1.51
	Cleveland	AL	6	20	0	2	2.21	1.43
1964	Portland	PCL	13	74	6	6	4.26	1.34
	Cleveland	AL	25	94	2	9	3.91	1.40
1965	Chicago	AL	39	183	14	7	3.09	1.20
1966	Chicago	AL	34	223	14	11	2.62	1.13
1967	Chicago	AL	31	178	10	13	2.47	1.07
1968	Chicago	AL	25	177	10	5	1.98	1.04
1969	Chicago	AL	33	232	9	11	3.25	1.38
1970	Chicago	AL	37	269	12	17	3.27	1.31
1971	Chicago	AL	38	229	13	16	3.61	1.32
1972	Los Angeles	NL	29	186	11	5	2.89	1.14
1973	Los Angeles	NL	36	218	16	7	3.10	1.16
1974	Los Angeles	NL	22	153	13	3	2.59	1.14
1975	Los Angeles	NL	(Injured—Did not play)					
1976	Los Angeles	NL	31	207	10	10	3.09	1.30
1977	Los Angeles	NL	31	220	20	7	2.78	1.25
1978	Los Angeles	NL	33	213	17	10	3.30	1.33
1979	New York	AL	37	276	21	9	2.96	1.21
1980	New York	AL	36	265	22	9	3.43	1.23
1981	New York	AL	20	140	9	8	2.63	1.24
1982	New York	AL	30	186	10	10	3.66	1.20
1982	California	AL	7	35	4	2	3.86	1.54
1983	California	AL	34	234	11	13	4.33	1.43
1984	California	AL	32	181	7	13	4.52	1.54
1985	California	AL	12	38	2	4	4.70	1.72
	Oakland	AL	11	48	2	6	6.19	1.65
	OAK-ML Rehab	(var)	3	17	0	0	4.76	1.53
1986	NYY-ML Rehab	A	3	13	2	0	0.00	0.59
	New York	AL	13	70	5	3	2.93	1.25
1987	New York	AL	33	187	13	6	4.03	1.38
1988	New York	AL	35	176	9	8	4.49	1.51
1989	New York	AL	10	63	2	7	5.80	1.71
26 Yrs	MLB Totals		760	4710	288	231	3.34	1.28

2

Hank Greenberg

World War II cut a wide swath through the careers of most of the great baseball stars of the 1940s. Many never made it back to the level of performance they had achieved before the hostilities. Future Hall of Famers like Ted Lyons, Red Ruffing, and Bill Dickey were already grizzled veterans when they entered military service and couldn't regain their form after returning. Many younger men also experienced difficulty resuming their careers. Johnny Beazley of the St. Louis Cardinals won 21 regular season games and two more in the 1942 Series as a 24-year-old rookie, but he added only nine more career victories after spending three years in the Air Force. Washington Senators infielder Cecil Travis hit .359 in 1941 before being drafted and suffering frostbitten feet in the Battle of the Bulge. Though he valiantly returned to play a couple of post-war seasons, he was never the same.

Fortunately most of the game's stars who entered the service at a relatively young age were able to successfully resume their careers. Top performers like Ted Williams, Bob Feller, Joe DiMaggio, Pee Wee Reese, Phil Rizzuto, Johnny Mize and Enos Slaughter were able to come back and complete lengthy, productive careers after sacrificing three or more years to the war effort.

But nobody sacrificed more years of his baseball career to the war effort than Detroit Tigers slugger Hank Greenberg, and nobody made a more stirring comeback.

Early in the 1941 season, Greenberg, the reigning American League Most Valuable Player (MVP), became the first major star to be inducted into the military. He was six months past his 34th birthday when he returned to resume his career almost 4½ years later. Despite having rarely picked up a bat while in Uncle Sam's employ, he jumped back into the Tigers lineup in mid-season to lead them to the 1945 world championship.

Greenberg was born in New York and grew up near Yankee Stadium. Both the New York Giants and Yankees scouted him in high school. Giants manager John McGraw thought the gangly 6'3" youngster was too awkward. The Yankees were interested, but young Hank astutely determined that his opportunities would be limited in the Bronx with Lou Gehrig around.[1] The Tigers signed him and agreed to let him attend New York University before beginning his baseball career. He lasted a semester at NYU before succumbing to the lure of professional baseball in the spring of 1930.[2] After a successful stint with the Raleigh Capitals in the Piedmont League, the 19-year-old was called up for a late-season cup of coffee in Detroit.

After two more years in the minors, Hank began the 1933 season on the Detroit bench. He soon took over the regular first base job, however, hitting .301 for the year with 12 homers and 87 RBIs in 117 games. Excluding the 1936 campaign, in which Hank was limited to 12 games by a broken wrist, he batted .329 while averaging 39 homers and an amazing 150 RBIs per season from 1934 through 1940.

Though the gangly youngster had worked hard to master first base, he unselfishly agreed to move to left field in 1940 to make room at first for hard-hitting Rudy York. Hank surprised everyone with a decent defensive job in the outfield and was rewarded with his second MVP trophy as the Tigers captured the American League pennant.

In September 1940, the United States had re-instituted the military draft as involvement in the war in Europe began to look inevitable. With the future of every mother's son at stake, the country became conscription conscious, vigilantly on the lookout for privileged duty shirkers. Attention focused on professional athletes, particularly major league baseball players. After all, these men were the best physical specimens the nation had to offer, and they were in the public eye.

A week after the Tigers lost a tough seven-game 1940 World Series to the Cincinnati Reds, Greenberg registered with the Selective Service System. The draft was a lottery type arrangement and, as luck would have it, he drew a low number. Married men and those with dependents or physical disabilities were deferred, but Hank didn't appear to fit those categories. That made him prime draft bait, especially with military and government leaders most eager to perpetuate the illusion that all able bodied young males would be treated equally, without regard to wealth, class, or status.

The Tigers star's draft status became a hot topic during the off-season between 1940 and 1941 for two obvious reasons. First, he was one of the top players in the game and second, he was Jewish.

Unfortunately, anti–Semitism was not confined to Nazi Germany during that era, and that aspect of what became known as "the Greenberg case" is difficult to ignore. Although Hank never requested a deferment from military service, he was publicly castigated when others suggested he might be able to get one. Industry was able to defer "necessary men" who were vital to the company's business, but the press howled when a draft official opined that the man voted most valuable in the American League might fit in that category. When Tigers manager Del Baker ventured that Greenberg might be kept out because of flat feet, the media attacked again. The unfortunate Greenberg became an undeserving target for armchair patriots across the country.[3]

"My number is 621. When it's called, I'll be ready. I have no intention of trying to get out of military training," Greenberg vowed. But his words did little to stem the irrational public outrage.[4]

The irony of the situation is that deferments for baseball players were relatively easy to come by in early 1941. After all, the United States wasn't at war. The attack on Pearl Harbor was still almost a year away. Yankees shortstop Phil Rizzuto received a deferment, while Washington stars Cecil Travis and Buddy Lewis were allowed to complete the 1941 season before reporting for duty. Philadelphia Athletics infielder Benny McCoy's requests for deferments were turned down three times, but appeals allowed him to finish out the 1941 season.[5]

Philadelphia Phillies hurler Hugh Mulcahy's deferment request was denied, however, and in March 1941, he became the first big leaguer inducted into the service. Contrary to the conjecture of the media wise guys, the fact that Mulcahy had been the losingest pitcher in the league in both 1938 and 1940 probably did not enter into the decision. A more plausible explanation for denial of his request and expeditious induction is that he was the last big leaguer scheduled to go in before Greenberg, and draft administrators didn't want to appear prejudiced by taking Hank first. Mulcahy, incidentally, was one of those who failed to make a successful return after the war.[6]

And then there was the matter of Hank's famously flat feet. In Lakeland, Florida, where the Tigers trained in preparation for 1941 season, Greenberg underwent the required physical examination to determine his fitness for military duty during spring training. The examining physician reported that Hank did indeed have flat feet and recommended a 1-B classification—available for limited service only. At that point the military was not drafting 1-B's. But an "impartial" review board subsequently determined that, flat feet notwithstanding, Greenberg was fit to serve in the army.[7]

On May 7, 1941, at 6:30 a.m. Greenberg became the second major league player to be inducted into the armed forces. As with the entire affair, the circumstances were unusual, to say the least. While many players were routinely being deferred for a year or more, Hank couldn't even buy a few extra hours. His induction date happened to fall on the very day that the city of Detroit had scheduled a ceremony to honor the 1940 American League champions and raise the pennant that Hank had done so much to help win. Local officials requested that his reporting date be delayed for 24 hours so he could participate in the festivities, but the army turned them down on the basis that it would set a bad precedent.[8]

Greenberg played the first 19 games of the 1941 season before his induction. He uncharacteristically refused to pose for photographers prior to his last game, in which he blasted two homers. Hank summed up his feelings as follows: "I'm bitter. Not about going into the army. I expected that. What I'm sore about is the way the papers hammered away at me, printing untruths and making a heel out of me. I'll be glad when this day is over and I'll be glad to get into the army. This has been an awful strain."[9]

He would be one of only five big leaguers who entered the armed forces during the 1941 baseball season.[10]

Hank made another statement after that last game that was less than prophetic. "I'll be back next year," he promised. "And there's no reason why I shouldn't be as good as ever." Unfortunately it would be more than four long years before he would don a Tigers uniform again.[11]

Although the country seemed to so desperately need the 30-year-old Greenberg's services in May, he was discharged seven months later when men over 28 years of age were released from duty. Two days later the Japanese attacked Pearl Harbor and Greenberg immediately re-enlisted—voluntarily.

He told an Associated Press reporter, "I have not been called back. I'm going back on my own accord.... Baseball is out the window as far as I'm concerned. I don't know if I'll ever return to baseball."[12]

Greenberg served his country with distinction, entering the army as a private and rising to the rank of Army Air Force captain. Since he had been one of the first players to be inducted, he was one of the first to be mustered out as the war began winding down in 1945. Now another challenge awaited him.

"Nobody has ever attempted to resume baseball operations after so long a lapse," warned *The Sporting News*.[13]

An Associated Press article cautioned, "He is the first of the really outstanding stars to try a comeback, after a prolonged service during which he and baseball were strangers. Many of the stars have had ample opportunity to at least keep in practice by playing on service teams. But Hank has had none of those assignments."[14]

"He is 34 years old," the article continued, "An age at which making a sports comeback after a long absence comes under the heading of almost super-human tasks. But he's the fellow [who] could do it if anyone could."[15]

Hank was discharged June 14, 1945, and was back in the Tigers lineup on July 1, playing left field and hitting in the cleanup spot. Almost 50,000 fans came to the park to welcome him back, curious to see if the missed seasons had eroded his great talent. He answered by blasting a home run to help win the game. The first-place Tigers were clinging to a 1½ game lead when Hank rejoined them, but extended it to 4½ lengths by the second week of July with Hank in the lineup. The surprising Washington club doggedly stayed on their heels for the entire stretch run, however. On September 30, the last day of the regular season, Detroit was scheduled to play a Sunday doubleheader against the St. Louis Browns, needing one victory to clinch the flag. With the Tigers down 3–2 in the ninth inning of the first game, Greenberg slammed a clutch grand slam home run to win the game and the pennant for Detroit. In his triumphant return to the major leagues, Greenberg batted .311, slugged the ball at a .544 clip, hit 13 homers, and drove in 60 runs in only 78 games. In the ensuing World Series, he batted .304 and belted two homers as the Tigers beat the Chicago Cubs in seven games.

Before the 1946 campaign, Rudy York was traded to the Boston Red Sox, clearing the way for Hank to return to his natural position at first base. He led the American League with 127 RBIs and hit a major league best 44 homers, but batted only .277. By his own admission, his defense at first base was lacking. Furthermore, he was feuding with Tigers owner Walter Briggs, who was annoyed about a photo of Greenberg in a Yankees uniform, taken while he was in the service, that appeared in *The Sporting News*.[16]

The Tigers fell to second place in 1946, and management felt the need to unload their aging, dissatisfied star and his hefty salary. In January, shortly after his 36th birthday, Hank's contract was sold to the second-division dwelling Pittsburgh Pirates of the National League. His first inclination was to retire, but Pirates ownership persuaded him to return for one more year as the highest paid player in baseball. He batted only .249, but banged 25 homers while drawing a National League high 104 walks. He also befriended young teammate Ralph Kiner and helped him develop into a Hall of Fame slugger himself.[17]

After the 1947 season, Greenberg retired as a player and went to work in the Cleveland Indians front office, helping to guide them to the 1948 pennant. He took over as general manager in 1950 and built the great pennant-winning team of 1954 that won 111 games. He later moved to the Chicago White Sox and was vice president of the team that captured the 1959 American League flag. Thus he was associated with the only three teams to interrupt the 1947–1964 Yankees dynasty. In 1963, he left baseball to pursue a successful career as an investment banker.

Greenberg, the first great Jewish major leaguer, was elected to the Baseball Hall of Fame in 1956. For his career, he batted .313, blasted 331 home runs, and drove in 1,276 runs in only 1,394 games. He finished with a .605 lifetime slugging percentage that stands as the sixth highest of all-time among retired players. The closest active veteran player is Albert Pujols who ended the 2013 season with a .599 career average. Since Pujols last topped .600 in 2009, however, Greenberg's sixth place standing seems secure.

But career totals don't do justice to Hank's magnificent accomplishments. Due to military service, injuries, and an early retirement, Greenberg completed only nine full seasons in the major leagues. Yet he led the league in homers and RBIs four times each, doubles twice, and slugging percentage and runs scored once each. In four of those nine seasons, Hank banged out 96 or more extra-base hits. Babe Ruth, who played 15 seasons as a full-time outfielder, is the only other hitter to reach that figure four times. For perspective, Lou Gehrig only did it twice, while Joe DiMaggio, Jimmie Foxx, Rogers Hornsby, Stan Musial and Barry Bonds only did it once, and Albert Pujols has only done it once, so far. Other notable slugging stars such as Ted Williams, Willie Mays, and Hank Aaron never reached that total, nor has active home run leader Alex Rodriguez.

During Greenberg's years of stardom with the Tigers, the team finished atop the American League four times and captured two world championships. In 1937, Hank challenged Lou Gehrig's American League RBI record before finishing one short at 183, and in 1938 he threatened Babe Ruth's record of 60 homers before ending up with 58 circuit blasts, a figure that's still tied for the American League high for a right-handed hitter. Interestingly, neither of those stellar performances gained him the MVP award, which he captured twice with less impressive stats. For his career, he averaged almost one RBI per game, tying Lou Gehrig and 19th century star Sam Thompson for the highest all-time. In addition to his proclivity for homers and RBIs, Hank was also something of a doubles machine. Though not generally considered to have the speed to stretch many singles, he slammed 63 doubles in 1934, the fourth highest total all-time.

Greenberg's 1945 comeback is one of baseball's most remarkable achievements. Hank was already past his prime when he rejoined the Tigers at the conclusion of a military stint that was much longer than most, and unlike many major leaguers who fulfilled their obligation playing for military teams during their enlistment, Greenberg had been stationed in China and India throughout much of the war, rarely getting a chance to play. Yet, after two weeks of batting practice, he came back to post a .311 batting mark that was higher than the .309 average rung up by official batting champ Snuffy Stirnweiss, Yankees second baseman. Furthermore, Hank's 13 homers and 60 RBIs in only 78 games project to league leading figures for a full campaign.

In other words, after all those years away from the game, rusty, aging Hank Greenberg returned to hit at a Triple Crown level for the remainder of the 1945 season and lead his team to the world championship. How could a comeback get much better?

Hank Greenberg

Born: 1/1/11

Year	Team	Lg	G	HR	RBI	SB	BA	OPS
1930	Hartford	EL	17	2	6	-	.214	-
	Raleigh	PIED	122	19	93	-	.314	-
	Detroit	AL	1	0	0	0	.000	.000
1931	Evansville	IIIL	126	15	85	-	.318	.851
	Beaumont	TL	3	0	0	-	.000	.000
1932	Beaumont	TL	154	39	131	-	.290	.863
1933	Detroit	AL	117	12	87	6	.301	.835
1934	Detroit	AL	153	26	139	9	.339	1.005
1935	Detroit	AL	152	36	170	4	.328	1.039
1936	Detroit	AL	12	1	16	1	.348	1.085
1937	Detroit	AL	154	40	183	8	.337	1.105
1938	Detroit	AL	155	58	146	7	.315	1.122
1939	Detroit	AL	138	33	112	8	.312	1.042

Year	Team	Lg	G	HR	RBI	SB	BA	OPS
1940	Detroit	AL	148	41	150	6	.340	1.103
1941	Detroit	AL	19	2	12	1	.269	.872
1942	Detroit	AL	(Military service—Did not play)					
1943	Detroit	AL	(Military service—Did not play)					
1944	Detroit	AL	(Military service—Did not play)					
1945	Detroit	AL	78	13	60	3	.311	.948
1946	Detroit	AL	142	44	127	5	.277	.977
1947	Pittsburgh	NL	125	25	74	0	.249	.885
13 Yrs	MLB Totals		1394	331	1276	58	.313	1.017

3

Smoky Joe Wood

There was no Cy Young Award back in 1912. After all, old Cy had only been retired a year. But if such an honor had existed, 22-year-old Smoky Joe Wood would certainly have been a top candidate. That year he won 34 games during the regular season and three more in the World Series to lead the Boston Red Sox to the World Championship.

Four years later, Wood was out of baseball, through at the tender age of 26. He'd been brought down by the bane of hurlers throughout the history of the game—a chronic sore arm.

Another four years later, the 1920 World Series opened in Brooklyn with Smoky Joe Wood in right field for the Cleveland Indians, cracking a double and scoring two runs to spark a 3–1 Tribe victory.

Over the decades, scores of pitchers have turned in their toe plate for a regular spot in the batting order. Most made the change because they weren't very good pitchers. Lefty O'Doul, who spent seven years futilely trying to establish himself as a pitcher before turning to the outfield, is a classic example. O'Doul, a one-game winner as a pitcher in the big time, was over 30 years old when he resurfaced in the major leagues as a hard hitting outfielder and went on to win two National League batting championships. Others were converted because their teams deemed their powerful bats or defensive talents more valuable than their pitching skills. The most prominent example is the great Babe Ruth, one of the best pitchers in the major leagues before he turned his prodigious talents from the pitching rubber to the batter's box. Jesse Burkett, George Sisler, Roger Bresnahan, Sam Rice, and Bobby Wallace were others who began their big league careers as promising moundsmen before turning into Hall of Fame position players.

Wood fit into neither category. When able to take the mound, he was still one of the best pitchers of his time. But when he could no longer pitch through the pain, he was forced to completely re-invent himself to stay in baseball. His return to center stage as an outfielder was more than a comeback. It was a complete transformation.

Joe's real name was Howard Ellsworth Wood. As youngsters, he and his brother were dubbed Joey and Petey after a pair of traveling circus clowns. The nicknames stuck and evolved into Joe and Pete.[1] As a teenager, he got his start as a professional with the Bloomer Girls, a barnstorming women's baseball team that wasn't above using young men in drag to stay competitive against male opponents. Joe broke into the majors with the Red Sox in 1908 at the age of eighteen and became a regular starter at nineteen, posting a respectable 11 wins against 7 losses. He progressed to 12 wins, with an impressive 1.68 ERA in 1910 and won 23 games the following year.[2]

In 1912, the young right-hander, who gained the "Smoky Joe" moniker in recognition of his over-powering fastball, enjoyed one of the most spectacular pitching seasons in the history of major league baseball. He won a major league high 34 games while dropping only 5 decisions as the Red Sox raced to the American League pennant. His .872 winning percentage also led the majors, as did his 35 complete games, and 10 shutouts. In addition, his 1.91 ERA was good for second place behind Walter Johnson of the Washington Senators, and he ranked third behind Johnson and Christy Mathewson of the New York Giants in strikeouts. In the World Series, his three complete victories led the Sox to victory over Mathewson's Giants.[3]

In competition with Walter Johnson, who was his senior by only two years and is generally regarded as one of the best hurlers of all time, Joe often came out on top. Early in the 1912 season, Johnson set an American League record with 16 consecutive victories, but Smoky Joe tied the mark later that same season. In fact, his 13th win in the streak was a 1–0 conquest over Johnson in a dramatic head-to-head matchup. During that momentous season, Sir Walter offered the following evaluation of his rival: "Can I throw harder than Joe Wood? Listen, my friend, there's no man alive who can throw harder than Smoky Joe Wood."[4]

After his sensational 1912 campaign, the future seemed limitless for the young hurler. But disaster struck in the spring of 1913 when Joe slipped on wet grass while fielding a grounder and broke his thumb. When he returned to action, he quickly developed a sore shoulder. He couldn't say whether he'd injured the shoulder when he fell or hurt it by altering his delivery to pitch with the tender thumb. Regardless, at the age of 23 he had irreparably damaged his magnificent throwing arm.[5]

Joe managed to keep pitching effectively for a few years, but he'd lost some velocity and the excruciating pain limited his workload. He posted an 11–5 won-lost record in 1913 and went 9–3 in 1914 with good ERAs both years. Though he was able to make only 32 starts over the two year period, he completed 23 of them. But pitching took so much out of his aching arm that he would have to lay off for an extended period after each assignment. In 1915, Joe had one last outstanding season as a pitcher. Appearing in 25 games as a spot starter and reliever, he won 15 games while losing only 5. Both his .750 winning percentage and microscopic 1.49 ERA led the league, but he was a mere shadow of his former self. In 157 innings, he struck out only 63 batters, the lowest

Former ace hurler Smoky Joe Wood starred in the World Series as an outfielder (Bain Collection, Library of Congress).

strikeouts-to-innings-pitched ratio of his career. Amazingly, the Red Sox had such a fabulous pitching staff that year that Joe spent the entire 1915 World Series sitting on the bench next to rookie pitcher Babe Ruth, who likewise didn't get a chance to throw despite posting 18 victories during the regular season.[6]

Ruth would get his chance in succeeding years and establish a Series record for consecutive scoreless innings pitched while winning three games without a loss. But there would be no more chances for Smoky Joe Wood the pitcher. The pain had become unbearable and, for all practical purposes, his spectacular career on the mound was over. By his own estimate he visited hundreds of doctors in an effort to cure his injured shoulder—to no avail. He ended up sitting out the entire 1916 season as the Red Sox captured another world championship.[7]

As the 1917 season approached, Joe was getting restless. The shoulder wasn't much better, but he was determined to return to the game in some capacity. Superstar outfielder Tris Speaker, Joe's old roommate and best friend on the Red Sox, had been traded to Cleveland the previous year, and he persuaded the Indians to acquire the sore-armed hurler. His contract was purchased for a reported $15,000—a considerable sum in those days.[8]

The Indians had acquired Wood to pitch, and he gave it a valiant effort. He pitched in five games during the 1917 campaign without much success. But he hung around through the season, pinch hitting and pinch-running occasionally, throwing batting practice, and shagging flies—generally just trying to make himself useful. "I'd have carried the water bucket, if they had water boys in baseball," he later admitted. "I wasn't the Invincible Joe Wood anymore. I was just another ball player who wanted a job and wanted it bad."[9] In fact, Joe declined his salary for most of the 1917 season because he didn't want to accept money under false pretenses.[10]

The next spring, Joe showed up at the Indians training camp in New Orleans without a contract for the 1918 season. Although the Cleveland brass may have still harbored hopes that the 28-year-old would be able to pitch again, Joe was intent on earning a spot on the roster as a position player. Even with the manpower and talent shortage resulting from the United States' entry into World War I, there was little reason for high expectations, however. Wood had been a decent hitting pitcher, but a career batting average of only .242 to date wasn't much to get excited about, and he'd never played another position.

In addition, the Indians were a solid team that had won 88 games the year before. The outfield was set with magnificent Speaker in center, flanked by hard-hitting Bobby "Braggo" Roth and leadoff man extraordinaire Jack Graney.

Wood began the season on the Cleveland bench. An opening presented itself when leftfielder Graney was injured in the first week of the season, but the Indians first turned to a couple of minor league first basemen, "Big Ed" Miller and Eddie Onslow, to replace him. Finally Joe was given a chance and he would not be denied. He took over the regular left field job and held onto it after Graney returned to action. In late July, with the second place Indians battling for the pennant, Joe moved to second base for 19 contests replacing injured Bill Wambsganss. He manned the keystone post well enough that the Indians narrowed the gap with the first place Red Sox by a couple of games. By the end of the campaign, the former hurler was filling the cleanup spot as the Tribe battled Boston down to the wire before finishing second.

For the war-shortened season, Joe played in 119 of the Indians' 129 games and hit a solid .296, second highest on the club behind Speaker among full-timers. His 5 homers and

66 RBIs may not sound like much, but both were enough for the team lead. In fact, he tied for fifth place in league rankings in both categories. Joe Wood had truly undergone an amazing metamorphosis, transforming himself from a washed-up, sore-armed hurler to a hard-hitting outfielder almost overnight.

It would be nice to report that Smoky Joe continued his progress and developed into as great an outfielder as he had a pitcher, but it didn't quite work out that way. When the war ended, the Indians found themselves with a glut of outfielders and began using him in a platoon arrangement. It was hard to argue with success as they barely missed out on the American League pennant to the ill-fated Chicago White Sox in 1919 and captured the flag in 1920.

Wood contributed batting averages of .255 and .270 as a valuable part-timer those two years, but perhaps more importantly, he provided inspirational veteran leadership to the team. When Cleveland's sterling shortstop, Ray Chapman, was killed by a beanball late in the 1920 season, Speaker, who'd become a player-manager, suffered an emotional breakdown and had to leave the team for several days in the middle of the pennant race. Joe Wood was the man who stepped forward to hold the team together as acting manager through that difficult period.[11]

In 1921, Joe enjoyed an outstanding season at the plate. Still being platooned, he played in only 66 games, but drove in 60 runs and posted a team-high .366 batting mark. The next year he won the regular right field job and drove in 92 runs to lead the Indians in that department, while hitting a creditable .297.

After the 1922 season, Yale University offered Joe the job of head coach of its baseball squad. In those days, the salaries of professional baseball players were more in line with the average working man, so the 33-year-old veteran, with nothing left to prove as a player, accepted the more secure position at the same salary he was making with the Indians. Over the next twenty years, he would become something of an institution at Yale.

During his abbreviated pitching career, Smoky Joe won 117 games against only 57 losses for a .672 winning percentage—a mark that is exceeded only by Whitey Ford and Lefty Grove among Hall of Fame hurlers. In addition, Joe's lifetime ERA of 2.03 ranks third behind Hall-of-Famers Ed Walsh and Addie Joss on the all-time list. In addition, he's one of only four 20th century performers to win at least 100 games and collect more than 500 hits in the major leagues. The others were Walter Johnson, Cy Young and Red Ruffing, all of whom collected their 500 hits as pitchers. Babe Ruth just missed the club, winning only 94 games before becoming the most prolific batter of all time.

It's interesting to speculate on what might have happened if Joe Wood had access to the medical treatment and expertise available to today's hurlers. He might have gained recognition as one of the greatest moundsmen of all time if he'd received proper attention for his ailing wing. Instead Joe got treatment from a chiropractor in New York who ordered him to fire a baseball as long and hard as he possibly could after each therapy session—no matter how much it hurt. After these throwing sessions, which often lasted an hour, Joe couldn't even lift his right arm and had to use his left hand to put his right one into his coat pocket. When that radical approach didn't work, Joe fashioned a trapeze in his attic and would hang on it for hours to stretch his arm out.[12] X-rays taken on Joe's shoulder years later would show that there was no lubrication left—it was bone on bone.[13]

For the Fenway Park 1982 home opener, the Red Sox honored Smoky Joe Wood by asking him to throw out the ceremonial first pitch. The 92-year-old former ace right-hander made the toss left-handed.[14]

Smoky Joe Wood

Born: 8/25/1889

Hitting

Year	Team	Lg	G	HR	RBI	SB	BA	OPS
1907	*Hutchinson*	*WA*	62	-	-	-	.190	-
1908	*Kansas City*	*AA*	32	-	-	-	.156	.338
1908	Boston	AL	6	0	0	0	.000	.000
1909	Boston	AL	24	0	3	0	.164	.407
1910	Boston	AL	35	1	5	0	.261	.673
1911	Boston	AL	44	2	11	1	.261	.764
1912	Boston	AL	43	1	13	0	.290	.784
1913	Boston	AL	25	0	10	1	.268	.674
1914	Boston	AL	21	0	1	1	.140	.376
1915	Boston	AL	29	1	7	1	.259	.692
1916	Boston	AL	(Did not play Organized Baseball)					
1917	Cleveland	AL	10	0	0	0	.000	.000
1918	Cleveland	AL	119	5	66	8	.296	.759
1919	Cleveland	AL	72	0	27	3	.255	.737
1920	Cleveland	AL	61	1	30	1	.270	.792
1921	Cleveland	AL	66	4	60	2	.366	1.000
1922	Cleveland	AL	142	8	92	5	.297	.809
14 Yrs	MLB Totals		697	23	325	23	.283	.768

Pitching

Year	Team	Lg	G	IP	W	L	ERA	WHIP
1907	*Hutchinson*	*WA*	29	196	18	11	-	1.25
1908	*Kansas City*	*AA*	24	178	7	12	2.38	1.00
1908	Boston	AL	6	22	1	1	2.38	1.32
1909	Boston	AL	24	160	11	7	2.18	1.02
1910	Boston	AL	35	196	12	13	1.69	1.07
1911	Boston	AL	44	275	23	17	2.02	1.10
1912	Boston	AL	43	344	34	5	1.91	1.02
1913	Boston	AL	23	145	11	5	2.29	1.24
1914	Boston	AL	18	113	10	3	2.62	1.13
1915	Boston	AL	25	157	15	5	1.49	1.04
1916	Boston	AL	(Did not play Organized Baseball)					
1917	Cleveland	AL	5	15	0	1	3.45	1.53
1918			(Did not pitch)					
1919	Cleveland	AL	1	0	0	0	0.00	0.00
1920	Cleveland	AL	1	2	0	0	22.50	3.00
11 Yrs	MLB Totals		225	1434	117	57	2.03	1.09

4

Monty Stratton

Baseball comebacks have long provided rich fodder for the film industry. And it probably comes as little surprise to all but the most naïve among us that artistic license has often been liberally employed by Hollywood screenwriters and directors to spice up the story.

In 1949 Metro-Goldwyn-Mayer (MGM) released *The Stratton Story*, the saga of Chicago White Sox pitcher Monty Stratton's heroic comeback to play professional baseball after losing his right leg in a hunting accident. Jimmy Stewart portrayed Stratton in the movie with June Allyson playing his wife, Ethel. Also featured was Jimmie Dykes, playing himself in a return appearance in a White Sox uniform after being dismissed as Sox manager a few years earlier. Former sportscaster-turned-actor Ronald Reagan had sought the title role. But he was under contract with Warner Brothers, which did not want to release him for the Stratton film because they thought it would be a failure. *The Stratton Story* became a box office hit, however, and won an Academy Award.[1]

After the film's release Stratton commented that "[Stewart] did a great job of playing me, in a picture which I figure was about as true to life as they could make it."[2]

Although the movie naturally focuses on Stratton's comeback, his baseball beginnings were also Hollywood stuff. He grew up in the tiny Texas town of Celeste, about fifty miles from Dallas. His father, a farmer, died when Monty was young, leaving the boy to help his mother operate the farm. Pitching for the town team, he gained local fame as "The Celeste Whirlwind" and was eventually signed by the White Sox at the age of 22 in 1934. He made his major league debut late that year after spending most of the campaign in the minors. He won 17 games for St. Paul of the American Association in 1935 and was called up to the Sox to stay the next year.[3]

Much was expected from the young 6'5" right-hander in 1936, but his first full year in the majors was a harbinger of the bad luck that would plague his career. Between bouts with tonsillitis and appendicitis, he made only 16 appearances and finished his first full season with a ho-hum 5–7 won-lost mark.[4]

After finishing third in 1936, their highest finish since the Black Sox scandal 16 years earlier, the White Sox opened the 1937 season anticipating a run at the American League pennant. And for a while it looked like they might make it, thanks largely to the work of young Monty Stratton. At the All-Star Game break, his won-lost record was 10–4 and he sported a sensational 1.95 ERA. He was named to the American League squad, but a twisted ankle kept him out of the game. On July 31 he won his seventh straight to push his record to 14–4 and put the second-place Sox 5½ games behind the powerful New York Yankees. But he injured his arm in his next start and had to leave the game in the fifth inning. He pitched fewer than five innings the rest of the season.

Monty came back to post a 15–9 won-lost record in 1938, despite missing the first month of the season with more arm trouble. Relying primarily on a trick pitch called the "Gander," which seemed to dart in and out as it approached the strike zone, the 26-year-old hurler seemed destined for greatness if his arm held up. Charlie Grimm, manager of the cross-town Cubs, ungrammatically called him "the nearest pitcher to Grover Cleveland Alexander I ever saw."[5]

But disaster struck in the off-season when Monty stumbled while rabbit hunting on the family farm. The .22 caliber automatic pistol he was carrying discharged into his right leg between the hip and knee. He crawled a half-mile back towards the farmhouse before he was able to hail his wife. He was rushed to a hospital in nearby Greenville and then on to Dallas.

Unfortunately, Stratton's bad luck held. The bullet pierced the femoral artery behind the knee, cutting off circulation to the his lower leg. Gangrene set in, and the leg had to be amputated above the knee the next day. The operating surgeon was quoted as saying, "Monty couldn't have hit that artery if he aimed at it. It probably wouldn't happen more than once in a hundred times."[6]

It looked like the end of a promising career to everyone except Monty Stratton. Equipped with a wooden leg, he doggedly attempted a comeback. On May 1, 1939, less than six months after the accident, the White Sox played the Cubs in a benefit game on Stratton's behalf. He was presented with an automobile and a crowd of over 25,000 paid a dollar each into the Monty Fund. In a gut-wrenching pre-game ceremony, Stratton took the mound to prove that he could still pitch. Despite the courageous demonstration, it was evident that he couldn't pivot on the artificial leg without losing his balance.[7]

According to *The Stratton Story,* the failure sent Monty into depression. He stopped wearing his prosthesis and spent his time moping around the house. Then one day he observed his infant son learning to walk. As he watched the boy determinedly clawing back up after each fall, Monty resolved that he wasn't going to stay down either. He strapped on his wooden leg and began helping out with the farm chores. Not long afterward, Ethel coaxed him into a game of catch and there was no stopping him after that. He secretly arranged to pitch in an exhibition game against topflight minor leaguers and won the game in dramatic fashion.[8]

In the real world, Stratton spent some time coaching for the Sox and managed the Lubbock Hubbers in the West Texas League in 1942, but his heart was in pitching.[9] He returned to the farm and began pitching for a local team in Greenville where he gradually overcame the balancing problem, which was no doubt exacerbated by his lanky frame, and became more proficient at handling bunts. By 1945 he was pitching for a top semipro team in Houston.[10]

In 1945, World War II veteran Bert Shepard, who'd lost a foot when his plane was shot down during the war, got a trial with the Washington Senators. Shepard, a minor league hurler before the war, made some exhibition appearances and relieved in one regular season game for the Nats, going 5⅓ innings and yielding only one earned run.

Shepard's performance may have given Monty some inspiration. Shepard did have some advantages over Stratton. For one, he was more than eight years younger. But more importantly, Shepard was only missing his right foot and part of his lower leg, while Stratton's right leg had been amputated above the knee. Furthermore, Shepard was a lefty which meant that his prosthetic foot was his landing foot. Stratton, being a right-hander had to balance on his wooden leg while shifting his weight during his delivery, and then push off on it—a much more difficult proposition. On the other hand, Monty was a former major league All-Star, while Shepard had never advanced out of the low minor leagues. And Stratton had several years to practice pitching with his disability.

Monty had rebuffed suggestions that he attempt a return to professional baseball during the war, saying that he'd rather stay in retirement than become a "4-F player," but after the war ended he caught on with the Sherman Twins in the Class C East Texas League for the 1946 season. At the age of 34, Stratton won 18 games for a losing team, walking only 43 batters in 218 innings pitched, an accomplishment that caught the attention of the national media—and subsequently Hollywood.[11]

The Stratton Story leaves viewers with the impression that Monty returned to the major leagues to resume his career with the White Sox, which was no doubt his dream. An article in *The Sporting News* maintained that "Monty is determined to earn his way back with the White Sox—not as a coach or pensioner, but as a winning pitcher." But the fact is that Monty's magnificent 1946 performance was the pinnacle of his comeback. A return to the major leagues was unrealistic given his age and condition. Reality set in when he moved up to the Waco Dons in the Class B Big State League for the 1947 season and was hit hard.[12]

There is still an amazing aspect of Stratton's 1947 campaign that bears mention. A fine hitting pitcher in the major leagues before the accident, Stratton was granted a special dispensation in the minors afterward. He could have a pinch-runner when he reached base without coming out of the game. He had to get there under his own power, though, which would take a long hit to the outfield. Monty managed to do just that 9 times in 41 at-bats for a decent .220 batting average.

Stratton retired as a player after the 1947 season to assist in the production of the movie, but his retirement didn't last long. During the 1949 campaign he suited up for the Vernon Dusters of the Longhorn League and Temple Eagles of the Big State League. In 1950, he posted four victories, all complete game efforts without a loss, pitching for his hometown Greenville Majors in the Big State League and the Corpus Christi Aces of the Rio Grande Valley League.

Monty reportedly netted more than $250,000 from *The Stratton Story*, which allowed him to retire to his farm in comfort.[13] Yet he was back in action in 1953 to try to help his Greenville hometown team. In June, *The Sporting News* reported: "Stratton kayoed in second inning of comeback try."[14] He also made another, more successful appearance back with the Sherman Twins, who were in the Sooner State League that year, but that was the end of his remarkable pitching career.

Despite the fact that Monty Stratton never returned to pitch in a regular major league game, his return to the mound to compete in the minor leagues on one leg still ranks as one of the greatest comeback stories of all time.

Monty Stratton

Born: 5/21/1912

Year	Team	Lg	G	IP	W	L	ERA	WHIP
1934	Omaha	WL	23	160	8	10	-	1.36
1934	Galveston	TL	9	40	1	4	4.28	1.25
	Chicago	AL	1	3	0	0	5.40	1.50

Year	Team	Lg	G	IP	W	L	ERA	WHIP
1935	St. Paul	AA	33	226	17	9	4.02	1.43
	Chicago	AL	5	38	1	2	4.03	1.29
1936	Chicago	AL	16	95	5	7	5.21	1.72
1937	Chicago	AL	22	164	15	5	2.40	1.09
1938	Chicago	AL	26	186	15	9	4.01	1.30
1946	Sherman	ETXL	27	218	18	8	4.17	1.44
1947	Waco	BSTL	15	103	7	7	6.55	1.80
1949	Vernon	LONG	1	9	1	0	-	-
1949	Temple	BSTL	1	4	0	1	-	-
1950	Corpus Christi	RGVL	2	18	2	0	-	-
	Greenville	BSTL	2	18	2	0	4.50	1.44
1953	Sherman-Denison	SOSL	1	8	0	1	-	-
	Greenville-Bryan	BSTL	1	1	0	1	-	-
5 Yrs	MLB Totals		70	487	36	23	3.71	1.31

5

Bo Jackson

From 1985 to 1990, Bo Jackson was the most spectacular athlete in the world, winning college football's Heisman Trophy and making both the Major League Baseball and the National Football League (NFL) All-Star Teams.

Yet Bo's most amazing athletic accomplishment came a few years later when he played in 160 major league games over the 1993 and 1994 seasons, hitting 29 homers and driving in 88 runs on an artificial left hip.

Jackson was the first athlete to simultaneously star in two major sports at the professional level. A running back at Auburn University, he culminated his fabulous college football career with the 1985 Heisman Trophy, awarded to the nation's top college player. A promising baseball player, who'd been drafted by the New York Yankees in the second round out of high school, he also played baseball at Auburn. As a junior, the right-handed hitting outfielder batted .401 for the baseball squad, but he played only part of his senior season before inadvertently violating an NCAA rule in a visit with the Tampa Bay Buccaneers, who held the first NFL draft pick. At Auburn, he also found time to qualify for the NCAA nationals in the 100-meter dash his freshman and sophomore years.[1] At the NFL draft combine, he ran a 4.12 second 40-yard dash, which unofficially topped the world record.[2]

The Kansas City Royals took a flyer on Jackson, drafting him in the fourth round of the 1986 amateur draft. When he announced that he was going to play professional baseball instead of football, most of the sports world assumed he was just posturing to gain a more lucrative NFL contract. But Bo turned down a guaranteed $2 million offer from football's Tampa Bay Buccaneers to sign a $200,000 baseball contract with the Royals. In a recent documentary, Jackson admitted that he decided not to sign with the Bucs because they lied to him about checking with the NCAA about the propriety of his Tampa visit.[3]

Bo dutifully reported to the Royals' Double A farm club, the Memphis Chicks, where he hit .277 in 53 games. In September, he was promoted to the parent club where he hit an uninspiring .207 in 25 games.

Of course, there was still considerable doubt in baseball circles about Bo's commitment to the National Pastime. It was widely suspected that he would quickly turn to football when he found that hitting major league pitching wasn't as easy as running over linebackers.

But Bo began the 1987 season as the Royals' regular left fielder, and by the All-Star break he was leading the club with 18 homers. Then, just as the baseball world was beginning to think he really was serious about a career on the diamond, Bo announced that he intended to play professional football for the Los Angeles Raiders in the fall. The press howled at his decision, as well as his unfortunate choice of words. He'd told reporters that his number one priority was still baseball; he'd just be adding football to his many off-season hobbies—like fishing and hunting.[4]

More than a few pro football players were deeply offended. A Washington Redskins linebacker threatened, "I'll put a good lick on him and see how he likes his new hobby." Even his new Raiders teammate Howie Long remarked, "Bo must have had a frontal and rear lobotomy."[5]

The reaction of the baseball community was just as intense. They were afraid they'd lost Bo, who'd already developed into a terrific gate attraction. Thomas Boswell, considered one of the most insightful sportswriters around, wrote: "To be a great baseball player you need a little humility. And that, to be blunt, is why Bo Jackson is heading for the door. If he has any significant success in cleats, you'll never see him back in spikes."[6]

Boswell's prediction looked even more prophetic when Bo slumped during the second half of his first full big league season and lost his regular outfield job. He finished his first full campaign in the majors with an impressive 22 homers, but hit a lowly .235 and struck out 158 times in only 396 at-bats.

The fear that Bo would not return to the diamond continued to grow when he found immediate success in professional football. He gained 14 yards on his first carry and ran for 98 yards and a touchdown in his first home game. The next week in Seattle, his defining moment as a professional football player occurred when he overpowered Brian Bosworth, simply running over the brash linebacker, who'd publicly promised to shut him down, for a touchdown. He also had a run of 91 yards from scrimmage and finished with 221 yards rushing for the day. Although a sprained ankle ended his campaign early, he averaged almost seven yards per carry and received considerable support for the league's Rookie of the Year honor despite playing less than half the schedule.

But Bo held to his word, returning to the Royals and concentrating on baseball. His batting average, slugging percentage, and homers per at-bat ratio improved every year until his hip injury. His popularity crested in 1989 when a spectacular first half made him an overwhelming choice for the American League All-Star Team. He led off the classic with a tremendous 448-foot home run and was named the game's MVP.

Bo's All-Star feats coincided with the introduction of the fabulously successful "Bo Knows" advertising campaign. Bo had already become a marketing icon the year before when he signed a lucrative contract to promote Nike shoes. The "Bo Knows" campaign capitalized on the young star's habit of referring to himself in the third person. It became his signature phrase and part of the era's pop vocabulary.

At the All-Star break it looked like Bo might join Jose Canseco as the only major leaguer to hit 40 homers and steal 40 bases in the same season, but he was slowed by nagging leg injuries in the

Bo Jackson homered in his first at-bat after hip replacement surgery (1988 Topps card).

second half of the season and missed significant playing time. He finished with 32 homers and 26 steals, while driving in 105 runs in only 135 games. The next year, more injuries limited him to 111 games, but he raised his batting average from .256 to .272 and belted 28 homers. His slugging average and home run percentage both ranked fourth in the league.

Meanwhile, Bo's performance on the gridiron was equally impressive. During the 1989–90 season he became the first NFL player to make two 90-yard touchdown runs from the line of scrimmage. In four seasons as a part-time running back, he averaged 5.4 yards per carry (the legendary Jim Brown's career average was 5.2) and scored 18 touchdowns in 38 games. After the 1990–91 season, in which he had an 88-yard run, he made the NFL Pro Bowl team—becoming the first athlete to be selected an All-Star in two major sports.

Unfortunately, he would never get the chance to duplicate his Major League All-Star Game heroics in professional football's All-Star extravaganza. On January 13, 1991, Bo's illustrious career as a two-sport star abruptly ended during a Raiders playoff victory over the Cincinnati Bengals when he injured his left hip on a routine play. Initially the injury wasn't considered that serious, but it didn't respond to treatment. A condition known as avascular necrosis developed, which caused the cartilage and bone around the partially crushed hip joint to deteriorate.

The severity of the injury didn't really register with the public until the Royals unconditionally released Jackson early in the 1991 spring training session. According to teammate George Brett, Bo promised, "I will be back," as he left the Royals training facility.[7]

The Chicago White Sox subsequently signed Bo as a long-term rehabilitation project and publicity magnet. After spending most of the 1991 campaign on the disabled list, he managed to get into 23 late season games with the Sox, but the results were disappointing. In the off-season, he undertook a rigorous conditioning program designed to build up the surrounding muscles to compensate for the damaged hip. In another advertising coup, Nike built a campaign around Bo's rehabilitation efforts. But when he reported to the White Sox camp in the spring of 1992, it soon became painfully evident that the hip would not permit him to perform at the big league level.

Bo returned to the disabled list and underwent an operation to replace his ruined hip with a prosthetic ball and socket. He vowed that he would resume his professional baseball career after rehab. But hip replacement surgery is usually performed to restore mobility for senior citizens. Playing a demanding professional sport on an artificial joint just didn't seem possible. A *New York Times* article thanked Bo for the memories and bid him a warm farewell. The article quoted Bo as saying he may have had his last at-bat in the major leagues, so even he had doubts.[8]

The general medical prognosis seemed to be that Bo would probably be able to run with the artificial hip, but not like a major leaguer. Encouraging stories of beer league softball players and ballet dancers continuing to perform after hip replacement surfaced, but no one had ever exposed an artificial hip joint to the rigors of professional sports. The 6'1" 225-pound Jackson would put the prosthesis to the ultimate test. His new rehabilitation program consisted of more than 10,000 pushups, 15,000 sit-ups, and 35,000 hip exercise repetitions in the five months before he reported to the White Sox 1993 spring training camp.[9]

Bo's first regular season appearance with his artificial hip was one of the most dramatic events in the annals of sports. The 30-year-old slugger came to the plate as a pinch hitter in the sixth inning of the Sox home opener against the Yankees and blasted a home run over the right field fence with his first swing of the bat. Fireworks exploded overhead and pandemonium reigned as Jackson triumphantly circled the bases. The roaring crowd demanded a curtain call and Bo came out of the dugout for another standing ovation. He recovered the home run ball and later had it bronzed and affixed to his mother's grave marker.[10]

Jackson always maintained that his mother, who died in 1992, imbued him with the strength to overcome his disability. She was the backbone of the family which lacked a father figure much of the time. Bo was born November 30, 1962, the eighth of ten children, and raised in the small town of Bessemer, Alabama. His real name is Vince Edward Jackson, named after the star of the *Ben Casey* soap opera, Vince Edwards. As a youngster he was so wild he was called "Boar Hog," which was eventually shortened to "Bo."[11]

The pinch-homer was the highlight of Bo's comeback. Although he'd lost his tremendous speed, his power was still imposing and he became a valuable part-time player. He served as the Sox' designated hitter in 36 contests but also played 47 games in the outfield, managing to post the highest fielding average of his career. He ended up with 16 homers in 284 trips to the plate, but his batting average was only .232 and he fanned 106 times.

The White Sox captured the 1993 American League Western Division Championship and faced the Toronto Blue Jays in the League Championship Series. The Sox lost in six games, due partly to Bo's abysmal performance. He was hitless in ten at-bats, striking out six times. The scouting report was that the artificial hip made him too stiff at the plate, so he wasn't able to bend down enough to hit the low strike.

Bo became a free agent in the off-season and signed with the California Angels for the 1994 campaign. Platooning in left field with rookie Jim Edmonds, he enjoyed a highly productive year, hitting a career-high .279 and blasting 13 homers with 43 RBIs in only 201 plate appearances. Those power numbers projected to 39 homers with a gaudy 129 RBIs over a full season of 600 at-bats.

In contrast to the rest of his incredible career, Bo's retirement from professional baseball was a non-event. The 1994 season was suspended at the two-thirds point by a labor strike which spilled over into spring training the next year and wasn't settled until shortly before the traditional opening day. Amid the furor over arranging a new schedule, hastily organizing mini training camps, and negotiating a backlog of contracts, 32-year-old Bo officially retired from baseball.

Bo Jackson ended his baseball career with a .250 lifetime batting average and 147 home runs in 694 major league games. But Bo could never be adequately measured by mere statistics. In the introduction to Bo's autobiography *Bo Knows Bo*, which came out just before his devastating injury, Royals teammate George Brett starts out with the statement, "Bo Jackson is my hero." Brett goes on to explain, "When he's at the top of his game, it's a sight to see. It's beyond your wildest dreams. It's beyond *my* wildest dreams." Noteworthy praise, coming from a man who won American League batting titles in three different decades and was elected to the Baseball Hall of Fame in his first year of eligibility.[12]

The only Hall of Fame honor that has come Bo's way, however, is a 1998 selection to the College Football Hall of Fame. His aborted baseball career is a monument to unfulfilled promise. His successful comeback to play baseball at the major league level with an artificial hip gives an indication of how great he could have been.

The first man to play professional baseball with an artificial hip will probably remain the only one for some time. The medical profession is now cautioning hip replacement candidates that the artificial joints do not last forever and are not designed for twisting, turning, high-impact activities. At a press briefing for the 2002 annual meeting of the American

Academy of Orthopedic Surgeons, Dr. Arlen Hanssen of the Mayo Clinic said that when Jackson "hit a home run in his first at-bat after having total hip replacement, it was an orthopedic surgeon's worst nightmare."[13]

Although promising new materials are being developed, 10 to 20 years is still considered a reasonable estimate for the life expectancy of an artificial hip under optimal conditions. Re-replacements are routinely performed, but the problem is that more bone is lost with each procedure, so the life of the succeeding joint is shortened every time another replacement procedure is performed.

"Surgically implanting replacement hips or knees in elite athletes and sending them back to the playing field is questionable medical practice and most orthopedic surgeons will not do it," warned Dr. Hanssen.[14]

Although there's been no official announcement, Jackson is presumed to no longer be on his first replacement hip. A few years after Bo retired, star outfielder Albert Belle developed a similar hip condition and elected to retire from the game at the age of 34 rather than undergo replacement surgery. He reportedly consulted with Bo before making the decision.

Bo did make one more comeback after hanging up his spikes. He returned to Auburn to complete his bachelor of science degree, fulfilling a promise he'd made to his mother years earlier.

Bo Jackson

Born: 11/30/1962

Year	Team	Lg	G	HR	RBI	SB	BA	OPS
1986	*Memphis*	*SOUL*	*53*	*7*	*25*	*3*	*.277*	*.841*
	Kansas City	AL	25	2	9	3	.207	.615
1987	Kansas City	AL	116	22	53	10	.235	.750
1988	Kansas City	AL	124	25	68	27	.246	.758
1989	Kansas City	AL	135	32	105	26	.256	.805
1990	Kansas City	AL	111	28	78	15	.272	.866
1991	*CHW-ML Rehab*	*(var)*	*6*	*0*	*2*	*1*	*.316*	*.732*
	Chicago	AL	23	3	14	0	.225	.742
1992	Chicago	AL	(Injured—Did not play)					
1993	Chicago	AL	85	16	45	0	.232	.722
1994	California	AL	75	13	43	1	.279	.851
8 Yrs	MLB Totals		694	141	415	82	.250	.784

6

Eric Davis

Can a player make a comeback three years in a row? Seems impossible, but from 1996 through 1998 Eric Davis accomplished it.

With the Cincinnati Reds for an all too brief period in the late 1980s, Davis was perhaps the best player in the game. But, after changing teams twice, he was forced into retirement at age 33 in 1995 due to injuries brought on by his all-out, wide-open style of play. He came back with the Reds in 1996 to win the Comeback Player of the Year Award. But the next year, 1997, after signing a lucrative two-year free agent contract with the Baltimore Orioles, he underwent surgery to remove a cancerous tumor six weeks into the season. Miraculously, he returned to action in September, while still undergoing chemotherapy, and helped the Orioles win the Eastern Conference championship. Never expected to be more than a part-timer again, he came back to regain a regular spot in the Orioles lineup and hit a career-high .327 in 1998.

In his prime, Eric Davis exhibited a historic blend of power and speed. In 1986, his first full big league season, the 24-year-old outfielder stole 80 bases and slammed 27 homers for the Cincinnati Reds. Until that season, no one had ever hit that many homers while stealing 80 bases in the same season at the major league level, nor has it been done since. But Rickey Henderson, then with the New York Yankees, accomplished the feat the same year. Henderson hit a few more homers (28) and stole a few more bases (87), but he went to the plate 701 times, while Davis, limited by injuries, compiled his numbers in only 487 plate appearances. Furthermore Eric was caught stealing only 11 times to Rickey's 18, giving him a higher success rate.

The next year "Eric the Red" became the seventh member of the elite 30–30 club: major leaguers who've slammed at least 30 homers and stolen 30 bases in the same season. In fact, he was on pace to become the first major leaguer to smash 40 homers and steal 40 bases in the same year when his season was interrupted by injury. On September 1, the right-handed hitting speedster banged home run number 36. He'd already swiped more than 40 bases and with 29 games to go in the regular season he seemed a lead-pipe cinch to become the inaugural 40–40 man. But three days later, he crashed into the brick wall at Wrigley Field, robbing Ryne Sandberg of an extra base hit and fracturing a rib in the process. He missed eight games and returned to the lineup too early. He hit only one more homer and batted a meager .156 before having to shut down again, missing the last seven games of the season and leaving the door open for Jose Canseco of the Oakland Athletics to become the first 40–40 player in major league history the next season.[1]

Injuries brought on by Eric's reckless style of play continued to take a toll and by 1990 his career was in decline. That year the Reds stunned the baseball world by capturing the National League pennant and sweeping the seemingly invincible Athletics in the World Series. Davis was still the team's big gun, leading the squad in runs batted in with 86 and finishing second in homers with 24. But bothered by injuries to his leg, hip, shoulder, and ribs, the 28-year-old star missed 35 games and hit only .260. Late in the season, he was moved from center to left field to compensate for his injuries.

Nevertheless, Eric drove in five runs and scored three times to spur the Reds to victories in the first three games of the Series. In the first inning of the fourth game in Oakland, he injured himself making a headlong dive for a sinking liner. The injury didn't seem that serious at the time. In fact, Eric finished the inning in the field after a visit from the trainer. But he collapsed in the dugout and was carried to the clubhouse by his teammates. When a urine sample produced mostly blood, he was rushed to the emergency room. The man who'd done so much to get the Reds to the championship wasn't able to join his teammates in celebration. He'd lacerated a kidney and remained hospitalized for the next 40 days.[2]

Eric Davis made three comebacks in three seasons (1989 Topps card).

The injury almost ended Eric's career. He was informed by his physician that the kidney would take 12 to 18 months to properly heal and advised to skip the entire 1991 baseball season. Unfortunately, he ignored the advice and reported to spring training on February 21, only four months after the injury. Just two days earlier, he'd managed to produce his first blood-free urine specimen since the injury, so the Reds team doctors gave him the green light. The Cincinnati brass, under the leadership of the infamous Marge Schott, had downplayed the seriousness of Eric's injury from the beginning. There were even hints that he was malingering. Laboring valiantly, he played poorly in his weakened condition. Finally, Eric's personal physician protested that his patient should not be playing baseball. The outfielder's 1991 campaign prematurely ended with a miserable .235 batting average in 89 games. Having played out his option, he became a free agent and signed with the Los Angeles Dodgers in the offseason.[3]

Still shy of his 30th birthday when the 1992 season began, great things were expected of Eric in Los Angeles. He'd grown up in the City of Angels and was returning home for a reunion with his close friend and former boyhood pal Darryl Strawberry, who'd signed with the Dodgers the preceding season. It seemed to be a dream come true for the two L.A. ghetto alums.

Unfortunately, the dream quickly turned into a nightmare. Early in the season, Eric broke his collarbone diving for a ball. When he returned, he damaged his wrist, hand, and shoulder—eventually undergoing shoulder surgery in September. For the year he got into only 76 games and posted a weak .228 average. The ballyhooed reunion with Strawberry never got off the ground as Darryl injured his back and played only 43 games himself.

While Strawberry continued to experience physical and emotional problems in 1993, missing all but 32 games, Davis stayed in the Dodgers lineup until being shipped to the Detroit Tigers in a late-season waiver deal. For the year, he played 131 games for the two clubs, slamming 20 homers and stealing 35 bases, but hitting only .237.

Eric began the 1994 season as the Tigers' regular center fielder until he ran into the outfield wall at Fenway Park early in the campaign and injured his neck. He tried to continue playing, even though he couldn't turn his head, but his season was ruined. After play was halted in mid–August by a season-ending player strike, Davis underwent surgery for a collapsed vertebrae and bulging disk in his neck. Due to the extensive damage found, medical experts advised Eric that there was possibility of paralysis if he continued to play. At the age of 32, after going under the knife eight times in seven years, Eric Davis retired from baseball—seemingly for good.[4]

But the year off did wonders for Davis, finally allowing his battered body to recover. As he started to feel better, he began to grow antsy and put out feelers to see if anyone was interested in signing him for the 1996 season. There was curiosity, but little real interest.

Back in Eric's old Cincinnati stomping grounds, however, Reds owner Marge Schott was under a barrage of criticism for comments denigrating minorities and advancing her sentiment that Adolph Hitler may have been somewhat misunderstood. Schott, a collector of Nazi rather than baseball memorabilia, had reveled in the attention the Reds had garnered while capturing the National League Western Division Championship in 1995. Under the glare of the spotlight, however, her mouth soon had her in deep trouble with the press and the commissioner of major league baseball.

Schott, who would eventually be forced to sell her interest in the Reds due to conduct unbecoming to baseball, was diligently trying to patch up her damaged reputation as preparations for the 1996 season began. After presumably scouring the globe for a Holocaust survivor with a good bat with no success, she was desperately searching for another embodiment of her new-found compassion for oppressed minorities.

When the Reds opened spring training with Eric Davis in camp, skeptics suspected nothing more than shameless posturing on the part of Schott. Years earlier when he was an emerging star, Schott had reportedly referred to Davis and teammate Dave Parker as her "million dollar niggers."[5] After Eric's injury in the 1990 Series, she'd balked at paying his transportation expenses home after his extended hospital stay.[6]

Even the more ingenuous baseball experts felt that Davis' presence in camp was nothing more than a courtesy look for a former Cincinnati favorite. There was really no reason to expect much from him. He was nearly 34 years old and had batted a dismal .183 in 37 games for the Tigers in 1994 before sitting out the entire 1995 season. Furthermore, he hadn't hit over .237 since 1990. He'd never been an iron man to begin with, never playing in more than 135 games in a season, but he'd averaged only 83 games per year from 1991 through 1994.

On top of that, the Reds manager, Ray Knight, didn't exactly have a warm, fuzzy feeling toward Davis. The two had been involved in an altercation when Knight played for the New York Mets a decade earlier, and apparently Ray still harbored a grudge.[7] Early on, he boosted Eric's morale with the statement, "Well, maybe he has got a possibility of making the team as a fifth outfielder."[8]

Yet, when the Reds broke camp, Davis was on the roster, having forced Knight to keep him by hitting around .400 for the spring. He started the season backing up the regular outfielders, but was a fixture in center field by the middle of May. For the year he batted .287

with 26 homers, 83 runs batted in, and 23 stolen bases in 129 games on his way to National League Comeback Player of the Year honors.

Despite his excellent 1996 performance, the Reds weren't convinced of Eric's staying power and again allowed him to leave as a free agent. After signing with the Orioles, Davis started the 1997 season where he left off. He captured Player of the Week honors for the last week in April and was batting .388 with a league leading .710 slugging percentage in the second week of May when he started having physical problems. He was tiring quickly and beginning to lose weight. In addition, he began suffering from cramps, queasiness, and pain in his right side. His once robust batting average had dwindled to a less imposing .302 figure before he doubled over in pain going from first to third on a routine play in Cleveland and had to be helped off the field.[9]

Davis' maladies were diagnosed as symptoms of cancer. Defying superstition, he underwent surgery on Friday the 13th of June, two weeks after his 35th birthday. Surgeons removed a malignant tumor the size of a baseball along with a third of his colon. The growth was classified as a Stage B tumor and the grim statistics put the expected survival rate at 60 percent to 70 percent. Eric was scheduled to begin chemotherapy immediately, and a return to baseball seemed out of the question for the near future and possibly forever.[10]

But Eric Davis had always been a magnificent physical specimen. Early in his career, he generated tremendous power from 175 pounds spread over a 6'3" frame. By the time he was stricken with cancer, he carried around 200 pounds easily and was as solid as a rock. Despite the debilitating effects of the chemotherapy, Davis began working out shortly after the surgery and was traveling with the team by August. He made an amazing comeback to play in the latter part of the 1997 season and contributed both inspirationally and physically to the Orioles stretch run for the division title. Against all odds, he gained a spot on the post-season roster with a 4 for 4 performance, including a homer, in the season finale. He followed with another home run in the League Championship Series, which the Orioles lost to the Cleveland Indians.

For the regular season, Davis finished with a .304 batting average and eight homers in 42 games. He was honored with the Roberto Clemente Award, which is given to the most inspirational player, and also received the Fred Hutchinson Memorial Award, presented to the player who best exemplifies the character, dedication, and competitive spirit of the former pitcher and manager.

Although doubts remained about his ability to withstand the rigors of a 162-game schedule, the Orioles picked up the option for the second year of Eric's contract. He finished his final chemotherapy treatment just before reporting to the Orioles 1998 spring training camp. The veteran outfielder began the season in a platoon role and performed well as his playing time gradually increased. At the All-Star break, the Orioles seemed hopelessly behind the red-hot Yankees in the pennant race and about 15 games behind the Boston Red Sox in the competition for the wild card berth. But Eric caught fire after the break and embarked on a 30-game hitting streak which established a franchise record and led the Orioles back into the thick of the wild card race.

Despite their heroic charge, the Orioles came up short, missing out on post-season play. But Davis did more than could have been expected in anyone's wildest dreams. In addition to his .327 batting mark, fourth highest in the American League, he slammed 28 homers, scored 81 times, and batted in 89 runs while playing 131 games.

The 1998 season was not all roses for Eric Davis, however. Just before the World Series, his old pal Darryl Strawberry was diagnosed with colon cancer. Fortunately, Eric was there to provide moral support and living proof that the disease could be overcome. Strawberry later said, "Knowing what he (Davis) went through probably saved my life." Ironically, when Davis and Strawberry teamed up in Los Angeles to form what was expected to be a dream outfield, the third outfielder was Brett Butler, also a cancer survivor. Butler underwent a serious operation for throat cancer in 1996 and returned to the game later that same year.[11]

Davis left the Orioles after the 1998 season and signed a two-year, eight-million-dollar contract with the St. Louis Cardinals. His first year in St. Louis was wrecked in late June when he tore his rotator cuff making a diving catch to save a no-hitter for young Jose Jimenez. But he engineered yet another comeback in 2000 to hit .303 platooning with young J. D. Drew in right field, and played a key role in the Cardinals drive to the National League Central Division Championship. After the season, Eric again became a free agent and was leaning toward retirement. But he couldn't pass up the chance to play for highly respected San Francisco Giants manager Dusty Baker and signed with the Bay area club for one last campaign.

Eric Davis finished his career with relatively modest lifetime stats. He played 17 seasons, although he never did appear in more than 135 games in a season. He ended up with 282 homers, 934 RBIs, and a .269 batting average. More impressive is his .841 on-base plus slugging percentage (OPS), better than contemporary Hall of Famers such as Eddie Murray and Dave Winfield. He also stole 349 bases while getting nabbed only 66 times. It was the highest success rate in history for a player with more than 300 steals at his retirement, although it's since been surpassed by Tim Raines. In addition to his accomplishments at the plate and on the bases, Eric captured three straight Gold Glove Awards from 1987 through 1989 for his spectacular defensive play in center field.

Perhaps the best gauge of Davis' extraordinary talent, however, is a quote attributed to a great center fielder from a previous era. During Eric's heyday, when he was often compared to Willie Mays, Willie himself remarked, "It's an honor to be compared to Eric Davis."[12]

Eric Davis is another example of "what might have been." He's the modern day answer to Pete Reiser, the former Brooklyn Dodgers center fielder who became the National League's youngest batting champ in 1941. Reiser also had a penchant for injuring himself with his daring style of play and was carried off the field on a stretcher eleven times according to one count. Cut from the same mold, most of his Eric's injuries occurred on defense, where he played with reckless abandon, challenging outfield walls and diving headlong for gappers. Reiser's injuries took him down at the age of 33, a year older than Davis was when he initially retired in 1995. But while Reiser's retirement was permanent, Davis managed to come back from adversity and to keep coming back again and again.

Eric Davis

Born: 5/29/1962

Year	Team	Lg	G	HR	RBI	SB	BA	OPS
1980	Eugene	NORW	33	1	11	10	.219	.619
1981	Eugene	NORW	62	11	39	40	.322	1.028
1982	Cedar Rapids	MIDW	111	15	56	53	.276	.803
1983	Waterbury	EL	89	15	43	39	.290	.918
	Indianapolis	AA	19	7	19	9	.299	1.003
1984	Wichita	AA	52	14	34	27	.314	1.025

Year	Team	Lg	G	HR	RBI	SB	BA	OPS
	Cincinnati	NL	57	10	30	10	.224	.786
1985	*Denver*	*AA*	*64*	*15*	*38*	*35*	*.277*	*.927*
	Cincinnati	NL	56	8	18	16	.246	.803
1986	Cincinnati	NL	132	27	71	80	.277	.901
1987	Cincinnati	NL	129	37	100	50	.293	.991
1988	Cincinnati	NL	135	26	93	35	.273	.852
1989	Cincinnati	NL	131	34	101	21	.281	.908
1990	Cincinnati	NL	127	24	86	21	.260	.833
1991	Cincinnati	NL	89	11	33	14	.235	.739
1992	Los Angeles	NL	76	5	32	19	.228	.647
1993	Los Angeles	NL	108	14	53	33	.234	.699
	Detroit	AL	23	6	15	2	.253	.904
1994	Detroit	AL	37	3	13	5	.183	.582
1995	Detroit	AL	(Injured—Did not play)					
1996	Cincinnati	NL	129	26	83	23	.287	.917
1997	Baltimore	AL	42	8	25	6	.304	.883
1998	Baltimore	AL	131	28	89	7	.327	.970
1999	St. Louis	NL	58	5	30	5	.257	.762
2000	St. Louis	NL	92	6	40	1	.303	.818
2001	San Francisco	NL	74	4	22	1	.205	.634
17 Yrs	MLB Totals		1626	282	934	349	.269	.841

7

Andres Galarraga

Since *The Sporting News* began consistently presenting the Comeback Player of the Year Award in 1965, six players have been honored twice. But Andres Galarraga is the only two-time winner whose nominations truly reflect the criteria for inclusion in these chapters.

While with the St. Louis Cardinals in 1992, the injury-plagued Galarraga had his second bad year in a row, finishing last in production among regular National League first sackers. After the Cards cut him loose at the end of the year, he managed to catch on with the Colorado Rockies expansion team where he raised his batting average an incredible 127 points, captured the National League batting crown, and won Comeback of the Year honors for the first time.

Eight years later, after three consecutive 40-homer seasons, Galarraga was diagnosed with lymphatic cancer in his back and missed the entire 2000 season undergoing treatment. The next year, at age 39, he returned to hit over .300, drive in 100 runs, make his first All-Star Game start and capture his second Comeback of the Year award.

The 6'3", 235-pound Galarraga was called "The Big Cat" for his extraordinary quickness at first base, in spite of his big frame. Long-time manager Whitey Herzog called him "the best-fielding right-handed first baseman I've seen since Gil Hodges." He began his professional career in his mid-teens with the Leones del Caracas club in the Venezuela Winter League. At the recommendation of his manager, Felipe Alou, he was signed by the Montreal Expos in 1979, despite the opinion of many scouts that he was too fat to play professionally. He worked his way up the Montreal chain before debuting with the parent club late in the 1985 season.[1]

The next year he captured the Expos' regular first base job, getting off to a promising start before injuries took a toll. He ended his rookie season hitting .271 with 10 homers and 42 RBIs in 105 games.

After a strong sophomore season in which he hit .305 and drove in 90 runs, Galarraga enjoyed a Silver Slugger season in 1988, batting .302 with 29 home runs and 92 RBIs, while leading the National League in hits and doubles and being named to the All-Star Team for the first time in his career. But pitchers began exploiting the free-swinging first baseman's impatience at the plate, and he endured disappointing seasons in 1989 and 1990, although he still posted decent power numbers and earned a pair of Gold Glove Awards for his stellar defensive play.

Slowed by injuries, Galarraga struggled through the worst offensive season of his career in 1991, hitting a weak .219 with only nine homers and 33 RBIs in 107 games. In the off-season, the Expos traded him to St. Louis for starting pitcher Ken Hill.

Great things were expected of Andres in St. Louis, but his wrist was broken by a wayward pitch early in the year and he didn't fully recover until July. He hit .296 after the All-Star break and swatted all ten of his homers after July 1, but the Cardinals brass was unimpressed with his overall .243 batting mark and measly 39 RBIs. He was cut loose after the season. At the age of 31, it looked like Galarraga's career as a front-line player was over.

The Big Cat had, however, made a good impression on Cards batting coach Don Baylor, who'd just been hired to manage the newly minted Colorado squad. Baylor convinced the organization to take a chance and sign Galarraga as a free agent.

Taking full advantage of the opportunity, Galarraga worked with Baylor to adjust his stance and flirted with the .400 mark for much of the 1993 season. He finished with a league-leading .370 mark, the highest average posted by a right-handed hitter in the major leagues since Joe DiMaggio hit .381 for the 1939 New York Yankees. Although he missed 42 games with injuries, Andres led the league with 56 multi-hit games, belted 22 homers, and drove in 98 runs. His .403 on-base percentage and .602 slugging average gave him an on-base plus slugging percentage (OPS) of 1.005, the second highest mark in the league behind Barry Bonds of the San Francisco Giants. He made the All-Star Team and captured the first of his two Comeback Player of the Year Awards.

Andres Galarraga was Comeback Player of the Year twice (1988 Topps card).

In the strike-shortened 1994 season, Galarraga set a new National League record by driving in 30 runs in April and seemed to be on his way to another spectacular year when he fractured his right hand on July 28. The Rockies had climbed to within a half-game of the first place Los Angeles Dodgers, but without The Big Cat in the lineup, they lost 10 of their next 13 games before the season ended prematurely. For the year, Andres paced the club with 31 homers and batted .319 with 85 RBIs in only 103 games.

From 1995 through 1997, Galarraga stayed relatively healthy, resulting in an average of almost 40 homers and more than 130 RBIs per season for the three-year period. He led the National League in homers and RBIs and won a Silver Slugger Award in 1996. In 1997 he led the league in RBIs while making the All-Star squad as a reserve for the third time.

Many skeptics disparaged Galarraga's accomplishments with Colorado, maintaining that his stats were greatly inflated by the thin, mile-high atmosphere at hitter-friendly Coors Field. But he silenced his critics in 1998 by hitting 44 homers and driving in 121 runs for the Atlanta Braves after signing a three-year contract with them as a free agent.

Galarraga, who'd first felt pain in his lower back at the 1998 All-Star Game, experienced more soreness in his back while preparing for the 1999 season. When traditional training room treatments such as hydrobaths, massages, stretching exercises, and muscle relaxers failed to alleviate the pain, he underwent a thorough physical exam that included an MRI shortly before spring training camp opened. The MRI revealed a tumor on his second lumbar vertebra in his lower back. The diagnosis was non–Hodgkin's lymphoma, a cancer of the lymph nodes that affects the body's immune system. The Big Cat missed the entire 1999 season, enduring a battery of six chemotherapy treatments every three weeks, as well as five weeks of radiation therapy. Although he couldn't play, he rejoined the Braves late in the season to lend moral support during the pennant drive and post-season. Always a popular clubhouse presence with his perpetual smile and effervescent personality, the veteran suited up and sat on the bench, sometimes offering a suggestion and generally playing goodwill ambassador. "I'm kind of a coach, kind of a fan," he said. "I'm here to support these guys."[2]

"Just to have his presence is an inspiration," teammate Ryan Klesko said. "Just look at what he's gone through this year. He's here and he has a smile on his face. That's inspiration."[3]

"It would be better if he were playing," said Andruw Jones, "but he's a great guy to be around. He enjoys the game and enjoys life. When he's on the bench, he motivates guys."[4]

Given his age and injury history, not to mention his bout with cancer, the Braves naturally harbored doubts about Galarraga's ability to come back, so they acquired former All-Star first baseman Wally Joyner in the offseason. But, after completing a chemotherapy regimen and a strict offseason workout routine, the Big Cat was in the lineup on Opening Day of the 2000 season, belting a game-winning homer in his third trip to the plate.

After battling for the National League home run lead in the early going, Galarraga's power tailed off in the second half of the season. He still finished with 28 homers and 100 RBIs to go with a .302 batting mark for a season highlighted by his All-Star Game appearance in front of the home fans at Turner Field.

Concerned about Galarraga's stamina, in light of his late season power outage, the Braves let him go as a free agent after the season. He signed with the Texas Rangers in the American League where he could conserve his strength by serving as a designated hitter. But he never warmed up to the role, hitting a disappointing .235 in 72 games before being dispatched to the San Francisco Giants in late July. His bat regained some life back in the familiar National League, but he again became a free agent after the season. He returned to Montreal for the 2002 season, but hit only .260 and was allowed to leave after the season.

Before the 2003 season, Galarraga signed up for another tour of duty with San Francisco and contributed handsomely to the Giants' National League Western Division title. Platooning with J.T. Snow at first base, he hit .301 average with 12 homers in only 272 at-bats.

In the winter of 2003, however, Galarraga's cancer returned. He had surgery that November and a stem cell transplant in February 2004. He also underwent two three-week rounds of chemotherapy and was hospitalized for 23 days of additional treatment. It was the same non–Hodgkin's lymphoma that had sidelined him in 1999, but he beat it for the second time and signed a contract with the Anaheim Angels in August 2004. He was assigned to the Angels' Salt Lake City Triple A affiliate but returned to the majors when rosters were expanded in September. Although primarily a bench player with the Angels, he was highly regarded in the clubhouse, especially among younger players such as Vladimir Guerrero, to whom he became something of a mentor. The Big Cat saw action in a few games and hit a pinch-homer.[5]

The New York Mets invited Galarraga to spring training before the 2005 season, not knowing if the 43-year-old would be a fit for their roster. Galarraga showed that he had some gas left in the tank offensively by socking three home runs, but he retired before the season started, saying it was "the right time to give a younger guy a chance to play."[6]

Andres Galarraga played 17 seasons and parts of two others in the major leagues, finishing with a .288 lifetime batting average and 399 home runs. During his career he led the league in RBIs twice, as well as batting average, home runs, base hits, total bases, doubles, and extra-base hits. A two-time Silver Slugger recipient and five-time All-Star, he is the first Venezuelan to win a big league batting title and still ranks as the all-time Venezuelan home run leader. Furthermore, his .370 mark in 1993 stands as the highest average ever recorded by a Hispanic-American major leaguer.

The first Rockies player to make the All-Star Team, he fittingly became the first Rockies player to be inducted into the Colorado Sports Hall of Fame in 2007.

More importantly, however, he's still baseball's most successful cancer survivor.

Andres Galarraga

Born: 6/18/1961

Year	Team	Lg	G	HR	RBI	SB	BA	OPS
1979	Calgary	PION	42	4	16	1	.214	.665
	West Palm Beach	FLOR	7	0	1	0	.130	.361
1980	Calgary	PION	59	4	22	3	.263	.733
1981	Jamestown	NYPL	47	6	26	0	.260	.800
1982	West Palm Beach	FLOR	105	14	51	2	.281	.837
1983	West Palm Beach	FLOR	104	10	66	7	.289	.777
1984	Jacksonville	SOUL	143	27	87	2	.289	.875
1985	Indianapolis	AA	121	25	87	3	.269	.854
1985	Montreal	NL	24	2	4	1	.187	.508
1986	Montreal	NL	105	10	42	6	.271	.743
1987	Montreal	NL	147	13	90	7	.305	.821
1988	Montreal	NL	157	29	92	13	.302	.893
1989	Montreal	NL	152	23	85	12	.257	.761
1990	Montreal	NL	155	20	87	10	.256	.715
1991	Montreal	NL	107	9	33	5	.219	.604
1992	STL-ML Rehab	AAA	11	2	3	1	.176	.612
	St. Louis	NL	95	10	39	5	.243	.673
1993	Colorado	NL	120	22	98	2	.370	1.005
1994	Colorado	NL	103	31	85	8	.319	.949
1995	Colorado	NL	143	31	106	12	.280	.842
1996	Colorado	NL	159	47	150	18	.304	.958
1997	Colorado	NL	154	41	140	15	.318	.974
1998	Atlanta	NL	153	44	121	7	.305	.991
1999	Atlanta	NL	(Cancer treatment—Did not play)					
2000	Atlanta	NL	141	28	100	3	.302	.895
2001	Texas	AL	72	10	34	1	.235	.734
	San Francisco	NL	49	7	35	0	.288	.863
2002	Montreal	NL	104	9	40	2	.260	.738
2003	San Francisco	NL	110	12	42	1	.301	.841
2004	Salt Lake	PCL	25	4	19	0	.304	.793
2004	Anaheim	AL	7	1	2	0	.300	.964
19 Yrs	MLB Totals		2257	399	1425	128	.288	.846

8

Ted Williams

"Ted, I think you ought to quit. You've had a great career ... why don't you just wrap it up?" advised Boston Red Sox owner Tom Yawkey after "The Splendid Splinter" had suffered through a miserable 1959 campaign. The 41-year-old Boston great had seen his batting average plummet to .254, 74 points off his 1958 average and more than 90 points below his career mark to that point. He'd asked Yawkey, who not only paid his salary but was also a close friend, what he thought about playing another year.[1]

He was not prepared for Yawkey's atypically blunt answer. "Well, that kind of burned my ass," Ted would write in his autobiography 10 years later.[2]

Red Sox star outfielder Ted Williams aspired to be the greatest hitter who ever lived, and he may well have achieved that goal. He never aspired to be the greatest comeback player of all time, but it's another distinction he may have earned. He came back from two extended military stints, rebounded from serious injuries, and stubbornly shook off the ravages of age, returning each time to the pinnacle of his profession. His stirring grand finale that capped his magnificent career was his best effort, however. After the worst season of his professional baseball career—by far—he came back to win the Associated Press Comeback Player of the Year award the next year, posting the top slugging, on-base, and home run percentages in the league in his grand finale.

Sensitive and defensive, Williams had always been a proud, defiant loner. He thought the world was against him and shunned the attention that his tremendous talent inevitably attracted. He was counted out many times, but always returned to "show 'em" what he was really made of.

"Quit" was not in Ted Williams' vocabulary! Sure, he'd been contemplating retirement for years. An avid fisherman, he'd been looking forward to permanently trading in his bat for a fishing rod. He'd even done it a few years earlier before an expensive divorce settlement forced him back into uniform.

But "quit!" He couldn't do that! Even though age and injuries had virtually slowed him to a walk in the field and on the bases. Even though he'd suffered the humiliation of being benched for the last month of the 1959 campaign, watching from the dugout as the Sox played their best ball of the season. Even though he'd heard rumors that the front office didn't want him back. Even though he was in line for a $30,000 pay cut. There was just no way he was going to go out with a bad season. He'd show 'em one more time. After all, he'd been doing just that for more than 20 years. Why stop now?

It started with Ted's first major league training camp with the Red Sox in 1938. The lanky, 19-year-old, left-handed batter from San Diego electrified the camp with his hitting and disgusted the older players with his cockiness. At the time, the Sox were set in the outfield with .300 hitters Joe Vosmik, Roger Cramer, and Ben Chapman. The veteran trio deeply resented the brash young busher who threatened their livelihood and rode him mercilessly. When he was farmed out to Minneapolis for more seasoning, his parting shot was: "Tell them I'll be back, and tell them that I'm going to wind up making more money in this frigging game than all three of them put together."[3]

"The Kid" showed 'em. The next year he was back, replacing Chapman and hitting .327 with 31 homers and a league leading 145 runs batted in. And it wasn't long before he was indeed making much more than all of them combined.

But he was no longer that confident young slugger when he reported to spring training camp before the 1960 season. Expectations were low. Boston manager Billy Jurges, who'd benched Williams shortly after taking over the previous year, said the most he expected from Ted was 100 games—and the least was pinch-hitting. Yet even those modest expectations began to seem like a pipe dream when Ted failed to hit one out of the park during the exhibition season.[4]

Ted Williams showed 'em for 22 years (1957 Topps card).

When the bell rang for Opening Day, however, Ted began "showing 'em" one more time, serving notice that he wasn't going away quietly. In his first at-bat, he crushed a tremendous home run off Washington Senators ace Camilo Pascual over the distant Griffith Stadium center field fence in Washington. The shot tied him with Lou Gehrig for fourth place on the all-time homer list behind Babe Ruth, Jimmie Foxx, and Mel Ott. The tie didn't last long, as Ted treated Boston fans to homer number 494 in the Sox home opener the next day.

Ted's 1960 comeback was simply phenomenal. Limited by age and nagging injuries to 87 games in left field and 26 pinch-hitting appearances, he finished with a .316 batting average, 29 homers, and 72 RBIs in 310 at-bats, while also drawing 75 walks. His batting mark was the second highest in the league behind teammate Pete Runnels' .320, although Ted didn't get enough plate appearances to qualify for the batting title. Likewise, he didn't play enough to get formal recognition for his .645 slugging average that beat official league leader Roger Maris' .581 or his .451 on-base percentage that was higher than "walking man" Eddie Yost's .414. Although on-base plus slugging percentage (OPS) wasn't something that anyone worried about back then, his 1.096 mark topped Mickey Mantle's league-high .957. Perhaps Ted's most impressive accomplishment that year was the 29 homers he slammed in part-time duty, the sixth highest total in the American League. He homered every 10.7 at-bats, easily eclipsing leader Maris' 12.8 rate and homer king Mantle's 13.2 mark. In fact, Ted's home run rate in his final season was more prolific than any full season of his career.

Williams' first big comeback wasn't as difficult or unexpected as his 1960 effort. Like many big leaguers, he served in the military during World War II and had to work hard to regain his skills upon his return. But his triumphant return after three years in the service was another "show 'em" performance.

The United States had instituted its first peacetime Selective Service draft in 1940 in preparation for a possible declaration of war. Ted, the sole support of his divorced mother, requested and received a deferment. But as the country's military involvement in the war became inevitable, patriotism reached a fever pitch. Any healthy, unmarried man who wasn't in the service fell under suspicion as a draft dodger with strapping, well-paid young athletes falling under particular scrutiny. Initially the spotlight fell on Detroit Tigers slugger Hank Greenberg. But when Greenberg was inducted early in the 1941 season, it was Williams' turn in the barrel.

In 1941, he had become the first major league hitter in a decade to top .400. He'd also led the league in homers, runs scored, walks, on-base percentage, and slugging—losing the Triple Crown by a mere five RBIs. On the last day of the season, with his average sitting at .3996, which rounded off to .400, Williams refused to sit out a meaningless doubleheader against the Philadelphia Athletics. Instead, he "showed 'em" by playing both games, rapping out six hits in eight at-bats to finish at .406 for the season, an average that hasn't been topped in the major leagues since.

Given the fact that few big leaguers actually entered the service before the end of the 1942 season, Ted's draft status seemed to receive an undeserved amount of attention. The criticism reached a crescendo after Pearl Harbor forced the United States' entry into the war. Though the fans and the media made his life miserable, Ted captured the Triple Crown in 1942.

Following his fabulous 1941 campaign, Ted had finished behind the New York Yankees' Joe DiMaggio in the voting for the American League MVP, despite the fact that DiMaggio's season totals were not as impressive as his. But Joe had hit in 56 straight games that year to set a major league record, and the Yankees had captured the pennant. And who could argue with the selection of the great DiMaggio? In 1942, however, Ted again found himself in the runner-up spot with the award going to Yankees second baseman Joe Gordon, who hit 34 points fewer than Williams with half as many homers. In fact, the only batting category in which Gordon led the league was strikeouts. Williams, on the other hand, not only paced the American League in the three triple-crown categories, he also bested all National Leaguers in those categories to win the Major League Triple Crown. In addition, he led all big league hitters in slugging, runs scored, walks, and on-base percentage.

Even though Ted had enlisted during the latter stages of the 1942 campaign, signing up for hazardous duty as a Navy fighter pilot, voters denied him the MVP award that year because of the controversy surrounding his military status.

After distinguishing himself as a pilot and flight instructor during the war, Ted returned to baseball in 1946 to "show 'em" again. Many top players had trouble rounding into form after being in the service. DiMaggio hit under .300 for the first time after three years in the Air Force. Gordon hit only .210 after missing two seasons. Detroit's Dick Wakefield missed only a year and saw his average decline from .355 to .268. Cecil Travis of the Senators, the 1941 batting title runner-up behind Williams, could muster only a .252 mark upon his return. Williams, however, forced baseball to give him his first MVP award by hitting .342 while slamming 38 homers and driving in 123 runs. He actually posted a higher OPS than he had in his pre-war Triple Crown campaign.

From 1947 through 1949, "The Thumper" (one of several unwanted nicknames Ted suffered) paced the league in slugging percentage, walks, and OPS all three years. He also led in batting average, home runs, runs scored, and runs batted in twice. He won his second Triple Crown in 1947 and barely missed another in 1949 when George Kell topped him in batting by a fraction of a point. He did, however, garner his second MVP trophy that year.

Ted was off to another incredible year in 1950, leading the league in homers and RBIs, when he broke his left arm crashing into the outfield wall in the All-Star Game. Amazingly, he stayed in the game and produced the game-winning hit, but when the game ended, the elbow swelled up and the full extent of the injury became apparent. In the operation that followed, thirteen bone chips were removed. The doctors feared Ted's career was over and offered him little hope that he would regain full use of the arm. But two months later he was back in the lineup. The elbow was still weak, however, and his batting average plummeted as the Red Sox dropped out of the American League pennant race. He came back to play 148 games in 1951, hitting .318 with 30 homers—great numbers for most players, but a significant decline from Ted's normal level.

Prior to the 1952 season, Uncle Sam decided that Ted Williams was just the man the country needed to end the Korean conflict. Ted had kept a reserve commission after World War II, and the Marines, who were desperately short of fliers, were recalling any former pilot they could get their hands on. He went to spring training knowing that he would be called up, but hoping something would happen to delay or cancel it.

Unlike his World War II service, Ted didn't expect to simply resume his baseball career after Korea. When he'd enlisted back in 1942, he was 24 years of age, just approaching his prime. He would begin his second tour of duty, however, as a 33-year-old veteran, already slowed by assorted injuries. And, unlike his prior military stint, he would be in combat, unable to get some playing time in with service teams.

Respected sportswriter Tom Meany, profiling Williams in his book *Baseball's Greatest Players* (published while Ted was in Korea), wrote: "Williams himself had little hope of returning to baseball. He figured when the Marines released him he would be past 35 and that his reflexes, rusted by inactivity, would be of no use for baseball." Meany left little doubt that he felt the same way by referring to Williams' baseball career in the past tense. "He left behind him a lifetime batting average of .346 and the record of never having hit under .300 while wearing the uniform of the Red Sox," he wrote.[5] Columnist Allen Lewis wrote in *The Sporting News*, "Most baseball men feel that Williams' great and controversial career is over if he misses the next two seasons."[6]

Ted reported for his physical on April 2, 1952, and, despite some doubt about the fitness of his damaged left arm, passed the exam.[7] Given the customary 30 days to get his affairs in order, he was in left field on Opening Day in Washington, but only made four sporadic pinch-hitting appearances until the 30th of April when baseball bade him an emotional farewell with a special "Ted Williams Day." Fittingly, he blasted a game-winning home run off the Detroit Tigers' Dizzy Trout, a clout that he thought at the time would be the last of his career.[8]

But fate intervened. Williams contracted pneumonia and was generally plagued by poor health while in Korea. After flying 39 missions, sustaining enemy fire, and surviving a fiery crash landing, he was sent stateside. Eventually he was mustered out when it turned out that he'd developed inner ear problems that required extensive treatment before he could fly again.[9]

The 1953 baseball season was already half over when Ted was discharged. Sick and weak, he wasn't really anxious to return to the baseball wars. But his appetite for the game returned when he saw his old teammates and rivals at Crosley Field in Cincinnati, where he received the honor of throwing out the first ball at the All-Star Game. He determined to "show 'em" that he was still one of the best.[10]

After a few weeks of batting practice, Williams returned to action on August 6 with an unsuccessful pinch-hitting appearance in St. Louis. Three days later he slammed a dramatic pinch homer in his return to Fenway Park. A week later he made his first start of the season in left field and treated Boston fans to another homer and a double. He ended his abbreviated season hitting .407, while smacking 13 homers in only 37 games.

The next year, Ted put the finishing touches on his Korean comeback by leading the league in slugging percentage and posting the league's highest batting average, despite missing the first month of the season with a broken collarbone. The injury, as well as his league leading 136 walks, kept him from getting the 400 at-bats needed to qualify for the batting title under the rule then in effect. This led to a change in the rules to base the minimum on plate appearances rather than official at-bats.

Plagued by personal problems and feeling that he had nothing more to prove on the field, Ted formally announced his retirement from major league baseball in September 1954. But a painful divorce left a void in Williams' personal life, as well as his bankbook. He rejoined the Red Sox in May 1955, with the season already well underway. Although he didn't have the benefit of spring training, his .356 average was the highest in the league, though once again he didn't go to the plate enough to qualify for the title. Ted's 1956 season was another fine one, but Mickey Mantle's spectacular .353 average beat his .345 mark for the batting title.

Ted thought 1957 would be his last season, but it turned out so well that he just couldn't walk away. The veteran slugger matched his age with 38 homers and led the league with a .388 average, the highest mark in the major leagues for a full season since his own .406 in 1941. Only five hits—hits that a younger Ted would surely have legged out—separated him from the magic .400 circle. After the season, he signed a new two-year contract and went on to capture his sixth batting title by passing teammate Pete Runnels on the last day of the 1958 season to finish with a .328 average.[11]

Reporting to the Red Sox Scottsdale, Arizona, spring training camp in the spring of 1959, Ted was full of optimism. But he suffered a pinched nerve in his neck and spent three weeks in traction. The season was a nightmare for him. Besides the embarrassing .254 batting average, he banged only 10 homers in 103 games.[12]

Everyone expected Ted to bow out gracefully after that ignominious performance. But instead "Teddy Ballgame" (yet another nickname that Ted hated) engineered one of the greatest comebacks in history in 1960. He drove his batting average up 60 points and slammed almost three times as many homers as he hit in 1959.

Williams had declared before the season that 1960 would be his last year—no matter what. The publicity guys wanted to make the last weeks of the campaign a farewell tribute to the veteran slugger, but Ted would have none of that. Late in the season, he decided to end his career in Boston, foregoing the seventh-place Sox' season-ending trip to New York. Much to the disappointment of Yankees fans and management, it was announced that the Sox' last home game against Baltimore on September 28 would be Ted's grand finale.

Ted desperately wanted to go out with a dramatic home run in his last game, but the elements seemed to be against him. He walked in his first appearance and flied out deep to the outfield against a stiff wind in his next two chances. When he came to the plate in the eighth inning he knew it was now or never. Facing hard-throwing young Jack Fisher, he caught a fast one on the seams and sent it over the right-center field fence for a dramatic career-ending home run.

Characteristically, he touched all the bases with his head down, refusing to tip his cap to the wildly cheering fans.

Throughout his career, Williams had stubbornly refused to cater to the fans by tipping his cap after a home run. Even in his last moment on the field, after having done what every player dreams of doing in his last at-bat, he couldn't find it in himself to acknowledge the applause of the fans. After he completed his circuit of the bases and returned to the dugout, the Fenway Park faithful continued to give him a standing ovation. His teammates implored him to go back out. "Come on Ted, give 'em your hat," they pleaded, but he just couldn't do it. Ted was sent out to left field in the top of the ninth to give him another chance to respond to the cheers, but when a substitute went out to take his place he just raced back to the dugout with his head down. Years later, he admitted in his autobiography that he should have let the fans know he appreciated their cheers, but "it just wouldn't have been me."[13]

Ted completed his marvelous career with a .344 lifetime batting average. No player has retired since with a mark approaching that figure. Despite losing almost five prime years to military service, he slammed 521 homers which placed him third on the all-time list, behind Babe Ruth and Jimmie Foxx, when he retired. If he hadn't lost all that time, he almost certainly would have threatened Ruth's career record long before Hank Aaron mounted his assault. His .482 career on-base percentage is still the all-time best, and he still ranks second to Babe Ruth in lifetime slugging percentage and OPS. He won six batting titles, twice fell short of the required number of appearances while registering the highest average, and lost another crown by a fraction of a point. In the counting stat categories, he led the league in homers and RBIs four times, runs scored six times, and walks eight times. In the qualitative department, he was the recognized American League leader in on-base percentage twelve times, slugging percentage ten times, and OPS nine times. Finally, he's the only major leaguer to star in four different decades.

He was a shoo-in his first year of Hall of Fame eligibility, named on 93.4 percent of the ballots cast in 1966.

Nine years after retiring as a player, Williams stunned the baseball world by taking over the managerial reigns of the moribund Washington Senators (second edition) in 1969. Ted was considered a great hitting instructor, but with his inflexible manner and knack for alienating the working press, he'd never been considered manager material. There was also considerable doubt that he would have the patience for dealing with ordinary players. Furthermore, the Senators were considered hopeless. They'd finished dead last in the American League in 1968 with the highest team ERA and the next-to-lowest team fielding and batting averages.

But Williams led his charges to 86 victories and a respectable fourth place finish in 1969, somehow extracting career years from slugger Frank Howard and a hodgepodge of marginal major leaguers. For his efforts, he was named Manager of the Year.

Ted had "showed 'em" yet again.

Ted Williams

Born: 8/30/1918

Year	Team	Lg	G	HR	RBI	SB	BA	OPS
1936	*San Diego*	*PCL*	*42*	*0*	*11*	-	*.271*	*.654*
1937	*San Diego*	*PCL*	*138*	*23*	*98*	-	*.291*	*.795*
1938	*Minneapolis*	*AA*	*148*	*43*	*142*	-	*.366*	*1.066*
1939	Boston	AL	149	31	145	2	.327	1.045
1940	Boston	AL	144	23	113	4	.344	1.036
1941	Boston	AL	143	37	120	2	.406	1.287
1942	Boston	AL	150	36	137	3	.356	1.147
1943			(Military service—Did not play)					
1944			(Military service—Did not play)					
1945			(Military service—Did not play)					
1946	Boston	AL	150	38	123	0	.342	1.164
1947	Boston	AL	156	32	114	0	.343	1.133
1948	Boston	AL	137	25	127	4	.369	1.112
1949	Boston	AL	155	43	159	1	.343	1.141
1950	Boston	AL	89	28	97	3	.317	1.099
1951	Boston	AL	148	30	126	1	.318	1.019
1952	Boston	AL	6	1	3	0	.400	1.400
1953	Boston	AL	37	13	34	0	.407	1.410
1954	Boston	AL	117	29	89	0	.345	1.148
1955	Boston	AL	98	28	83	2	.356	1.200
1956	Boston	AL	136	24	82	0	.345	1.084
1957	Boston	AL	132	38	87	0	.388	1.257
1958	Boston	AL	129	26	85	1	.328	1.042
1959	Boston	AL	103	10	43	0	.254	.791
1960	Boston	AL	113	29	72	1	.316	1.096
19 Yrs	MLB Totals		2292	521	1839	24	.344	1.116

9

Stan Musial

For much of the 1940s and 1950s, Stan Musial was the best player in the National League, if not all of Major League Baseball. From 1943 to 1957, he captured seven batting titles and became the first National Leaguer to win three MVP awards. During the 1958 season, he lashed out his 3,000th career hit, and early the next year he slammed his 400th career home run, becoming the first major leaguer to attain both milestones.

A little more than a year later, however, it looked like the end of line for the greatest player in the St. Louis Cardinals' rich history. Almost 19 years after breaking in with two hits to lead the Cards to victory, the 39-year-old icon was riding the pines with a batting average south of .250. He was even contemplating announcing his retirement at the upcoming All-Star break two weeks later.

Instead, Musial rallied to regain a regular spot in the Cardinals lineup. His 1960 batting average ended up 20 points higher than his final 1959 mark. He raised it another 13 points in 1961. And, at the age of 41 in 1962, he capped his comeback skein by driving his average up another 42 points.

Musial began his illustrious career in professional baseball while still a high school student in the mining town of Donora, Pennsylvania, about 25 miles south of Pittsburgh. After starring for Donora High on the basketball court as well as the diamond during the school year, he spent the summers of 1938 and 1939 pitching in the Cardinals minor league system with middling success.

In 1940, his first full professional season, he posted an 18–5 won-lost record for the Daytona Beach Islanders in the Class D Florida State League. The Islanders were managed by Dickey Kerr, the hero of the 1919 World Series who'd won two games for the Chicago White Sox while some of his teammates were trying to throw the Series. Recognizing Stan's natural hitting ability, Kerr used him in the outfield when he wasn't on the mound, and the youngster responded with a creditable .311 average in 113 games. But late in the season, Stan seriously injured his left shoulder diving for a ball in center field.

When Stan reported to the Cardinals minor league training camp the next spring, it was apparent that his pitching arm was shot. But there was nothing wrong with his bat. He impressed the brass enough to begin the 1941 season in the outfield for Springfield in the Class C Western Association. A dead-armed Class D pitcher switching to the outfield and rocketing all the way up to the major leagues sounds like storybook stuff, yet that's exactly what happened to young Musial. After hitting .379 for Springfield, he was promoted to Rochester where a .326 mark led to a late season call-up to the parent Cardinals.

At the time, the Cards were in a ferocious battle with the Brooklyn Dodgers for the

National League flag. Their outfield had been decimated by injuries, so Musial was installed in left field. Though the Cards failed to overtake the Dodgers, Stan established himself as a major league hitter with a sensational .426 in 12 games during the heat of the pennant race. The next year he batted .315 as the world champion Cardinals regular left fielder and in 1943 he lashed out 220 hits, won his first batting title with a .357 average, and was named the league's MVP as the Cardinals again captured the pennant, although they lost to the New York Yankees in the World Series. He followed that performance with a .347 average in 1944 as the Cardinals won a third straight pennant and subdued the neighboring St. Louis Browns in the Series. Stan returned from a year of military service to hit .365 in 1946 and again capture the MVP Award. In the Fall Classic, the Cards won yet another world championship with a victory over Ted Williams' Boston Red Sox.

After a down 1947 season, when he played through a ruptured appendix, Stan recaptured MVP honors in 1948, enjoying his greatest year. He led the league in batting (.376), slugging (.702), hits (230), doubles (46), triples (18), runs scored (135), and RBIs (131). In addition, his 39 homers left him one short of the Triple Crown as Ralph Kiner and Johnny Mize tied for the league lead with 40 circuit shots. After tailing off to .338 in 1949, Stan rebounded to lead the league in hitting each year from 1950 through 1952. At the conclusion of the 1952 campaign, the 31-year-old star's career batting average stood at .346.

From 1953 to 1957 there was a modest decline in Stan's batting stats. His career batting mark dipped to .340, yet he still led the league in doubles, walks, and on-base percentage in 1953; average, doubles and runs scored in 1954; and RBIs in 1956. Then, at age 36 in 1957, he captured his seventh National League batting championship while pacing the circuit in on-base plus slugging percentage (OPS) and on-base percentage as well.

Musial's power numbers slipped noticeably in 1958, although he did make a heroic run at an eighth batting title, which would have tied Honus Wagner's National League record. He tailed off at the end of the campaign and finished third behind future Hall of Famers Richie Ashburn and Willie Mays. Although his .337 mark wasn't that far off his career norm, his 17 homers and 62 RBIs were well below the 31 homers and 112 RBIs he'd averaged the previous five seasons.

The 1959 season would be Stan's worst, by far. His batting average plummeted to a mediocre .255 after 16 straight .300 seasons, and his slugging average fell to a career-low .428 in 115 games.

Ironically, events that took place while Stan was vying for the 1958 batting crown contributed greatly to his disastrous 1959 season. With less than two weeks to go in the campaign, impetuous Cards owner Gussie Busch fired popular and respected manager Fred Hutchinson, replacing him with interim manager Stan Hack. Busch had already decided to hire former Cardinals infielder Solly Hemus, then playing second base for the Philadel-

Stan Musial wasn't called "The Man" for nothing (1959 Topps card).

phia Phillies, as his manager for the upcoming 1959 campaign. After being traded by the Cards in 1956, Hemus had impressed Busch with a fawning letter praising the organization and expressing a desire to return if the circumstances were right. The day after the conclusion of the 1958 regular season, the Cards acquired Hemus' player contract in a lop-sided trade for hard-hitting young infielder Gene Freese. He was officially named manager a few days later.[1]

In *The Spirit of St. Louis*, Peter Golenbock wrote: "Hemus was determined to run things his way. One of his decisions concerned how much and where to play Stan Musial.... Hemus insisted that Musial ride the bench or retire."[2]

Four days after getting Hemus, the Cardinals acquired veteran first baseman George Crowe, a 1958 All-Star, from the Cincinnati Reds. It was a mystifying deal since the Cards already had the best first base combination in baseball. Waiting in the wings behind Musial was Joe Cunningham, a smooth fielding first baseman who'd hit .300 the previous two seasons in part-time duty. Furthermore, Crowe was a left-handed hitter, as were Musial and Cunningham.

Then, two weeks before the season started, the Cards further muddled their first base situation by trading pitcher Sam Jones to the San Francisco Giants for another talented lefty-swinging first sacker, Bill White. White was a 25-year-old budding star whose future with the Giants was blocked by Orlando Cepeda.

On Opening Day of the 1959 season, the 38-year-old Musial found himself stationed in the outfield for the first time in almost three years with White manning first base. A fine defensive outfielder in his prime, Stan had moved to first base during the 1946 campaign at the behest of the club, a move that helped the Cards capture the world championship. Over the next decade, he unselfishly shifted between first base and all three outfield positions according to the needs of the team, but he had been used exclusively at first base since June 1956. His return to the outfield lasted only two games. Stan gave it the old college try, but he misplayed a few balls and banged himself up on the left field wall before he was returned to first base. He started 88 of the Cards' remaining 152 games at first, sharing time with White, Cunningham, Crowe, and rookie Gene Oliver. The unsettled situation certainly played a part in Stan's poor performance that year.

Brushing off suggestions that he retire, Stan vowed to whip himself into better condition for the 1960 season. The previous spring he'd taken it easy in training camp—an attempt to try to stay fresh for the regular season that backfired. He'd reported to camp late and slightly overweight, didn't run as much, and played less than usual during the exhibition season. Therefore, he wasn't in top shape when the season started. As a result, he got off to a slow start and never really got going.[3]

During the 1959–1960 offseason, Stan followed a rigorous conditioning program and "already had lost an inch or two at the waistline" before reporting for spring training. In camp, he did more running and calisthenics on the side and played more in the exhibition games.[4]

After enjoying an excellent exhibition season, he felt good going into the regular season. But once the season opened, the hits suddenly stopped falling in.

Unfortunately, the Cards had done nothing to ease their first base logjam in the offseason. Crowe, Cunningham and White were still around. In fact, the problem had been compounded by the acquisition of outfielders Leon Wagner and Bob Nieman, a couple of weak defenders who figured to take playing time at the corner outfield spots away from Cunningham and White. Musial began the 1960 campaign at first, while first sacker types Cunningham and White were stationed in right and center field respectively, with Wagner manning left—undoubtedly one the worst defensive outfield alignments in major league history.

When the Cardinals found themselves occupying seventh place in mid–May, Stan was dropped from the lineup. A week later, he was reinserted at first base after criticism over the way he was being handled from leading St. Louis columnists Bob Broeg of the *Post-Dispatch* and Bob Burnes of the *Globe-Democrat*. But on May 27, with his batting average languishing around .250, the veteran was again sent to the sidelines. He would never play first base for the Cardinals again. White moved in from center field to take over first, freeing up center for sharp-fielding young Curt Flood. Both White and Flood would go on to become outstanding players, and each would also gain fame for their off-field endeavors. After retirement, White would go into baseball administration and eventually became National League president, the first black man in organized baseball to hold such a high office. Flood would pave the way for players' rights to free agency by mounting the first serious challenge to Major League Baseball's reserve clause after being traded by the Cardinals years later.[5]

With a rejuvenated defense, which also benefited from the acquisition of young second baseman Julian Javier, the Cards began winning. In early June, the Associated Press carried an article in which Hemus and General Manager Bing Devine confirmed that Musial had indeed lost his regular job, with Hemus indicating that he considered the demotion to be permanent.[6]

Meanwhile, Stan continued working hard to stay in shape running and shagging flyballs in the outfield. He knew that many regarded him as "washed-up," but he was convinced that he could still swing the bat and thought he could help the team in the outfield if given a chance.[7]

Always the consummate pro, he refused to criticize Hemus or the team, but he was chafing under the forced idleness. He toyed with the idea of requesting his release from the Cardinals so he could join the Pittsburgh Pirates in their pennant quest. But pride wouldn't let him do it, and he began thinking more and more about retiring at the All-Star break.[8]

In late June, *The Sporting News* featured a front page article entitled "Father Time Pressing Standout Seven" in which Musial, Ted Williams, Warren Spahn, Early Wynn, Duke Snider, Gil Hodges, and Carl Furillo were identified as prime candidates for retirement at the end of the season—if not sooner. The article suggested that Musial might either be joining his boyhood favorites, the Pirates, or he might retire soon in response to pressure being exerted on him by management. The Cardinals brass denied that Musial would be traded, but his days with the team certainly seemed to be numbered and it just wasn't the way the proud old warrior had planned to go out.[9]

Then on June 24, Cards manager Hemus, desperate for some production from the left field slot, or perhaps giving in to front office pressure, gave the popular star a chance in left field against the Phillies. The veteran didn't immediately distinguish himself with the bat, going 1 for 8 his first two games, but he proved that he was in good enough shape to handle the job defensively despite his advancing years. When he proceeded to bang out two or more hits in each of his next five games, he re-established himself in the starting lineup. Stan's average had dropped to .238 while he was riding the bench, but by the July 11 All-Star break he was back up to the .300 mark. Furthermore his spectacular clutch hitting had spurred a St. Louis surge into the first division.

Baseball held two All-Star Games in 1960, giving Stan, a sentimental selection to the

National League squad, a chance to show he was still among the best in the game with the bat. He lined out a pinch single in the first contest in Kansas City and following up with a pinch homer two days later in the second game in New York.

With a revitalized Musial contributing down the stretch, the Cards made a valiant run at the Pirates. In August, Stan beat Pittsburgh three times with homers, but after getting within three games of the front-runners, the Red Birds faded to third place—still an impressive achievement after their seventh place finish in 1959.

For the year, Musial batted .275 with 17 homers and 63 RBIs in little more than part-time action, even garnering some support for MVP honors. Starting 58 of the Cardinals' final 92 games, Musial hit .292, slammed 13 home runs and drove in 50 runs in only 226 at-bats after winning back a spot in the lineup. More importantly, to a team player like Stan, the Cards went 56–36 during that stretch after starting the season with a 30–32 record. At season's end, the Associated Press voted him National League Comeback Player of the Year.

Stars of Musial's age and accomplishment often choose to retire after enjoying a late career comeback, opting to walk away on their own terms with their heads held high. Others, all too often, tarnish their legends by sticking around for one more encore or paycheck.

Not so with "The Man," a soubriquet his battered opponents had grudgingly bestowed on him.

Though many urged him to quit while he was ahead, Stan returned in 1961 because he still liked to play and because the Cards asked him to. In addition, he believed the Cardinals could improve on their 1960 success and challenge for the pennant. He did his part, hitting .288, driving in 70 runs, and belting 15 homers in platoon duty, but the club got off to another poor start before rallying under new manager Johnny Keane to take fifth place.[10]

There were no thoughts of retirement that offseason. At the end of the season, Keane had approached the veteran with the idea of increasing his playing time, and Stan welcomed the challenge. In addition, the National League was expanding into New York in 1962, and he was excited about performing in The Big Apple again. As an added incentive, the Cards swapped Cunningham for Minnie Minoso, and Stan was looking forward to playing with the veteran American League star, even though it meant shifting to right field so Minoso could play left. Unfortunately, Minnie went down with an injury early in the year, bringing the Cards' pennant hopes down with him.[11]

Musial began the 1962 season with a 3-for-3 day to welcome the expansion New York Mets to the big time. Keane kept his promise of more playing time. In early May, Stan played a doubleheader for the first time in nearly four years and he got three hits, including a home run, in the second game. Later that month, he knocked out hit number 3,431 to surpass Honus Wagner's National League record. In June, he passed Ty Cobb's major league record of 5,863 total bases. Just before the All-Star Game in July, he slammed homers in four consecutive at-bats at the Polo Grounds, three on Sunday afternoon after homering in his last at-bat to beat the Mets the previous day. Later that month, he broke Mel Ott's National League career RBI record of 1,860.

Amazingly, Stan found himself again competing for a batting crown. On August 1, he was leading the league in hitting, although he wasn't projected to get enough plate appearances to qualify for the title. So, with the Cards out of contention, his playing time was increased. Though his average slipped, allowing Tommy Davis and Frank Robinson to pass him in the competition for the title, he was still in contention until the final week of the season. He ended up with the third highest average in the league, a robust .330 for 135 games, and blasted 19 homers while driving in 82 runs. He rounded out one of the most amazing seasons in history by an over–40 player by reaching base 14 times in 19 pinch hitting appearances and even stole 3 bases in 3 tries. At season's end, the Associated Press honored him as National League Comeback Player of the Year for the second time in three years..

In his autobiography, Musial acknowledges that maybe he should have quit after his sensational 1962 performance, "...but, heck, I was having too much fun hitting to want to quit," he wrote.[12]

In addition, Stan thought the Cards had a good chance to win the 1963 National League pennant after picking up star shortstop Dick Groat and slugging outfielder George Altman in the offseason. Stan played in the World Series in each of his first four full years in the major leagues, but he hadn't made it back since. He desperately wanted one more trip to the Fall Classic. Unfortunately, the Cards fell short again, finishing in second place, six lengths behind the Dodgers.

In his last season, at the age of 42, Musial hit a deceptively productive .255, driving in 58 runs in only 337 at-bats. Early in the season, he broke yet another all-time record when he passed Babe Ruth's career total of 1,356 extra base hits.

Musial retired with seven National League batting crowns and also led the league in slugging percentage, total bases, and hits six times, doubles eight times, triples five times, runs scored five times, runs batted in twice, and base on balls once. Although OPS wasn't an official stat in Stan's day, he is retroactively credited with leading the league in the category seven times. His lifetime totals still rank in the all-time top ten in games played, hits, doubles, runs scored, and RBIs. He finished with a .331 lifetime batting average, blasted 475 homers, and slugged the ball at a .559 clip for 21 full major league seasons and a portion of another. In addition, he was second on the all-time hit list behind Ty Cobb and was the sole member of the 3,000-hit–400-homer club, a status he would enjoy until he was joined by Hank Aaron in 1970.

Though the Cardinals failed to win a pennant in Musial's last 17 years with them, his retirement after the 1963 season probably secured the 1964 flag. When the Cards farm system couldn't produce a replacement for "The Man," they were forced to trade 18-game-winner Ernie Broglio to the Chicago Cubs for an unheralded young outfielder named Lou Brock. Brock sparked the Cardinals to the 1964 World Championship and handled left field for the next 16 years, ending a Hall of Fame career with more than 3,000 hits and setting single season and lifetime major league records for most steals.

Moving into the Cardinals front office after his playing days were over, Stan served as general manager in 1967 when the Cards again captured the world championship. A bronze statue of him stands in front of Busch Stadium in St. Louis as a permanent tribute to the greatest Cardinal. He was elected to the Hall of Fame in 1969, his first year of eligibility, and in 1972 he became the first foreigner to receive the Polish government's highest sports award, the Merited Champions Medal.

Stan's refusal to give in to Father Time was rewarded with one of his most personally memorable and satisfying moments. When the Dodgers and Giants called "The Big Apple" home, Musial feasted on New York pitching. He gained the grudging admiration of the hardened New York fans to such an extent that when the expansion Mets brought the city back into the National League, they honored him with a special day at the Polo Grounds late in the 1962 season. It may have been the first time an active player was so honored by the opposition.

When Stan finally retired after the 1963 season, it was because he realized, "My liabilities were about to outweigh my assets as a ballplayer." It's too bad all great players aren't able to recognize that they've reached that point on their own—and a good thing that Stan Musial didn't arrive at that conclusion too early.[13]

Stan Musial

Born: 11/21/1920

Year	Team	Lg	G	HR	RBI	SB	BA	OPS
1938	*Williamson*	*MTNS*	*26*	*1*	*6*	-	*.258*	-
1939	*Williamson*	*MTNS*	*23*	*1*	*9*	-	*.352*	-
1940	*Daytona Beach*	*FLOR*	*113*	*1*	*70*	-	*.311*	-
1941	*Springfield*	*WA*	*87*	*26*	*94*	-	*.379*	-
	Rochester	*IL*	*54*	*3*	*21*	*2*	*.326*	*.817*
	St. Louis	NL	12	1	7	1	.426	1.023
1942	St. Louis	NL	140	10	72	6	.315	.888
1943	St. Louis	NL	157	13	81	9	.357	.988
1944	St. Louis	NL	146	12	94	7	.347	.990
1945	St. Louis	NL	(Military service—Did not play)					
1946	St. Louis	NL	156	16	103	7	.365	1.021
1947	St. Louis	NL	149	19	95	4	.312	.902
1948	St. Louis	NL	155	39	131	7	.376	1.152
1949	St. Louis	NL	157	36	123	3	.338	1.062
1950	St. Louis	NL	146	28	109	5	.346	1.034
1951	St. Louis	NL	152	32	108	4	.355	1.063
1952	St. Louis	NL	154	21	91	7	.336	.970
1953	St. Louis	NL	157	30	113	3	.337	1.046
1954	St. Louis	NL	153	35	126	1	.330	1.036
1955	St. Louis	NL	154	33	108	5	.319	.974
1956	St. Louis	NL	156	27	109	2	.310	.908
1957	St. Louis	NL	134	29	102	1	.351	1.034
1958	St. Louis	NL	135	17	62	0	.337	.950
1959	St. Louis	NL	115	14	44	0	.255	.792
1960	St. Louis	NL	116	17	63	1	.275	.841
1961	St. Louis	NL	123	15	70	0	.288	.860
1962	St. Louis	NL	135	19	82	3	.330	.924
1963	St. Louis	NL	124	12	58	2	.255	.728
22 Yrs	MLB Totals		3026	475	1951	78	.331	.976

10

Grover Cleveland Alexander

The success of *The Stratton Story* in 1949 turned the eyes of Hollywood producers to baseball. Within a few years, Warner Brothers Pictures placated Ronald Reagan for not allowing him to portray Stratton by starring him in a popular 1952 film, *The Winning Team*.

The movie was based on one of baseball's legendary comeback stories in which aging drunkard Grover Cleveland Alexander, formerly one of the greatest pitchers of all time, climbs out of the gutter to pitch the St. Louis Cardinals to the 1926 world championship. The climax, of course, is when Alexander shuffles out of the bullpen to strike out hard-hitting Tony Lazzeri of the New York Yankees with the bases loaded to save the final game of the World Series—an event that took on epic proportions over time.

Commander-in-Chief-to-be Reagan played Alexander, while perky Doris Day portrayed his wife, Aimee. The movie chronicles Alexander's release by the Chicago Cubs due to excessive drinking and his subsequent humiliation as he bounced around with various semi-pro clubs, including the bearded House of David team. He finally hits rock bottom working as a warm-up act for a flea circus before being rescued by Doris Day/Aimee, who persuades evangelistic Cardinals general manager Branch Rickey to give him another chance.[1]

A great comeback story if there ever was one, but it is somewhat technically flawed.

It's true that Alexander was an alcoholic and his drinking caused problems that led to the Cubs getting rid of him.

It's also true that Alexander, after joining the Cards during the season, helped them win the pennant. And he did strike out Lazzeri in a crucial spot in the Series.

But some of the details of Alexander's comeback are clouded by Hollywood hyperbole.

The fact is the Cubs didn't release Alexander, or "Old Pete" as he was often called. They asked waivers on him, since it was past the trade deadline, and he was claimed by the Cardinals. The Pittsburgh Pirates and Cincinnati Reds also put in claims, but the Cards' bid prevailed because they were behind the other two in the standings on the day the waiver listing period ended.[2]

Though the veteran right-hander, already a 300-game-winner, was 39 years old, he'd led the Cubs with 15 victories the previous year. He'd started the 1926 season well before developing a sore arm. After getting hit hard for a second consecutive start on May 22, he was removed from the rotation and left in Chicago to "get back in shape" when the Cubs went on the road a week later. He rejoined the squad in New York at the end of the first week of June, but was still in no condition to pitch. When Alex reported for a game in Philadelphia several days later, obviously inebriated, Cubs rookie manager Joe McCarthy barred him from the clubhouse and sent him home.[3]

Grover Cleveland Alexander never made it all the way back (Bain Collection, Library of Congress).

McCarthy, who would later enjoy a Hall of Fame career as manager of the Yankees, was not an Alexander fan. He knew that, despite a successful managerial record in the minors, he was still considered an unproven busher by most of the veteran Cubs since he'd never made the big leagues as a player. He had to gain their respect, and he simply couldn't abide Alexander's drinking or his casual approach to the game.

Alex reportedly sealed his fate with the serious, meticulous McCarthy early in the 1926 season. The Cubs were scheduled to play the Brooklyn Dodgers for the first time, and an intense skull session was already in full swing when the veteran hurler made his appearance. He ambled unsteadily to the rear of the room, finally located a seat, and immediately dozed off to the ill-concealed amusement of his teammates.[4]

McCarthy, studiously ignoring Alexander, eventually got around to discussing signs. "Maranville is with Brooklyn now," he said referring to Rabbit Maranville, the hard-partying, light-hitting former Cubs infielder who'd been sold to the Dodgers during the offseason. "Rabbit is a smart baseball operator. He knows all our signs from last season, so we'll have to change them today. Otherwise, the first time he gets to second he'll have every one of them."[5]

Alexander, roused from his nap by the mention of his former drinking companion, contemplated McCarthy's shrewd insight and unwisely elected to share his own strategy for dealing with the Maranville situation. In his characteristic soft, whispery voice he broke up the meeting by advising a red-faced McCarthy, "I wouldn't worry about Rabbit, Joe. He won't even reach second base."[6]

In St. Louis, Alexander would join a hungry, star-studded, young team assembled by Rickey and player-manager Rogers Hornsby. He recorded 9 wins, many of them clutch performances down the stretch, against 7 losses, and was a major factor as the Cards captured the pennant by a slight two-game margin. After St. Louis dropped the World Series opener, Alex won the second game at Yankee Stadium by a 6–2 score, retiring the last 21 batters in order. Back in New York, after the Cards lost two of three in St. Louis, Alex evened the series up again with another complete game victory in the sixth contest, once again holding the mighty Yankees to two runs.

As with the true circumstances surrounding Alexander's comeback, many of the facts of the Lazzeri confrontation have become somewhat blurred as the event evolved to the mystical realm. The popular myth is that Alex spent most of the night celebrating his sixth game victory and was still drunk (or at least hungover) when called in to face Lazzeri. Some claimed that Hornsby's pat on the butt when the old-timer entered the game was to see if he was carrying a flask rather than to convey encouragement.

To his dying day Alex denied he'd been drinking before the decisive game. "I was cold sober the night before I relieved Haines in the seventh game," he said shortly before his death. "After Saturday's game, Hornsby came over to me in the clubhouse and asked me not to celebrate, telling me he might need me in the seventh game. So I stayed in my hotel room all night."[7]

Hornsby did indeed require the veteran's services. Jesse Haines started for the Cards and pitched effectively. The Cards held a slim 3 to 2 lead going into the bottom of the seventh, but the Yankees' lead-off hitter, Earle Combs, walked to start the inning and was sacrificed to second. The next hitter, Babe Ruth, who'd already slammed four homers in the series, was intentionally walked. Ruth was forced at second by clean-up hitter Bob Meusel, sending Combs to third and bringing up 23-year-old Lou Gehrig, playing in his first of many championship series. The Cards decided to walk Gehrig and take their chances with Lazzeri, a 22-year-old rookie second baseman and a future Hall of Famer himself.

Haines had developed a blister on his finger from pitching so many knuckleballs, so after a short mound conference, Hornsby signaled to the bullpen. There was a murmur of surprise from the crowd as Alexander, who hadn't even been warming up, sauntered to the mound to face Lazzeri.

Alex slipped a called strike past Lazzeri on the first pitch. Tony jumped on the next offering, but was a split second early. He smashed a drive down the third base line that would have cleared the bases if it hadn't curved foul at the last minute. On the next pitch, Alex fired a quick sidearm curve to send Lazzeri down swinging and retire the side. He held the Bronx Bombers scoreless for the next two innings to preserve the Cardinals' 3 to 2 margin of victory. The last out was recorded in the bottom of the ninth when Ruth, who had walked with two down, was thrown out trying to steal second base.

Though Alexander may have been sober when he retired Lazzeri, his alcoholism was no secret in baseball circles. But Alex was also afflicted with epilepsy, a widely misunderstood disease at the time, and many incidents attributed to excessive drinking may have actually been seizures. The affliction first surfaced during World War I, when Alex was serving in an artillery brigade in France, and continued to plague him for the rest of his life. Ironically, Lazzeri also suffered from epilepsy and died in a convulsion at the age of 43. However, while Lazzeri never had an attack on the field, Alex would suffer several episodes a year. His teammates had a pragmatic approach to dealing with the seizures that probably didn't serve Alex well in the long run. The remedy was to pour whiskey down his throat until he calmed down and a bottle was always kept handy for this purpose.[8]

Despite his problems, Alexander was one of the most successful pitchers in baseball history. At 6'1" he was a big man for his time, and despite an awkward, disheveled appearance, he had a smooth, effortless pitching motion. He took a short, economical windup and delivered the ball from a slightly sidearm angle with extraordinary control.

The Philadelphia Phillies acquired him for $750 in 1911, and he led the National League with 28 wins, 367 innings pitched, and 7 shutouts as a raw rookie. His greatest years were from 1911 to 1917 when he won 190 games for the Phillies (including 30 or more wins for three straight years) and led the league in every important pitching statistic at least once. Despite toiling in Philadelphia's tiny Baker Bowl, with a right field wall only 272 feet from home plate, he hurled 16 shutouts in 1916, which is still a major league record. Economics forced his trade to Chicago after the 1917 season and he won another 128 games for the Cubs before his sale to the Cardinals.

After his 1926 Series heroics, Alexander got his best contract ever ($17,500) and responded with 21 wins in 1927 at the age of 40. In 1928, he helped the Cardinals to another pennant, winning 16 games against 9 losses, but losing his only start in the Series.

In 1929, Alexander seemed to be on his way to another successful season. He captured victory number 373 in Philadelphia to surpass Christy Mathewson, whose career was winding down when Alex broke in, for the National League lead in lifetime victories. The win was Alexander's 9th of the young season, but sadly it would be his last. An overly enthusiastic celebration with some old cronies from his early days with the Phillies turned into an extended binge. When the 42-year-old veteran wasn't in shape to take his next turn on the mound, manager Bill McKechnie suspended him and sent him back to St. Louis.

Actually, Alex had been drinking heavily all year and had even been admitted to a sanitarium earlier in the season. McKechnie sent him home, hoping he would dry out and rejoin the rotation. But he couldn't stay sober and was eventually suspended for the rest of the season as the Cardinals floundered in fourth place.[9]

Alexander would, however, receive another chance to add to his final victory total. In the offseason, the 43-year-old hurler was traded back to Philadelphia, where he'd begun his fabulous career nineteen years earlier. That season the Phillies would finish last in the standings while setting major league records for both highest team batting average (.315) and highest team ERA (6.71). But old Pete couldn't even hold a spot on that most horrendous of pitching staffs and was released early in the year with an 0–3 record and 9.00 ERA. When packing to leave the Phillies and major league baseball for the last time, Alexander muttered to a veteran sportswriter, "I'm leaving the same way I came—with nothing."[10]

After being cut by the Phils, Alex caught on with the Dallas Steers in the Texas League, but was ineffective and soon drew his release. Through with organized baseball, he pitched on and off for various touring teams, including The House of David, until he was over 50 years old. He also found occasional employment as an instructor at former manager Rogers Hornsby's baseball school in Texas. As times worsened, he began picking up a few bucks demonstrating his pitching technique as a carnival sideshow act, and for a time, he really did share the bill with performing fleas at Hubert's Museum in New York.[11]

For his career, Alexander threw a National League record 90 shutouts, while winning 373 games, losing 208, and registering a marvelous 2.56 lifetime ERA. He had a rubber arm, twice winning both ends of a doubleheader, and never turned in a losing record in either the majors or the minors until his last season.

But Alex had difficulty with everything in life other than pitching. He was inducted into the Hall of Fame in 1938 and came away from the ceremony with a replica of the tablet that had been placed there in his honor. "You know I can't eat tablets or nicely framed awards," he later grumbled to renowned sportswriter Fred Lieb. Alex took great pride in the fact that he'd finished one win ahead of Mathewson for the most career National League victories. But that distinction, like everything else, slipped away from him when statistical researchers in the 1940s added another victory to Matty's win column. In 1950, Alexander was found dead in a rented room in St. Paul, Nebraska, penniless and alone—an unfinished letter to his former wife on the table.[12]

The sad truth is that Grover Cleveland Alexander never really did complete that great comeback. Tremendous natural ability fueled his meteoric rise to stardom and kept him at the top for many years. What followed was a steady downward slide, occasionally slowed by sheer talent, but never reversed. Despite the film depiction, he was still a valuable pitcher, and his status as a major leaguer was not in jeopardy when he was sold to the Cardinals during the 1926 season. His comeback that year ranks high on this list based more on the notoriety of the event than its true merit. Alex's opportunity for a truly remarkable comeback came years later, and he failed miserably.

Grover Cleveland Alexander

Born: 2/26/1887

Year	Team	Lg	G	IP	W	L	ERA	WHIP
1909	Galesburg	ILMO	24	219	15	8	1.36	0.76
1910	Syracuse	NYSL	44	345	29	11	1.85	0.95

Year	Team	Lg	G	IP	W	L	ERA	WHIP
1911	Philadelphia	NL	48	367	28	13	2.57	1.13
1912	Philadelphia	NL	46	310	19	17	2.81	1.27
1913	Philadelphia	NL	47	306	22	8	2.79	1.19
1914	Philadelphia	NL	46	355	27	15	2.38	1.14
1915	Philadelphia	NL	49	376	31	10	1.22	0.84
1916	Philadelphia	NL	48	389	33	12	1.55	0.96
1917	Philadelphia	NL	45	388	30	13	1.83	1.01
1918	Chicago	NL	3	26	2	1	1.73	0.85
1919	Chicago	NL	30	235	16	11	1.72	0.93
1920	Chicago	NL	46	363	27	14	1.91	1.11
1921	Chicago	NL	31	252	15	13	3.39	1.27
1922	Chicago	NL	33	245	16	13	3.63	1.29
1923	Chicago	NL	39	305	22	12	3.19	1.11
1924	Chicago	NL	21	169	12	5	3.03	1.23
1925	Chicago	NL	32	236	15	11	3.39	1.27
1926	Chicago	NL	7	52	3	3	3.46	1.19
	St. Louis	NL	23	148	9	7	2.91	1.08
1927	St. Louis	NL	37	268	21	10	2.52	1.12
1928	St. Louis	NL	34	243	16	9	3.36	1.23
1929	St. Louis	NL	22	132	9	8	3.89	1.30
1930	Philadelphia	NL	9	21	0	3	9.14	2.12
	Dallas	*TL*	*5*	*24*	*1*	*2*	*8.25*	*1.92*
20 Yrs	MLB Totals		696	5190	373	208	2.56	1.12

11

Rabbit Maranville

Rabbit Maranville actually enjoyed the type of comeback that his old teammate Grover Cleveland Alexander was never able to complete.

The colorful Maranville was often quoted as saying, "There's much less drinking in baseball now than there was before 1927, because I quit drinking on May 24, 1927"—or something to that effect. The exact wording varies, but in each rendition of the quote the date remains constant.

That date is important because on May 24, 1927, 35-year-old Rabbit Maranville was toiling for the Rochester Tribe in the International League. Exactly one year later he would take over as the regular shortstop for the St. Louis Cardinals, helping the Cards win the National League pennant and resurrecting a ruined career.

Walter James Vincent Maranville was dubbed "Rabbit" as a minor leaguer by a young girl in the stands who appreciated his hippity-hoppity movements around the infield. Only 20 years old when he debuted with the Boston Braves late in the 1912 season, he hit only .209 in 26 games and failed to nail down a regular spot. The following spring his main competition for the shortstop job happened to be a nephew of newly appointed Braves manager George Stallings. After a fine spring performance, Rabbit went to Stallings and brashly inquired, "Do I have to beat out your whole family?" Impressed by his spunk, Stallings adopted Maranville as his regular shortstop and personal favorite.[1]

Rabbit has been called the real miracle behind the 1914 "Miracle Braves" who made an incredible dash to the pennant after being in last place on July 19. Although he hit only .246 for the season, the diminutive infielder drove in a team-leading 78 runs and often manned the fourth spot in the batting order. Standing only 5'5" and weighing about 150 pounds, he may be the smallest clean-up man to ever grace a major league lineup. In the World Series, he hit .308 as the Braves swept the heavily favored Philadelphia Athletics. Displaying tremendous range in the field, the flashy fielder handled more chances in 1914 than any shortstop before him and teamed with the veteran Johnny Evers to lead the league in double plays. In fact, Evers participated in far more twin killings teaming with Maranville that year than he had ever turned during his years as the middle man of the Chicago Cubs' fabled Tinker-to-Evers-to-Chance double play combination. For his efforts, Rabbit finished second behind Evers in voting for the Chalmers Award, the forerunner of the Major League Baseball MVP award.

Although the Braves couldn't maintain the pace of that fabulous 1914 season and soon faded into the depths of the National League, Maranville remained the darling of Braves fans and proceeded to embellish his reputation as baseball's finest defensive shortstop. From 1914 to 1919, he led National League shortstops in putouts each year, except for the 1918 campaign that he spent in the Navy. He also led in assists twice, double plays three times, and fielding average once during that period.

In addition to being a great shortstop, Maranville was a natural crowd pleaser. With his Lilliputian stature and impish face, he reveled in the role of baseball clown. He would pull his cap sideways and jump into the arms of his biggest teammate to delight the fans. His most memorable antics on the field including handing the umpire a pair of glasses after a questionable call and pantomiming opposing players and coaches. But he was most famous for his "vest pocket" catches of infield flies, a difficult feat in the era of tiny gloves that weren't much of an improvement over bare hands.

Much to the dismay of the Boston faithful, Maranville was traded to Pittsburg before the 1921 season for three players and $15,000 in cash. Sporting a modest .251 career average to that point, he surprised everyone by hitting .294 and .295 his first two years with the Pirates. In 1922 he set a still-standing ML record by going to the plate 672 times (the league high) without a home run, although he did belt an impressive 15 triples. In 1923, he led National League shortstops in fielding before shifting over to second base the next year to make room for rookie sensation Glenn Wright and posting the top fielding mark among the loop's second sackers in his first season at the new position.

Rabbit Maranville won the battle with the bottle to save his career (Bain Collection, Library of Congress).

The mischievous Rabbit was also an ardent late night carouser and incorrigible prankster. After a few drinks with kindred souls, he became the life of the party—swallowing goldfish, walking hotel ledges, and terrorizing baseball writers and teammates alike with an arsenal of practical jokes. His antics invariably began to grate on management, but didn't seem to affect his performance until 1925, when his fortunes took an abrupt downturn. Before the season, the 33-year-old infielder had been traded to the Chicago Cubs where he joined a rather loosely disciplined, second division club that featured the hard-drinking Alexander as the ace of its pitching staff. The club was managed by Bill Killefer, Alex's long time pal and old battery mate.

Maranville was expected to be the Cubs' regular second baseman, provided enigmatic Charlie Hollocher, a career .300 hitter, was healthy enough to man shortstop. But Hollocher never made it to spring training—in fact, he would never play again. So Rabbit moved over to shortstop early in the exhibition season, and promptly broke his right ankle. He'd finally returned to the lineup on a regular basis in early July, when the Cubs, despite his long history of distinctively non-managerial deportment, named him to replace Killefer as manager just before the team left on an extended eastern trip.

Chicago general manager Bill Veeck, Sr. must have thought that the responsibility of managing a major league club would have a sobering effect on the playful shortstop. He was wrong. After celebrating his appointment on the train in his customary manner, the inebriated new manager made his way through the team's Pullman berths pouring ice water on his sleeping players while bellowing at the top of his lungs: "No one sleeps on Maranville's team!" It's surprising that he lasted 53 games before being relieved of his managerial duties with the Cubs in the same eighth place position they occupied when he got the job. Rabbit was also on his way out as a player. He played only 75 games that year, and in the offseason he was waived to the Brooklyn Dodgers.[2]

Maranville and the Dodgers seemed to be a match made in heaven. He joined a memorable cast of characters known as the "Daffiness Boys," led by the infamous Babe Herman with a supporting cast that included the likes of Dazzy Vance, Jacques Fornier, Jess Petty, and Burleigh Grimes. Their "handler" was the immortal Wilbert Robinson, who often dozed through late afternoon games and sometimes had trouble remembering his lineup. Though the Dodgers had gladly suffered their share of eccentrics down through the years, they soon had their fill of Rabbit. In late June, he was removed from the lineup for breaking training, and 33-year-old rookie Johnny Butler was installed at shortstop. Rabbit was given a crack at second base, but played only sporadically before being unconditionally released in late August.[3]

Rabbit had hit rock bottom. Despite acknowledgment as one of the finest glove men in the game, he found no takers for his services at the major league level after his release by the lowly Dodgers. It wasn't until the next season that the Rochester club, managed by his old skipper George Stallings, gave him a shot.

Though Rochester was technically an independent outfit in 1927, they had a working relationship with the Cardinals. In fact, they would officially join Branch Rickey's farm system and change their name to the Rochester Red Wings the next year. Apparently Rickey, who was always looking for a soul to save, promised Rabbit that he'd get a chance at a regular job in St. Louis if he stayed off the booze for a year. And Rickey stuck to his guns. Even though the Cardinals had a glaring weakness at shortstop and Rabbit performed sensationally for Rochester, hitting .298 in 135 games, he remained in the minors for most of the season.

Rabbit was finally called up and inserted into the Cards lineup in place of error-prone rookie Heinie Schuble on September 2. At the time the club was in third place, only two games behind the front-running Cubs and a game behind the Pirates. But five games later Rabbit went down with a injury suffered in a collision with center fielder Ernie Orsatti. He missed three weeks, returning to help the Cards win two of their last three games. It wasn't enough as the Cards finished in second place, 1½ games behind the Pirates.

Rabbit went to spring training with the Cardinals in 1928 and made the team. But the 36-year-old glove magician warmed the bench for the first month of the season watching weak-hitting Tommy Thevenow handle shortstop duties. Finally, on May 26, after a full year of sobriety, he replaced Thevenow with the Cards in third place. With Maranville at short, the Cards overtook the Cubs and Cincinnati Reds within a month and cruised to the pennant. Though he hit only .240, his .969 fielding average was a career high and the second best mark among league shortstops. At season's end, Rabbit finished 10th in voting for the National League's top player. The Cards lost the World Series to the New York Yankees in four games, but Rabbit led the St. Louis regulars in hitting with a .308 average.

Maranville's stay in St. Louis would be short-lived, however. Highly regarded rookie Charley Gelbert, who would later stage a remarkable comeback himself, was waiting in the wings to take over the shortstop post. Fortunately Rabbit had re-established himself as a dependable major leaguer. In the offseason, his contract was sold to the Boston Braves for a magical homecoming with the franchise he'd begun his career with many years earlier.

Rabbit enjoyed remarkable prosperity in his second tour of duty with the Braves. He was the top fielding shortstop in the league in 1930 at age 38 and was the league's best glove man at second when he moved back to that position in 1932. Despite his advanced age, he never played fewer than 142 games a season from 1929 through 1933.

Just when it seemed that he would go on forever, the 42-year-old wonder broke his leg sliding into the plate during an exhibition game against the Yankees in the spring of 1934. The serious fracture caused him to miss the entire season, but he was primed for another comeback in the spring of 1935. The Braves had finished a promising fourth in 1934, and Maranville was eagerly anticipating being in the lineup of a contender along with 40-year-old Babe Ruth, who'd signed with the Braves in the offseason. Alas, neither old-timer would be around long. Babe staggered through 28 games before retiring in late May, while Rabbit couldn't regain his old form and bowed out after playing only 23 games in his final major league season.

His big league career over, the Braves offered Rabbit the chance to manage their Elmira farm club in the New York–Pennsylvania League in 1936. In this endeavor, he was much more successful than in his previous managerial opportunity more than a decade earlier. He led the Pioneers to a winning record and batted .323 in 123 games as their second baseman. Three years later, at age 47, he was still at it, appearing in six games while skippering the Eastern League Albany Senators. That same year he garnered a respectable 82 Hall of Fame votes in his first year on the ballot. He was eventually elected to the Hall in 1954, but didn't live to enjoy the honor, dying shortly before the ballots were counted.

There has been a tendency among modern baseball historians to malign Maranville's career and question his Hall of Fame selection based on his rather ordinary .258 career batting mark. But the experts of his era, who had the advantage of seeing him perform, recognized his brilliance beyond offensive statistics. He was the most sensational defensive player of the era—the Ozzie Smith of his time. In tribute to his fielding ability, Rabbit did surprisingly well in various MVP award balloting. Before finishing second in the Chalmers voting in the Miracle 1914 season, he'd finished third in 1913, his first full campaign in the majors. The Chalmers Award was discontinued after 1914, but in 1924 a National League Award for the top player was introduced, and Rabbit finished a strong seventh in the running despite an ordinary .266 batting average. Following his tenth place finish for the top player award in 1928 the 39-year-old veteran ranked tenth in the first MVP voting by the Baseball Writers Association of America that was held in 1931. The next year he finished eighth on the *Sporting News* MVP ballot, and as a 41-year-old .218 hitter in 1933, he still rated thirteenth place in the voting.

Rabbit Maranville engineered a genuinely heroic comeback. When it looked like he was about to lose everything, he won the battle with the bottle and managed to regain control of his life and his career. After his banishment to the minor leagues, he fought his way back to the big time and starred for six more years. His ultimate reward was a place among baseball's immortals in the Hall of Fame—an honor that wouldn't have been possible if he hadn't succeeded in conquering his addiction.

Rabbit Maranville

Born: 11/1/1891

Year	Team	Lg	G	HR	RBI	SB	BA	OPS
1911	*New Bedford*	*NENL*	117	2	-	-	.227	.552
1912	*New Bedford*	*NENL*	122	4	-	-	.283	.659
	Boston	NL	26	0	8	1	.209	.524
1913	Boston	NL	143	2	48	25	.247	.638
1914	Boston	NL	156	4	78	28	.246	.632
1915	Boston	NL	149	2	43	18	.244	.632
1916	Boston	NL	155	4	38	32	.235	.620
1917	Boston	NL	142	3	43	27	.260	.668
1918	Boston	NL	11	0	3	0	.316	.749
1919	Boston	NL	131	5	43	12	.267	.696
1920	Boston	NL	134	1	43	14	.266	.676
1921	Pittsburgh	NL	153	1	70	25	.294	.727
1922	Pittsburgh	NL	155	0	63	24	.295	.733
1923	Pittsburgh	NL	141	1	41	14	.277	.673
1924	Pittsburgh	NL	152	2	71	18	.266	.706
1925	Chicago	NL	75	0	23	6	.233	.602
1926	Brooklyn	NL	78	0	24	7	.235	.624
1927	*Rochester*	*IL*	135	1	63	-	.298	.690
	St. Louis	NL	9	0	0	0	.241	.566
1928	St. Louis	NL	112	1	34	3	.240	.652
1929	Boston	NL	146	0	55	13	.284	.710
1930	Boston	NL	142	2	43	9	.281	.711
1931	Boston	NL	145	0	33	9	.260	.646
1932	Boston	NL	149	0	37	4	.235	.579
1933	Boston	NL	143	0	38	2	.218	.539
1934	Boston	NL	(Injured—Did not play)					
1935	Boston	NL	23	0	5	0	.149	.365
1936	*Elmira*	*NYPL*	123	0	54	-	.323	.691
1939	*Albany*	*EL*	6	0	2	-	*.118*	.235
23 Yrs	MLB Totals		2670	28	884	291	.258	.658

12

Willie McCovey

"Playing first base for the San Francisco Giants ... Willie McCovey!" boomed the Candlestick Park loudspeaker on Opening Day of the 1977 season. Those words had first echoed through "The Stick" 17 summers earlier, but it had been three long years since Giants fans had heard them. They responded with an enthusiastic standing ovation that moved the 39-year-old veteran to tears.[1]

It's said that "you can't go home again." The phrase originated as the title of a popular 1940 novel by Thomas Wolfe and has become embedded in popular American vernacular. Though it's actually not Wolfe's original message, the phrase has come to mean that you can't resurrect the past, that attempts to relive youthful memories will inevitably fail. The words can also be interpreted as a warning that you can't return to your origins without being deemed a failure.

But McCovey's surprising comeback with the Giants, a return to the scene of his greatest triumphs to reclaim his former glory, belied that message.

From 1959 through 1973, Willie slammed 413 homers for the Giants. He made six National League All-Star Teams and led the league in home runs, slugging percentage, and on-base plus slugging percentage (OPS) three times each, and RBIs twice. In addition, he captured Rookie of the Year and MVP honors in a San Francisco uniform. His big bat was key to the 1962 pennant, as well as the 1971 Western Division title and helped the club consistently contend during his tenure. His trade to the San Diego Padres before the 1974 campaign devastated Giants fans.

After two relatively productive seasons with the lowly Padres, McCovey slumped badly in 1976. He lost his regular spot and was waived to the Oakland A's late in the season, where he failed to produce as a designated hitter. For the year, he compiled a woeful .204 batting average and slammed only seven home runs. At the end of the season, he was unconditionally released by the A's.

At 39 years of age, with balky knees and a tired bat, Willie McCovey's career seemed about to end with a career total of 465 home runs.

But in Willie's old San Francisco stomping grounds, new owners who had taken charge were anxious to rekindle fan interest after a disappointing 1976 season. In what initially appeared to be little more than box office pandering, McCovey was invited to the Giants spring training and given a shot as a reserve first baseman and pinch-hitter. After spending his entire career playing for California teams, he could end his tremendous career in the bay area where it began.[2]

In addition to a publicity boost, the Giants were counting on McCovey for a strong veteran presence in a clubhouse that had been torn by dissent. "Just sitting there in the dugout, he'll give rival managers something to think about in the late innings," said team owner Bob Lurie shortly after he was signed. Obviously, his on-field contributions were expected to be minimal.[3]

But Willie had bigger plans. He not only secured a spot on the roster, but also grabbed the regular first base job and held it the entire season. In 141 games, he slammed 28 homers and drove in 86 runs to lead the club in both categories. In addition, his .280 batting average was the highest mark he'd achieved since 1970. After the season, he was the hands-down winner of the National League Comeback Player of the Year award.

Years later Willie would state simply, "Being in good shape at that age was no big deal. I was able to do it by not burning the candle at both ends during my career. I worked hard to stay in shape, and it paid off."[4]

McCovey's 1977 comeback is one of the greatest stories in Giants history, as is his sensational debut 18 years earlier in the midst of the 1959 pennant race. The raw-boned, 21-year-old left-handed hitter was ripping the ball at a phenomenal .372 clip for Phoenix in the Pacific Coast League when he was called up. On July 30, manager Bill Rigney tried to wake up his slumping team by inserting him in the third spot in the lineup between fellow future Hall of Famers Willie Mays and Orlando Cepeda. In his first game, he blasted two triples and went 4 for 4 against Robin Roberts, another future Hall of Famer. The youngster kept up the sensational pace as the surprising Giants led the race for the pennant until a late season collapse dropped them back to third place. Willie ended the year with a .354 batting average along with 13 homers in only 52 games, capturing Rookie of the Year honors despite playing little more than a third of the season in the majors.

A long and successful career was predicted for the young slugger, but the promise was not immediately fulfilled. Willie had the misfortune to arrive in San Francisco only one year after the talented Cepeda, who had captured the Rookie of the Year award himself the previous season. Cepeda, only a few months older than McCovey, was also a first baseman and the darling of San Francisco fans. The careers of these two young stars soon became unfortunately intertwined to the detriment of both, especially McCovey.

To make room for McCovey, Cepeda was originally tried, and found wanting, at third base. He was then moved to left field where he was better, but not exactly proficient. When McCovey slumped badly in 1960 and Cepeda sulked through a so-so season shuttling between the outfield and first base, the two become the center of controversy. Critics cried that the Giants were ruining the careers of both young stars and demanded that one or the other be traded. Most felt it should be McCovey. But, Giants management either stuck to their guns or simply couldn't make a decision and held on to both players for six years.

It's doubtful that a similar situation ever has been or will ever be allowed to exist on a major league roster. Cepeda and McCovey were both budding superstars in their early twenties, both destined for the Hall of Fame, and each obviously more comfortable and productive at first base. Cepeda, who had earned the nicknames "Cha Cha" for his flamboyant style and "The Baby Bull" for his tremendous power, was a polished defender at first base. The more awkward McCovey suffered greatly in comparison. His defensive shortcomings were duly noted, if not exaggerated, and he was booed frequently.

Playing half-time, McCovey had a decent 1961 season while Cepeda, splitting time between first and the outfield, led the league in homers and RBIs. Essentially Willie was platooned with former batting champ Harvey Kuenn. McCovey usually sat against lefties with

Cepeda at first and Kuenn in left field. With a righty on the mound, Cepeda went to left, McCovey took first, and Kuenn either sat out or played third base. In 1962, Giants manager Al Dark decided to simplify things by returning Cepeda to full time duty at first and converting McCovey from a weak-fielding first sacker to a terrible left fielder. The experts howled, but Willie, still in platoon with Kuenn, didn't do too badly in the outfield. He also blasted 20 homers in only 229 times at bat as the Giants captured their first West Coast pennant. In the World Series, Willie came within inches of becoming a Giants hero in the "Bobby Thomson mode." Trailing the New York Yankees 1–0 in the bottom of the ninth inning of the seventh game, the Giants put runners on second and third and two outs with McCovey up. Willie couldn't have hit the ball much harder, but his line drive to the right side was speared by second baseman Bobby Richardson to end the Series.

Nineteen sixty-three was a breakthrough year for McCovey. Playing left field on a regular basis, he tied Hank Aaron of the Milwaukee Braves for the National League home run lead with 44 circuit shots while besting the Milwaukee slugger in homers-per-times-at-bat.

Willie McCovey proved you can come home (1968 Topps card).

The Cepeda–McCovey controversy, which had subsided with McCovey's apparently successful conversion to the outfield, began simmering again in 1964 when Willie experienced knee and foot troubles and slumped badly both at the plate and in the field.

The situation finally sorted itself out when an injury disabled Cepeda for most of the 1965 campaign. McCovey moved back to first base and slugged 39 homers. Early the next season, Cepeda was traded to the St. Louis Cardinals and the Giants' first base job finally belonged to Willie. But the controversy wasn't over. After years of refusing lucrative offers for either of their star first basemen, the Giants ended up peddling Cepeda for Ray Sadecki, a mediocre lefthander who would win only 32 games for the Giants over the next four seasons. Fans and writers decried the wisdom of trading the popular Baby Bull for years.

Naturally, Cepeda aggravated the situation by staging a big comeback with St. Louis. He won the National League MVP award and drove the Cardinals to the world championship in 1967 and another pennant in 1968. In the meantime, McCovey quietly continued to build a reputation as one of the most feared sluggers in the game, averaging 34 homers and 97 RBIs per year from 1966 through 1968.

But Willie put the controversy to rest and won the hearts of Giants fans by winning the 1969 MVP Award. He led the National League with 45 homers, 126 RBIs, and a .656 slugging percentage. In addition, he placed fifth in the league with a .320 batting average and paced the senior circuit to a 9–3 victory with two home runs in the All-Star Game.

At last McCovey enjoyed the adulation of the hometown fans. It had been a long road. In his early years, the shy, soft-spoken slugger was overshadowed by more colorful teammates like Cepeda and pitcher Juan Marichal, who joined the Giants a year after McCovey. And, of course, there was always the incomparable Willie Mays to monopolize the attention of the fans and media. In addition, the long-running Cepeda controversy had forced Giants fans to take sides, turning many against Willie. And, although no fair minded fan considered him the goat of the 1962 Series ... he *had* failed to bring that run in.

But with Cepeda gone, Mays nearing the end of his fabulous career, and Marichal forever tarnished by an attack on Los Angeles Dodgers catcher John Roseboro with a bat, McCovey became the fan favorite. He was the consummate slugger, respected and feared by opposing teams. In 1970, when he banged 39 homers and led the league in home run percentage for the fourth consecutive season, he was walked a league leading 137 times, including a then-record 45 intentional passes.

Chronic knee problems and other assorted injuries reduced McCovey's productivity after the 1970 season. He rallied to hit 29 homers in 1973 but was traded to the Padres after the season to make room for underachieving Dave Kingman. To the horror of San Francisco fans, all the Giants got for him was journeyman southpaw Mike Caldwell in a trade eerily reminiscent of the Cepeda fiasco almost eight years earlier.

With the Giants, the lanky 6'4" McCovey had proudly worn the nickname "Stretch." In San Diego, he manfully endured the indignation of being rechristened "Big Mac" after the hamburger creation of Padres owner Ray Kroc, who also happened to own the McDonald's restaurant chain.

With the Padres, McCovey ran square into another Cepeda-type situation. The incumbent first baseman was Nate Colbert, a premier power hitter who'd led the team in homers every year since its inception. Naturally, Colbert was moved to left field—like Cepeda had been. Unlike Cepeda, however, Colbert defused the touchy situation by completely falling apart at the plate and forcing a trade to Detroit after the season.

Still, McCovey never found a home in San Diego. Kroc almost moved the franchise to Washington in 1974 and at least part of his reason for acquiring Willie was to give the franchise's new fans a recognizable face. When the move failed, "Big Mac" was stuck in a pitcher-friendly stadium performing before sparse crowds until his return to the Bay area.

After his inspiring comeback season, Willie spent two more years as the Giants' regular first baseman. Although his average declined, he continued to be an effective run producer and pushed his career home run total over the coveted 500 mark. But even his golden years were not without controversy as he again became part of a competitive platoon arrangement with power-hitting young Mike Ivie.

In 1980, the 42-year-old favorite was relegated to the bench before he retired midway through the season. Willie did reach two milestones that final year, however: he became a rare four-decade player, and his lone homer that year, number 521, tied him with the great Ted Williams for eighth place (at the time) on the all-time list.

Willie was elected to the Hall of Fame in 1986, his first year of eligibility. He probably would have eventually made the Hall, but he probably wouldn't have achieved the first ballot honor without those last years in San Francisco. After coming back to the Giants, he surpassed Stan Musial, Lou Gehrig, Mel Ott, Eddie Mathews, and Ernie Banks in homers to secure a top ranking among the game's all-time greats. In addition, McCovey's 18 grand slams established a National League record that still stands. In fact, he smacked all of his homers in the National League, retiring with the third highest all-time total for the league behind fellow Alabamians Hank Aaron and Willie Mays.

McCovey's comeback incorporated all of the features of the classic sports comeback described in the introduction to this work. He'd been a major star until age and injuries took their toll. He returned to the city of his youth, the scene of his greatest triumphs and his long rise to popularity, in a final attempt to hang on to the remnants of a great career. After being waived out of the National League and released shortly thereafter, his career as an active player appeared at an end, yet he was able to exact one more big season from his aching body and again bask in the cheers of the crowd.

Willie McCovey proved beyond a doubt that you can come home.

Willie McCovey

Born: 1/10/1938

Year	Team	Lg	G	HR	RBI	SB	BA	OPS
1955	*Sandersville*	*GASL*	*107*	*19*	*113*	-	*.305*	*.812*
1956	*Danville*	*CARL*	*152*	*29*	*89*	-	*.310*	*.892*
1957	*Dallas*	*TL*	*115*	*11*	*65*	*11*	*.281*	*.836*
1958	*Phoenix*	*PCL*	*146*	*14*	*89*	*4*	*.319*	*.894*
1959	*Phoenix*	*PCL*	*95*	*29*	*92*	*0*	*.372*	*1.219*
	San Francisco	NL	52	13	38	2	.354	1.085
1960	San Francisco	NL	101	13	51	1	.238	.818
	Tacoma	*PCL*	*17*	*3*	*16*	*1*	*.286*	*.900*
1961	San Francisco	NL	106	18	50	1	.271	.841
1962	San Francisco	NL	91	20	54	3	.293	.957
1963	San Francisco	NL	152	44	102	1	.280	.915
1964	San Francisco	NL	130	18	54	2	.220	.748
1965	San Francisco	NL	160	39	92	0	.276	.920
1966	San Francisco	NL	150	36	96	2	.295	.977
1967	San Francisco	NL	135	31	91	3	.276	.913
1968	San Francisco	NL	148	36	105	4	.293	.923
1969	San Francisco	NL	149	45	126	0	.320	1.108
1970	San Francisco	NL	152	39	126	0	.289	1.056
1971	San Francisco	NL	105	18	70	0	.277	.876
1972	San Francisco	NL	81	14	35	0	.213	.719
1973	San Francisco	NL	130	29	75	1	.266	.966
1974	San Diego	NL	128	22	63	1	.253	.922
1975	San Diego	NL	122	23	68	1	.252	.805
1976	San Diego	NL	71	7	36	0	.203	.633
	Oakland	AL	11	0	0	0	.208	.505
1977	San Francisco	NL	141	28	86	3	.280	.867
1978	San Francisco	NL	108	12	64	1	.228	.694
1979	San Francisco	NL	117	15	57	0	.249	.720
1980	San Francisco	NL	48	1	16	0	.204	.586
22 Yrs	MLB Totals		2588	521	1555	26	.270	.889

13

Eddie Waitkus

One of the most popular baseball flicks in history is the 1984 hit *The Natural*, starring Robert Redford as fictional baseball player Roy Hobbs. According to the story line, Hobbs was a talented young pitcher on his way to baseball stardom when he was shot in the abdomen by a deranged temptress. His promising career on the mound was over, but he surfaced again years later as a middle aged outfielder and slugger who set the baseball world on fire. Alas, the bullet which still remained in his body after all those years suddenly started to cause him problems, and he was forced to retire from the game after clinching the pennant with one last heroic performance.

The movie *The Natural* is based on a 1952 novel of the same name written by Bernard Malamud. It's widely presumed that Malamud's inspiration was the 1949 shooting of Philadelphia Phillies first baseman Eddie Waitkus, who, like Roy Hobbs, made a remarkable comeback to lead his team to the pennant.

Waitkus, then with the Chicago Cubs, had been a National League All-Star in 1948. The next year, after an off-season trade to Philadelphia, he was once again on an All-Star track when he was shot by a female admirer. There were fears that he would never play again, but he returned to action the next year and, despite a weakened condition, was one of the key ingredients of the Phillies pennant-winning squad.

A smooth, stylish, left-handed hitter and thrower, Waitkus came up with the Cubs in 1941 for a 12-game trial after three years in their minor league system. He spent the 1942 campaign with the Cubs' Los Angeles farm team before entering the U.S. Army for three years. Returning from wartime service in 1946, he claimed the Cubs' regular first base job and hit a solid .304. For his efforts, he was selected Major League Rookie of the Year by the Chicago chapter of the Baseball Writers Association of America (BBWAA), which stirred up considerable controversy. Many felt the selection was somewhat biased in favor of the hometown boy, since Phillies rookie Del Ennis outperformed Waitkus in every major hitting category and garnered the competing *Sporting News* Rookie of the Year Award. As a result, the National BBWAA organization took over the task of bestowing Rookie of the Year honors beginning with the 1947 season.

Holding down the Cubs first base job, Waitkus hit in the .290s in both 1947 and 1948. Never a power hitter, he banged a career high of only seven homers in 1948 when he made the All-Star Team as a backup to slugging Johnny Mize. Before the 1949 season, he was swapped to the Phillies, along with veteran hurler Hank Borowy, for pitcher Dutch Leonard, who would become a Chicago favorite, and former Yankees moundsman Monk Dubiel. The 29-year-old was clipping along at a .306 pace for the Phils and leading National

League first sackers in balloting for the 1949 All-Star Team when his season came to an abrupt halt.

During his years with Cubs, Waitkus had unknowingly acquired a dedicated and dangerous fan, a tall, attractive teenage girl named Ruth Ann Steinhagen. She had, in fact, become fixated on him. She built a mini-shrine to him in her bedroom and developed a strange obsession with number 36, his uniform number, as well as the city of Boston where he was born.[1] When she discovered that Eddie was of Lithuanian heritage, she attempted to learn the language.[2]

On June 14, 1949, 19-year-old Ruth Ann checked into Chicago's Edgewater Beach Hotel, where the visiting Phillies were staying for their series with the local Cubbies. She ordered three drinks and sent a message to Waitkus. The note said that they weren't acquainted, but implored Eddie to see her as soon as possible on a matter of some importance.[3]

Later that night, Waitkus knocked on the door to Ruth Ann's room. After admitting him, she pulled a .22 caliber rifle from the closet and pointed it at him. Before firing a bullet through his chest, she is purported to have said, "For two years you've been bothering me and now you're going to die." The impact knocked him against the wall and he rolled onto his back as he went down, a pool of blood forming around him.[4]

Apparently Ruth Ann's original plan was to stab Eddie to death with a paring knife and then kill herself with the gun. But she panicked when he breezed into the room and shot him instead. After that, she didn't have the courage to finish him off or commit suicide. She called the front desk to report that she had just shot a man in her room. When help arrived, Waitkus was rushed to the hospital where it was discovered that the bullet had entered under his heart and lodged close to his spine, causing his right lung to collapse. He received two blood transfusions as doctors desperately worked through the night to save his life.[5]

Several versions of Waitkus' reason for making his fateful visit were offered by teammates. Andy Seminick said that Ruth Ann coaxed Eddie to her room under the pretext that she was a friend of some of his neighbors and had a message from them. According to Del Ennis, Waitkus was on another date when he received a message from Ruth Ann claiming that she had just seen Eddie's father in Boston and that he was sick. It's also possible that Eddie, a bachelor at the time, merely decided to check out an intriguing invitation.[6]

Whatever Eddie Waitkus' motives, Ruth Ann Steinhagen's became quite clear after her arrest. She admitted to being insanely obsessed with him since she first saw him play for the Cubs two years earlier. She knew she didn't have a chance with him and decided that if she couldn't have him, nobody else could either. She'd made her hotel reservations a month earlier, under an assumed name, and told her best friend that she intended to kill the ballplayer. Understandably, the friend didn't take her seriously

Eddie Waitkus was the inspiration for *The Natural* (1949 Bowman card).

since Ruth Ann had previously been obsessed with Cubs outfielder Peanuts Lowrey, as well as various performers in the entertainment world. She was subsequently judged insane and spent three years in a state mental hospital.[7]

After absorbing the startling news of Waitkus' shooting and learning the extent of his injuries, the baseball world assumed that he was through as a player. He remained hospitalized for weeks, undergoing several operations to remove coagulated blood from his right lung and later re-inflate it while the offending bullet remained lodged near his spine.[8]

Seminick recalled that when Waitkus first appeared in the clubhouse to visit his teammates almost two months after being shot, "He looked like a ghost. He looked terrible."[9] Eddie spent the winter recuperating and working with the Phillies trainer in Clearwater, where the Phillies held spring training camp, as a guest of the city.[10]

Surprisingly Waitkus recovered enough to begin spring training with the Phillies in 1950, although he was still somewhat underweight. In addition to his frail condition, Eddie didn't have a job. When he joined the Phillies in 1949, he had to beat out Dick Sisler, son of Hall of Famer George Sisler, for the regular first base post. But, Sisler had reclaimed the spot while Waitkus was recuperating from his wounds, hitting .289 for the season.

Incredibly, Eddie again wrested the position away from the hard-hitting Sisler, who volunteered to move to left field, giving the Phils another valuable bat in the lineup. Waitkus went on to have a solid season, lending invaluable veteran leadership to the youthful Phillies, who became known as the "Whiz Kids" on their way to the National League pennant. He hit .284 and scored 102 runs while finishing second among National League first basemen in fielding percentage. His gutsy performance earned him acclaim by the Associated Press as baseball's Comeback Player of the Year.[11]

Although Waitkus played 154 games in 1950, sustaining his energy level was difficult. And the fact that he hit only two homers and led the National League with 143 singles is evidence that he still hadn't fully recovered his strength. In fact, he would only hit six homers in the remaining five years of his career. In addition, adhesions in his lower back muscles resulting from the surgery to remove the bullet were painful and made his back stiff.[12] His best friend on the Phillies, pitcher Russ Meyer, later admitted that Waitkus was never the same player after the shooting.[13] Jim Fridley, a teammate with the Orioles years after the shooting said, "He had a hole going in the front and coming out the back. You could put your arm in it. It was grotesque."[14]

As a result of his tremendous comeback, Waitkus became a huge fan favorite in Philadelphia, where he continued his steady work at first base for the next three years. He served as the Phillies' regular first baseman through 1952 and shared the post with Earl Torgeson in 1953. In 1954, he was sold to the Baltimore Orioles and spent that season and the first part of the 1955 campaign with them before returning to the Phillies for his swan song. He finished out the 1955 season and his baseball career by hitting .280 in 33 late season games before retiring at the age of 36 with a .285 lifetime batting average to show for 11 major league seasons.

Unfortunately, Eddie, who'd survived four island invasions in the Pacific during the war, didn't make a totally successful emotional comeback from the trauma.[15] Five months after the shooting he said, "If I'd known all I had to go through, I sometimes wish she had not missed."[16] Alcohol would become a problem that would plague him throughout the rest of his life.[17]

His son, Edward Waitkus, Jr., or Ted, later said, "The shooting changed my father a great deal, as you might imagine. Before he was a very outgoing person. Then he became paranoid about meeting new people, and pretty much stopped going out drinking with his teammates, which is what I guess they did in those days."[18]

In 1952, after a little less than three years in Kankakee State Hospital, where she'd reportedly "responded favorably to electric shock treatment," Ruth Ann Steinhagen was transferred to the Cook County jail to await a sanity hearing and prosecution for assault with intent to kill. Waitkus, who'd given up bachelorhood the previous year, was concerned for his safety. Shortly after the shooting, Steinhagen had threatened, "If I ever get out of here I'll kill him for sure if he ever gets married." Nevertheless, Eddie decided not to press charges. A short time later, Ruth Ann was declared sane and freed from confinement. Waitkus would never hear from her again.[19]

After the end of his baseball career, Waitkus returned to the Boston area where he'd grown up. Other than working summers as an instructor for the Ted Williams baseball camp, he was pretty much retired, living off his baseball pension and savings. "After baseball, Dad had some trouble finding himself," said Ted Waitkus.[20]

Eddie Waitkus died in 1972, just after his 53rd birthday. An autopsy revealed that his death resulted from cancer, although he'd never been diagnosed with the disease.

According to Ted Waitkus, "Different doctors through the years have expressed the theory that the stress of the shooting combined with the four operations allowed the cancer to take hold."[21]

As with the fictional Roy Hobbs, Eddie Waitkus' assailant may also have left a "time bomb" in her victim.

Eddie Waitkus

Born: 9/4/1919

Year	Team	Lg	G	HR	RBI	SB	BA	OPS
1939	Moline	IIIL	122	3	70	4	.326	.763
1940	Tulsa	TL	162	1	91	18	.303	.722
1941	Tulsa	TL	125	1	50	5	.293	.690
	Chicago	NL	12	0	0	0	.179	.385
1942	Los Angeles	PCL	175	9	81	7	.336	.834
1943	Chicago	NL	(Military service—Did not play)					
1944	Chicago	NL	(Military service—Did not play)					
1945	Chicago	NL	(Military service—Did not play)					
1946	Chicago	NL	113	4	55	3	.304	.748
1947	Chicago	NL	130	2	35	3	.292	.717
1948	Chicago	NL	139	7	44	11	.295	.764
1949	Philadelphia	NL	54	1	28	3	.306	.829
1950	Philadelphia	NL	154	2	44	3	.284	.700
1951	Philadelphia	NL	145	1	46	0	.257	.636
1952	Philadelphia	NL	146	2	49	2	.289	.745
1953	Philadelphia	NL	81	1	16	1	.291	.686
1954	Baltimore	AL	95	2	33	0	.283	.724
1955	Baltimore	AL	38	0	9	2	.259	.638
	Philadelphia	NL	33	2	14	0	.280	.762
11 Yrs	MLB Totals		1140	24	373	28	.285	.718

14

Tony Conigliaro

Boston Red Sox star right fielder Tony Conigliaro (a.k.a. Tony C), was on top of the world as he confidently dug in at the plate on the night of August 18, 1967. The surprising Sox, who were hosting the California Angels in front of a packed house at historic Fenway Park, were fighting for their first American League Pennant since 1946. The wildly popular, 22-year-old Conigliaro, who'd recently become the youngest American Leaguer in history to reach 100 career home runs, was enjoying another banner season, batting a solid .287 with 20 homers in 95 games.

Seconds later he lay bleeding in the dirt, beaned by hard-throwing Angels hurler Jack Hamilton. Originally expected to be out of the lineup for about a month, he ended up missing the remainder of the 1967 regular season and the World Series due to blurred vision. When his vision seemed to be worsening the next spring, even Conigliaro conceded that he was through, announcing his retirement from baseball shortly before the start of the 1968 season.

Yet, when the curtain rose on the 1969 season, Tony was back in right field for the Red Sox. He went on to hit 20 homers that year, and the next season he reclaimed his place among the American League home run leaders.

The pages of the *Baseball Encyclopedia* tell the story of many big league hitters who never fully regained their form after a serious beaning. Some suffered permanent physical injuries that ended their career immediately. Hall of Fame catcher Mickey Cochrane never played another big league game after a 1937 beaning, and 28-year-old Chicago White Sox infielder Cass Michaels was through after being hit in 1954. But for most, the most severe injury was psychological. Joe Medwick, shook off the physical effects of a 1940 beaning, but was never the same hitter. Likewise, Paul Blair became plate-shy after a 1970 beaning, and rising star Ellis Valentine's career went into a steep decline after he was hit in the face in 1980.

But Conigliaro seemed to overcome both the physical and psychological effects of his beaning. His was not an ordinary comeback. But then, Tony had never been an ordinary talent.

Tony signed with the Red Sox out of high school and hit .363 with 24 homers in only 83 games for Wellsville of the New York–Pennsylvania League in 1963, his first year of professional baseball. Ominously, his professional debut had been delayed a few months when his Uncle Vinnie broke Tony's thumb with a backyard batting practice offering just before he was due to report to Wellsville.[1]

The next year, at the age of 19, Tony captured a regular job in the Red Sox outfield.

Limited to 111 games because of injuries, including a six-week stay on the disabled list courtesy of a wayward Pedro Ramos fastball, he hit .290 and slammed 24 homers, a new all-time record for homers by a teenager.

Conigliaro was more than just another slugger, though. A local kid from Swampscott, Massachusetts, he was the idol of every baseball-playing boy and the heartthrob of thousands of young ladies in the Boston area. On the field Tony had style. He was one of those hitters who seemed to swagger while just standing in the batter's box, and he invariably saved his best efforts for the most dramatic moments, like the home run he slugged in his first plate appearance at Fenway Park. Tony was exciting off the field as well. His love life was tabloid fare and it was headline news when he was fined for missing curfew.

In 1965, Conigliaro became the youngest major league home run champ ever with an American League leading 32 circuit shots, despite again missing significant time with injuries. In 1966, he was voted the Red Sox' most valuable player after slamming 28 home runs and driving in 93 runs in 150 games.[2]

Everything seemed to be coming together for Tony and the Red Sox in 1967. After ending up the 1966 season in ninth place, their eighth straight second division finish, the young club was challenging for the pennant under rookie manager Dick Williams. Carl Yastrzemski was enjoying a fabulous season at the plate and in left field, while Jim Lonborg led a surprising young pitching staff. And Tony was doing his part in the cleanup spot. He missed two weeks while on Army Reserve duty early in the season, but had otherwise managed to stay in the lineup. In July, he was named to the American League All-Star squad for the first time.

Going into the fateful August 18 contest, Tony had been in a slump with only one hit to show for his last 23 at-bats. His batting average had declined 18 points and he'd been dropped from fourth to the sixth spot in the order. Before the game, he told his younger brother Billy, an outfielder in the Red Sox farm system, that he was going to move up on the plate and look for something inside to pull.[3]

Of course, Tony had always challenged pitchers. Darrell Johnson, a Red Sox coach during Conigliaro's heyday, called him a "matador" at the plate. "Nobody had more courage," recalled Johnson. "He'd get hit and stick his head right back in there the next time." In his brief career, he'd already suffered a broken finger, thumb, wrist, hand and shoulder blade from inside pitches. But crowding the plate and taking aim at Fenway Park's short left field fence was his bread and butter."[4]

The game was scoreless when Tony came to the plate in the bottom of the fourth inning with two out and the bases empty. He'd singled to center in his first appearance, but Angels hurler Hamilton had yielded only one other hit and seemed to be cruising along.

Just before Conigliaro stepped into the batters box, a smoke bomb was thrown on the field and the

Tony Conigliaro could have been the greatest (1969 Topps card).

game was delayed for several minutes as a cloud of smoke hung over the diamond. That black cloud may have been a portentous omen or even a direct cause of the ensuing calamity. Tony would later speculate that the delay may have caused Hamilton's arm to tighten up.[5]

When play resumed, Hamilton fired a fastball that sailed towards Tony's chin. His batting helmet flew off as he fell away from the plate and the pitch hit him squarely on the left side of his head. He suffered a fractured cheekbone, a broken jaw, and a badly bruised and swollen left eye. Doctors ventured that if the pitch had been two inches higher he might have been killed.[6]

Thirty years later, Bill Rigney, the Angels' manager in 1967, would say, "The sound is what I'll always remember.... The sound [of the ball hitting Tony's head] seemed to carry everywhere in that ballpark. Of all the things I've experienced in baseball, that's what I can't get out of my head. That's the sound that still wakes me up at night."[7]

Tony's eye remained swollen shut for days, and after the swelling went down his vision was cloudy. The trauma to the eye had caused the formation of a cyst on a portion of the retina called the macula, resulting in a blind spot. Nothing could be done other than wait for the natural healing process to take place and see how much damage remained.

In Conigliaro's absence, Carl Yastrzemski stepped up to lead the Cinderella Red Sox through a wild four-team race to the pennant that wasn't decided until the last day of the season. In one of the greatest World Series of all time, Tony could only watch helplessly from the bench as St. Louis Cardinals ace Bob Gibson dominated the Boston hitters. Thanks to Jim Lonborg's own spectacular mound work, the Red Sox took the Cardinals to seven games before Gibson shut them down for his third victory of the classic. Overall, the free swinging Sox batted only .216, with Tony's right field replacement, Ken Harrelson, hitting an embarrassing .077 for the Series.

In the off-season the condition of Tony's eye seemed to gradually stabilize. His vision, which had been measured at 20/100 shortly after the injury, had improved to the 20/50 range (his right eye was 20/15 by the time he reported to the Sox 1968 spring training camp in Winter Haven, Florida.[8] He seemed okay at first, but it soon became painfully obvious that he wasn't seeing the ball well. He was sent back to Boston, where an examination revealed that the cyst on the macula had burst, creating a small hole. It was determined that his eyesight had deteriorated to 20/300 and he was advised to find another line of work.[9]

While sitting out the 1968 campaign, Tony decided he wasn't ready to completely give up on baseball. He couldn't hit anymore, but he was only 23 years old and possessed a strong throwing arm. He'd been a star pitcher, as well as a slugger, in high school. Maybe he could become a major league pitcher. The Red Sox organization was supportive of the idea, so Conigliaro eagerly reported to Sarasota, Florida, where the Red Sox had a team in the Winter Instructional League.

As a pitcher, Tony was a bust, but in those pre-designated hitter days hurlers were required to take a turn at the plate. Miraculously, when Tony picked up a bat he was able to see the ball again, and he promptly started blasting it all over the park. He rushed back to Boston for new tests, where the mystified doctors discovered that, somehow, the hole in the macula had healed, leaving only a small scar. The vision in his left eye had improved to almost normal.[10]

To the delight and amazement of the baseball world, Tony was in the 1969 Opening Day lineup against the Baltimore Orioles. As usual, he rose to the occasion by slamming a home run in the top of the tenth to put the Sox ahead. Later, after the Orioles tied it up, he drew a walk and scored the winning run in the twelfth inning. Incredibly, Tony C. was back! He banged 20 homers and drove in 82 runs in 141 games while capturing the American League Comeback Player of the Year Award.

Conigliaro's 1970 season was even more successful from a statistical standpoint as he set personal records with 36 home runs and 116 runs batted in. But his eyesight seemed to be deteriorating again. He was having trouble with flyballs in the field, and he seemed to be bailing out on certain pitches. His depth perception seemed to be worse, and he had virtually become a one-eyed hitter.[11]

Before the 1971 season, Conigliaro was traded (ironically) to the California Angels. In some respects, California seemed like an ideal match for the handsome slugger. After all, he'd sung on the *Merv Griffin Show*, performed a duet with Dionne Warwick, and dated Mamie Van Doren. But his West Coast experience quickly turned into a disaster.[12]

"There's a spot on my eye. I can't see some pitches," he confided to columnist Dick Miller early in the season." Bothered by a pinched nerve in his neck and failing vision both at the plate and in the field, Tony C. left baseball after a humiliating 0-for-8, 5-strikeout performance in a 20-inning 1–0 loss. In a half-season with the Angels he hit a meager .222 with only 4 homers and 15 runs batted in 74 games.[13]

Still only 26 years old, Tony returned to Boston where he remained a popular public figure, but he still couldn't completely turn his back on baseball. There was an abortive comeback try with the Angels and rumors of a comeback attempt with the New York Yankees. Finally in 1975, at the age of 30, Tony resolved to give it one more try—back home with the Red Sox, as a designated hitter.

"It's a long road back, but who knows? If anyone can do it, it's Tony Conigliaro," said Red Sox general manager Dick O'Connell when the announcement was made that Tony C. would be back in a Boston uniform.[14]

Conigliaro was the "feel-good story" of the spring. On Opening Day, he was back in his old clean-up spot behind Yaz. And again he came through for opening day fans, singling in his first big league plate appearance in almost 3½ years. In the third game of the season, he slammed a homer to give the Sox the lead in a game they eventually won by one run. But three days later he suffered a pulled groin that kept him out of action for a month. Unfortunately for Tony, the Red Sox had come up with a couple of sensational rookie outfielders named Fred Lynn and Jim Rice. These youngsters, who would lead the Sox to the pennant that year, made it difficult for Conigliaro to get much playing time when he returned. Hitting a scant .123 in 21 games with Boston, he accepted a demotion to Pawtucket of the International League in June. He got off to a good start with the Triple A club before nagging injuries again brought him down. In September, after hitting only .203 with a trio of homers in 37 minor league games, Tony finally retired for good to accept a sportscaster's job.

To this day Conigliaro is often cited as a prime example of the "Curse of the Bambino"—the fabled hex that supposedly befell the BoSox after the unfortunate trade of Babe Ruth in 1920. If not for the beaning, Tony might have been one of the all-time greats. Hall of Famer Jim Palmer, one of the outstanding pitchers of the era, said, "He might have been the guy to break Ruth's and Aaron's record. With that swing, in that ballpark, there's no telling how many he would have hit."[15]

Conigliaro's career ended with a .264 career batting mark and 166 homers and in 876 games—which projects to 31 homers and 96 RBIs for a full 600 at-bat season. Not bad numbers in an era when pitching dominated. He was only 22 years old when he was beaned in

1967, but had already slammed 104 homers in only 494 games. He still holds the distinction of being the youngest player to win the home run crown, and his 24 homers as a 19-year-old rookie still stand as the high for a teenager. He's also still the youngest man to reach 100 homers in the American League. National League Hall of Famer Mel Ott was about two months younger than Conigliaro when he stroked his 100th homer in 1931, but by then "Master Melvin" had 250 at-bats more than Tony C. had when he reached triple figures.

Youth, charisma, enormous talent, a flair for the dramatic, and a swing perfectly suited for Fenway Park—Tony C. had it all before that fateful day in 1967. But the beaning changed everything. His life would never be perfect again. During his comeback, he routinely hit 300 or more balls a day, preferring to take batting practice in private to conceal his failing eyesight. Even after his playing career ended, tragedy stalked him. He drifted to the West Coast working in television and radio. At the age of 37, he came home to Boston to pursue a broadcasting job with the Red Sox, but he suffered a severe heart attack following a promising audition. The resulting brain damage confined him to a chronic-care hospital for the remainder of his life. He died on February 24, 1990, at the age of 45.[16]

It's regrettable that Conigliaro was not able to sustain the remarkable comeback he forged in 1969. In lieu of a Hall of Fame plaque in Cooperstown, there's the Tony Conigliaro Award, given annually to the player who best overcomes an obstacle and continues to thrive through the adversity.

Tony Conigliaro

Born: 1/7/1945

Year	Team	Lg	G	HR	RBI	SB	BA	OPS
1963	*Wellsville*	*NYPL*	83	24	74	6	.363	1.093
1964	Boston	AL	111	24	52	2	.290	.883
1965	Boston	AL	138	32	82	4	.269	.850
1966	Boston	AL	150	28	93	0	.265	.817
1967	Boston	AL	95	20	67	4	.287	.860
1968			(Injured—Did not play)					
1969	Boston	AL	141	20	82	2	.255	.748
1970	Boston	AL	146	36	116	4	.266	.822
1971	California	AL	74	4	15	3	.222	.620
1972	California		(Injured—Did not play)					
1973	California		(Injured—Did not play)					
1974	California		(Injured—Did not play)					
1975	Boston	AL	21	2	9	1	.123	.466
	Pawtucket	*IL*	37	3	12	1	.203	.554
8 Yrs	MLB Totals		876	166	516	20	.264	.803

15

Charley Gelbert

"Charley Gelbert, St. Louis Shortstop and Hero of the 1930 World Series Played 239 Major League Games with a Broken Leg," according to the 1941 issue of *Ripley's Believe It or Not* magazine.[1]

Gelbert didn't actually star in the 1930 World Series with a broken leg, as the *Ripley's* banner might lead one to believe. In fact, Charley's days of stardom pretty much came to an end when he blew away a portion of the lower part of his left leg in a hunting mishap after the 1932 season. But, he did stage an amazing comeback to return to professional baseball two years after the accident, playing 239 major league games, as well as 249 minor league contests, before calling it a career in 1942.

The accident occurred in November 1932, when the 26-year-old Gelbert, the St. Louis Cardinals regular shortstop, and four companions were hunting near his Fayetteville, Pennsylvania, home. Charley's shotgun discharged into his left leg about four inches above the ankle when he snagged his foot on a vine and toppled to the ground. Fortunately, the gun had been right up against his leg when it fired. Had it been a few inches away, his foot might have been blown off. Instead, the charge went all the way through his leg, almost completely destroying the sheath of tendons connecting the upper leg muscles to the ankle and obliterating a section of the fibula, the smaller of the two bones that extend from the knee to the foot.[2]

Initially, it was feared that his foot would have to be amputated, but the doctors agreed to hold off when Charley stubbornly resisted. The first hours were critical. If there wasn't enough circulation remaining to keep the foot warm, it would have to come off to prevent gangrene. Charley's wife, Jerry, spent a sleepless night rubbing the foot to make sure it remained warm. To everyone's relief, the narrow strip of tendon that remained intact proved to be enough to provide an adequate supply of blood.[3]

The first media reports minimized Gelbert's injury, so it was some time before the full extent became known. Several weeks after the accident, *The Sporting News* reported: "Medicos who are familiar with the injury say only a miracle in healing will make it possible for the popular young man to play big league ball again." Meanwhile Charley was bravely predicting: "Out of the hospital by January 15 and at training camp with the other fellows in March."[4]

In February, a *Sporting News* column headline proclaimed, "Cards not figuring on Charley Gelbert," while Charley allowed that he might not make in back until mid-season.[5] But in April, it was announced that Gelbert was facing another operation and would be out for the season.[6]

The loss of their superb young shortstop was a tremendous blow to the Cardinals. The right-handed hitting infielder had joined the club in 1929 after a sensational season at Rochester, replacing aging Rabbit Maranville at the key shortstop post.

Like most young players he was somewhat error prone, but his fielding was spectacular at times, and he hit a promising .262 as a rookie. He improved his average to .304 in 1930 as the Cards captured the National League pennant. In the World Series, he hit .353 and played errorless ball, but the Cardinals went down in six games before the powerful Philadelphia Athletics.

In 1931, Gelbert batted .289 and dramatically reduced his errors. In that fall's World Series rematch with the Athletics, Pepper Martin earned the colorful nickname "The Wild Horse of the Osage" by belting out a Series record 12 hits and running wild on the bases. But, Charley led the Cards' defense, setting records for shortstops in a seven-game series by accepting 42 chances, including six double plays, without an error, as the underdog Cardinals denied the mighty A's a third straight championship.

The 1932 season was a disappointing one for Gelbert and the Cardinals. His average fell to .268 and the club dropped to seventh place. But the outlook was far from grim. Dizzy Dean had been called up from Houston to solidify the pitching staff, Ripper Collins supplanted veteran Jim Bottomley at first base, and Joe Medwick took over left field. Gelbert, who'd already established himself as one of the game's top shortstops, figured to be a key man in the anticipated resurgence.

When Gelbert went down, however, the Cards didn't have a ready replacement. They initially tried to replace him with utility infielder Gordon Slade and 38-year-old Sparky Adams, who'd missed most of the previous season with an injury. When that didn't work, veteran second baseman Frankie Frisch moved to shortstop and 37-year-old slugger Rogers Hornsby, signed as a free agent in the offseason, was plugged in at second. The flaw in the plan soon became painfully apparent. Although still a great hitter, the leg-weary Hornsby could no longer handle second base, while the versatile Frisch, no spring chicken himself at 34, couldn't adequately cover short. On May 7, the Cards acquired Leo Durocher from the Cincinnati Reds to play shortstop, allowing Frisch to return to second base and sending Hornsby to the bench. Though much improved with the fancy-fielding Durocher at shortstop, the club never challenged for the pennant, ending the season in fifth place.

Back in Pennsylvania, Charley Gelbert was still unable to walk without the aid of crutches or a cane. He'd remained hospitalized for more than three months after the accident. Four inches of posterior artery and nerve had been completely destroyed, leaving his leg supported only by the shin bone or tibia and a single remaining blood-supplying tendon. The remains of the fibula hung suspended from the knee area, totally disconnected from the foot.[7]

In late November 1933, *The Sporting News* reported, "There is virtually no hope of Charley Gelbert getting in the game next year.... The general belief is that he will never play major league ball again."[8]

Apparently, Charley didn't get the memo. Underneath a photo of him with a cane that appeared in the January 4, 1934, edition of *The Sporting News,* it was noted that he "plans to go to Florida in a short time to await the arrival of his old Cardinal mates."[9]

Gelbert did make it to camp, but Cards physician Dr. Robert Hyland quickly doused any hopes he entertained of getting back into action anytime soon. Nevertheless, Charley continued to work out with the team. Disappointed that the Cards "dropped him from the roster" (carried him on their "voluntarily retired" list, actually), he vowed to "be ready" by the Fourth of July.[10]

Six weeks into the season, *The Sporting News* noted that "Charley Gelbert works out lightly every day with the Cardinals," going on to say "there is tragedy in his efforts." The article likened him to former boxing champ Al Wolgast, who, after suffering a debilitating nervous breakdown, continued training diligently for years for another bout that would never come.[11]

On May 29, the Cardinals allowed Gelbert to take the field in an exhibition game. He played four innings at shortstop and blasted a drive that would have gone for extra bases had he not been under orders to simply jog to first base. Afterward, he was reported to be "more optimistic than ever over his comeback chances."[12]

Charley's determination and grit earned him the respect and admiration of his teammates. Though he didn't appear in a regular season game for the 1934 Cardinals, he was voted a $1,000 share of the post-season pot—no trivial gesture from a notoriously underpaid team during the reign of penny-pinching general manager Branch Rickey and owner Sam Breadon.

When the Cardinals pre-season training camp got underway in the spring of 1935, Charley Gelbert was there, sporting a special rubber stocking, which he had designed himself, to provide support for the damaged leg. He took infield with the scrubs, shagged flies, and pitched batting practice—anything to make himself useful.[13]

The defending world champs really weren't expecting much from him, though. Durocher was entrenched at short and the rest of the infield was set with player-manager Frisch at second, Pepper Martin handling third base, and smooth fielding Burgess Whitehead ably backing everyone up.

Though Gelbert made the opening day roster as a utility infielder, it appeared to be no more than an act of sympathy early in the season. The campaign was almost a month old before he got a chance to play in the field. Inserted at shortstop after Durocher was lifted for a pinch-hitter, he promptly muffed an easy grounder to let the tying run score. After the Cardinals lost by a run, manager Frisch's strategy was roundly criticized by the press, and Frisch seemed to lose whatever confidence he had in the veteran. For the next three weeks, Charley stayed on the bench except for a single pinch-hitting appearance in which he struck out.

On June 2, Charley finally got another chance, as a late-inning replacement for Frisch at second base with the Cards down by four runs. In only his second plate appearance of the season he banged a single and scored a run to help the Cards overtake the Chicago Cubs with a 5-run ninth inning rally.

After three straight losses, Frisch shook up the lineup, inserting Gelbert at shortstop on June 8 in place of Durocher and his anemic .215 bat. Charley went hitless in his first two starts, but the Cardinals won both games, so the superstitious Frisch stayed with him and was rewarded with three more victories. The skein ended with a 3–1 loss to the Boston Braves and Charley, despite solid hitting, was back on the bench the next day.

But a week later, with the Cards floundering, Frisch called on Charley again, and again he responded. After five games at shortstop, four of which the Cards won, Gelbert had his average up to .340 when he was again replaced by Durocher. Charley started two more games at shortstop in late June but remained glued to the bench as the Cards began the month of July with a 14-game winning streak, and Frisch stuck with the winning lineup.

In fact, Charley didn't get another opportunity until the first day of August when Frisch sent him to third base in place of sore-armed Pepper Martin. Again, the move worked like a charm, as the Cardinals reeled off eight consecutive wins with Gelbert at the hot corner. Naturally, when the Cards finally lost one, it was back to the bench for Charley, despite hitting close to .300.

Three weeks later, Frisch once again turned to his hot-streak igniter after the Cards had dropped four of seven. And once again the Cards went on a tear, winning seven in a row with Gelbert manning third base. Charley ended the season as the Cards' regular third sacker, more or less, starting 19 of the last 29 games, playing great defense and keeping his average around .300. Unfortunately, the Cubs got even hotter, ripping off 21 straight victories to overtake the Cardinals in the closing weeks of the season. St. Louis ended up winning 96 games, one more than the previous year, but finished in second place, four games behind Chicago.

For the year, Gelbert batted a solid .292 and committed only five errors splitting time between shortstop and third base. At short, his .959 fielding average was only slightly below Durocher's .963 mark which ranked second among regular National League shortstops. At third base his .978 average was well above Red Rolfe's major league leading .964 percentage and light years ahead of the .904 figure that Cards regular third sacker Pepper Martin registered. With part of his leg missing, Charley's range was limited at shortstop, but he was brilliant at the hot corner where range is not as critical. Still possessing a strong arm and sure hands, he fielded everything hit his way and turned in many spectacular plays.

Charley was also the team's good luck charm. Their winning percentage was .690 for games he was in the starting lineup, as opposed to .598 when he was on the sidelines. After the season, the Philadelphia Sport Writer's Association nominated him the "Most Courageous Athlete" in the country.

Gelbert's 1935 performance was so impressive that the Cards returned Pepper Martin to the outfield in 1936 and installed the stout-hearted 30-year-old hero at third. But Charley got off to a poor start at bat and was hitting only .182 when he was benched at the end of May. He never got his regular job back though he raised his average almost 50 points by the end of the season to finish at .229 for 93 games.

Prior to the 1937 season, Gelbert was sent to Cincinnati, where he backed up young Billy Myers at shortstop. His hitting was awful, however, and he was claimed off waivers by the Detroit Tigers late in the year and subsequently released. His composite average was a paltry .161 for the season.

Once again, it looked like the end of the line for Charley, but he had another comeback left in him. The 1938 season found the 32-year-old infielder manning third base for the Toledo Mud Hens, where he hit .284 and drove 91 runs across the plate. This led to another major league opportunity in 1939 with the Washington Senators. He served as a productive sub for the Senators, until the contending Boston Red Sox acquired him during the 1940 season to fill in for injured Jim Tabor at third base. But a .198 average in 30 games for the Sox ended his big league career.

Charley was through as a major leaguer after the 1940 season, but he hung on for two more seasons in the high minors. He subsequently turned to working with youngsters and became a highly successful baseball coach for Lafayette College in Pennsylvania. Over a 21-year stretch, his team took seven post-season tournaments and five District II titles. Of course, Charley still wanted to be on the field. During his career at Lafayette, he battled for and eventually succeeded in getting a rule change allowing college coaches to man the coaching lines during games.

Although Charley never regained his pre-injury status as a major league star, his comeback to play five seasons at the major league level after such a devastating injury was nothing short of miraculous.

After the accident, physicians gave Gelbert "a chance" of regaining full use of his injured leg. But that only meant walking without the use of a cane, not resuming a career in professional baseball. Few honestly believed he would play ball again.

But Charley Gelbert, like his father, who'd been an All-American football star at Pennsylvania, was made of tough stuff.

Charley Gelbert

Born: 1/26/1906

Year	Team	Lg	G	HR	RBI	SB	BA	OPS
1926	*Syracuse*	*IL*	*1*	*0*	-	-	*.250*	-
1927	*Topeka*	*WA*	*46*	*3*	-	-	*.286*	-
1927	*Syracuse*	*IL*	*5*	*0*	-	-	*.333*	-
1928	*Rochester*	*IL*	*164*	*21*	-	-	*.340*	*.895*
1929	St. Louis	NL	146	3	65	8	.262	.696
1930	St. Louis	NL	139	3	72	6	.304	.801
1931	St. Louis	NL	131	1	62	7	.289	.748
1932	St. Louis	NL	122	1	45	8	.268	.706
1933	St. Louis	NL	(Injured—Did not play)					
1934	St. Louis	NL	(Injured—Did not play)					
1935	St. Louis	NL	62	2	21	0	.292	.750
1936	St. Louis	NL	93	3	27	2	.229	.620
1937	Cincinnati	NL	43	1	13	1	.193	.541
	Detroit	AL	20	0	1	0	.085	.285
1938	*Toledo*	*AA*	*143*	*8*	*91*	-	*.284*	*.722*
1939	Washington	AL	68	3	29	2	.255	.754
1940	Washington	AL	22	0	7	0	.370	.961
1940	Boston	AL	30	0	8	0	.198	.482
1941	*Louisville*	*AA*	*40*	*0*	*10*	*1*	*.270*	*.724*
1942	*Montreal*	*IL*	*66*	*2*	*23*	*3*	*.217*	*.642*
9 Yrs	MLB Totals		876	17	350	34	.267	.709

16

Dennis Eckersley

Just before the 1987 season began, the Chicago Cubs sent Dennis Eckersley, a sore-armed, 32-year-old pitcher two months out of an alcohol rehabilitation program, to the Oakland Athletics for three minor leaguers whose names would never grace a major league scorecard.[1]

Eckersley, once one of the premier starting pitchers in baseball, was on the last season of a three-year contract. After winning only 6 of 17 decisions in 1986, the Cubs were so anxious to get rid of the 12-year veteran that they were willing to eat part of his $800,000 salary.[2]

Years later, Eckersley was still sober and had become the top relief pitcher in major league baseball. He led both leagues with 45 saves in 1988, then the second highest save total in major league history.

Many pitchers have made the transition from starter to reliever, but none as successfully as "Eck." Under the deft handling of Oakland manager Tony LaRussa, Eckersley re-defined the role of bullpen ace and ushered in the era of the modern closer.

Eckersley, who grew up in Fremont, California, signed with the Cleveland Indians after high school. After three years in their minor league system, he bypassed Triple A to join the Indians staff as a 20-year-old in 1975. He opened the season as a reliever. "I wanted to start him, but the front office wouldn't let me," said manager Frank Robinson. "I figured that having Dennis in the bullpen was better than not having Dennis at all."[3]

The young fireballer justified Robinson's faith in him by hurling 14⅓ innings in 10 appearances without yielding an earned run, winning one game and saving two.

Eckersley made his first big league start on May 26, 1975, against the defending world champion Oakland Athletics, blanking the mighty A's on three hits in a 6–0 complete game victory. Five days later, he again beat the A's, this time in Oakland, about 35 miles down the road from his hometown. Pitching in front of family and friends, the local boy scattered six hits and walked only one to win 4–1. And he finally showed a hint of mortality, yielding his first earned run 28⅔ innings into his budding career. For his rookie season, he posted a 13–7 won-lost record and his 2.60 ERA was the third lowest in the league. *The Sporting News* named him the American League Rookie Pitcher of the Year.

Dennis barely finished over .500 in won-lost percentage the next two years, despite ranking among the league leaders in most strikeouts, fewest walks, and fewest hits per nine innings. The Indians offense simply did not provide their young ace with much run support. But, in early 1977, Eckersley demonstrated how truly dominating he could be. On Memorial Day, he threw a no-hitter against the California Angels, yielding a lone first inning walk and fanning 12 batters.

The great Cy Young is generally credited with the record for consecutive hitless innings in 1904, although the exact number varies from 23 to 25⅓ depending on the source. Having held the Seattle Mariners hitless for the last 7⅔ innings of a twelve-inning 2–1 complete game victory in his outing immediately prior to the no-hitter, Dennis had 16⅔ hitless frames to his credit. Therefore, he was gunning for Old Cy's record when he faced the Mariners at the Kingdome on June 3. He managed to get through 5⅔ innings before giving up a hit to total 22⅓ innings of hitless ball, a little shy of Young's amazing 73-year-old record.

Dennis Eckersley's move to the bullpen resurrected his career (1987 Topps card).

Though Eckersley had demonstrated the potential for stardom, rumors that the Indians were trying to move him persisted. The Cleveland front office noted that he gave up the long ball much too often, had trouble against left-handed batters, and allowed baserunners to run on him too easily. They were also concerned about his pitching mechanics. He used a high leg kick, followed by a side-winding delivery that the Tribe brass worried could eventually cause him arm problems. Remember, this was the same franchise that had the same concerns about Luis Tiant a decade earlier.[4]

Just prior to the start of the 1978 season, Cleveland sent the 23-year-old hurler to the Boston Red Sox, along with backup catcher Fred Kendall, for starting pitchers Rick Wise and Mike Paxton and promising prospects Bo Diaz and Ted Cox. It was an expensive package, but the Sox felt they were only a "Number 1" starter—a staff leader—away from overtaking the New York Yankees for the Eastern Division title.

The excitement of going to a contender was dampened significantly when Eckersley's wife and former high school sweetheart asked for a divorce upon news of the trade. Apparently, she'd become romantically involved with Cleveland outfielder Rick Manning, Dennis' long-time teammate and best friend, whom she later married.[5]

Nevertheless, Eckersley did an excellent job in the role of Boston's "Number 1" guy, posting a 20–8 won-lost record with a 2.99 ERA. Nine of his victories came after a Red Sox loss, each time giving Boston a victory when they needed it. And he went 11–1 in the hitter-friendly confines of Fenway Park. He won his last four starts, allowing only three earned runs in 33⅓ innings, as the Sox won 12 of their final 14 scheduled contests, including the last eight in a row, to catch the Yankees on the last day of the regular season. Of course, the Yankees won the one-game playoff on a clutch three-run homer by light-hitting shortstop Bucky Dent (ever after known in Boston as Bucky "&%#$ing" Dent).

Eckersley continued to pitch well the next season, posting 17 wins against 10 losses and matching his previous years' 2.99 ERA. He won eight straight starts from July 11 to August 14. The first seven were complete games, and he left the eighth after six scoreless frames with the Sox ahead 9–0. Thanks to the heavy workload, he developed a sore arm and won only one game the rest of the campaign.

"I was just tired from all the pitching (246⅓ innings for the season)," Eck said later. "It usually happens to me every year, although only once before did it really hurt. That was either my first or second year when I was in Cleveland, but the arm bounced back after the long winter rest."[6]

But the soreness didn't go away. Over the next four years in Boston, Eckersley's won-lost record was only 43–48 with a 4.43 ERA. Far from being the staff ace, he was a less than .500 hurler for a team with a winning record, and his ERA was well above the league average for those years.

In late May 1984, the Red Sox were floundering along with a 19–25 record when they traded Eckersley, who'd split eight decisions while posting a 5.01 ERA, to the Cubs, along with infielder Mike Brumley, for first baseman Bill Buckner.

In the National League, Dennis enjoyed a resurgence, winning 10 while losing 8 and posting a fine 3.03 ERA as a starter for the remainder of the 1984 campaign. He helped the Cubs capture the National League's Eastern Division title and go to the postseason for the first time since 1945. But, Eckersley was chased in the sixth inning by the San Diego Padres in Game 3 after the Cubs had won the first two games of the National League Championship Series at Wrigley Field. When San Diego won the next two games, the Cubs' season was over.

In 1985, Dennis was off to a good start until shoulder problems flared up again, sending him to the disabled list for the first time in his career. The soreness persisted in 1986, resulting in a career worst 6–11 won-lost record along with a 4.57 ERA, well above the National League average of 3.73. He gave up 58 doubles to lead the league that year and also yielded 21 homers to finish among the league's worst in that department.[7]

With his miserable pitching and the free nights due to the Cubs day-game schedule at Wrigley Field, it was easy for Dennis to start drinking heavily, a problem he'd dealt with off and on in his career.

He'd started drinking at an early age. As a teenager growing up in Oakland, California, he spent a lot of time hanging around with his older brother Wally, who naturally exerted a great influence over his little bro.

"We were out to get drunk, not to have a couple of beers," he would recall.[8]

Nancy Eckersley, Dennis' second wife whom he married while stationed in Boston, had noticed that he had started over-imbibing again, "The first year in Chicago wasn't too bad," she said. "But then Dennis started drinking again. I could see it in his eyes; hear it in his voice on the phone." Soon Nancy began attending Al-Anon meetings to try to cope with her husband's drinking, but she couldn't convince Dennis to get help.[9]

Eckersley's day of reckoning came that offseason when he watched a video of himself reeling drunkenly around his in-laws' house at a family get-together. He was horrified by the sight, especially since it had taken place in front of his young daughter. Dennis was forced to face the fact that he was an alcoholic and decided to do something about it. In January, he entered an alcohol rehabilitation clinic in Newport, Rhode Island, for a 30-day treatment program.[10]

While he was striving to overcome his addiction and put his life and career back together, the Cubs swapped him to Oakland shortly before the start of the 1987 season. He would be returning home to his old stomping grounds, not always a good thing for a recovering alcoholic.

In addition, Eck had experienced more arm problems in spring training with the Cubs and was unsure of his role with the A's. His new manager, Tony LaRussa, who'd taken over the reins in Oakland midway through the previous campaign, had once called him "gutless"—hardly a foundation for a good player-manager relationship. Eckersley still considered himself a starter, but LaRussa dispatched him to the bullpen despite a paucity of top-shelf starting talent on the A's staff.[11] Though he considered the move a demotion, Dennis figured he'd reached the twilight of his career and accepted it.[12]

As he had at the beginning of his big league career, Eckersley flourished in the bullpen. After only eight relief appearances, he'd registered his first save and first relief win in more than a decade. With his excellent 2.21 ERA, he was rewarded with his first start of the season on May 6. He gave up three runs and nine hits in 6⅓ innings, absorbing the loss and earning a return trip to the bullpen. But, after throwing more than twelve consecutive scoreless innings in long relief, he complained to LaRussa about his role and got another start on May 31. Again he took the loss, giving up six runs on two homers in 5⅓ innings. So it was back to the bullpen—this time for good. In fact, Eckersley would go on to take the mound 680 more times in the major leagues without ever making another start.[13]

Working exclusively in relief, Dennis posted a 2.60 ERA for the remainder of the 1987 season to finish with an overall 3.03 mark. In late June, he took over closer duties from Jay Howell and finished the season with 16 saves to tie Howell for the team lead. For the year, he fanned 113 batters and walked only 17 in 115⅔ innings. In the off-season, Howell was traded, leaving the closer job in Eckersley's hands.

In the last half of the 1980s, the Athletics put together a powerful dynasty. In a mere four years, from late 1985 through mid–1989, they brought in LaRussa, a certain Hall of Fame manager, future MVPs Jose Canseco and Rickey Henderson, future Cy Young winner Bob Welch, record-setting homer run hitter Mark McGwire, and four-time 20-game-winner Dave Stewart. But none were more integral to the team than Dennis Eckersley, both a future MVP and Cy Young award winner.

Beginning the 1988 season as LaRussa's stopper, Eckersley didn't yield a single earned run in his first 13 appearances covering 15⅔ innings. He saved 12 games in as many opportunities and held opposing hitters to a microscopic .098 batting mark. At that point, the Athletics' record stood at 24–7, and they held an imposing eight-game lead that would grow to 13 lengths by the end of the season.

For the year, Eckersley saved a major league-leading 45 games, tying Dan Quisenberry for the second highest yearly total to date behind Dave Righetti's 46, and posted a 2.35 ERA. He made the All-Star Team and finished second in the league in Cy Young voting and fifth in MVP balloting as the A's romped to the first of three straight American League pennants.

In the 1988 American League Championship Series, Eck saved all four Oakland victories and was named series MVP as the A's swept Boston. Disaster struck in Game 1 of the World Series against the Los Angeles Dodgers, however, when he came in for the bottom of the ninth inning to preserve a 4–3 Oakland lead. After easily retiring the first two batters, he walked pinch-hitter Mike Davis, bringing Kirk Gibson to the plate to pinch-hit. Gibson, the National League MVP that year, was out of the lineup with a sore leg. After hobbling up to the plate and taking a few ugly hacks, Gibson hit a 3–2 slider over the right-field wall for a 5–4 walk-off victory.

"When he hit it, I just sank," said Eckersley. "I guess I'm glad it wasn't a Ralph Branca job that ended the season, but it was bad enough. Usually when you give one up, teammates will pat you on the behind, and say 'Go get 'em next time.' We were all so stunned, no one said a thing." With the momentum on their side, the Dodgers took the Series, four games to one.[14]

Some pitchers never recover from such a dramatic failure. Branca was never the same after giving up Bobby Thomson's pennant-winning shot in 1951. Donnie Moore dropped out of the majors and committed suicide a few years after Dave Henderson's dramatic walk-off homer in the 1986 American League Championship Series.

In addition to contending with the stigma of being the World Series goat, Eckersley was also forced to publicly admit his alcoholism that offseason. In a drunken stupor, his brother Wally had stolen a car, with the owner, a 50-year-old woman, still in it. He was charged with kidnapping and assault. Dennis agreed to testify about his brother's, as well as his own, addiction at the trial.[15]

But, Eckersley handled his outing as a alcoholic well and shook off the Gibson homer. In fact, he lowered his ERA to 1.56 in 1989 and then to an ungodly 0.61 with 48 saves in 63 appearances in 1990. The Athletics made the World Series both years, sweeping the San Francisco Giants first and then falling to the Cincinnati Reds in four games the next year.

After a mediocre (by his standards) 1991 season, when his ERA rose to 2.95 and the A's fell to fourth place in the American League West, Eckersley bounced back with the best year of his career, from an awards standpoint, in 1992. He again led the major leagues in saves with 51, then the second highest total of all time. His ERA was 1.91 and opponents hit a meager .158 against him with runners in scoring position. The A's regained the American League West championship, but lost the League Championship Series to the Toronto Blue Jays. After the season, he captured both the American League MVP and Cy Young awards, as well as *The Sporting News* American League Fireman of the Year and the Rolaids Relief Man of the Year awards.

The 1992 season marked the end of the A's dynasty as they posted a lowly .443 winning percentage over the next three years. Eckersley's performance followed suit as his ERA jumped to 4.41 for the three seasons.

Following the 1995 campaign, LaRussa left Oakland to take over as manager of the St. Louis Cardinals and immediately acquired the 41-year-old Eckersley to head the Cards bullpen. In two years with St. Louis, Eck saved 66 games including all three games in the National League Division Series against San Diego in 1996. But he was hardly a dominant closer any more. After the 1997 season, the Cardinals let him go and he signed with the Red Sox for a final campaign.

Eckersley's 24-year major league career can be divided neatly down the middle. He spent his first 12 big league seasons as a regular starter, compiling a 149–130 won-lost record in 361 starts, completing 100 games and throwing 20 shutouts, and making the All-Star Team twice.

The next dozen years were spent working out of the bullpen, all but the last as his team's closer. Despite not switching to relief until he was 32 years old, Eckersley was a four-time All-Star as a reliever and finished up with 390 saves, which is still good for a solid sixth place on the all-time list. In his final game, he broke Hoyt Wilhelm's all-time record for career pitching appearances. In fact, his 1,071 games pitched in the big leagues still ranked fifth at the close of the 2013 season.

At his peak as Oakland's closer from 1988 through 1992, Eckersley became something of an iconic figure, brashly striding in from the bullpen with his unstyled, shoulder length black hair and trademark mustache, to put the game away. He may have been the most dominating reliever ever. In those five seasons, he averaged 44 saves a year with an ERA of 1.91. In 359⅔ innings, he fanned 378 batters while walking only 38 (12 intentionally), an incredible strikeout-to-walk ratio of just under 10-to-1. During that period Dennis recorded four 40-save seasons, the first reliever to do so.

For his career, Eckersley won 197 games, while losing 171 and posting a 3.50 ERA in the major leagues. Only 14 other big league hurlers have both won and saved more than 100 games, including Hall of Famers Hoyt Wilhelm, Rollie Fingers, Goose Gossage, and possible future Hall of Famer John Smoltz. All had at least 49 fewer saves, as well as 49 fewer victories than Eck, except Smoltz who registered 213 wins, but only 154 saves. In fact, Eckersley's combined wins plus saves total of 587 was the highest in big league history when he retired, although it's since been surpassed by all-time saves leaders Mariano Rivera and Trevor Hoffman, both career relievers who didn't get many wins.

Eckersley was the first pitcher to record both a 20-win and a 50-save season, a most select club with Smoltz the only other member. As a starter, Dennis finished fourth and seventh in Cy Young voting during his career. As a reliever, he won the award and also earned second, fifth, and sixth place rankings.

In retirement, Eckersley stayed in the game as a popular studio analyst and color commentator and came to be called "Honest Eck" for his blunt observations.

Dennis Eckersley's comeback from alcoholism and arm problems to successfully make the conversion to reliever had a tremendous impact on the game. The way Eckersley was used, and the success he and the A's enjoyed, transformed the way bullpens were deployed. The creation of the one-inning closer job eventually led to clearly defined roles for the rest of the relief corps.

LaRussa credited Oakland pitching coach Dave Duncan with coming up with the idea of first using Eckersley as a reliever, and then a stopper. According to Duncan, "Eck always throws strikes, and he has the heart of a giant. His natural response is to challenge a crisis head-on. That's what makes him such a great reliever. And it's not tough on his arm if he's used right. Think of it this way: Aren't you less likely to break down running two miles every day than 10 miles every fifth day?"[16]

But, it was Eckersley who made it work. "A year earlier, I don't think it would have worked," he admitted. "I couldn't have been an every-day pitcher when I was drinking. But at Oakland I changed jobs at precisely the right time, and I give the A's credit for that."[17]

Of course, other clubs quickly copied the Oakland plan, and the one-inning closer is now the rule in most organizations.

Dennis Eckersley was inducted into the Hall of Fame at Cooperstown in 2004, his first year of eligibility. He was only the third hurler, behind Wilhelm and Fingers, to be inducted largely for his work out of the bullpen. In offering thanks to the many people who supported him during his climb to the pinnacle of baseball success, he said: "I'm being inducted into the Hall of Fame in large part because of Tony LaRussa and Dave Duncan. Not only did they change how late innings of a baseball game would be played, they carved out a role that was tailor-made for my personality, aggressiveness, competitiveness and intensity. They created a platform for me to pitch another 12 years. And it is those 12 years that were my ticket to Cooperstown."[18]

A comment made by Eckersley's after he'd blown a save early in first full year as the A's closer pretty well sums up his comeback. "I wouldn't be any good if I couldn't rebound. I wouldn't be a big leaguer."[19]

Dennis Eckersley
Born: 10/3/1954

Year	Team	Lg	G	IP	W	L	ERA	SV
1972	*Reno*	*CALL*	*12*	*75*	*5*	*5*	*4.80*	*0*
1973	*Reno*	*CALL*	*31*	*202*	*12*	*8*	*3.65*	*0*
1974	*San Antonio*	*TL*	*23*	*167*	*14*	*3*	*3.40*	*0*
1975	Cleveland	AL	34	186	13	7	2.60	2
1976	Cleveland	AL	36	199	13	12	3.43	1
1977	Cleveland	AL	33	247	14	13	3.53	0
1978	Boston	AL	35	268	20	8	2.99	0
1979	Boston	AL	33	246	17	10	2.99	0
1980	Boston	AL	30	197	12	14	4.28	0
1981	Boston	AL	23	154	9	8	4.27	0
1982	Boston	AL	33	224	13	13	3.73	0
1983	Boston	AL	28	176	9	13	5.61	0
1984	Boston	AL	9	64	4	4	5.01	0
	Chicago	NL	24	160	10	8	3.03	0
1985	Chicago	NL	25	169	11	7	3.08	0
1986	Chicago	NL	33	201	6	11	4.57	0
1987	Oakland	AL	54	115	6	8	3.03	16
1988	Oakland	AL	60	72	4	2	2.35	45
1989	Oakland	AL	51	57	4	0	1.56	33
1990	Oakland	AL	63	73	4	2	0.61	48
1991	Oakland	AL	67	76	5	4	2.96	43
1992	Oakland	AL	69	80	7	1	1.91	51
1993	Oakland	AL	64	67	2	4	4.16	36
1994	Oakland	AL	45	44	5	4	4.26	19
1995	Oakland	AL	52	50	4	6	4.83	29
1996	St. Louis	NL	63	60	0	6	3.30	30
1997	St. Louis	NL	57	53	1	5	3.91	36
1998	Boston	AL	50	39	4	1	4.76	1
	BOS-ML Rehab	*AAA*	*2*	*2*	*0*	*0*	*4.50*	*0*
24 Yrs	MLB Totals		1071	3285	197	171	3.50	1.16

17

Red Schoendienst

When the 1959 baseball season got underway, Albert "Red" Schoendienst, the premier National League second baseman through much of the 1950s, was bed-ridden—a victim of tuberculosis (TB).

Most baseball men assumed the 36-year-old second baseman's brilliant career was over. No one had ever come back from TB. Almost a quarter of a century earlier Bill DeLancey, the sterling young Gashouse Gang catcher who Branch Rickey always named to his personal All-Star team, was sidelined by the disease at age 24. After a four-year absence, DeLancey recovered enough that he was able to briefly return to the Cardinals as a bullpen catcher, appearing in 15 games in 1940. But he suffered a relapse and died a few years later on his 35th birthday. If a strapping young man like DeLancey couldn't make it back, what chance did an aging veteran like Schoendienst have?

Yet on Opening Day of the 1960 campaign, Schoendienst was manning second base and batting in his familiar number two spot for the powerful Milwaukee Braves.

From a statistical standpoint, Schoendienst's comeback may not seem like a great success story since he never again approached his earlier Hall of Fame form. But his battle to overcome TB was one of the most dramatic and highly publicized stories of its time, resulting in a popular 1961 biography, *The Man Who Fought Back* by Al Hirshberg. Schoendienst became the first prominent baseball player to overcome tuberculosis and make a successful return to the diamond. He made a contribution to the Braves' 1960 campaign, and served the St. Louis Cardinals as a valuable pinch-hitter for two more seasons before embarking on a long career as a big league manager and coach.

In what might pass for a Ring Lardner story, the switch-hitting Schoendienst was signed at a 1942 Cardinals' tryout camp after hitchhiking from his Germantown, Illinois, home to St. Louis with a quarter in his pocket. The freckle-faced Huck Finn look-alike began his professional baseball career as a 19-year-old Class D shortstop, but the next year he was manning the position for the Rochester Red Wings, the top farm club in the Cardinals' vast system. He hit an impressive .337 for the Red Wings in 1943, becoming, at age 20, the youngest player to win an International League batting title since Hall of Famer "Wee Willie" Keeler in 1892.[1]

The youngster returned to Rochester in 1944 and hit .373 in 25 games before Uncle Sam beckoned. A few years earlier, Red almost lost his left eye in a carpentry accident working for the Civilian Conservation Corps. The eye was spared, but vision problems would plague him throughout his career. Army doctors approved him for limited duty only—which meant playing baseball for the post team. When he hurt his right shoulder playing ball, the brass saw no reason to keep him around. He was mustered out with a medical discharge in January 1945 after only eight months in the service.[2]

Reporting to the Cardinals training camp in the spring of 1945, the 22-year-old rookie faced significant challenges, aside from his bothersome eyesight and sore arm. The Cardinals, world champions in 1944, had a tough roster to crack even with the wartime talent shortage. Marty Marion, the reigning National League MVP, had a death grip on the shortstop position, power-hitting All-Star Whitey Kurowski manned third base, and smooth-fielding Emil Verban handled the keystone sack. But superstar Stan Musial had been inducted into the service, leaving his left field spot vacant. So Schoendienst became an outfielder, and a good one at that. He hit .278 at the top of the Cardinals batting order and led the National League with 26 stolen bases.

The versatile Schoendienst began the next season filling in wherever he was needed, eventually taking over at second base after Verban was traded to Philadelphia and returning vet Lou Klein jumped to the outlaw Mexican League. The redhead would remain the Cardinals' regular second baseman for the next decade, making the National League All-Star Team nine of those years.

On June 14, 1956, Schoendienst was swapped to the New York Giants for shortstop Alvin Dark in a trade that included several other players. The Cards had young Don Blasingame ready to take over second base and needed someone to handle shortstop. The deal touched off the fiercest fan reaction in the city of St. Louis since the trade of Rogers Hornsby (also to the Giants) almost 30 years earlier, and caused a rift between Cardinals owner Gussie Busch and general manager Frank "Trader" Lane that led to Lane's ouster the next season. A year later, after hitting .301 in 149 games in a Giants uniform, Schoendienst was again dealt in a deadline deal, this time going to the Milwaukee Braves.[3]

In Milwaukee, Red joined a talent-laden team that featured future Hall of Famers Hank Aaron, Warren Spahn, and Eddie Mathews. He slid seamlessly into the lineup, instantly becoming a fan favorite. Milwaukee had finally gained a major league franchise when the Braves moved from Boston in 1953, and the fans now thirsted for a championship banner to decorate County Stadium. The Braves were in the thick of a pennant fight, half game ahead of the Cincinnati Reds with the Brooklyn Dodgers, Cardinals, and Phillies also within three lengths, when Red was installed at second base. By August, they'd pulled away from the pack. With Schoendienst contributing a .310 batting mark and brilliant fielding, they won the pennant by eight games and bested the powerful New York Yankees in the Series to bring the world championship to Milwaukee.

Red started off strong in 1958, but began experiencing respiratory problems early in the sea-

Red Schoendienst was the first to overcome TB (1960 Topps card).

son. He caught a cold in May and couldn't seem to completely shake it. His chest bothered him, he had a slight cough, and he tired easily. He was diagnosed with pleurisy and sat out 19 games in late May and early June, but still felt weak when he returned to the lineup. His batting average was down to .252 when a broken finger sidelined him in mid–July. The injury may have been a blessing in disguise. He was rested when he returned to the lineup after a three-week absence and started to hit the ball like the Schoendienst of old. His chest still hurt, however, and he still suffered from occasional coughing fits. In addition, the 6-footer, who usually played at 170 pounds, was losing weight from his already slender frame.[4]

The Braves repeated as pennant winners in 1958, but lost to the Yankees in an exciting seven-game classic. In the Series, the 35-year-old Schoendienst seemed at the top of his game, batting .300 and fielding brilliantly. But something was wrong. Although he led National League second basemen in fielding, he'd hit only .262 for the regular season, his lowest average in more than a decade. What's worse, he played only 106 games, the fewest ever at that point in his major league career. Even as he starred in the Series, it was obvious to his teammates that something was seriously wrong with him. After each game, Red would sit in front of his locker exhausted, hardly able to catch his breath. "The guy's living on guts!" Eddie Mathews told another teammate. "I don't know what keeps him going."[5]

Despite the urging of friends, family, and teammates, Red refused to see a doctor until the Braves clinched the pennant. Only then did he submit to some chest X-rays, which were negative, although there were still signs of pleurisy. Again, rest was recommended, but Red intended to play in the World Series regardless of doctors' orders.

After the Series, Red continued to resist a thorough medical examination until November 8, when he finally entered St. Louis Hospital. Several days later, he was transferred to Mount St. Rose Sanitarium, where he was finally correctly diagnosed with tuberculosis.

The news that Schoendienst had TB shocked the nation. Thanks to medical advances, the disease was no longer the dreaded killer it had been in the early part of the century when Hall of Famers Rube Waddell and Christy Mathewson had been among its victims. Though tuberculosis sufferers were no longer shunned and strictly quarantined, it still remained a serious and frightening disease in 1958. There were no guarantees that Red could be cured, much less resume a career as a professional athlete at the relatively advanced age of 36.

The doubters obviously hadn't checked with Red Schoendienst, who resolutely vowed to rejoin the Braves during the 1959 season.

After months of lying flat on his back in the sanitarium, rest and medication finally started to do the job, although not as quickly as Red would have liked. He was finally allowed to go home a few days before Easter 1959, but was still confined to bed much of the time.

Amazingly, Red did make it back before the close of the 1959 season, but just barely. He rejoined the club September 2, although he wasn't in condition to play much. He pinch-hit and filled in at second, getting into only five games without a hit in three at-bats. Nevertheless, the popular veteran's mere presence seemed to give the team a lift. They closed with a rush, winning 16 of 23 regular season games after Schoendienst rejoined them. The real test, however, was yet to come.

Schoendienst reported to the Braves camp in the spring of 1960, determined to recapture his old second base post. Thanks to their late season surge, the Braves had finished the 1959 season tied with the Los Angeles Dodgers for first place before losing a playoff for the pennant. Second base had been a glaring trouble spot in an otherwise star-studded lineup, and there was little doubt that a healthy Schoendienst would have made the difference.

New manager Charlie Dressen, however, was a Schoendienst doubter. "Even if the guy hadn't had TB," he said in an off-the-record conversation. "He's 37—and that's too old for a ballplayer. I figure my second baseman has got to be either (Mel) Roach or (Chuck) Cottier."[6]

But the feisty manager seemed to become a convert after Schoendienst's impressive performance in exhibition games. "I didn't count on Red," he admitted. "I wasn't sure he'd play at all, let alone every day. He's not only been hitting every pitcher hard, but he looks as good as he ever did. As of right now, he's my second baseman. And if he can keep it up, nobody else will even come close to the job."[7]

Schoendienst opened the season at second base, playing brilliantly. By the time May rolled around, he was hitting .333 and was the talk of the league. Apparently forgetting his spring training vow to make sure Red got enough rest, Dressen started him in 30 of the club's first 31 games. Gradually, the physical grind of playing so much took its toll, and Red began sharing time with utility infielder Felix Mantilla as his average dwindled down to the .230 range.

For all practical purposes, Red's season ended on July 1. The previous day he'd knocked out two hits in three at-bats, but in the top of the fifth inning, with the Braves behind by six runs, Dressen sent light-hitting Chuck Cottier, recently recalled from the minors, up to pinch-hit for him.

Clearly Dressen had lost faith in Schoendienst, who found himself riding the pines and watching Cottier handle second base. In fact, Dressen seemed determined to bury the veteran, especially after Red confronted him over some statements attributed to him in the press.[8]

With Cottier hitting under .200, Red finally got another start at second in the first game of a July 24 doubleheader. After sitting for 20 games, he shook off the rust and contributed two hits in a victory over the Chicago Cubs that put the Braves in a first place tie with Pittsburgh. The next day he was back in his familiar seat on the bench. A week later, the Braves had fallen two games behind the Pittsburgh Pirates and Cottier's average had slipped to .180, when the redhead was given another chance. Again he lashed out a pair of hits, forcing Dressen to give him some more playing time. He started six of the next nine games and hit at a .429 clip, but the Braves encountered a rough patch and fell seven games behind the hard-charging Pirates. Despite his hot bat, Schoendienst was exiled to the bench again. In fact, he would only get on the field once over the last 50 games of the season, pinch-hitting for Cottier once and finishing out the game at second base. He ended the season with a .257 batting average in 68 games, as Milwaukee finished a distant second behind Pittsburgh.

After 1960, Schoendienst could easily have retired to the sidelines and rested on his laurels. But he still didn't think he was through as a player. He asked the Braves for his release and hooked up with his old Cardinals buddies in St. Louis. Though Red's days as a regular second baseman were over, he became a premier pinch-hitter, recording a .333 average in the pinch in 1961 and leading the league with 22 pinch-hits in 1962. Overall he hit .300 in 1961 and .301 in 1962.

Red finally retired to the coaching lines at the age of 40 early in the 1963 campaign. In 1965 he was named Cardinals manager, beginning the longest managerial tenure in club history prior to Tony LaRussa's reign. He guided the Cards to back-to-back pennants in 1967 and 1968 and remained on the job through 1976, consistently keeping the club in contention. After a two-year absence spent as a coach with the Oakland Athletics, he once again returned to the Cardinals and remained with the organization as a coach and front office representative well into the 1990s. He even served two stints as interim manager, the last in 1990 at 67 years of age.

For his career, Red Schoendienst played 17 full seasons and brief portions of two others. He posted a career batting average of .289, led National League second basemen in fielding seven times, and was named to ten All-Star squads. One of the finest switch-hitters in the game, he led the league in stolen bases, doubles and hits in different seasons, and batted a career high .342 in 1953 to finish runner-up to Brooklyn's Carl Furillo for the batting title.

Tuberculosis definitely cost Schoendienst some good years. The 1957 campaign, the year before the first symptoms appeared, was one of the best of his career. He played 150 games and batted .309 with a career-high 200 hits. In addition, his 15 home runs tied his previous best and in the field he ranked a close second to Brooklyn's Jim Gilliam in fielding percentage.

Despite the time lost to TB, Red was selected for induction into the Baseball Hall of Fame by the Veterans Committee in 1989. He had received consistent support in the balloting after his retirement, but never amassed enough votes for election by the writers.

Although Red Schoendienst never regained his place as a major league All-Star after his bout with tuberculosis, he did come back to be a productive major league player. More importantly, he demonstrated that an athlete could come back from the disease. This would be especially important to future Braves star Rico Carty, who contracted TB in the late 1960s but recovered to continue a long, successful career. Schoendienst also become a spokesman for the National Tuberculosis Association and for years served as "Exhibit A" for TB patients in need of proof that the disease could be overcome.[9]

Red Schoendienst certainly lived up to the title of his biography, *The Man Who Fought Back*.

Red Schoendienst

Born: 2/2/1923

Year	Team	Lg	G	HR	RBI	SB	BA	OPS
1942	Albany	GAFL	68	1	-	-	.269	-
1942	Union City	KITL	6	0	-	-	.407	-
1943	Lynchburg	PIED	9	0	-	-	.472	-
1943	Rochester	IL	136	6	37	20	.337	.807
1944	Rochester	IL	25	2	14	16	.373	.943
1945	St. Louis	NL	137	1	47	26	.278	.648
1946	St. Louis	NL	142	0	34	12	.281	.665
1947	St. Louis	NL	151	3	48	6	.253	.636
1948	St. Louis	NL	119	4	36	1	.272	.691
1949	St. Louis	NL	151	3	54	8	.297	.707
1950	St. Louis	NL	153	7	63	3	.276	.717
1951	St. Louis	NL	135	6	54	0	.289	.740
1952	St. Louis	NL	152	7	67	9	.303	.772
1953	St. Louis	NL	146	15	79	3	.342	.907
1954	St. Louis	NL	148	5	79	4	.315	.794
1955	St. Louis	NL	145	11	51	7	.268	.711
1956	St. Louis	NL	40	0	15	0	.314	.738
	New York	NL	92	2	14	1	.296	.721
1957	New York	NL	57	9	33	2	.307	.813

Year	Team	Lg	G	HR	RBI	SB	BA	OPS
	Milwaukee	NL	93	6	32	2	.310	.782
1958	Milwaukee	NL	106	1	24	3	.262	.641
1959	Milwaukee	NL	5	0	0	0	.000	.000
1960	Milwaukee	NL	68	1	19	1	.257	.630
1961	St. Louis	NL	72	1	12	1	.300	.764
1962	St. Louis	NL	98	2	12	0	.301	.717
1963	St. Louis	NL	6	0	0	0	.000	.000
19 Yrs	MLB Totals		2216	84	773	89	.289	.724

18

Rico Carty

It usually takes some good luck for a player to make a successful comeback in major league baseball. On the other hand, it often takes some bad luck to put a player in position to engineer a comeback.

Rico Carty was one of the most consistently unlucky men to ever play major league baseball. His entire career consisted of a series of disasters followed by remarkable comebacks. If he hadn't been so unfortunate, he might be remembered today as one of the greatest right-handed hitters in the history of the game.

While with the Atlanta Braves in 1970, Carty won the National League batting championship by more than 40 points over his nearest competitor. At the conclusion of that season, he was barely 31 years old and boasted an impressive .322 career batting mark—which compares most favorably with the averages of some guys named Hank Aaron (.320), Willie Mays (.315), and Roberto Clemente (.309) at the same age.

Only three years later, Carty was out of a job. Before the 1973 season, the Braves shuffled him to the lowly Texas Rangers for an undistinguished relief pitcher. Five months into the campaign, he was waived to the Chicago Cubs, and another month later he was waived again, to the Oakland Athletics, who gave him his walking papers after the season ended. At age 34, illness and injuries had reduced him to a shell of his former self. Deemed washed-up by major league baseball, he had to turn to the Mexican League for a job.

Fast forward five years to 1978. That season, at the advanced age of 38, a rejuvenated Carty slammed 31 home runs to become the fourth oldest slugger in major league history (at the time) to hit 30 homers in a season. Hank Aaron, Ted Williams, and All-Star Team slugger Cy Williams attained that level at a slightly more advanced age, while the Babe himself was only a few months younger than Rico the last time he reached the 30 mark.

Rico Carty was born September 31, 1939, in San Pedro de Macoris, the Dominican Republic town that would spawn so many fine middle infielders that it came to be known as "The Cradle of Shortstops." He claimed his parents wanted him to be a doctor, but he fainted at the sight of blood—an affliction that may also have short-circuited his ambitions as a boxer after he suffered his first loss.

His often torturous professional baseball career began when he first commanded the attention of big league talent scouts as a hard-hitting catcher in the Dominican Republic. And he commanded it in a big way! Anxious to please, the agreeable, naive youngster with a limited grasp of the English language signed with at least three major league organizations, in addition to several top Dominican teams, before his prolific pen was stilled. When the mess was finally straightened out, he was awarded to the Milwaukee Braves.[1]

Starting out with the Class D Davenport Braves in 1960, Rico worked his way up the Milwaukee chain, soon distinguishing himself as the top hitting prospect in the organization. The Braves, however, were blessed with the best catching corps in baseball at the time. The number one receiver was Del Crandall, the National League's starting All-Star catcher and Gold Glove winner in 1962, his eighth All-Star and fourth Gold Glove selection. Backing Crandall up was young Joe Torre, who would subsequently appear in nine All-Star Games, win a National League batting championship, RBI title, and MVP award before achieving his greatest fame as manager of the New York Yankees. Last (and most definitely least) in the Braves catching hierarchy was rookie Bob Uecker, a 27-year-old defensive specialist who would later gain fame as a baseball comedian and television personality.

In order to get Carty's big bat into the Braves' lineup as soon as possible, the promising young catcher was converted into a slow, awkward outfielder. Playing the outfield for the first time as a professional for the Texas League Austin Senators in 1963, he enjoyed a tremendous campaign and earned a brief late season look with the parent club.

In 1964, Rico was ticketed for another year of outfield experience in Triple A ball, but he earned a spot on the Braves' Opening Day roster by stroking the ball at a .408 clip in training camp. When the opening bell sounded, however, the 24-year-old rookie found himself warming the bench. In the offseason, the Braves had acquired hard-hitting, sharp-fielding Felipe Alou from the San Francisco Giants to fill their troublesome center field spot, flanked by the great Hank Aaron in right and steady Lee Maye in left.[2]

But the big Dominican was not to be denied. Playing sporadically early in the season, he sported an ordinary .273 batting average on June 26 when he was installed in left field on a regular basis with Maye shifting over to center. From that point on, Rico pounded the ball relentlessly, finishing with a .330 batting average, the second highest batting mark in major league baseball that year, trailing only Roberto Clemente of the Pittsburgh Pirates. Rico also slammed 22 homers and drove in 88 runs, impressive totals for only 455 at-bats.

As a 1964 rookie, Carty was a member of a class of sensational freshman sluggers that included Tony Oliva, Richie Allen, Jim Ray Hart, and Tony Conigliaro. The group rewrote the rookie record books, but they were dogged by subsequent ill fortune. Oliva, Hart, and Conigliaro suffered devastating injuries that prematurely ended their careers, while Allen's personal problems brought an early end to his days as a star. When it came to bad luck, however, Rico Carty could match any of them.

Plagued by back problems and other assorted injuries as a sophomore in 1965, Rico started only 70 games in the field but posted a .310 batting average. The next year, the "Beeg Boy" rebounded to hit .326, the third highest average in the major leagues, behind a couple of his countrymen, Matty Alou of the Pirates, the leader, and his brother Felipe, a

Rico Carty may be the unluckiest man alive (1965 Topps card).

Braves teammate. No player from the Dominican Republic had ever led either major league in hitting, but in 1966 a trio of them placed in the top three spots.

Ironically, if Carty had been an American Leaguer, he might have been the first Dominican champ, as well as the first rookie to win the batting title. In 1964, fellow freshman Tony Oliva became the first rookie batting champ, capturing the American League title with a .323 average that trailed Rico's mark that season by seven points. In fact, if Carty had come up in the American League, he might well have captured two batting titles in his first three years in the majors, since Frank Robinson won the 1966 American League crown with a .316 average that was ten points less than Carty's average that year.

Entering the 1967 season, Carty seemed poised for stardom, but it would be a campaign of frustration and disappointment as his average tumbled to .255 in 134 games. During the season, he fought with mild-mannered Braves superstar Hank Aaron.[3] And in the offseason, veteran third baseman Clete Boyer publicly blasted him for loafing and not working to improve his game.[4]

After a fine season in the Dominican Winter League, Carty reported to the Braves' 1968 spring training camp 10 to 15 pounds underweight. Though he hit well, he felt weak and began having trouble keeping food down. Tests were ordered, and a few weeks before the season began the baseball world was stunned by the news that the hearty-looking young slugger was suffering from tuberculosis.[5]

Fortunately for Carty, much had been learned about TB and its effect on professional athletes since former Braves All-Star second baseman Red Schoendienst had contracted the disease nine years earlier. Though Schoendienst recovered to continue his baseball career, his play never returned to its former level. But Schoendienst had been almost 36 years old when he was diagnosed, while Carty was only 28, so there was reason for optimism. Carty was treated at the Southeast Florida Tuberculosis Hospital in Lantana, missing the entire 1968 campaign.[6]

Despite dislocating his shoulder several times, Rico made a spectacular comeback in 1969 to hit .342 in part-time duty. His late season slugging helped the Braves capture first place in the National League West division, and he starred in the League Championship Series loss to the "Miracle" New York Mets. After the season, *The Sporting News* ignored Carty in awarding Comeback Player of the Year honors to Tommie Agee of the world champion Mets, a healthy young player rebounding from a couple of sub-par seasons.

In 1970, Rico managed to put the injury jinx on hold and enjoy a career year. He led the majors in hitting with a .366 average, 41 points ahead of National League runner-up Joe Torre and 37 points higher than American League champ Alex Johnson. In fact, it was the highest mark recorded in the National League between Stan Musial's .376 in 1948 and Tony Gwynn's .370 in 1987. Furthermore, it was the highest average by a right-handed batter in either major league since Joe DiMaggio of the New York Yankees hit .381 in 1939, and it wouldn't be surpassed by another righty until Andres Galarraga batted .370 for the 1993 Colorado Rockies. Even after his great comeback the previous year, Carty was so underappreciated that he'd been left off the 1970 preseason All-Star ballot. The oversight turned into a cause celebre, and Rico became the first player to be elected to the starting All-Star lineup via write-in vote. Finally, he was gaining some recognition for his prodigious hitting. As Rico basked in the glory of his magnificent season, it seemed that his health problems were finally behind him and his best years lay ahead

But once again misfortune beset him—with a vengeance. Playing winter ball in his homeland, Rico collided with center fielder Matty Alou and shattered his left knee. The defending batting champ missed another entire season as he went through an arduous rehabilitation program.

Though there had initially been some doubt that he would ever play again, Carty worked hard to rehabilitate his knee and made it back for the 1972 season. But he was not the same player, limping through 78 games in the field and hitting a soft .277. In keeping with Rico's established pattern of rotten luck, Ralph Garr had stepped in to take over left field during his absence and developed into a star. So Carty found himself bound for Texas in the American League shortly after the season ended.[7]

The American League had adopted the designated hitter (DH) for the 1973 season, a position that seemed tailor made for Carty. As DH, his dangerous bat could be in the lineup every day, and he wouldn't be hampered by the burden of playing the field. The Rangers, who'd hit for a meager .217 team average in 1972 while finishing with the worst record in the major leagues, desperately needed a big bat like Rico's in the middle of their lineup.

But just prior to the start of the season, Rico's personal black cloud again rumbled and rained ill fortune upon him. His new employers made a deal with the Cleveland Indians to acquire another former batting champ, enigmatic outfielder Alex Johnson. Johnson, who'd captured the American League title the same year Carty reigned as National League champ, was three years younger and much healthier than Rico. Though Johnson still possessed good speed, he seemed to harbor an aversion to playing defense. Apparently the Rangers empathized with Alex more than Rico. Despite his .239 average the previous year, Johnson was handed the DH spot with Carty hobbling off to play the outfield. Rico struggled through 53 games in left field for the Rangers, getting only 31 chances to serve as the DH. After a horrible start at the plate, he'd finally started to get hot when he broke a bone in his foot sliding in late July. He went on the disabled list with a disappointing .232 batting average and was sent to the contending Chicago Cubs upon being activated in mid–August. He failed to regain his batting eye in his return to the National League and was shipped back to the American League a month later, joining the Oakland A's who were on their way to their third straight Western Division Championship. The big guy contributed little to the Oakland effort and wasn't included on the postseason roster. In mid–December, he received an early Christmas present—his unconditional release and what appeared to be a one-way ticket to oblivion.[8]

When no major league opportunity materialized the next spring, Rico swallowed his pride and accepted an offer to play for the Mexican League Cordoba Cafeteros. After belting the ball at a .354 clip for Cordoba, his contract was sold to the Cleveland Indians in August 1974, and the veteran slugger was back in the big leagues again. Sharing the DH position with left-handed hitting Oscar Gamble and filling in occasionally at first base, he hit for a lusty .363 average for the remainder of the season.

Predictably, Lady Luck reached out to slap Rico down again by throwing another major obstacle in his path. A month after signing Carty, the Indians traded for Frank Robinson, the only man to win the MVP Award in both leagues and already the author of 572 major league home runs. Immediately after the end of the 1974 season, Robinson was named major league baseball's first black manager by the Indians. The veteran superstar, who'd spent the past two years serving as the primary DH for the California Angels and had his eye on 600 lifetime homers, was expected to be a playing manager for the Tribe—an arrangement that didn't bode well for the 35-year-old Carty.

Despite his fine work with the bat in 1974, Carty's prospects were not good when he reported to the Indians spring training camp in 1975. Even if Robinson wasn't making out the lineup card, Rico didn't figure to budge the future Hall of Famer out of the DH role. In addition, Gamble, also a productive DH, was still on the roster. To further complicate Carty's situation, the Indians had traded for Robinson's old Oriole teammate, Boog Powell, to man first base. And if Rico were to entertain visions of returning to left field, he would find his path blocked by talented young Charlie Spikes, the Indians' best all-around player. Hanging on as a pinch-hitter seemed to be his only hope.

So Rico did the only thing he could under the circumstances. He pounded out base hits at every opportunity, making it impossible for the Indians to ignore him. Starting the campaign on the bench, he banged out six hits in eight tries as a pinch hitter while also filling in at first base and left field. Eventually he replaced an injured Robinson as the Indians primary DH and finished the year with a .308 batting average while hitting 18 homers and driving in 64 runs in less than 400 times at bat.

At year's end, Carty again lost out on Comeback Player of the Year honors. This time the award went to teammate Boog Powell. Though Powell had a big year in 1975, Rico had certainly come back further, virtually climbing off the scrap heap to win a job with Indians.

Carty held on to the Indians DH job in 1976 despite manager Robinson's continued presence on the active roster. His .310 batting average and 83 RBIs were both team highs. Yet after the season, he was left unprotected in the expansion draft and quickly snapped up by the fledgling Toronto Blue Jays. Realizing their mistake, the Indians paid dearly to get him back a month later. He enjoyed another solid season with Cleveland in 1977, again leading the team in RBIs, but was shipped back to Toronto in the spring of 1978 after the Tribe acquired Willie Horton to serve as DH.

Five years after being left for dead by the major leagues, in 1978 Carty became the oldest major leaguer to enjoy the first 30-homer season of his career. He began the campaign with the Jays and was traded to Oakland in mid–August. Fortunately, his second tour of duty with the A's went much better than his first as he blasted 11 out of the park in only 41 games to finish with a combined 31 homers and 99 RBIs on the season.

Rico, who'd played out his option in 1978, re-enlisted with the Blue Jays for the 1979 campaign. Although 39 years old, he had no plans to retire as evidenced by the five-year partially guaranteed contract he signed. But he batted a mediocre .256 as the Jays DH in 1979 and followed that with a disappointing Dominican Winter League performance.[9] Carty reported to spring training with Toronto in 1980, but was slowed by injuries and drew his release before the season got underway. This time there would be no comeback for the "Beeg Mon," as he'd come to be called, and he accepted an offer to scout Latin American talent for the Jays.[10]

Rico Carty's major league career spanned 17 seasons from 1963 through 1979. Despite playing in an era when pitching ruled, he finished his career with 204 homers and 890 RBIs in 5606 at-bats, which projects to roughly 22 homers and 95 RBIs for a full 600 at-bat, season.

But illness and injury cost him two prime seasons and significant parts of several others. In fact, he managed only three relatively healthy campaigns—1964, 1966, and 1970—out of his first ten years in the big leagues. Those three seasons, however, provide a good indication of what might have been as he hit a cumulative .340 and placed among the top three hitters in major league baseball each year.

Naturally, Carty's impossibly bad luck would hold to the bitter end of his career. In the closing weeks of his final season, his career batting average slipped under .300 for the first time since the beginning of his rookie year. In the Jays' 155th game of the season, Carty slammed a pinch homer and a single to raise his lifetime mark to .29918. But a one-for-four performance the next day would be his last chance to raise his average to the magic .300 level as he sat out the last six games of the season. His major league career ended with a .299 career batting average, a paltry two hits short of the magic .300 mark.

Rico Carty

Born: 9/1/1939

Year	Team	Lg	G	HR	RBI	SB	BA	OPS
1960	*Davenport*	*MIDW*	25	3	15	0	.233	.717
1961	*Eau Claire*	*NORL*	110	11	39	4	.298	.754
1962	*Yakima*	*NORW*	108	17	79	12	.366	1.038
1963	*Austin*	*TL*	111	27	100	5	.327	1.066
	Toronto	*IL*	21	4	11	1	.222	.791
	Milwaukee	NL	2	0	0	0	.000	.000
1964	Milwaukee	NL	133	22	88	1	.330	.942
1965	Milwaukee	NL	83	10	35	1	.310	.849
1966	Atlanta	NL	151	15	76	4	.326	.859
1967	Atlanta	NL	134	15	64	4	.255	.730
1968	Atlanta	NL	(Tuberculosis—Did not play)					
1969	Atlanta	NL	104	16	58	0	.342	.951
1970	Atlanta	NL	136	25	101	1	.366	1.037
1971	Atlanta	NL	(Injured—Did not play)					
1972	Atlanta	NL	86	6	29	0	.277	.780
1973	Texas	AL	86	3	33	2	.232	.612
	Chicago	NL	22	1	8	0	.214	.533
	Oakland	AL	7	1	1	0	.250	1.150
1974	*Cordoba*	*Mex*	122	11	72	-	.354	-
	Cleveland	AL	33	1	16	0	.363	.846
1975	Cleveland	AL	118	18	64	2	.308	.882
1976	Cleveland	AL	152	13	83	1	.310	.821
1977	Cleveland	AL	127	15	80	1	.280	.787
1978	Toronto	AL	104	20	68	1	.284	.821
	Oakland	AL	41	11	31	0	.277	.928
1979	Toronto	AL	132	12	55	3	.256	.713
15 Yrs	MLB Totals		1651	204	890	21	.299	.833

19

Dave Dravecky

"Dave, if you have this operation I think your chances of returning to professional baseball are zero," said the surgeon who would remove a cancerous tumor, as well as half of the surrounding deltoid muscle from Dave Dravecky's pitching arm. "My greatest hope is that after intensive therapy you will regain a normal range of motion and be able to play catch with your son in your backyard."[1]

Ten months later, Dravecky stood on the mound at Candlestick Park preparing to face the Cincinnati Reds.

Dave Dravecky's book, *Comeback,* chronicles his incredible return to the pitcher's mound less than a year after radical surgery to remove a cancerous tumor from his pitching arm. And it would be positively negligent for a piece about baseball's great comeback players to not include the hero of the book entitled *Comeback*.

Dravecky was a 32-year-old left-handed hurler who seemed to be coming into his own as a starter for the San Francisco Giants when his cancer was diagnosed after the 1988 season. He broke into the major leagues with the San Diego Padres midway through the 1982 campaign after an apprenticeship in the Padres and Pittsburgh Pirates organizations. Used mostly as a starter, he posted a mediocre record of 53 wins against 50 losses with San Diego.

A mid-season swap sent Dravecky to San Francisco in July 1987 along with outfielder Kevin Mitchell and Craig Lefferts for enigmatic third baseman Chris Brown, future Cy Young winner Mark Davis, and a couple of lesser lights. The trade keyed the Giants' charge to the Western Division title, with Mitchell starring in place of Brown at third base and Dravecky helping to stabilize the starting rotation, winning 7 games against 5 losses with a 3.20 ERA. In the League Championship Series against the St. Louis Cardinals, Dravecky fired a masterful two-hit shutout to win game number two and even the series, but he was the loser in game six despite giving up only one run in six innings. The Giants lost in seven games.

Late in the season, Dave had noticed a small lump on his throwing arm about the size of a quarter. The Giants' trainer looked at it and told him not to worry, but in the offseason he decided to have it tested. A magnetic resonance image (MRI) procedure was performed, and the results indicated the growth was benign, but he was advised to have it checked again in six months.[2]

After a solid spring training performance, Dravecky started the 1988 season full of optimism. He was named to start Opening Day and fired a three-hitter to beat the Los Angeles Dodgers 5 to 1. But the season quickly turned sour for the veteran lefty when his shoulder started to ache, and he had trouble getting loose. After only seven starts, he underwent routine arthroscopic surgery on his shoulder in June. Amazingly, with all this medical attention, the growth on Dravecky's achy left arm didn't warrant a closer look.[3]

Dravecky began rehab immediately after surgery, but something was still wrong. His arm was killing him, and he couldn't break a pane of glass with his fast ball. After an embarrassing minor league rehab assignment in August, complete rest was prescribed and he was shut down for the season.

By the end of the 1988 season, the lump on Dave's arm had become clearly visible, about the size of half a golf ball. Even then, the Giants trainer thought that the lump only looked bigger because the surrounding muscles had atrophied during his layoff. But Dravecky decided to have it examined again. This time the word was that further testing was in order. He visited the Cleveland Clinic, near his Youngstown, Ohio, home, and got the first indication that the curious lump could be cancerous. A follow-up biopsy proved the diagnosis. The growth was identified as a fibrous tumor called a desmoid tumor. It was not considered life threatening, but it was certainly a threat to Dravecky's pitching arm.[4] Ominously, the doctor added that a desmoid tumor was also the most likely to come back after an operation.[5]

Surgery was scheduled for October 7, 1988. Due to the position of the tumor and the need to make sure every single cancerous cell was destroyed, a wide margin around the tumor would have to be removed. This included about half of the deltoid, one of the three most powerful muscles in the arm, the muscle at the front of the upper arm that young boys and body builders clench to show off their strength. The procedure was expected to render the remaining deltoid muscle almost useless. Where the tumor actually sat on the humerus bone, the doctors elected a procedure whereby the bone was scraped and the portion adjacent to the tumor frozen with liquid nitrogen to kill all living cells, including bone cells. The bone would be brittle, but it was believed that it would eventually regenerate and regain its full strength.[6]

Dave Dravecky gave his left arm for his career (1988 Topps card).

Nearly eleven hours after he'd been wheeled into the operating room, Dravecky was moved to recovery, but the ordeal wasn't over. Complications arose due to the length of the surgery, and he had to undergo the knife again to restore circulation in his leg.

Afterward, the surgeon repeated his grim prognosis to Dave's wife, Janice. "Short of a miracle," he said, "he will never pitch again."[7]

The miracle began two weeks after the surgery, when Dravecky displayed remarkable range of motion in the arm. The virtual loss of the deltoid was expected to drastically affect certain kinds of movement. It was only hoped that he would eventually be able to lift his arm over his head. To the shock of his doctors, however, Dave was able to lift his left arm straight up over his head two weeks after surgery. A few weeks later, he was able to duplicate his pitching motion and began to feel the first faint stirrings of hope that he would actually pitch again someday.

The doctors were still understandably cautious. It wasn't until mid–March, about two weeks before the start of the 1989 baseball season, that Dave was permitted to pick up a baseball for the first time. He made it to Arizona for the last two days of the Giants' spring training and attracted the morbid fascination of his teammates with the appearance of his mangled arm. "Man, you look like Jaws took a bite out of you!" exclaimed Kevin Mitchell, welcoming him back.[8]

The medical experts really couldn't understand how Dave was managing to throw with the same motion he'd used before the operation. Dravecky had always had a muscular build, and the only explanation they could venture was that the other muscles had somehow adapted and were compensating for the loss of the deltoid muscle function.

Dave's explanation for the phenomena was much simpler. He attributed it to "a miracle of God."[9]

Throughout his career, Dravecky had been a deeply religious man. He was known to roll back the eyes of sportswriters with biblical rather than baseball quotes. In San Diego, he was associated with a collection of devout Christian players, some of whom gained notoriety as members of the ultra-conservative John Birch society.

Whether Dravecky's incredible progress was made possible by divine intervention or the over-developed muscles of his left arm, he was soon pitching in simulated games, and in late July he began a tremendously successful rehabilitation assignment in the Giants minor league system that culminated with three complete game victories.

On August 10, 1989, the miracle reached its zenith. Dravecky jogged to the mound to face the Reds in front of 34,810 wildly cheering Giants fans, as the scoreboard in center field flashed a gigantic "WELCOME BACK, DAVE!"

The game would be no walk in the park for Dravecky. The Giants held a scant two-game lead in the midst of a heated pennant race. The Reds had been picked by many to take the flag and were eager to gain a game on the front-runners. Before the game, Cincinnati manager Pete Rose was asked what he thought about Dravecky's upcoming comeback effort.

Pete's thoughtful and succinct response was: "He's back, and it's great for him. I hope he loses."[10]

Dravecky throttled the Reds for seven innings, giving up only one bloop hit. The Reds chased him in the eighth, but the Giants hung on to win 4–3 and preserve Dave's first victory in more than 15 months. Veteran Giants manager Roger Craig, who'd earned his baseball spurs during some rather thrilling times with the old Brooklyn Dodgers, claimed it was the most emotional baseball game he'd ever seen.[11]

On August 15, Dravecky took his next turn against the Montreal Expos under their domed stadium. After five innings, he'd held them to three hits and hadn't allowed a run, but in the dugout after the top of the fifth his arm felt strange. Dave's doctors, nervous about the still-fragile humerus, had warned him to stop immediately if anything didn't feel right, but he was intent on his pitching and ignored the signs. In the top of the sixth inning, Dave gave up a lead-off homer and then hit Andres Galarraga with a pitch.

Dravecky's first pitch to the next hitter, Tim Raines, was the last he would ever throw. He took his stretch, pivoted on his left leg, raised his arm and fired. In Dave's words, "Next to my ear I heard a loud popping noise. The sound was audible all over the field . It sounded as though someone had snapped a heavy tree branch... I felt as though my arm had separated from my body and was sailing off towards home plate."[12]

To the horror of onlookers, Dravecky instinctively clutched his left arm and tumbled headfirst to the ground as the ball flew high over the catcher's head. He screamed in pain as he did a complete somersault landing flat on his back. The grisly action was captured on film and rolled endlessly before television audiences for days thereafter. Despite the tremendous pain, Dravecky refused to be taken off the field lying down, and in another gut-wrenching scene he was carried off sitting up on a stretcher. Giants relievers preserved the Giants' lead so that Dave was able to go out with a win. Dravecky was through for the year, though, at the time, it was felt that the broken arm was no more than a setback. The doctors expected it to fully heal and finish regaining strength, allowing Dave to return to action—possibly the next spring.

The Giants were on their way to the 1989 National League pennant, and Dave stayed with the team to cheer them on. After the Giants won the deciding game of the League Championship Series from the Chicago Cubs, he couldn't resist joining his teammates in a post-game celebration on the field, and re-fractured his arm during the ensuing melee.

The second break itself was not considered serious, but X-rays showed that a mass had formed in the area where the tumor had been removed. Further tests revealed that the worst had come to pass: the tumor had grown back. Additional surgery would be required, and the doctors feared that there would not be enough muscle left to support the bone. A few days later, Dave made his retirement from professional baseball official.

Afterward, when Dravecky was asked if the comeback was worth it, a year of rehab and all that pain to pitch only twice at the major league level, he answered without hesitation: "Yes, it was worth it a million times over.... I got to live out the greatest boyhood dream of all. I got to do what the experts said was impossible, to come back from cancer and pitch a major league baseball game.... What more would anybody want out of baseball?"[13]

In retirement, Dave became a popular motivational speaker. He endured two more surgeries, but the condition of his arm continued to deteriorate. On June 18, 1991, less than two years after his comeback with the Giants, Dave's left arm and shoulder were amputated.

Dravecky left baseball with a 64–57 won-lost record and impressive 3.13 career ERA. He was an All-Star in 1983, his first full big league season, pitching two scoreless innings for the National League. That year he won a career high 14 games. He excelled in post-season play, posting a microscopic 0.35 ERA in just under 26 innings for the 1984 Padres and 1987 Giants.

Though Dave was never a major star, and his comeback was short-lived, it was unequaled in drama. The final words in *Comeback* reflect the magic of the accomplishment.

"Every year in America hundreds of thousands of kids go out to play Little League, and every year each of them dreams of playing in the major leagues," Dravecky wrote. "The odds are so slim. It's as if you had a huge stadium jammed full of kids, each wearing a uniform and a glove, and just one out of all those thousands got picked to come down and play with the big boys.

"I was that kid. I got to play with the big boys.

"And even more: I got the chance to come back."[14]

Dave Dravecky

Born: 2/14/1956

Year	Team	Lg	G	IP	W	L	ERA	WHIP
1978	Charleston	WCRS	20	52	4	2	4.15	1.65
1979	Buffalo	EL	35	114	6	7	4.26	1.61

Year	Team	Lg	G	IP	W	L	ERA	WHIP
1980	*Buffalo*	*EL*	*27*	*161*	*13*	*7*	*3.35*	*1.40*
1981	*Amarillo*	*TL*	*30*	*172*	*15*	*5*	*2.67*	*1.17*
1982	*Hawaii*	*PCL*	*16*	*36*	*4*	*1*	*2.48*	*1.16*
	San Diego	NL	31	105	5	3	2.57	1.13
1983	San Diego	NL	28	183	14	10	3.58	1.23
1984	San Diego	NL	50	156	9	8	2.93	1.12
1985	San Diego	NL	34	214	13	11	2.93	1.20
1986	San Diego	NL	26	161	9	11	3.07	1.26
1987	San Diego	NL	30	79	3	7	3.76	1.29
	San Francisco	NL	18	112	7	5	3.20	1.32
1988	San Francisco	NL	7	37	2	2	3.16	1.11
	SFG-ML Rehab	*AAA*	*1*	*2*	*0*	*1*	*16.88*	*4.13*
1989	*SFG-ML Rehab*	*(var)*	*3*	*25*	*3*	*0*	*1.80*	*0.84*
	San Francisco	NL	2	13	2	0	3.46	0.92
8 Yrs	MLB Totals		226	1062	64	57	3.13	1.21

20

Jack Quinn

Reporting on Jack Quinn's release by the New York Highlanders (later the Yankees) during the 1912 season, *The Sporting News* described Quinn as a victim of Father Time, saying the veteran hurler "went down before the assault of years."[1] That same year, an article in a New York daily publication claimed he was 42 years old.[2]

No less than 20 years later, the same Jack Quinn led the National League in saves pitching for the Brooklyn Dodgers.

Quinn didn't make any one particularly sensational or dramatic comeback. His whole career was essentially one unlikely comeback after another. In fact, he won more than 300 games in the majors and minors after the "washed-up" label was hung on him for the first time.

According to *Baseball Reference*, Jack Quinn had just turned 50 years of age when he made his last major league appearance for the Cincinnati Reds on July 7, 1933. But no one is absolutely sure when or where he was born. For that matter, no one really knows what his real name was, or what nationality he was, or how long he pitched. Quinn shrouded himself in mystery. Though he prided himself on a simple, no-nonsense approach to pitching, nothing else about the enigmatic hurler was straightforward.

Jack Quinn's full baseball name was John Picus Quinn, but he reported his name as John Quin Picus to the Social Security Administration in 1939. But his surname may have originally been either Paykos or Pajkos, depending on his actual ancestry—with Welsh, Polish, Russian, Greek, and a few others in contention.[3] To add to the confusion, he spelled his last name "Quin" when he signed his autograph[4]

Then there's the matter of his age. It's generally accepted that Quinn was born in Pennsylvania mining country around Hazelton and he celebrated his birthday every 5th day of July, but the exact year of birth is the subject of much conjecture. Like *The Baseball Encyclopedia*, *Baseball-Reference.com* lists the date of Jack's worldly debut as July 5, 1883. But Quinn's 1933 Goudey Baseball Card and his 1946 obituary credit him with an 1885 birthdate. Karst and Jones' *Who's Who in Professional Baseball* lists his date of birth as July 5, 1884, as does the *Biographical Dictionary of American Sports*. Recently, researcher Michael D. Scott reported in the publication *Nine* that the old pitcher was born on July 1, 1883, in Stefurov, in the northwestern part of what is now the Republic of Slovakia.[5] Even the earliest of the above mentioned dates, however, can be rightfully regarded with suspicion since, in his obituary, *The Sporting News* reported that he served in the Spanish-American War (also known as the War of 1898).[6] It's also been reported that the New York club thought the ex-coal miner was a rather aged rookie when he first reported to them in 1909, and some old-timers suspected that he'd trimmed as many as ten years from his true age.[7]

Since authoritative modern sources seem to have gingerly settled on 1883 as the year of Quinn's birth, that date will be used as the basis for subsequent age references in this profile. That would put Quinn's age at 15 when and if he served in the Spanish-American War, which is possible given his size and his claim that he left home at the age of 14. It would also make him a mere 31 years old when he made the first of his many major league comebacks in 1914.

Growing up, Quinn's educational opportunities were limited, as he apparently began working in the mines when he should have been in grade school. He barely survived a mining accident before leaving home to seek his fortune—or at least a better way of life. He claimed he was being paid to play ball as a 14-year-old. His inconsistent recollections of his early years in baseball sound like something out of one of Zane Grey's early baseball novels as he rode the rails around the country. Among the jobs he held, in addition to baseball player, were blacksmith, boilermaker, plumber, steel mill hand, and machinist.[8] His travels took him out West, but after five years on the road he'd failed to

Jack Quinn's career lasted 20 years after he was too old (Bain Collection, Library of Congress).

find his pot of gold and returned to Pennsylvania, where, according to legend, he finally got his big break. Several variations of the story exist, but one of the best is that young Jack hopped off a train in Dunbar, Pennsylvania, and came across a baseball game in progress. A loose ball happened to come his way, and he threw it back with such force that it greatly impressed the visiting Connellsville team, and he was recruited to pitch the second game of the afternoon's doubleheader. Quinn claimed he was to be paid twice as much if he won the game, which was all the incentive he needed to overpower the locals. He subsequently joined the Connellsville nine and spent the 1903 through 1906 seasons pitching for them in the semi-pro Pennsylvania State League.[9]

Jack began his documented career in organized baseball with the Macon Brigands in the South-Atlantic League in 1907. He caught the attention of big league scouts when he went undefeated in 14 decisions the next year for the Virginia League's Richmond Colts, and his contract was purchased by the New York franchise in the American League. After a fine 1909 rookie season, splitting his time between starting and relieving, he won 18 games for the second-place Highlanders in 1910. But the following year, his won-lost record fell to 8–10, followed by a 5–7 record and 5.79 ERA in 1912 that led to a demotion to the minors in August.

He finished the 1912 campaign with the Rochester Hustlers of the International League and won 19 games for them in 1913 before the Boston Braves picked up his contract. Quinn proved he still belonged in the big time with a 4–3 won-lost record and 2.40 ERA in a late season trial with the Braves, but he missed an opportunity to pitch for the 1914 Miracle

Braves when he jumped to the Baltimore Terrapins of the newly organized Federal League. Though the Federal League was an outlaw league—not recognized by organized baseball—its rosters featured many of the top players in the game and it's retrospectively considered to have been a major league. Quinn became the ace of a Baltimore staff that included former major league stars George Suggs, Kaiser Wilhelm, and Frank Smith, and won 26 games, the second highest total in the league. But in 1915, the financially strapped Terrapins dropped from third place to last, and Quinn led the league with 22 losses while winning only 9 times. When the Federal League disbanded after the campaign, most of its top players were returned to their former American or National franchises. But there was no demand for old Jack Quinn's services, and he again found himself without a big league job.

Before the 1916 season, Jack hooked on with the Vernon Tigers of the Pacific Coast League and pitched solid ball for them until World War I caused the circuit to shut its 1918 season down early. Never one to remain idle for long, the 35-year-old hurler signed on with the American League Chicago White Sox for the remainder of the season. In six starts for the Sox, he again proved his big league worthiness by winning 5 games against a single loss. He averaged over eight innings per outing and posted a fine 2.30 ERA.

Suddenly Jack Quinn was a desired commodity again. The White Sox assumed that the Coast League had forfeited their rights to him when the league disbanded, and he was theirs. In the meantime, the Yankees, who'd dropped him seven years earlier, had formally purchased his contract from Vernon and claimed him as their property. The contentious dispute ended up in the hands of American League president Ban Johnson, who awarded Jack to the Yankees.

That decision may have played a major part in baseball history. The relationship between former allies Johnson and White Sox owner Charles Comiskey had already been strained before the Quinn decision. Afterward, open hostility broke out, and many baseball experts attribute Johnson's strange behavior in dealing with the Black Sox scandal during the 1919 World Series to the Quinn dispute.[10]

Johnson's decision denied Quinn the infamy of a spot on the roster of the notorious White Sox squad that forever earned the Black Sox tag when several of its stars tried to fix the World Series. If Jack had remained with the Sox, he likely would have filled the fourth starter role that went to rookie Dickey Kerr. Kerr, of course, who ended up gaining lasting fame by twice besting the rival Cincinnati Reds, while several of his teammates were intent on throwing the game.

Instead, Jack put the finishing touches on his second major league comeback by winning 14 games for the 1919 Yankees. The next year, the 37-year-old veteran won 18 games as the franchise seriously contended for the American League pennant for the first time since he'd won 18 for them a decade earlier.

After the 1920 season, Major League Baseball adopted a radical new rule forbidding the application of foreign substances, such as saliva, to the ball. But a handful of established spitball artists were grandfathered in and permitted to continue loading up the ball for the rest of their careers. Quinn, who'd long been throwing the spitter, was one of those allowed to continue. But it looked like it would only be a short run when he registered a disappointing eight victories for the 1921 pennant winners and lost his starting spot. After the World Series, he was dispatched to the lowly Boston Red Sox in a seven-player deal that brought Everett Scott, Joe Bush, and Sam Jones to the Yankees.

Jack staged another comeback to capture a regular spot in the Red Sox starting rotation.

In both 1922 and 1923, he won 13 games for last place squads. In 1924, he won 12 and posted the best ERA on the staff as the Sox rocketed all the way up to seventh place.

But midway through the 1925 season, Quinn's ERA for the Red Sox was more than a run per game higher than his 1924 mark. The front office types again decided that the aging hurler must be through, and he was waived through the league before winding up with the contending Philadelphia Athletics. The A's finished that season in second place, but Quinn pitched credibly, causing canny manager-owner Connie Mack to suspect that the old guy might have a few more good years left.

Old Connie was right. For the next five years, Jack was one of the mainstays of his pitching staff. The Athletics squad of the era was a rising young club that would go on to capture the American League pennant from 1929 through 1931. The grizzled veteran Quinn fit right in, helping solidify the young staff. Pitching mostly as a starter, Jack progressed from 10 wins in 1926 to 15 victories in 1927 and then 18 triumphs in 1928 at the age of 45.

Although he started 18 times in 1929, Quinn began making more and more appearances out of the bullpen to bail out the starters, and by 1930 he was being used almost exclusively in relief. With the veteran spitballer anchoring the bullpen, the club captured back-to-back world championships in 1929 and 1930.

Despite evidence to the contrary, Connie Mack decided that Quinn couldn't keep going forever and gave him his unconditional release after the 1930 World Series. But Jack was still far from through. Uncle Wilbert Robinson, manager of the National League Brooklyn Robins, loved veteran pitchers and persuaded Quinn to move his act to the Robins' bullpen. In an era of inflated scoring, the 48-year-old spitballer proceeded to post a brilliant 2.66 ERA in 1931. Although the save statistic wasn't recognized at the time, a later-day compilation revealed that he led the National League with 15 saves in 1931, more than doubling the total of his closest competitor. Amazingly, the veteran reliever finished 13th in balloting for the National League MVP award, the oldest player to ever finish that high.

Quinn had another good season in 1932, again leading the league in saves, this time with eight. But Uncle Robby had moved on after 18 years at the Brooklyn helm, and the new regime sent the old-timer packing once again after the season. Jack latched on with Cincinnati for the 1933 season, but this time Father Time finally had caught up with him, and he was let go in mid-season, shortly after celebrating his 50th birthday.

Jack thought he might have one more comeback left in him and joined Hollywood of the Pacific Coast League for the 1934 season. His signing became a source of controversy since league rules contained no provision allowing ex-major league spitballers to do their "wet work" on the coast. Finally, Quinn and another former major league spitball expert, Clarence Mitchell, were cleared for spitter usage. Quinn, however, was released after six appearances because he had difficulty fielding his position and couldn't go longer than a few innings on the mound.[11]

Quinn reportedly pitched for the bearded House of David team in 1935 and served as manager of Johnstown Johnnies, pitching one Mid-Atlantic League game for them before disappearing from organized baseball.[12]

In a professional baseball career that spanned almost 30 years, Quinn pitched 23 seasons in the major leagues, despite starting out as a somewhat mature rookie and spending two full mid-career seasons in the minors. He pitched for eight different major league franchises in three difference major leagues, recording 247 victories against 218 defeats with a fine 3.29 career ERA.

Quinn holds several longevity-related distinctions. Although several older players have made cameo appearances after their regular careers ended, Quinn, at age 50 in 1933, was the oldest regular major league performer. He was the oldest pitcher to win a major league game, until Jamie Moyer edged him out in 2012, and he's still the oldest reliever to record a save. With Philadelphia in 1929, he became the oldest pitcher to start a World Series game and his relief appearance in the 1930 classic made him the oldest to pitch in the Series. With Brooklyn in 1931, he became the oldest hurler to make an opening day start. He was the last active Federal Leaguer, but missed becoming the last hurler to deliver a legal spitball in the majors because Burleigh Grimes, his junior by a decade, hung on until 1934 to nab that honor.

A fair hitting pitcher, Jack was a month shy of his 47th birthday when he belted a round-tripper on June 27, 1930, to become the oldest man to homer in the major leagues. He was to hold that distinction for more than 75 years until 47-year-old Julio Franco cranked one out of the park on April 20, 2006. In 1930, Quinn teamed with 40-year-old catcher Wally Schang to form the oldest battery in the history of the game.

Probably the most impressive age-related distinction that Quinn holds, however, is his league leading 1932 saves total which makes him, at 49, the oldest man to ever lead a major league in a significant statistical category. Yet, his 1928 season was probably his crowning achievement. At age 45, the oldest player in majors that year by a good margin, Jack posted an 18–7 won-lost record for the seventh highest win total and sixth best winning percentage in the league. His 2.90 ERA was good for fifth place and his four shutouts were the second highest total in the league. The old-timer also threw an amazing 18 complete games and had one of the lowest walk-to-innings-pitched ratios in the major leagues.

Though he was always circumspect about his age, Jack did have a simple answer to one frequently asked question. To the inquiry: "What keeps him pitching after 20-some years?" he always responded with the quip: "That's easy. A wife and six children."[13]

Jack Quinn

Born: 7/1/1883

Year	Team	Lg	G	IP	W	L	ERA	WHIP
1907	Macon	SALL	14	107	6	5	2.35	1.03
1908	Richmond	VIRL	16	146	14	0	1.10	0.83
1909	New York	AL	23	118	9	5	1.97	1.13
1910	New York	AL	35	235	18	12	2.37	1.15
1911	New York	AL	40	174	8	10	3.76	1.40
1912	New York	AL	18	102	5	7	5.79	1.58
	Rochester	IL	13	108	8	4	2.33	1.00
1913	Rochester	IL	38	267	19	13	2.76	1.21
	Boston	NL	8	56	4	3	2.40	1.10
1914	Baltimore	FL	46	342	26	14	2.60	1.17
1915	Baltimore	FL	44	273	9	22	3.45	1.29
1916	Vernon	PCL	51	289	16	13	2.93	1.30
1917	Vernon	PCL	52	409	24	20	2.35	1.22
1918	Vernon	PCL	26	213	13	9	1.48	0.88
	Chicago	AL	6	51	5	1	2.29	0.88
1919	New York	AL	38	266	15	14	2.61	1.15
1920	New York	AL	41	253	18	10	3.20	1.26
1921	New York	AL	33	119	8	7	3.78	1.60

20. Jack Quinn

Year	Team	Lg	G	IP	W	L	ERA	WHIP
1922	Boston	AL	40	256	13	16	3.48	1.26
1923	Boston	AL	42	243	13	17	3.89	1.46
1924	Boston	AL	44	228	12	13	3.27	1.28
1925	Boston	AL	19	105	7	8	4.37	1.58
	Philadelphia	AL	18	99	6	3	3.88	1.36
1926	Philadelphia	AL	31	163	10	11	3.41	1.39
1927	Philadelphia	AL	34	201	15	10	3.26	1.23
1928	Philadelphia	AL	31	211	18	7	2.90	1.29
1929	Philadelphia	AL	35	161	11	9	3.97	1.37
1930	Philadelphia	AL	35	89	9	7	4.42	1.46
1931	Brooklyn	NL	39	64	5	4	2.66	1.38
1932	Brooklyn	NL	42	87	3	7	3.30	1.44
1933	Cincinnati	NL	14	15	0	1	4.02	1.60
1934	*Hollywood*	*PCL*	*6*	*17*	*1*	*1*	*6.35*	*1.88*
1935	*Johnstown*	*MATL*	*1*	*2*	*0*	*0*	*0.00*	*1.00*
23 Yrs	MLB Totals		756	3920	247	218	3.29	1.00

21

John Hiller

At age 27, John Hiller was a pudgy, underperforming reliever and spot starter when he suffered a serious heart attack. It seemed improbable that he would ever pitch again. But, if he did return to the mound, at least he wouldn't have that far to climb back up to reach his former level.

Instead, he came back as a record-setting relief ace, putting together one of the most amazing seasons in baseball history two years after it looked like his career was over.

The Canadian-born Hiller was discovered pitching sandlot ball in Toronto and signed by the Detroit Tigers in 1962. After a couple of cups of coffee in the majors, he came up to stay in 1967, joining a talented Detroit team in the midst of a spirited battle for the American League pennant. The Tigers ended up losing the flag to the Cinderella Boston Red Sox on the last day of the season, but the rookie earned his keep, posting a 2.63 ERA in 23 appearances, including two complete games in six starts.

The next season, the 25-year-old lefthander was even better, registering a tidy 2.39 ERA and a 9–6 won-lost mark for the 1968 world champion Tigers. He started 12 games, relieved in 27 others, and set a modern major league record by striking out the first six batters he faced in an August 6 start.

In 1968, Tigers ace Denny McLain won 31 games in the regular season and number two starter Mickey Lolich logged 3 victories in the World Series against the St. Louis Cardinals, but the rest of the staff was uninspiring. The Tigers were hoping that Hiller would grab a spot in the 1969 rotation, but he pitched poorly in spring training and found himself back in the bullpen.

Pitching mostly out of the bullpen the next two years, Hiller posted a mediocre record of 10 wins against 10 losses, settling into a middle-relief role, with an occasional spot start. His attitude, as well as his weight, seemed to be a problem. Generally regarded as lazy and lacking ambition, he didn't seem to have enough desire to stay in shape. The six-footer pitched at a beefy 200 pounds or more, but over the offseason he would balloon up to 220 pounds and inevitably have a bad spring as he struggled to drop the excess weight.[1]

On January 11, 1971, Hiller sat down at the breakfast table in his Duluth, Minnesota, home, to enjoy his first smoke of the day. He began feeling a strange heaviness in his chest, so he crushed the cigarette out, deciding it would be best to give his well-abused lungs a little break. Two hours later, he fired up again and felt the chest pain return. When his condition worsened, he went to the emergency room, concerned that he might be coming down with pneumonia, as he had in 1966. After a 15-minute exam, he was admitted to the cardiac care unit for further tests, and three days later his doctor told him, "I don't want you to worry, but you've had a heart attack."[2]

Hiller's first reaction was, "I'm a baseball player and ... will I be able to go back and play ball?"³

His hospital stay stretched to four weeks. The physicians were not exactly encouraging about his chances of resuming his baseball career. "The doctors were asking me what else I could do except pitch, how much education did I have, stuff like that," remembered Hiller a few years later.⁴

Meanwhile, Hiller did not even let the Tigers know what was going on until spring training was underway. Upon hearing the news, his roommate, the famously pot-bellied Mickey Lolich, said, "Guess it can happen to anyone. Maybe John knew something—he used to run less than I did." Another pitcher, Mike Kilkenny, a fellow Canadian, said, "Too bad John wasn't a little thinner when he pitched."⁵

Early in the season, Hiller talked optimistically about returning in mid-year, but admitted, "The doctors have never even hinted that I'll be able to pitch again." Evidently, the medical community in general felt that pitching in the pressure-packed world of professional baseball was not the ideal occupation for a recovering coronary patient.⁶

John Hiller's heart attack made him a better pitcher (1974 Topps card).

In early May, he underwent surgery for the removal of seven feet of small intestine. "This is a new kind of operation," said Tigers general manager Jim Campbell at the time, apparently unaware of the full extent of the procedure. "Doctors think Hiller's recovery chances are better after removing some fatty tissues in the intestines."⁷

Hiller, in fact, seemed intent on downplaying the whole episode as much as possible. In interviews, he dismissed it as a minor heart attack, but other sources reported it as a massive stroke that almost took his life.

John ended up sitting out the entire 1971 season when, at age 28, he should have been in the prime of his career. He religiously obeyed his doctor's orders to quit smoking, watch his diet, and get plenty of exercise. With his weight down around 170 pounds, he got medical clearance to attend the Tigers 1972 spring training camp in Lakeland. John wanted to begin pitching immediately, but the team wouldn't allow it. Just a few months earlier, Detroit Lions wide receiver Chuck Hughes had died of a heart attack on the field at Tiger Stadium, so the front office was understandably leery. They did, however, offer him a job as a special coach, working with young players at their minor league complex.

But Hiller was anxious to get back in action. Economics, as well as competitive desire, were driving him to return to active player status. The coaching job just wasn't enough to pay the bills. Finally, after the season started, he got a heart specialist to give him the go-ahead to pitch again—and put it in writing. That took the liability onus off the Tigers, and they allowed him to start throwing batting practice and work out with the team. On July 8, 1972, he saw his first action in a year and a half when he relieved against the Chicago White Sox at Wrigley Field. He was roughed up in three innings of work but returned two days later to earn a save against the Texas Rangers in Detroit.

When John came in from the bullpen for his first post-heart attack appearance, Tigers catcher Bill Freehan innocently asked the umpire, "Suppose Hiller has a heart attack while he's in his windup. Is it a balk?" After a moment's hesitation, the quick-thinking arbitrator replied, "Yeah, if he falls forward, it's a balk. So if you see him grab at his chest and start to go down, you run out there and push him backwards." Tigers manager Billy Martin had already warned his pitcher, "If you have another heart attack, have it during the offseason. If you die during the season, you'll make me look bad."[8]

Despite his teammates' reservations, Hiller saw action in 24 games for the Tigers in the second half of the 1972 season. He posted a stellar 2.03 ERA with three saves in 44 innings of work to help the Tigers capture the 1972 Eastern Division Championship. In the League Championship Series, he pitched three scoreless innings to win the fourth game, although the Tigers ultimately lost to Oakland in five contests.

Hiller seemed to be back where he was before, but the 1973 season would be a breakout season for the 30-year-old southpaw. In one of the best seasons ever enjoyed by a relief pitcher, he set a since-broken major league record with 38 saves and won 10 games against 5 losses to give him a hand in 56 percent of the Tigers' victories. His ERA was a sensational 1.44 for 125 innings of relief work, and he struck out almost one batter per inning while surrendering only 89 hits. His 65 appearances also led the league, and his combined total of 48 wins and saves stood as the major league record for 10 years. For his efforts, he won the Fireman of the Year Award, the Comeback Player of the Year Award, the Hutch Award, and the Tiger of the Year Award, while finishing fourth in voting for the Cy Young and MVP Awards.

Unlike today's closers, relief pitchers of Hiller's era were workhorses, and John was one of the most durable. In 1974, he threw 150 innings in 59 relief appearances and had the distinction of establishing an American League season record for relief wins with 17, while simultaneously tying the record for relief losses with 14. Both records still endure, although the victory record was later equaled by the Minnesota Twins' Bill Campbell. As a point of interest, Roy Face holds the major league mark for relief victories with 18 for the Pittsburgh Pirates in 1959, while Gene Garber lost a record 16 games out of the bullpen for the Atlanta Braves in 1979. Hiller is still tied for second in both categories.

Hiller continued as the ace of the Detroit bullpen through 1979 before retiring early in the 1980 season at the age of 37. His lifetime won-lost record was 87–76, and he still held the Tigers club record with 125 career saves going into the 2014 season.

Comebacks are generally considered a huge success if the player merely approaches his former level of accomplishment. Seldom does a comebacker actually exceed his earlier standards. Hiller was one of those rare exceptions. And, he not only improved his performance on the field, he became a better person, to boot. By his own admission, John was a "selfish bastard." He hated dealing with autograph seekers, usually in too much of a hurry to find a cold beer to sign after games. Fan mail went unanswered, often tossed in the garbage without a glance. He just didn't care.[9]

But after his illness, he gained a new appreciation for life, realizing that baseball was just a job, rather than a life or death proposition. Furthermore, he realized that it was a pretty good job, one that would be over all too soon. He started to oblige the fans and began answering mail from heart patients and their relatives from all over the country—sometimes telephoning them directly at his own expense.[10]

In total, Hiller pitched in 15 major league seasons, all with the Detroit Tigers. For the first part of his major league career he was a mediocre reliever and spot starter, saving 13 games and posting a 3.26 ERA. After suffering a serious heart attack which threatened to end his baseball career, he came back to become one of the top firemen in baseball, amassing 112 saves with a 2.77 ERA.

Instead of ending his career, the heart attack allowed him to finally reach his full potential. In fact, he often joked that he wished he'd had the heart attack ten years earlier because it might have made a better pitcher out of him.[11]

John Hiller

Born: 4/8/1943

Year	Team	Lg	G	IP	W	L	ERA	SV
1963	Jamestown	NYPL	29	181	14	9	4.03	-
1964	Duluth-Superior	NORL	30	167	10	13	3.45	-
1964	Knoxville	SOUL	3	15	0	3	3.60	-
1965	Montgomery	SOUL	47	103	5	7	2.53	-
	Detroit	AL	5	6	0	0	0.00	1
1966	Syracuse	IL	54	87	3	7	4.45	-
	Detroit	AL	1	2	0	0	9.00	0
1967	Toledo	IL	13	45	5	1	3.00	-
1967	Detroit	AL	23	65	4	3	2.63	3
1968	Detroit	AL	39	128	9	6	2.39	2
1969	Detroit	AL	40	99	4	4	3.99	4
1970	Detroit	AL	47	104	6	6	3.03	3
1971	Detroit	AL	(Heart attack—Did not play)					
1972	Detroit	AL	24	44	1	2	2.03	3
1973	Detroit	AL	65	125	10	5	1.44	38
1974	Detroit	AL	59	150	17	14	2.64	13
1975	Detroit	AL	36	70	2	3	2.17	14
1976	Detroit	AL	56	121	12	8	2.38	13
1977	Detroit	AL	45	124	8	14	3.56	7
1978	Detroit	AL	51	92	9	4	2.34	15
1979	Detroit	AL	43	79	4	7	5.22	9
1980	Detroit	AL	11	30	1	0	4.40	0
15 Yrs	MLB Totals		545	1242	87	76	2.83	125

22

Steve Howe

Steve Howe, an outstanding relief pitcher for four major league teams from 1980 to 1996, epitomizes the image of the immensely talented but drug-tormented athlete. No one would dream of holding Howe up as an example for American youth, but you have to admire his persistence.

In *Baseball Babylon,* author Dan Gutman likens Howe to Rasputin, an early twentieth century Siberian monk whom political assassins found almost impossible to kill. Legend has it that Rasputin was initially fed wine and cake flavored with enough potassium cyanide to kill a horse. When that failed to bring him down, he was shot with a pistol and then stabbed several times, yet he still wouldn't die. Finally, he was tied up and thrown into a river where he drowned.[1]

Howe might have been a little tougher. Major League Baseball tried for more than a decade to get rid of him, but it was a worn-out throwing arm that finally killed his baseball career rather than the determined efforts of the baseball establishment.

Steve Howe broke into the majors in 1980 with the Los Angeles Dodgers and captured Rookie of the Year honors with a 2.65 ERA and 17 saves. The stylish southpaw from Pontiac, Michigan, had been signed as a starter out of the University of Michigan the previous year and had only a half season of minor league baseball under his belt when he reported to the Dodgers' Vero Beach spring training complex. At the time, the Dodgers were woefully short of lefthanders in their bullpen, so when Howe proved he could get major league hitters out, he was converted into a relief pitcher. Despite his inexperience, he soon took over as the club's bullpen ace.

Howe may have lacked experience on the mound, but he was already a seasoned cocaine user the day he first reported to the Dodgers. He'd experimented with coke for the first time in college and took an immediate liking to the drug. Marijuana, mescaline, and LSD were also sampled but found less satisfying.[2]

Through the 1981 and 1982 seasons, Howe's cocaine usage grew steadily, although it didn't seem to hurt his performance on the field. In fact, his ERA improved from a fine 2.65 rookie mark to 2.50 in 1981, and then down to an outstanding 2.08 in 1982. Steve's interest in recreational pharmacology didn't publicly surface until after the 1982 season, when he checked into The Meadows, an Arizona drug and alcohol rehabilitation clinic.[3]

Unfortunately, rehab didn't work for him. A day after leaving The Meadows, he raided a stash he'd hidden away at home and proceeded to get high. In 1983, Steve was making $325,000 a year, but most of it was going up his snout. He was soon forced to declare bankruptcy, and separated from his wife. In May, he broke down in manager Tommy Lasorda's office and was voluntarily admitted to the CareUnit, an Orange County rehab center, a way station for some of the best players of the era.⁴

When Steve got out a month later, Baseball Commissioner Bowie Kuhn demonstrated his support for the emotionally and financially troubled young man by docking him a month's salary of $53,867, the largest fine in baseball history to that point.⁵

Amazingly, the young reliever pitched effectively in 1983, even as his personal life was spinning wildly out of control. Amid all the distractions, he relieved 46 times and his ERA was a sparkling 1.44 when he went AWOL in late September, drawing a suspension for the remainder of the season. The Dodgers managed to hang on to first place in the National League Western Division without him, but they succumbed to the Philadelphia Phillies in the League Championship Series. In his biography, *Between the Lines*, Howe admits to feeling responsible for the loss.⁶

Steve Howe came back from seven drug-related suspensions (1991 Topps card).

Howe re-enlisted at the CareUnit for another month, but he just didn't have the willpower to stop using drugs. In December 1983, Commissioner Kuhn decided to make an example out of Steve by suspending him for the entire 1984 season. Apparently, the thinking under major league baseball's emerging drug enforcement program was that wayward professional athletes needed more idle time to cope with their drug dependency problems. The policy, which makes most professional substance abuse counselors cringe, was to isolate the offending player from baseball, the very thing that often provided his only discipline and direction, not to mention his livelihood.

Not surprisingly, without baseball to channel his energies, the high-strung Howe continued his cocaine use. Eventually he entered Palmdale Hospital, a Christian chemical dependency center. Steve professed to be a deeply religious man who'd accepted Jesus Christ into his life about the same time his cocaine consumption was kicking into high gear. He was regularly reborn between subsequent bouts with drug addiction, and for a time he belonged to a church whose members believed in speaking in tongues.⁷

After sitting out the entire 1984 season, the 27-year-old Howe reported back to the Dodgers in the spring of 1985. He brought along the familiar old promises to behave and something new—a sore arm. He'd developed it playing winter ball in the Dominican Republic and had undergone an operation shortly before reporting to camp. Steve was being frequently tested for drugs through training camp and the early stages of the season, but managed to stay clean by drinking heavily.⁸ By late June, he'd gained weight and was pitching ineffectively when he came to the conclusion that the fast-lane L.A. lifestyle was the real problem. He asked the Dodgers to trade him, and when they refused to comply, he jumped the team.⁹

The Dodgers had finally had enough. On July 3, 1985, Howe was unconditionally released after posting a mediocre 4.91 ERA in 19 games. He was unemployed for about six weeks before signing a generous $450,000 contract with his home state Minnesota Twins. His arm was still bothering him, however, and his ERA skyrocketed to a horrendous 6.16 in Minnesota. Inevitably, he suffered another drug relapse and the Twins voided his contract in September. This time he tried St. Mary's Hospital in Minneapolis, another drug abuse treatment facility.

Howe was figuring he'd just complete another rehabilitation and negotiate another lucrative major league contract, but there was a slight problem. Since Steve's last suspension, Peter Ueberroth had been elected commissioner of baseball. Ueberroth was a political animal who'd tasted celebrity as organizer of the successful 1984 Olympics and developed an appetite for it. Many felt he had national political aspirations and was using the commissioner's post as a springboard to elected office. He quickly latched onto the drug abuse issue and made cleaning up baseball's drug problem a highly visible crusade.

Since Howe was no longer under contract with organized baseball, Ueberroth had no direct control over him. But the commissioner seemed committed to doing everything in his power to keep him out of the game. After all, another relapse would be an embarrassment to the "Grand Old Game," not to mention the game's ambitious new leader.

Therefore, when Howe approached major league teams prior to the 1986 season, their initial interest quickly dissipated and no contract offers were forthcoming. Steve finally landed with the San Jose Bees of the independent California League, whose roster was dotted with a colorful collection of ex–major leaguers with drug and alcohol abuse histories, including Mike Norris, Derrel Thomas, Ken Reitz, and Daryl Sconiers.

Howe pitched spectacularly for the Bees, but was unceremoniously kicked out of the league when he failed a urine test that he maintained was bogus. After an aborted attempt to pitch in Japan, he found employment south of the border with the Tabasco Ganaderos in the Mexican League for the last month of the 1986 season.[10]

But hard-throwing lefthanders with big league talent have always been in short supply, so it was no surprise when the pitching-poor Texas Rangers began showing an interest in Howe in 1987. Against Commissioner Ueberroth's "advice," they signed him and farmed him out to Oklahoma City in the American Association. Shortly thereafter, the Rangers openly defied Ueberroth, and earned a $250,000 fine, by bringing Steve up to the majors without the commissioner's approval. It proved to be an unwise investment for the Rangers when Howe flunked yet another drug test after a lackluster half-season in their bullpen. The disenchanted Texans terminated his contract and it looked like Howe was history after six relapses in as many seasons.

Three years later, however, the resilient Howe was back knocking at the door of major league baseball. Except for a brief California League fling in 1990, the 33-year-old lefty had been out of organized baseball since 1987. Given his age and track record, a team would have to be either desperate or deranged to risk giving him another chance. Fortunately, Steve found an organization that qualified on both counts and signed with the New York Yankees for the 1991 season. The Yankees, coming off their worst season since 1912, were definitely desperate. As for the second criteria—they were owned and operated by George Steinbrenner.

Signing Howe actually proved to be an uncharacteristically sound move by the Yankees for that era. He went to the minors to prove he could still pitch and earned a quick promotion to the parent club, where he recorded a sensational 1.68 ERA in 37 outings.

But the reliever just couldn't stand success. Back in his new offseason Montana home, he was arrested on a cocaine-related charge. The lords of baseball didn't know how to handle this. Howe hadn't admitted to using drugs, and, as much as they wanted to kick him out of baseball, they didn't dare try it until he'd been convicted. Consequently the lefthander was still with the Yankees when the 1992 season started. Seemingly oblivious to the legal problems swirling about him, he appeared in 20 games, gathered 6 saves, and was rolling along with a 2.45 ERA before he pled guilty to cocaine possession and was immediately permanently suspended from organized baseball.

Certainly Steve Howe was finally through with organized baseball. What could be more final than "permanently suspended?" That's the term they used when they banished Shoeless Joe Jackson and his Black Sox buddies from the game more than seventy years earlier.

But when the Yankees reported to training camp the next spring, Steve Howe was back in pinstripes throwing 93 MPH fastballs. In November 1992, his "permanent suspension" had been reduced to time served by an arbitrator who said that Howe suffered from Attention Deficit Disorder. Howe was reinstated, and kindly George Steinbrenner, ever a model of tolerance and forgiveness, promptly inked him to a new contract. "The Boss" was rewarded with a mediocre 1993 performance.

The Scouting Report: 1994, produced by Stats, Inc., included the following prophetic analysis of the 36-year-old Howe's prospects for the upcoming season: "He still has good stuff and no arm problems, but then his arm was never the problem. He will always be a risk to himself and his team. Nevertheless, yet another comeback shouldn't be ruled out."[11]

Sure enough, Howe vaulted all the way back to closer status with the first place Yankees. He'd appeared in 40 games, recorded 15 saves, and sported an ERA of 1.80 when the infamous 1994 strike brought the baseball season to an abrupt close in mid–August.

Before the 1995 season, the Yankees signed Montreal Expos relief ace John Wetteland as a free agent, a move that immediately downgraded Howe's status to lefty relief specialist. He was fairly effective in the role, appearing in 56 games with a 6–3 won-lost mark and appearing in the World Series for the first time since his sophomore year. Though Howe was a model citizen that year, when the Yankees signed veteran slugger Darryl Strawberry, fresh off a drug abuse suspension, the joke was, "The Yankees are the first team in history to have two players forbidden by law from associating with one another."

The 1995 campaign would be Howe's last as an effective hurler. The 38-year-old veteran was hit hard in 1996, and the Yankees released him in mid-season after an unsightly 6.35 ERA in 25 appearances. He returned to his adopted home, Whitefish, Montana, but didn't altogether disappear from the public eye. He attempted another comeback with a South Dakota minor league team in 1997, where his trusty left arm finally failed him.

Then in August 1997, word came that the former reliever was seriously injured in a motorcycle crash in Kalispell, Montana. For some reason, the accident wasn't reported for several days, but when the local police finally got wind of it, they discovered that Howe's blood-alcohol content was 0.16, a tad above the legal limit of 0.10. He was charged with driving under the influence, but wiggled out of it when prosecutors concluded that they had not had probable cause to subpoena the hospital records.[12]

On April 28, 2006, Howe died in an early morning single-vehicle traffic accident in Coachella, California. To no one's surprise, the toxicology report subsequently revealed that he had methamphetamine in his system. He was 48 years old.[13]

Steve Howe's major league career spanned 17 campaigns, but he appeared in the big time in only 12 of those years. Actually, he only pitched five complete seasons in the majors, losing five full years and portions of six others to substance abuse problems and part of another year to the 1994 strike. For his career, he relieved 497 times without a single start, saved 91 contests, and posted a solid 3.03 lifetime ERA.

Rolling Stone magazine once referred to Howe as "John Belushi in a jockstrap."[14] He was an irreverent, fun-loving, life-of-the-party type who just couldn't help destroying himself. By most accounts, he wasn't a bad guy. Ron Perranoski, his old pitching coach from his glory days in Los Angeles, made these comments two years after Steve left the Dodgers: "He was a great competitor and just thrived on coming into tight situations....A lot of times he would be in a save situation and we would take him out and bring a righthander in, and the righty would get the save. It never really fazed him. He wasn't a selfish individual when it came to his business."[15]

Baseball old-timers will be aghast at the comparison, but in many ways Steve Howe was a modern-day Grover Cleveland Alexander. Like Alexander, he had an addictive personality and little self-control. Also like Alexander, his undeniable talent carried him for a long time, but psychological weakness eventually overcame his physical prowess.

Steve Howe

Born: 3/10/1958

Year	Team	Lg	G	IP	W	L	ERA	SV
1979	*San Antonio*	*TL*	*13*	*95*	*6*	*2*	*3.13*	*0*
1980	Los Angeles	NL	59	84	7	9	2.66	17
1981	Los Angeles	NL	41	54	5	3	2.50	8
1982	Los Angeles	NL	66	99	7	5	2.08	13
1983	Los Angeles	NL	46	68	4	7	1.44	18
1984	Los Angeles	NL	(Suspended—Did not play)					
1985	Los Angeles	NL	19	22	1	1	4.91	3
	Minnesota	AL	13	19	2	3	6.16	0
1986	*San Jose*	*CALL*	*14*	*49*	*3*	*2*	*1.47*	*2*
1987	*Oklahoma City*	*AA*	*7*	*20*	*2*	*2*	*3.48*	*0*
	Texas	AL	24	31	3	3	4.31	1
1988			(Suspended—Did not play)					
1989			(Suspended—Did not play)					
1990	*Salinas*	*CALL*	*10*	*17*	*0*	*1*	*2.12*	*0*
1991	*Columbus*	*IL*	*12*	*18*	*2*	*1*	*0.00*	*5*
	New York	AL	37	48	3	1	1.68	3
1992	New York	AL	20	22	3	0	2.45	6
1993	*Columbus*	*IL*	*2*	*2*	*0*	*1*	*10.12*	*0*
1993	New York	AL	51	50	3	5	4.97	4
1994	New York	AL	40	40	3	0	1.80	15
	Albany-Colonie	*EL*	*1*	*1*	*0*	*0*	*0.00*	*0*
1995	New York	AL	56	49	6	3	4.96	2
1996	New York	AL	25	17	0	1	6.35	1
1997	*Sioux Falls*	*NORL*	*12*	*13*	*1*	*1*	*1.98*	*1*
12 Yrs	MLB Totals		497	606	47	41	3.03	91

23

George McQuinn

Seventeen years is a long time to pursue a dream. George McQuinn's 17-year-old dream finally came true on April 16, 1947, Opening Day at Yankee Stadium, when the 36-year-old first baseman took the field wearing the famous pinstripes of the mighty New York Yankees.

When McQuinn entered pro baseball as a 19-year-old Yankees prospect in 1930, his dream was to succeed the great Lou Gehrig as the Bronx Bombers' first baseman. But in the winter of 1946, after eight years in the Yankees farm system followed by nine seasons of battling the Yankees in enemy flannels, the possibility of that dream ever being realized seemed remote. Though he could look back proudly on a career that included four All-Star squad selections and World Series stardom, he'd just been released by the lousiest team in major league baseball after completing the worst season of his career. Plagued by back problems, he posted the worst average of any regular on Connie Mack's Philadelphia Athletics team that won only 49 games in 1946.

In fact, kindly old Connie all but administered the last rites to McQuinn's career during the campaign with the deadly observation: "The boy has played a year too long."[1]

But McQuinn begged to differ. Veteran manager Bucky Harris had just been named to lead the Yankees in the upcoming 1947 season when he received an intriguing phone call that would end up having a tremendous impact on that year's pennant race.

"If you're still interested in winning that pennant, I know how you can do it," said the familiar voice on the other end of the line. "Sign me!"[2]

The caller was George McQuinn, who went on to explain that he was in fine condition despite his age and felt he had at least one good year left. Fortunately for the Yankees, Harris took a chance and came out looking like a genius. Bucky later explained, "I figured if he had enough confidence in himself to come to me like that I couldn't lose trying him."[3]

The Yankees deeply regretted letting McQuinn go almost a decade earlier. While he was starring as the St. Louis Browns' regular first baseman from 1938 through 1945, the Bombers scrounged for a successor to Gehrig. They seemed to audition a new first sacker every year with Babe Dahlgren, Johnny Sturm, Buddy Hassett, Ed Levy, Bud Souchock, as well as second sackers Jerry Priddy and Joe Gordon and outfielders Tommy Henrich and Johnny Lindell trying their hand at the post. The 1943 to 1945 war years offered the only stability at the position, with veteran National League refugee Nick Etten supplying a strong bat but weak glove.

Ironically, the Yankees had tried to re-acquire McQuinn prior to the 1940 season in exchange for Dahlgren. But Major League Baseball had just instituted a rule barring championship clubs from making interleague deals the following season. Though the rule lasted only one year, it cost McQuinn a chance to join the Yankees years earlier.[4]

McQuinn was born and raised in Ballston, Virginia, close to Arlington. As a teenager, he often worked out with the New Haven Profs in the Eastern League, who trained about 40 miles away at Annapolis, and he signed his first contract with them in 1930. The Profs were owned by future Yankees farm system director and general manager George Weiss and had a working agreement with the Yankees. McQuinn proved to be overmatched at the Class A level and was soon sent down to the Yankees' Class C Wheeling farm club, where he hit .288 for the season. By 1934, he'd worked his way up the chain to Class AAA, although he had to play for the Toronto Maple Leafs on loan because the first base spot on the Yankees top farm club, the Newark Bears, was handled by ex-big leaguers Johnny Neun and Dale Alexander.[5]

In 1935, McQuinn finally took over the Newark first base job, but he wasn't about to supplant Gehrig in New York. After the season, the Yankees sold him to the Cincinnati Reds on a conditional basis, and he started the 1936 campaign as the Reds' first baseman. Hitting only .201 six weeks into the season, he was returned to the Yankees and spent the remainder of the season in exile with Toronto before rejoining Newark in 1937.

The 1937 Newark Bears are considered by many to be the strongest minor league club in history. Teaming with future Yankees stars Charlie Keller, Joe Gordon, Tommy Henrich, Spud Chandler, Babe Dahlgren, and Atley Donald, McQuinn hit a robust .330 with 21 homers to help the Bears sew up the International League flag with a fantastic 109–43 won-lost record.

But McQuinn, who would turn 28 early the next season, wasn't getting any younger, and the indestructible Gehrig was showing no sign of slowing down. In fact, "The Iron Horse" had never missed a day in the lineup during George's years in the Yankees farm system. In 1937, at the age of 34, Gehrig hit .351 with 37 homers and 159 RBIs. As team officials explained: "It would be unfair to the player to keep him (McQuinn) out of the major leagues any longer. Lou Gehrig goes right along and there's simply no place for McQuinn, except on the Yankee bench." So the Yankees permitted him to be drafted by the Browns in the off-season.[6]

After taking the first base job away from veteran "Stinky" Davis, McQuinn enjoyed an outstanding 1938 season with the perennial second-division Browns. He notched an excellent .324 batting average that featured a 34-game hitting streak. Ironically, while McQuinn was establishing himself as a star in St. Louis, Gehrig slumped to .295, showing the first signs of the debilitating illness that would take his life within three years.

Eight games into the 1939 season, a struggling Gehrig would pull himself from the Yankees lineup forever, ending his consecutive games played streak at 2,130 contests. A short time later he was diagnosed with amyotrophic lateral sclerosis (ALS), a rare and incurable disease resulting in a progressive atrophy or wasting of the muscles, and inevitably death. Meanwhile, in his second season as a big

George McQuinn finally realized his dream after 17 years (1949 Bowman card).

league regular, McQuinn hit .316, blasted 20 homers, and drove in 94 runs for the Browns. He did replace Gehrig in one aspect that year when he was selected to back up Boston slugger Jimmie Foxx at first base on the 1939 All-Star Team—an assignment that had gone to Gehrig the previous season.

McQuinn became a big fan favorite with the Browns. From 1938 through 1945, he averaged .283 at the plate and led American league first basemen in fielding three times and in assists twice. Although not a big power hitter, he averaged almost 80 RBIs per season. After the Browns stunned the baseball world by winning the American League pennant in 1944, McQuinn firmly established himself as an all-time Brownie hero in the World Series against the cross-town Cardinals. His opening game home run gave the Browns their first Series victory and, though the Cardinals prevailed in the end, he led all hitters on both teams with a .438 average.

But like a true Brownie, McQuinn's heroics did not go unpunished. George, who wore a bulky back brace while playing, was originally classified 4-F in the draft because of a congenital back condition. However, his newfound notoriety attracted the attention of draft system officials, and he was reclassified to eligible status along with several other similarly deferred athletes. It was only through the intervention of Senator Happy Chandler, who later became the commissioner of major league baseball, that McQuinn and others who were legitimately unfit for military service were allowed to stay with their teams. McQuinn went on to enjoy a solid 1945 season in his last year in St. Louis.

In the offseason, George was traded to the Athletics, last place finishers in 1945. The Athletics were even worse in 1946, and McQuinn was not blameless. He batted only .225 and drove in a paltry 35 runs in 136 games, while leading the league in errors at first base. After the season, the Athletics gave him his unconditional release.

McQuinn passed up an opportunity with Detroit Tigers, who were searching for a replacement for Hank Greenberg, to report to the Yankees' spring training base in St. Petersburg, Florida, without a contract.

The 1946 Yankees had finished third, a distant 17 games behind the pennant-winning Boston Red Sox. In the first season after the end of World War II many of their returning stars had failed to recapture their prewar form. Joe DiMaggio, 1941 MVP, and 1942 winner Joe Gordon experienced the worst seasons to date of their Hall of Fame careers, while Tommy Henrich, Phil Rizzuto, Billy Johnson, and Johnny Lindell also experienced disappointing seasons.

Though they expected DiMaggio, et al., to return to form, the Bombers desperately needed help at first base. Nick Etten had developed into one of baseball's premier sluggers during the war, leading the American League in homers in 1944 and runs-batted-in in 1945. But at age 32 in 1946, he slipped to a .232 average with only 9 homers.

When Etten faded, the Yankees brass began to seriously consider "Old Reliable" Tommy Henrich as their future first baseman, especially since they had DiMaggio, Johnny Lindell, and Charlie "King Kong" Keller available in the outfield. In fact, Henrich ended the 1946 season as the regular first sacker and was considered the front runner for the regular job going into spring training. Etten was still around, hoping to recapture his old job, and youngsters Souchock and Jack Phillips were also on hand. McQuinn was a long shot to make the big club. In fact, his training camp invitation appeared to be little more than an uncharacteristically sentimental gesture on the part of the Yankees.

Or maybe it was guilt that motivated the Yankees brass to give McQuinn an opportunity. After all, he'd languished in their farm system for years without getting a shot with the big club. Maybe they figured they owed him at least one belated chance to prove he was Yankees material.

Whatever the reason, McQuinn wasn't about to let his long-awaited chance to be the New York Yankees' first baseman slip away. Despite his advanced age and back problems, he moved to the head of the pack in the first base competition with an outstanding spring training performance.

Even with Opening Day at hand, the skeptics refused to believe the Yankees would give the first base job to McQuinn. "The rich Yankees with their opulent chain would never take the chance of inviting adverse comment by opening with a first baseman who had not been good enough to play for Connie Mack," was the consensus in the press box according to *The Sporting News*.[7]

But McQuinn invoked the power of the famous "Yankee Magic."

"My back will not hamper me," he promised, "And I count on my Yankee uniform to do things for me as it had done for others."[8]

"It is a tremendous thrill to be, at last, at the position I had hoped to cover so many years ago," he added. "Lou Gehrig chased me away from the stadium in 1936, and again in 1938. And now I must contend with the pattern and the spirit of 'Larruping Lou.'"[9]

Harris certainly didn't lose gambling on George McQuinn. In fact, he won all the marbles—the American League pennant and the World Series. McQuinn became a fixture in the important fifth spot in the batting order. Appearing in 144 games, he finished second on the team to DiMaggio in hitting with a solid .304 average and drove home 80 runs. For the season, he ranked tenth in the American League in batting, sixth in on-base percentage, and eighth in slugging. He also fielded his position superbly and beat out the likes of Ferris Fain, Rudy York, and Mickey Vernon, whom the Yankees had desperately tried to acquire before the season, for the starting first base spot on the American League All-Star squad.

The 1947 Yankees finished 12 games ahead of the second place Tigers. They may have captured the pennant without McQuinn at first, but it wouldn't have been easy. Keller was out most of the year, and DiMaggio and Lindell also missed significant time with injuries, so Henrich's services were badly needed in the outfield, and he was no match for the smooth fielding McQuinn at first, anyway. In addition, McQuinn's bat helped fill the void from the left side of the plate caused by Keller's absence. His contributions were duly noted by the sporting press. He finished sixth in voting for the American League MVP award, getting three first place votes, the same number as Triple Crown winner Ted Williams, who placed second to DiMaggio in the overall voting.

McQuinn started well in 1948 and was again elected to the All-Star Team, where he played the entire game and established an All-Star Game record with 14 errorless chances at first base. But he tired, and tailed off badly after midseason. In August, Henrich was moved in from the outfield to replace him at first for the remainder of the season. George finished with a .248 average and 11 homers while playing in only 94 games, his lowest total since coming up with the Browns.

Released by the Yankees after the 1948 season, McQuinn devoted himself to his new sporting goods store in Arlington and designed a new first baseman's mitt for Rawlings that became very popular.

In 1950, he returned to organized baseball as a playing manager for the Quebec Braves in the Canadian-American League and hit .318 at the age of 40 to finish among the league leaders. He moved to the Provincial League with the franchise in 1951, planning to retire as a player, but ended up rejoining the active ranks and again hitting over .300. He managed to stay on the bench throughout most of the 1952 season, but he still had another comeback left in him. When his regular first baseman broke a leg in the sixth game of the Provincial League Championship Series, George was pressed into service and he ended his playing days driving in two runs in the seventh and final game of the series to lead Quebec to victory.[10]

George McQuinn finished his career with a lifetime batting average of .276 for 11 full major league seasons and a portion of a 12th. The stylish left-hander was a brilliant gloveman and a consistent clutch hitter, versatile enough to place among the league leaders in singles, doubles, triples, homers, walks, and sacrifice hits during his career. He also finished his career with a reputation as a money player and a sense of satisfaction that too few competitors find. Though it took 17 years, he finally succeeded in fulfilling his dream of starring in Yankees pinstripes.

It's no wonder that he earned the nickname "The Patient Scot."

George McQuinn

Born: 5/29/1910

Year	Team	Lg	G	HR	RBI	SB	BA	OPS
1930	New Haven	EL	8	0	-	-	.105	-
1930	Wheeling	MATL	97	5	58	9	.288	.681
1931	Scranton	NYPL	133	5	101	5	.316	.795
1932	Albany	EL	78	5	-	-	.345	-
	Binghamton	NYPL	62	1	35	4	.319	-
1933	Binghamton	NYPL	129	7	102	14	.357	.894
	Toronto	IL	14	1	10	0	.351	-
1934	Toronto	IL	138	4	77	16	.331	.787
1935	Newark	IL	148	11	77	7	.288	.705
1936	Cincinnati	NL	38	0	13	0	.201	.546
	Toronto	IL	108	9	61	6	.329	.854
1937	Newark	IL	114	21	84	2	.330	.907
1938	St. Louis	AL	148	12	82	4	.324	.861
1939	St. Louis	AL	154	20	94	6	.316	.898
1940	St. Louis	AL	151	16	84	3	.279	.802
1941	St. Louis	AL	130	18	80	5	.297	.867
1942	St. Louis	AL	145	12	78	1	.262	.737
1943	St. Louis	AL	125	12	74	4	.243	.701
1944	St. Louis	AL	146	11	72	4	.250	.733
1945	St. Louis	AL	139	7	61	1	.277	.762
1946	Philadelphia	AL	136	3	35	4	.225	.633
1947	New York	AL	144	13	80	0	.304	.832
1948	New York	AL	94	11	41	0	.248	.757
1949			(Did not play)					
1950	Quebec	CAML	74	7	-	-	.318	.806
1951	Quebec	PROV	59	1	-	-	.301	.735
1952	Quebec	PROV	12	0	-	-	.083	.167
12 Yrs.	MLB Totals		1,550	135	794	32	.276	.781

24

Luis Tiant

On May 15, 1971, 30-year-old Luis Tiant, barely two years removed from a spectacular 21-win campaign, drew his second unconditional release of the young season, having been found wanting by the Richmond Braves after a one-month trial. The Richmond club was in Louisville to play the Colonels, a Boston Red Sox farm club, so the former ace trudged across the field to see Louisville manager Darrell Johnson about a job with the Boston organization.[1]

By the end of the next season, Tiant was being treated to adoring cries of "Loo-Eee, Loo-Eee" reverberating through Fenway Park.

Tiant experienced one of the steepest declines and sharpest rebounds in major league baseball history. In 1968, his fifth year in the league, he burst into stardom with 21 victories against 9 losses for the Cleveland Indians. The Cuban right-hander led the league with a spectacular 1.60 ERA, the lowest mark by a regular American League starter since the legendary Walter Johnson posted a microscopic 1.49 mark almost 50 years earlier. In 1972, Tiant would again post the American League's lowest ERA, a sensational 1.91 mark, accompanied by a 15–6 won-lost record. He thus became the first starter to enjoy a pair of sub 2.00 ERA seasons since Hall of Famer Hal Newhouser accomplished the feat in back-to-back 1945 and 1946 campaigns.

In the three intervening years between these two incredible seasons, however, Tiant suffered a sore arm, broke a bone in his right shoulder, and absorbed the maximum allowable salary cut. He passed through three organizations, being traded once and unconditionally released twice, and almost drew a third release from the Red Sox before re-establishing himself. From 1969 through 1971, his major league won-lost record was a dismal 17–30, and he went a combined 3–5 with two minor league clubs.

The saga of "El Tiante," as he came to be known, began in Marianao, Cuba. The son of a Cuban and Negro League pitching star, Luis began his professional career in 1959. He was 18 years old at the time, or so he claims. Tiant's age has always been the subject of some speculation, with suspicions that he may have fudged his birthdate by several years. From 1959 to 1961, he spent his summers pitching for the Mexico City Tigers in the Mexican League and returning home to play in the Cuban Winter League in the offseason.

Purchased by the Cleveland organization in 1962, he didn't attract much attention until he set a Pacific Coast League record with 15 wins against a single loss for Portland in 1964. Called up by the tribe in mid–July, he went 10–4 for the remainder of the campaign. Pitching both as a starter and reliever from 1965 through 1967, he won 35 games, while losing 31 and yielding just over three earned runs per game for the Indians.

The 1968 season was the infamous "Year of the Pitcher," when hurlers throughout the majors turned in extraordinary performances. Denny McLain, of the Detroit Tigers, bagged a record 31 wins against 6 losses to become major league baseball's first 30-game-winner since Dizzy Dean in 1934. But Tiant matched the Tigers ace for most of the campaign, despite anemic offensive support from his Cleveland teammates. In July, Luis was named to start the All-Star Game for the American League, and a few weeks after the break his record stood at 17 wins against 6 losses. But poor support and arm trouble stalled him short of twenty wins for weeks. He finished with a flourish, fanning 16 hitters to win his 20th game, then closing the season with a one-hit, 11-strikeout shutout. But he missed several starts due to a sore arm between those last two masterpieces.

Although McLain captured the Cy Young Award as the American League's top pitcher in 1968, many felt that Tiant was at least his equal. The world champion Tigers backed McLain with the league's best defense and most potent offense. Meanwhile, the Indians ranked eighth in the ten team league in runs scored. In the eight starts Tiant lost (he lost one game in relief), his teammates never gave him more than two runs to work with, and he left several games with the score tied or a lead that eventually evaporated. His 21 victories included a league high 9 shutouts—often the only way he could secure a win.

Luis Tiant won 20 games three times after two unconditional releases (1977 Topps card).

Overall, 1968 was a successful year for the Indians who won 86 games and finished in third place, largely on the strength of the superb pitching of Tiant and staff-mate Sam McDowell. In the offseason, Luis was feted as the Tribe's Man of the Year. But trouble was brewing.

Tiant's distinctive pitching motion had always been controversial. He was often described as a whirling dervish on the mound, delivering pitches from a variety of angles ranging from over the top to sidearm to submarine. He intimidated hitters with a jerky, twisting windup, virtually turning his back on hitters and executing a pirouette before delivering the ball. His delivery often included a distinct hesitation where he would pause with his back to the batter looking toward center field. He would hold that position for a few disconcerting beats before wheeling and firing plateward. Opposing teams often protested his deliveries, but they were rarely ruled illegal by the men in blue. Despite his effectiveness, many baseball men were concerned that Tiant's contortions would eventually ruin his arm.

One of these men was Alvin Dark, the Indians manager. Dark was a former star shortstop and L.S.U. football hero who harbored deeply held convictions about religion and Tiant's pitching style, not necessarily in that order. Dark was a baseball traditionalist who fervently believed that Tiant's valuable arm was threatened by his unorthodox delivery as well as by his pitching winter league baseball in Latin America.

Upon taking over the Indians in 1968, Dark immediately locked horns with Tiant over his delivery, but he was forced to keep his silence while Tiant was winning. However, tension between the two escalated when Luis experienced arm trouble late in the 1968 season, and Dark convinced the Cleveland front office to forbid Tiant from pitching winter ball. Luis objected vehemently, claiming that his arm would tighten and his muscles would shorten if he stopped throwing year around. He even predicted a poor performance for himself in 1969, but in those days players had little voice in such matters, so Luis spent his first winter on the mainland.[2]

Whether an inevitable result, self-fulfilling prophesy, or mere fate, Tiant endured a miserable 1969 campaign. His ERA more than doubled as he lost a league-leading 20 games while winning only 9 times, nearly reversing his brilliant record of the previous year. His relationship with Dark and the Tribe front office deteriorated along with the team's record as the Indians tumbled into the American League East cellar. In the offseason, the disenchanted hurler was dispatched to the defending American League West Champion Minnesota Twins in a five-player deal that brought former Cy Young winner Dean Chance and unheralded young infielder-outfielder Graig Nettles to Cleveland.[3]

When the 1970 campaign started, Luis didn't seem to be throwing as hard as usual. Yet, he won his first six decisions to help the Twins jump out to a commanding division lead. Luis later admitted that his shoulder felt stiff all year, but the club trainer assured him that the tight muscle would loosen up and eventually pop back into place. A few days later, something did pop in his arm while he was pitching against the Milwaukee Brewers. Unfortunately, the sound was Tiant's scapula, or shoulder blade, cracking. The injury perplexed the doctors since this type of injury was unheard of for a baseball pitcher. Although a fractured scapula is usually the result of an extreme effort to throw an object, it's an injury usually associated with javelin throwers—not baseball players. Of course, this lent credence to the notion that Tiant's arm couldn't stand up to the rigors of his unorthodox deliveries.[4]

Tiant missed several months, returned too early, and pitched ineffectively when reactivated. During his absence, 19-year-old future Hall of Famer Bert Blyleven, who would go on to win 287 games in a 22-year career, took his place in the rotation.

In the spring of 1971, Luis pulled a back muscle in his first exhibition action and was out three weeks. He pitched well in his first outing after his return, but got bombed for six runs on ten hits in four innings the next time out. The Twins decided he wasn't worth risking a roster spot or the salary dollars on, so they released him before breaking camp.

The Twins weren't the only team unwilling to take a chance on the man who'd dominated the league only two years earlier. Unbelievably, no other club was willing to sign Tiant to a major league contract. Eventually the Atlanta Braves, a franchise not known for the quality of its pitching staff at the time, extended him a 30-day trial with their Richmond farm club to prove he could still pitch. Luis won his first start, but at the end of the trial period his won-lost record was 1–3 with an ugly 6.26 ERA when he was once again handed his walking papers. But Louisville Colonels manager Darrell Johnson saw something in Tiant that the Braves had missed, and recommended that the parent Red Sox sign him. With Louisville, he started rounding into shape, and in early June, he was called up to Boston.

Like the Braves, the Red Sox didn't enjoy a reputation as masters of spotting hidden pitching talent. Throughout their history, they seemed more adept at converting high profile winners into confused, sore-armed losers, but they'd recently had good luck with reclamation projects such as Ray Culp, Dick Ellsworth, and Gary Peters. Manager Eddie Kasko exhibited an inordinate amount of patience with Tiant, and the outcome would far exceed the wildest dreams of anyone in the Sox family.

But first, there were some rough waters to navigate. After his first Boston appearance on June 11, in which he yielded five runs in one inning, columnist Cliff Keane wrote in the *Boston Globe*: "The latest investment by the Red Sox looked about as sound as taking a bagful of money and throwing it off Pier 4 into the Atlantic."[5]

Two months later, Keane's comment looked positively psychic. When Kasko finally removed him from the rotation, Tiant was winless in 10 starts and a single relief appearance, giving him and 0–6 won-lost record with a 6.44 ERA.

Unexpectedly, Tiant seemed to find himself in the Boston bullpen. Pitching in relief the rest of the season, he posted a terrific 1.23 in 22 innings to salvage a spot on the Sox off-season roster.

Entering spring training before the 1972 season, however, Luis' prospects appeared none too bright. The Red Sox seemed to have a surplus of veteran starters and a bumper crop of promising youngsters. Despite his impressive finish, Tiant sported a gruesome 1–7 won-lost record and uninspiring 4.88 ERA for the previous year. He was again fighting for his baseball life.

Luis' chances improved greatly on March 22, 1972, a date that will live in infamy for Boston fans. On that fateful Wednesday, the Red Sox presented relief ace Sparky Lyle to the hated New York Yankees in a deal for first baseman Danny Cater. Lyle would develop into a Cy Young Award winner in New York, while the unfortunate Cater would take a place at the head of an extraordinary line of Red Sox failures. It would have been difficult to convince long-suffering Sox fans of this at the time, but the deal did have a bright side for Boston in that it created an opening on the staff for Tiant.

The veteran hurler started the season as a middle reliever and spot starter. He pitched effectively out of the bullpen and gradually started getting the call with the game on the line. He'd won four games against four losses and had an ERA around 3.00 when Kasko inserted him into the regular starting rotation in late July.

The Red Sox had been languishing in the middle of the pack throughout the year. At the end of July, they were in fourth place with a sleepy 47–46 record. But they caught fire in August and won 38 of 62 games the rest of the way, fueled by Luis Tiant's fabulous pitching. During that streak, El Tiante won 11 of his 13 starts, each victory a complete game—including 6 shutouts. His ERA was a glittering 1.22 for the period.

Through no fault of Tiant's, the Sox lost the 1972 pennant to the Tigers under unusual circumstances. A brief player strike had delayed the start of the season, resulting in an unbalanced schedule. Detroit ended up playing 156 games to Boston's 155 and recorded one more victory for their winning margin.

Despite not joining the starting rotation until late July, the 6 shutouts Tiant numbered among his 15 victories represented the fourth highest total in the league. During one stretch, he fired 4 straight shutouts and 6 in 7 games. In addition to posting the lowest ERA in the league, he had the second highest winning percentage. After the season he was a shoo-in for the league's Comeback Player of the Year nomination.

Tiant ended up becoming one of the most revered players in Red Sox history. Pete Gammons, the dean of Boston sportswriters, called him "the most popular pitcher on any team of my 35 years covering baseball."[6] Luis reveled in the honorific title "El Tiante" and the cries of "Loo-Eee, Loo-Eee" that filled Fenway Park when he took the mound. The balding, paunchy hurler with the thick Spanish accent was also an incurable locker room prankster, who often teamed with venerable Carl Yastrzemski to liven the clubhouse atmosphere. Off the field, his ever-present smile was usually adorned by a fat cigar that he smoked even in the shower.[7]

"El Tiante" was the undisputed ace of the Boston staff in the mid–1970s, topping 20 wins in 1973, 1974 and 1976. His victory total fell to 18 in the pennant-winning 1975 season. But he was the star of the postseason that year, starting the Sox on a three-game sweep of the Oakland Athletics team (managed by his old antagonist Alvin Dark) with a three-hitter. In the 1975 World Series, considered one of the greatest classics of all-time, he twice beat the heavily favored Cincinnati Reds, although the Sox finally lost in seven thrill-packed games.

Although Luis' effectiveness diminished after 1976, he remained a dependable, winning pitcher for the remainder of his years with the Red Sox. After the 1978 season, the 38-year-old twirler became a free agent and broke the hearts of long-suffering BoSox fans by signing with the Yankees. After two mediocre years in the New York starting rotation, he was released at the age of 40. He signed on with the Pittsburgh Pirates organization and won 13 games, including a no-hitter for their Portland farm club in 1981, but won only 2 of 7 decisions when called up by the parent club. He continued to pitch in the Latin American Leagues and earned another big league trial with the California Angels in 1982. But he was ineffective in 6 appearances to close out his big league career.

Luis Tiant finished with a lifetime 229–172 won-lost record and accompanying 3.30 career ERA for his major league career. These stats compares quite favorably to Jim Bunning's 224–184, 3.27, Don Drysdale's 209–166, 2.95, and contemporary Catfish Hunter's 224–166, 3.26. Yet, while Bunning, Drysdale, and Hunter—all of whom pitched most of their careers in more pitcher-friendly parks than Fenway—are in the Hall of Fame, Tiant has never received serious consideration. In balloting by the writers, he topped out at 31 percent of the vote in 1988, his first year of eligibility, far short of the 75 percent required for induction. In 2012, the Hall's Historical Overview Committee listed him on a special ballot for overlooked players who made their greatest contribution between 1947 and 1972. Possibly due to the fact that 57 percent of Tiant's wins came after 1972, he didn't come close to being selected.

Tiant recorded 147 of his 229 career victories after he'd been left for dead by major league baseball. As extraordinary as El Tiante's comeback was, however, it may have been topped by another member of the Tiant family. Luis Tiant, Sr. hadn't seen his son since Castro closed Cuba to emigration. But in 1975, he was allowed to travel to the United States to see him pitch professionally for the first time. Before an August 26 contest that Luis Jr. was scheduled to start, the Red Sox asked Luis Sr. to throw out the ceremonial first pitch. Not about to make a wimpy, half-hearted toss, the 70-year-old southpaw went into a smooth, graceful windup and delivered a pitch low and away. Dissatisfied with that effort, the former Negro League ace asked for another chance and split the plate with a surprisingly lively fastball to the delight of the capacity crowd.

"He told me he was ready to go four or five innings anytime," Luis Jr. quipped later.[8]

Luis Tiant Sr., returning to be honored by a baseball world that had rejected him due to the color of his skin in his prime, may have achieved the ultimate comeback.

Luis Tiant

Born: 11/23/1940

Year	Team	Lg	G	IP	W	L	ERA	WHIP
1959	*Mexico City*	*Mex*	*41*	*184*	*5*	*19*	*5.92*	-
1960	*Mexico City*	*Mex*	*41*	*180*	*17*	*7*	*4.65*	-
1961	*Mexico City*	*Mex*	*24*	*145*	*12*	*9*	*3.78*	-
1962	*Charleston*	*EL*	*29*	*139*	*7*	*8*	*3.63*	*1.53*
	Jacksonville	*IL*	*1*	*1*	*0*	*0*	*0.00*	*1.00*
1963	*Burlington*	*CARL*	*31*	*204*	*14*	*9*	*2.56*	*1.14*
1964	*Portland*	*PCL*	*17*	*137*	*15*	*1*	*2.04*	*0.93*
	Cleveland	AL	19	127	10	4	2.83	1.11
1965	Cleveland	AL	41	196	11	11	3.53	1.18
1966	Cleveland	AL	46	155	12	11	2.79	1.10
1967	Cleveland	AL	33	213	12	9	2.74	1.14
1968	Cleveland	AL	34	258	21	9	1.60	0.87
1969	Cleveland	AL	38	249	9	20	3.71	1.43
1970	Minnesota	AL	18	92	7	3	3.40	1.35
1971	*L'ville, Richm'nd*	*IL*	*9*	*54*	*3*	*5*	*4.17*	*1.39*
	Boston	AL	21	72	1	7	4.85	1.45
1972	Boston	AL	43	179	15	6	1.91	1.08
1973	Boston	AL	35	272	20	13	3.34	1.09
1974	Boston	AL	38	311	22	13	2.92	1.17
1975	Boston	AL	35	260	18	14	4.02	1.29
1976	Boston	AL	38	279	21	12	3.06	1.21
1977	Boston	AL	32	188	12	8	4.53	1.38
1978	Boston	AL	32	212	13	8	3.31	1.14
1979	New York	AL	30	195	13	8	3.91	1.24
1980	New York	AL	25	136	8	9	4.89	1.39
1981	*Portland*	*PCL*	*21*	*146*	*13*	*7*	*3.82*	*1.36*
	Pittsburgh	NL	9	57	2	5	3.92	1.27
1982	California	AL	6	29	2	2	5.76	1.58
19 Yrs	MLB Totals		573	3486	229	172	3.30	1.20

25

Robin Roberts

"It was one of the hardest, most difficult things I've ever had to do," said New York Yankees manager Ralph Houk. "Roberts is one of the real great pitchers... but he... he... he just doesn't fit into the overall picture for us."[1]

It looked like it was all over for Robin Roberts. What was supposed to have been the comeback story of the 1962 season had been aborted two weeks into the campaign. Before the 35-year-old right-hander had pitched an inning for the Bronx Bombers, he'd been handed his unconditional release, baseball's death knell.

The Yankees had purchased Roberts from the Philadelphia Phillies after the Yanks dominated the underdog Cincinnati Reds in the 1961 World Series. It seemed too good to be true for the classy veteran hurler. He was moving from the worst team in the major leagues to the best, a just reward for years of suffering with the hapless Phils.

From 1948 through 1961, Roberts won 234 games for the Phillies, second most in the history of the franchise. But the Phils were in the midst of a long-term rebuilding program. In 1961 they'd lost 107 games, including a modern National League record of 23 in a row. Roberts' record for the season was a single win against 10 defeats. After beginning the campaign with 7 straight losses, he was dropped from the regular rotation in late June and made only 6 more starts over the last three months of the season. There was little room for a struggling legend when strong young arms like Chris Short, Art Mahaffey, Dallas Green, and Johnny Buzhardt were ready and available.

The Yankees, on the other hand, were in the midst of another dynasty, one that would produce five straight pennants from 1960 through 1964. The 1961 edition is considered by many baseball historians to be one of greatest teams of all time. On their way to the world championship, they'd won 109 games and set a major record with 240 home runs. The attack was led by Roger Maris with a record setting 61 homers and Mickey Mantle with 54 circuit blasts. Yogi Berra, Moose Skowron, Elston Howard, and Johnny Blanchard also contributed to form the most potent offensive machine in the game. The infield, featuring sure-handed Bobby Richardson, Tony Kubek, and Clete Boyer, turned in the most double plays in the American League. Overall, the club committed the fewest errors in the league and tied for the lead in fielding percentage.

If the Bombers had an Achilles' heel, it was their pitching. For an ace, there was no one better than Whitey Ford, who'd posted a career best 25 wins against only 4 losses in 1961. But after Whitey, the staff was somewhat suspect. Ralph Terry (16–3), sophomore Bill Stafford (14–9), and rookie Rollie Sheldon (11–5) formed the rest of the "big four," but they were all young and their 1961 victory totals represented career highs for each of them. Veteran

Luis Arroyo, a National League castoff, had been the surprise of the year, winning 15 games and saving a league leading 29 others out of the bullpen. But Arroyo was 34 years old and had never given previous indication that he possessed that kind of ability.

The situation seemed ideal. "The Yankees and Robin Roberts seemed made for each other," according to *The Sporting News*. Backed by the finest team in baseball, he figured to slide into the rotation behind Ford and provide a stabilizing veteran influence while winning a lot of ballgames. After all, Robin had won 44 games for last place Phillies squads in the three years preceding his abysmal 1961 season.[2]

In addition, the Yankees seemed to have a knack for acquiring aging veteran stars and coaxing additional productive seasons out of them. From 1947 through 1961, they captured twelve pennants in fifteen years, with much of the credit owing to comebacks by rejuvenated cast-offs such as George McQuinn, Bobo Newsom, Johnny Sain, Johnny Mize, Jim Konstanty, Enos Slaughter, Bobby Shantz, and the aforementioned Arroyo.

Robin Roberts learned to change speeds after 234 major league victories (1962 Topps card).

In the spring of 1962, however, the Yankees were suddenly flush with promising young pitching arms, and Roberts didn't get much of a chance to show if he had anything left in spring training. Always the consummate professional, he summed up the situation while packing his gear in the Yankee clubhouse: "They picked me up from the Phillies on speculation, but their own kids from the farms looked awfully good at Ft. Lauderdale, and naturally they've got to look ahead.... I told them, pitch me or let me go. And they took me at my word."[3]

It's the oldest story in baseball. The old pro Roberts was sent packing so the Yankees could free up a spot on their roster for a fast-rising young rookie named Jim Bouton.

Roberts still thought he could pitch effectively, but no one called. Even the newly formed National League expansion teams, the New York Mets and Houston Colts, weren't interested. He was about to give up when he got a call from his old Phillies coach, Cy Perkins, whose encouragement early in Robin's career helped put him on the right track.

"You'll be pitching shutouts when you're forty," Perkins predicted. "I'm telling you, kid, don't quit. There's no way that you can't keep pitching."[4]

Inspired by Perkins' call, Robin started calling around. Finally, a month into the season, the Baltimore Orioles decided to give him a tryout.

Orioles general manager Lee MacPhail admitted that he called Roberts back just as a courtesy. "But Robin sounded so convincing that I decided there would be no harm in letting him come down and throw for us." Though impressed, the Orioles deliberated for 10 days before offering him a contract.[5]

After a couple of relief appearances, Robin made his first Baltimore start on May 27, holding the Boston Red Sox to two runs through 7⅔ innings. The Orioles eventually won in 11 innings, and the performance temporarily earned Roberts a spot in the rotation. After two tough losses, he beat the Yankees on June 11, his first victory in more than a year, and embarked on a four-game winning streak which solidified his rotation spot. By mid–July he'd won 5 games, including 3 route-going efforts, against 3 losses, while posting a 2.50 ERA.

In his latter years with the Phillies, Robin was often criticized for not accepting the fact that his fastball wasn't what it once was, stubbornly trying to power the ball past enemy hitters rather than changing speed. Apparently, the shock of being released led to a change in his approach. Orioles player-coach Darrell Johnson, who'd been a catcher with the Phillies in 1961, claimed, "He (Roberts) re-discovered himself."[6]

"It's no secret he wasn't too successful last year," Johnson went on, "and Robin was pitching the same as when he was a young man. The edge was off his fastball. But something happened before he came to Baltimore ... he came here with the idea he had to throw other pitches. He always had the fastball and a little breaking ball. He's using a different type of change of speed and a more sizeable curve ball. He features the other stuff to make his fastball the 'out' pitch. The new way he's pitching is almost second nature to him now."[7]

"It's like starting all over, but that's what I have to expect," said Roberts.[8]

With Baltimore, Roberts was able to adopt the role that he'd anticipated with the Yankees. The Orioles were contenders with a young and talented pitching staff. They'd recorded the best staff ERA in the big leagues in 1961 and would lead the American League again in 1962. The bullpen was anchored by veteran knuckleballer and future Hall of Famer Hoyt Wilhelm, but starters Steve Barber, Chuck Estrada, Milt Pappas, and Jack Fisher were all under 25 years of age.

Robin would be more than just a mentor to the Orioles' "Kiddie Korps," however. For the 1962 season, he wound up with a 2.78 ERA, the second best mark in the league, and his 10 wins included a pair of extremely satisfying victories over the Yankees. He lost 9 times, but the Orioles scored only 18 runs in those losses and 8 of them were so close that a timely hit could have won them. In addition, Roberts threw 6 complete games in 25 starts, the second highest total on the staff.

And his success with his new-found pitching style continued. In 1963, Robin started 35 times, won 14 games, and walked a mere 40 batters in 251 innings pitched. Nineteen sixty-four was another solid year for the veteran right-hander. He posted a 13–7 won-lost record to go with an excellent 2.91 ERA as the Orioles won 97 games and battled the Yankees and Chicago White Sox down to the wire for the pennant.

Roberts started off well in 1965 but was banished to the bullpen when he faltered in mid-season. In late July, he was cut loose to make room for 19-year-old, future Hall of Famer Jim Palmer. At the time of the second unconditional release of his career, his won-lost record was only 5 and 7, though his ERA was a respectable 3.37.

Again Robin made the team that released him regret their decision. The 38-year-old competitor was picked up by the National League Houston Astros (formerly the Colts) and embarrassed the Orioles decision makers by hurling shutouts in his first two starts for his new team. Starting 10 games for the Astros in the last half of the 1965 campaign, he won 5 times while losing 2 contests and recording a dazzling 1.89 ERA. Meanwhile, Baltimore's young pitching faltered down the stretch, and they finished in third place.

Roberts had his sights set on 300 lifetime victories, needing only 19 more after the 1965 season. He'd experienced some arm problems late in the campaign, however, and underwent surgery in the offseason. Yet he started the home opener in the year-old Astrodome, gaining the distinction of being the first pitcher to perform on the newly installed AstroTurf. His arm hadn't returned to full strength, however. Despite some good performances for the light-hitting Astros, he won only 3 games and lost 5 before being released again in July.

This time, Robin failed to make his former employer look bad. He hooked on with the Chicago Cubs, where he was reunited with his old Phillies pitching partner, Curt Simmons. Sadly, the reunion wasn't a smashing success. Roberts won only 2 games for the Cubs and was generally ineffective, as evidenced by a 6.19 ERA. He was released at the end of the season.

At the age of 40, Robin still wasn't ready to hang it up. Whether for sentimental or practical reasons, the Phillies gave him a chance with their Reading farm club in 1967. He won 5 games and posted an excellent 2.48 ERA, but decided to hang up his spikes when June rolled around and he hadn't been offered another big league opportunity. He retired with a major league record of 286 wins and 245 losses, 14 victories shy of his goal.[9]

The real shame is that Roberts truly deserved to be a 300-game-winner and certainly would have entered that charmed circle but for the prejudice of Phillies management.

In 1950, Roberts' second full year in the major leagues, the Phillies captured the pennant with a nucleus of outstanding young players dubbed the "Whiz Kids." Robin, a 20-game-winner was only 23 years old, while 17-game-winner Curt Simmons was a mere 21. Bob Miller, age 24, Russ Meyer, age 26, and Bubba Church, age 25, filled out the starting rotation. Shortstop was manned by 23-year-old Granny Hamner and 24-year-old Willie Jones handled third base. Richie Ashburn, age 23, and Del Ennis, age 25, were the mainstays in the outfield and 24-year-old Stan Lopata platooned behind the plate. The rest of the front-liners weren't exactly graybeards. First baseman Eddie Waitkus was 30, while left fielder Dick Sisler and catcher Andy Seminick were only 29. The oldest regular was relief pitcher and 1950 MVP Jim Konstanty, who was 33 years old. With this wealth of young talent, the Phillies seemed to be poised for the dynasty of the 1950s.

It didn't happen because Phillies management resisted signing black ballplayers, while the integrated teams in the National League, the Brooklyn Dodgers, New York Giants, and Milwaukee Braves continued to augment their rosters with quality black players. Not coincidentally, these three teams dominated the remainder of the 1950s, with the Dodgers winning five flags and the Giants and Braves capturing two each. While these franchises were adding players like Junior Gilliam, Joe Black, Willie Mays, Ruben Gomez, Hank Aaron, Bill Bruton and Wes Covington to rosters that already included the likes of former Negro League stars like Jackie Robinson, Roy Campanella, Don Newcombe, Hank Thompson, Monte Irvin, and Sam Jethroe, the Phillies stood pat with their all-white roster.

In fact, the 1950 Phillies were the last segregated team to win a National League pennant. After that season, they hung around the fringes of the first division for a few years before falling into the depths of the second division; 1953 would be their last winning season of the decade. The club remained segregated until 1957 and didn't have a top-flight black star until Dick (then known as Richie) Allen's 1964 rookie season, the year in which the Phillies returned to the upper echelon of the National League for the first time since the days of the Whiz Kids.

Roberts paid dearly for management's bias. He won more than 20 games every year from 1950 through 1955 while the Phillies remained a respectable team. But after winning 179 games before reaching age 30, he won only 55 times while racking up 79 losses over the next five years as the Phillies plummeted to the depths of the National League standings.

Certainly Robin would have picked up another 14 victories with a decent supporting cast, which would have been much easier to assemble if the Phils hadn't limited themselves to a "whites only" policy.

By the time the Cy Young Award was first presented in 1956, Robin was past his peak. But he probably would have earned a few of the trophies if it had been introduced a few years earlier. A true workhorse, he led the National League in victories from 1952 through 1955, as well as complete games and innings pitched. His 1952 season stands as one of the best pitching performances of all time. He won 28 games that year, a total that hasn't been topped since in the National League, and finished a close second to Cubs' slugger Hank Sauer in a controversial MVP vote. He did garner the 1952 *Sporting News* Major League Player of the Year award and was also the publication's choice for National League Pitcher of the Year in 1955.

Interestingly, Roberts actually posted a better ERA (3.20 to 3.46) after his release by the Yankees and subsequent change in his pitching philosophy. Surprisingly, his strikeout rate per nine innings was also slightly better, as was his strikeout-to-walk ratio, after he began mixing in more off-speed deliveries. Even his hits-per-inning ratio was a little better.

Despite finishing his career with 286 victories, which at the time was the eighth highest total among pitchers who began their careers after 1900, Robin Roberts was not immediately elected to the Hall of Fame when he became eligible in 1973. He was inducted in 1976, but he might not have made it at all if he'd quit with the 234 wins he had under his belt when the Yankees dumped him. The 52 victories he captured afterward solidified his place among baseball's greats.

Robin Roberts

Born: 9/30/1926

Year	Team	Lg	G	IP	W	L	ERA	WHIP
1948	*Wilmington*	*ISLG*	*11*	*96*	*9*	*1*	*2.06*	*0.85*
	Philadelphia	NL	20	146	7	9	3.19	1.43
1949	Philadelphia	NL	43	226	15	15	3.69	1.34
1950	Philadelphia	NL	40	304	20	11	3.02	1.18
1951	Philadelphia	NL	44	315	21	15	3.03	1.11
1952	Philadelphia	NL	39	330	28	7	2.59	1.02
1953	Philadelphia	NL	44	346	23	16	2.75	1.11
1954	Philadelphia	NL	45	336	23	15	2.97	1.03
1955	Philadelphia	NL	41	305	23	14	3.28	1.13
1956	Philadelphia	NL	43	297	19	18	4.45	1.24
1957	Philadelphia	NL	39	249	10	22	4.07	1.16
1958	Philadelphia	NL	35	269	17	14	3.24	1.19
1959	Philadelphia	NL	35	257	15	17	4.27	1.17
1960	Philadelphia	NL	35	237	12	16	4.02	1.22
1961	Philadelphia	NL	26	117	1	10	5.85	1.51
1962	Baltimore	AL	27	191	10	9	2.78	1.13
1963	Baltimore	AL	35	251	14	13	3.33	1.07
1964	Baltimore	AL	31	204	13	7	2.91	1.25
1965	Baltimore	AL	20	114	5	7	3.38	1.13
	Houston	NL	10	76	5	2	1.89	0.93
1966	Houston	NL	13	63	3	5	3.82	1.40
	Chicago	NL	11	48	2	3	6.14	1.51
1967	*Reading*	*EL*	*11*	*80*	*5*	*3*	*2.48*	*1.03*
19 Yrs	MLB Totals		676	4688	286	245	3.41	1.17

26

Babe Adams

Old-school baseball purists have long bemoaned the lack of team loyalty from modern players. To hear them talk, today's stars are simply ingrates, greedily pursuing top dollar. In point of fact, the old-time stars rarely stayed in place for their entire careers, while modern all-time greats like Carl Yastrzemski, Tony Gwynn, Robin Yount, and Cal Ripken established records while staying with the same team throughout their lengthy careers. In fact, the 2013 season ended with Derek Jeter and Mariano Rivera still with the same New York Yankees franchise they began their careers with 19 years ago, while Todd Helton concluded his 17th season with the small-market Colorado Rockies.

But early 20th century hurler Charles "Babe" Adams set a standard for team loyalty that will probably remain unchallenged. After a false start with the Cardinals in St. Louis, Adams pitched for the Pittsburgh Pirates for nine seasons before being unceremoniously dumped in 1916 when his effectiveness waned. The Pirates may have considered themselves through with Babe Adams, but Adams was a long way from being through with the Pirates. He worked his way back from the deep minor leagues to regain his old place in the Pirates rotation and spent another nine years with them before again being summarily (many say unfairly) discharged.

In his first full big league season, Adams took the baseball world by storm. In the 1909 World Series, he almost single-handedly vanquished the great Ty Cobb and the mighty Detroit Tigers, capping a spectacular rookie season with three complete game victories to lead Pittsburgh to the world championship. His sensational performance made the 27-year-old pitcher an overnight celebrity, and his name became a household word throughout the nation. Following the final game, a brass band led revelers through the streets of Pittsburgh, and store windows proudly displayed his portrait.[1]

Seven years later, his career hit rock bottom. He'd proven that he was no flash in the pan by winning 99 games from 1910 through 1915 while keeping his ERA below 3.00 every year. But midway through the 1916 campaign, he'd won only 2 games against 9 losses and his ERA was a dismal 5.72, more than twice as high as his career mark going into the season. In August, the Pirates unconditionally released the 34-year-old veteran. The Pittsburgh brass and the rest of the baseball world thought he was through. The suspicion was that he'd ruined his arm in a grueling 21-inning marathon duel against Rube Marquard of the New York Giants two years earlier.[2]

But two years later, Babe Adams was back in a Pirates uniform, pitching as effectively as ever. In fact, the old war-horse had another 81 victories left in his rejuvenated pitching arm.

Babe Adams had two different careers with the Pirates (Bain Collection, Library of Congress).

Babe stood almost six feet in height and weighed about 180 pounds in his prime. He had coal black hair and piercing dark eyes to match. His handsomeness, rather than his skill on the baseball field, reputedly led to his nickname.[3] On the mound, he threw with a smooth over-the-top delivery that made the ball appear to descend on the batter, and he pitched with such ease that he was often compared to the great Christy Mathewson. He possessed a good fastball, but his best pitch was an overhand curve.[4]

Adams was born on a farm in Tipton, Indiana, on May 18, 1882, and moved to Mt. Moriah, Missouri, with his family while still in school. Legend has it that young Charley was originally a lefty, but a childhood injury to his left hand forced him to become a right-hander. He reportedly developed his strong right arm throwing stones at rabbits and tree stumps. His family was so poor that when Adams was 16, he was taken in by a local farmer who encouraged the boy's baseball aspirations.[5]

While pitching for town teams in the area, Adams mastered the curveball and gained the pinpoint control that would become his calling card. Eventually he signed on with the Parsons, Kansas, club of the old Missouri Valley League. The 23-year-old won 21 games for Parsons and made the jump from Class D to the majors when St. Louis purchased his contract. He began the 1906 campaign with the Cardinals but was demoted to Louisville of the American Association after one ineffective start. Louisville subsequently assigned him to the Denver franchise in the Class A Western League, where he posted a 9–10 won-lost record.

After winning 24 games against 11 losses for Denver in 1907, leading the league in victories as well as winning percentage, Babe found himself the property of the Pittsburgh Pirates, who'd purchased his contract for $5,000. He was unimpressive in four late season appearances for the Pirates, so his services were loaned back to Louisville for the 1908 season. He won 22 games for Louisville and walked only 40 batters in 312 innings to earn another shot with the Pirates.

The 1909 Pirates employed one of the finest pitching staffs in baseball, featuring future Hall of Famer Vic Willis, who posted 22 victories, and 25-game-winner Howie Camitz. With former 20-game winners Lefty Leifield, Nick Maddox, Deacon Phillippe, and Sam Leever also on the staff, it was difficult for a rookie to get much work, so Adams pitched only 130 innings his first full big-league season. But his work was nothing short of spectacular. He recorded 12 victories against only 3 losses, and his microscopic 1.11 ERA was better than Christy Mathewson's league-leading mark, although he didn't pitch enough innings to qualify for the title.

The World Series of 1909 was billed as a showdown between Detroit's Ty Cobb and Pittsburgh's Honus Wagner, who were almost unanimously considered to be the top players in the game. Cobb was a rising 22-year-old superstar who had already captured his third American League batting crown that season with a .377 mark. Wagner was 35 years old, but the veteran shortstop had just won his fourth straight National League batting championship—his seventh title overall. Despite the Pirates' great pitching and the presence of Wagner and player-manager Fred Clarke in their batting order, the Tigers were considered the favorites. In addition to the intimidating Cobb, their lineup featured another future Hall of Famer, Sam Crawford, and their pitching staff was led by 29-game-winner George Mullin, 21-game-winner Ed Willett, and 19-game-winner Ed Summers. They had captured the American League pennant the previous two seasons, only to lose the World Series to the National Leaguers—losses they were eager to avenge.

Pirates manager Fred Clarke's decision to start Adams in the first game of the Series was a shocker. Despite his success during the regular season, Babe was still relatively unknown—little more than a raw rookie and no better than the fourth ranked hurler on the staff. But Clarke thought Adams, who relied mostly on a devastating overhead curve, was the type of pitcher who could give the Tigers a run for their money despite his relative inexperience. Starting him in the initial game of the Series would be risky, but Clarke was willing to take the gamble.

According to baseball lore, Clarke was influenced by an ad-hoc scouting report from National League president John Heydler. Heydler had reportedly seen a nondescript young Washington Senators twirler by the name of Dolly Gray shut down the Tigers during the season and mentioned to Clarke that Adams and Gray had similar styles. However, given the fact that Gray was a lefthander, this may be nothing more than a myth. Babe's brilliant pitching down the stretch might have had more to do with the decision.[6]

Babe, who was notified of his assignment the day of the game, was understandably nervous as he toed the rubber before a hometown crowd of almost 30,000 fans. He walked the leadoff man on four pitches and then walked Cobb after the second batter had sacrificed. Seconds later the Tigers had their first run, and Clarke's gamble was looking like a bad one. But the youngster vindicated his manager's faith in him by retiring Detroit without further damage and holding them the rest of the way. In the meantime, the offensive efforts of Clarke and Wagner gave the Pirates the lead and they prevailed 4–1.

After Camnitz and Leifield failed in games two and three, the Pirates won game five behind Nick Maddox and sent Adams back to the mound with the Series tied at two apiece. This time Babe wasn't quite as effective, but he hung on to win 8 to 4 for his second victory. The Tigers rebounded to win a hard-fought sixth game over Vic Willis by a score of 5–4. It was down to the final game. Incredibly, the Pirates' three biggest winners—Camnitz, Willis, and Leifield—had combined for three losses and no wins. Again, Clarke rolled the dice and laid the responsibility squarely on the broad young shoulders of Babe Adams, who would be pitching with only two days of rest.

Adams was up to the assignment. Working easily and confidently, he threw a masterful six-hit shutout to nail down the world championship for the Pirates. For the Series, he pitched three complete game victories, yielding only 18 hits and 5 runs in 27 innings. Furthermore, he had held the celebrated Cobb to a mere .091 batting average in the three contests.

In the off-season, the Pirates sold Vic Willis to the Cardinals, relying on Adams to take his place at the top of the rotation. Though the team fell to third place in 1910, Babe didn't disappoint, winning a staff-high 18 games. The next year he won 22 contests, while leading the league with 7 shutouts, and after a down season in 1912, he rejoined the exclusive 20-win club in 1913.

The Pirates were struggling mightily on their way to a seventh place finish, their worst season since the turn of the century, when Adams hooked up with Marquard on July 17, 1914. At the time, it was reported to be the longest game in National League history. Babe went the distance but ended up losing 3–1 when the Giants scored a pair of runs on a tainted inside-the-park home run. He yielded only 6 hits and set a record that still stands by not walking a single batter.[7]

While it's a matter of record that Adams' won-lost record declined precipitously after his duel with Marquard, there's no proof that it led to the sore arm that would derail his career two years later. After winning 21 games and posting a 2.15 ERA for the fourth place

Pirates in 1913, he won only 13 games while losing 16 in 1914. But his fine 2.51 ERA that year would seem to indicate that the drop off was due to the team's disappointing performance (they fell to seventh place) rather than Babe's pitching. The next season, he went 14–14 with a 2.87 ERA for another losing Pittsburgh squad before collapsing completely in 1916. It's likely that his shoulder woes were the result of an average 258-inning yearly workload between 1910 and 1915 rather than the one game.

After the Pirates let him go, Babe decided to sit out the rest of the 1916 season rather than go to the minors.[8] But he wasn't ready to retire to the farm just yet. He'd tried all the usual treatments for his ailing wing that were available in those days, but nothing seemed to work. He didn't think he'd suffered a torn ligament or strained muscle, so he figured the problem was nerve damage that might be cured with rest.[9]

When his arm felt better the next year, Babe caught on with the St. Joseph, Missouri, squad in the Western League for the 1917 season. Although he wanted to play close to home, he stayed with the team when operations were shifted to Hutchinson, Kansas, in mid-season. In his return to the circuit where he'd pitched a decade earlier, he won 20 games.

Though Babe had failed to attract the attention of big league scouts, he did move up to Kansas City in the American Association in 1918, where he won 13 of 17 decisions and posted a 1.67 ERA. After the American Association season ended early due to the manpower demands of World War I, the Pirates reacquired Babe's contract. In retrospect it might seem like a sentimental gesture—a fitting tribute to an old hero. But the Pirates were still in the National League pennant race at the time and the wartime talent drain made a draft-exempt 36-year-old hurler look like a top prospect. In three starts, Babe proved he could still pitch effectively at the major league level, throwing two complete games and splitting two decisions with an excellent 1.19 ERA.

By the time the 1919 season opened, the Great War was over and the first-stringers were back home. But Adams not only managed to win back his old spot in the Pirates starting rotation, he also regained his place among baseball's elite hurlers. The 37-year-old workhorse was the oldest and one of the best pitchers in the league, winning 17 games with an outstanding 1.98 ERA and walking only 23 batters in 263 innings.

The next year, Babe again won 17 games and again pitched 263 innings. Incredibly, he reduced his already remarkable base-on-balls total to only 18 and rang up a league-leading 8 shutouts. At the age of 39 in 1921, his 14–5 won-lost record gave him the best winning percentage in the National League. Though his record fell to 8–11 in 1922, he issued the fewest walks-per-game in the major leagues for the fourth straight year.

Babe rebounded to post a 13–7 won-lost mark at the age of 41 in 1923. Still one of the most popular Pirates in the team's history, he came to be regarded as a kind of talisman or good luck charm. Working mostly out of the bullpen, he hung around for another two seasons compiling a winning record. The 43-year-old icon even pitched a scoreless inning in the 1925 World Series.[10]

In the spring of 1926, the Pittsburgh press trumpeted the signing of the 44-year-old veteran to another Pirates contract. But unfortunately, his last season in a Pittsburgh uniform would end in disappointment and acrimony for the classy veteran hurler.[11]

The Pirates had captured the 1925 pennant and gone on to win the World Series under the capable leadership of 39-year-old Bill McKechnie, in only the fourth year of his Hall of Fame managerial career. But Fred Clarke, who'd managed the Pirates from 1897 through 1915, had returned to the organization as a vice president and stockholder during the campaign. The 1926 season found the former skipper back in uniform as an assistant manager. Several of the Pirates felt that the 54-year-old Clarke was overly critical of them and often second-guessed McKechnie.[12]

By August, the situation had become a source of dissention on the club. The players sought Clarke's removal from the dugout, and the press got involved in the controversy. When his opinion was sought, Adams simply commented: "The manager should manage and no one else should interfere." This forthright opinion, which has been validated by veteran baseball men through the ages, brought down the wrath of the Pittsburgh front office. Babe was accused of insubordination and branded as one of the ringleaders of the insurrection, along with veteran outfielders Carson Bigbee and Max Carey. Carey, the team captain and a future Hall of Famer, was suspended without pay and soon peddled to the Brooklyn Dodgers, while Adams and Bigbee drew their unconditional releases. The irony of the situation was not lost on the press, where it was pointed out that Adams and Carey, the most senior members of the team, had begun their Pirates careers and risen to stardom under Clarke. They had once been among his favorites and had no reason to go against him, other than for what they considered the good of the team.[13]

The three players appealed the team's actions to league president John Heydler, who probably came as close as he could to backing a player in those days by exonerating them of insubordination. Heydler, however, upheld the club's right to dispose of unwanted personnel as they saw fit.[14]

Not ready to give up baseball, Adams signed on as a player-manager with Johnstown of the Mid-Atlantic League for the 1927 season. But he was frustrated by injuries and pitched only twice before turning in his resignation. He then joined Springfield of the Western Association, which was much closer to his home, and won 4 of 5 decisions. Springfield wanted him back the next year, but the veteran hurler had invested wisely in farmland throughout his career and decided to remain home in Mt. Moriah. He later became a sportswriter and a respected foreign correspondent, going overseas to report on both World War II and the Korean War.[15]

For his major league career, Babe Adams amassed 194 victories against 140 losses. He completed 206 of his 355 starts and finished with an excellent lifetime ERA of 2.76. One of the greatest control pitchers of all time, he issued an average of less than one walk per game from 1919 through 1922. In fact, he handed out only 430 bases-on-balls in 2,995 innings during his career, for an average of 1.29 walks-per-game, the second lowest figure in big league history among pitchers with more than 2,000 innings pitched. And his incredible 1.11 ERA in 1909 is still the lowest mark ever for a rookie pitcher. Many modern day statistical gurus prefer a measure of pitcher effectiveness called WHIP which is a computation of base runners allowed via hit or walk per inning. Since 1900, among pitchers with more than 1,500 innings pitched in the big leagues, only Hall of Famers Addie Joss, Ed Walsh, Christy Mathewson, Walter Johnson, and Mordecai "Three Finger" Brown have retired with better WHIPs than Babe's 1.092 career average.

In modern times, with Tommy John surgery, rotator cuff repair, bone chip removal, and other procedures routinely performed on pitchers' arms, Babe Adams' comeback may not seem that noteworthy. But in his day, the only courses of action available to a sore-armed moundsman were to rest the ailing wing or throw through the pain. Unfortunately, club owners of the era were not inclined to pay a pitcher to rest his arm, and too many hurlers were forced to choose the latter. Few made it back, and many ruined their precious arms forever. Adams had the courage to shut it down before he irreparably damaged his arm and had the determination to fight his way back to the big leagues. He may have actually come back as a better pitcher. He left the major leagues in 1916 with a fine .574 winning percentage and raised it to .581 after coming back. He had the lowest WHIP in the National League from 1919 through 1921 before slipping to second place as a 40-year-old in 1922.

A statement attributed to Adams in 1920 is incredibly ironic in light of his later treatment by the Pirates, and it accentuates the difference between the attitudes and circumstances of the players of that time versus modern stars. When the Hutchinson team sold his contract to Kansas City while he was on the comeback trail in 1918, he reluctantly agreed to report and later commented, "The Hutchinson club had treated me with great generosity and I wished to see them make a dollar." He also added that the American Association was a "step back to my old job with the Pirates."[16]

The fact that Babe's big league days would eventually end in acrimony was a grievous injustice. His career with the Pittsburgh Pirates spanned 20 seasons, with time out for additional seasoning at the beginning and a minor league rehab in the middle. All of his 194 major league victories went to the Pittsburgh cause, yet he was banished for supporting his manager.

"I am 18 years in baseball without ever opening my mouth, and then when I answer a question, I find myself chucked off the club," he remarked on his way out the door.[17]

It took Babe Adams 18 years to find out what the modern athlete instinctively knows.

Babe Adams

Born: 5/18/1882

Year	Team	Lg	G	IP	W	L	ERA	WHIP
1905	*Parsons*	*MOVL*	*32*	*276*	*21*	*9*	*2.05*	*-*
1906	*Denver*	*WL*	*21*	*155*	*9*	*10*	*3.01*	*1.20*
	St. Louis	NL	1	4	0	1	13.50	2.75
1907	*Denver*	*WL*	*39*	*325*	*24*	*13*	*1.99*	*1.14*
	Pittsburgh	NL	4	22	0	2	6.95	1.96
1908	*Louisville*	*AA*	*41*	*312*	*22*	*12*	*2.08*	*0.97*
1909	Pittsburgh	NL	25	130	12	3	1.11	0.85
1910	Pittsburgh	NL	34	245	18	9	2.24	1.13
1911	Pittsburgh	NL	40	293	22	12	2.33	1.01
1912	Pittsburgh	NL	28	170	11	8	2.91	1.20
1913	Pittsburgh	NL	43	313	21	10	2.15	1.02
1914	Pittsburgh	NL	40	283	13	16	2.51	1.03
1915	Pittsburgh	NL	40	245	14	14	2.87	1.07
1916	Pittsburgh	NL	16	72	2	9	5.72	1.42
1917	*St. Jos/Hutch'son*	*WL*	*35*	*308*	*20*	*13*	*1.75*	*0.90*
1918	*Kansas City*	*AA*	*19*	*167*	*14*	*3*	*1.67*	*0.90*
	Pittsburgh	NL	3	22	1	1	1.19	0.84
1919	Pittsburgh	NL	34	263	17	10	1.98	0.90
1920	Pittsburgh	NL	35	263	17	13	2.16	0.98
1921	Pittsburgh	NL	25	160	14	5	2.64	1.08
1922	Pittsburgh	NL	27	171	8	11	3.57	1.20
1923	Pittsburgh	NL	26	158	13	7	4.42	1.39
1924	Pittsburgh	NL	9	39	3	1	1.13	0.86
1925	Pittsburgh	NL	33	101	6	5	5.42	1.44
1926	Pittsburgh	NL	19	36	2	3	6.14	1.61
1927	*Springfield*	*WA*	*7*	*53*	*4*	*1*	*1.36*	*0.96*
	Johnstown	*MATL*	*2*	*18*	*2*	*0*	*-*	*-*
19 Yrs	MLB Totals		482	2995	194	140	2.76	1.09

27

Mark Koenig

In the 1927 World Series, shortstop Mark Koenig hit an even .500 to lead the powerful New York Yankees regulars as they swept the over-matched Pittsburgh Pirates in four games.

Five years later, he again played a major World Series role, although this time he was on the wrong end of a sweep as a member of the 1932 Chicago Cubs. In between the two classics, he'd lost his regular Yankees shortstop job to brash, young Leo Durocher, was traded to the Detroit Tigers after he was spotted wearing glasses off the field, tried becoming a pitcher with the Tigers, and was sent to the minor leagues before resurfacing to spark the Cubs pennant drive.

Some comebacks are more noteworthy for their contribution to baseball lore and legend rather than the actual achievement. Mark Koenig's comeback with the Cubs falls into this category. It directly led to one of the most widely celebrated and controversial events in baseball history—Babe Ruth's called shot.

The story begins early in the morning of July 7, 1932, when a young woman named Violet Valli entered the hotel room of Cubs shortstop Billy Jurges and shot him in the hand and through the ribs. This unfortunate incident set in motion a series of events that spawned one of the most fascinating chapters in baseball annals.

Apparently, the 24-year-old Jurges had exercised the requisite poor judgment to become involved with Ms. Valli, a dancer and model. When he tried to break it off, she didn't take it well. In circumstances that eerily presaged the shooting of Philadelphia Phillies first baseman Eddie Waitkus in the same city seventeen years later, Violet downed a few healthy shots of gin and set out to kill Jurges. She even left a note that read, "To me, life without Billy isn't worth living, but why should I leave this earth alone? I'm going to take Billy with me."[1]

The wounded Jurges managed to subdue Ms. Valli, who was shot in the wrist herself in the ensuing struggle. She was taken away by police and booked for attempted murder, but soon freed when the forgiving ballplayer magnanimously declined to press charges. A week later Violet, who was rumored to have encountered difficulty dating Cubs players after the incident, was back at Wrigley Field, staring at the owner's box behind the third base dugout where the recuperating Jurges sat.[2]

At the time of the shooting, the Cubs were in a tight race with Pittsburgh and Boston for the National League pennant. Jurges was an integral part of the club. The slick fielding shortstop, in his first year as a regular, teamed with rookie second baseman and future Hall of Famer Billy Herman to form a brilliant double play combination. The emergence of the duo allowed the Cubs to move Woody English over to fill their troublesome third base spot and let 36-year-old player-manager Rogers Hornsby run the team from the bench.

After Jurges was wounded, the Cubs initially returned English to shortstop and installed another rookie, Stan Hack, at the hot corner. Hack would go on to a lengthy career with the Cubs and become a huge fan favorite in Chicago, but he failed to hit with authority as a freshman. This led Hornsby to try his hand at third for a few games, but the Cubs continued to falter due to weakness at the all-important shortstop position. Though Jurges returned to action before the end of July, the shooting had left him severely weakened and his play suffered.

Meanwhile, the cantankerous, blunt-spoken Hornsby, who was intensely disliked by his players, had lost the backing of the Cubs front office as well. On August 2, with the Cubbies clinging to first place with a 53–44 record, the former star was fired as manager and released as a player. Popular veteran first baseman Charlie Grimm picked up the managerial reins, and three days later the club purchased the contract of ex–Yankees shortstop Mark Koenig from the Mission club of the Pacific Coast League to shore up their infield.

The switch-hitting Koenig was the Yankees' regular shortstop from 1926 through 1928 as they captured three straight pennants. He joined the Yankees near the end of the 1925 season after being purchased from St. Paul of the American Association. Despite a penchant for errors, he was a key ingredient to the Bombers' success. He enjoyed an excellent sophomore season in 1927, batting a solid .285, scoring 99 runs, and driving in 62 from the second spot in the famous Murderer's Row lineup, before starring in the World Series.

Koenig improved his batting average to .319 in 1928 as the Yankees won the world championship again, but his glovework continued to be a problem. Mark had led American League shortstops in errors in 1926 and 1927, and finished with the second highest total in the league in 1928. The next year his playing time decreased despite a .292 batting average, as the sharp fielding Durocher began getting most of the playing time at short.

Early in the 1930 season, Koenig was traded to Detroit along with pitcher Waite Hoyt. Although he was more or less the regular shortstop for the Tigers that year, he began experiencing problems with his eyesight, and his average plummeted to .238. Always known for a strong, if somewhat erratic, throwing arm, he even tried pitching—with little success. Koenig spent the 1931 season shuffling around the Tigers infield while continuing the pitching experiment. But a .253 batting mark, mediocre defense, and the emergence of Billy Rogell as the Tigers' regular shortstop led to his sale to the Pacific Coast League San Francisco Missions as the 1932 season was getting underway. The return to his hometown brought Koenig's bat back to life, as he hit .335 in 89 games before getting the call from Chicago.

After a few pinch-hitting appearances, Koenig started at shortstop on August 19 and contributed two hits to a Cubs loss that shrunk their lead over Pittsburgh to 1½ games. The next day, the club embarked on 14-game winning streak that blew the race wide open. Koenig, starting every game at shortstop, fueled the streak with his sensational hitting.

For the season, Koenig hit .353 in 33 games for the Cubs and was a key to their successful pennant drive. They won 37 of 57 games under Grimm to finish four lengths ahead of Pittsburgh. Yet, when it came time to allot shares of the World Series proceeds, the players voted Koenig only a half share of the Series money. When word of this penuriousness hit the press, some of the players try to justify it by reasoning that Koenig wasn't entitled to a full share since he hadn't been with the club the whole year. That excuse, however, was compromised by the fact that the players didn't allocate a penny to Hornsby, who managed the club more than half the season and had them in first place when he was replaced.

The Yankees, of course, weren't about to ignore a slight to their old teammate. Before the first game, Babe Ruth set the tone for the Series when he hollered across the field, "Hey Mark, who are those cheapskates you're with?" Through the first two games in New York, the Cubs were subjected to merciless bench jockeying. The Yankees won both contests and traveled to Wrigley Field to face a hostile Chicago crowd for the third game. In the first inning, the Babe belted a three-run homer to give the Yankees the lead, but the Cubs rallied to tie the score at 4–4 by the time he came to bat in the fifth inning.[3]

As the Babe stepped to the plate, Cubs reserves lined the top step of the dugout shouting insults while their fans hurled fruit and invectives at the Bambino. According to legend, Babe held up one finger when Cubs pitcher Charlie Root fired strike one. After taking the next pitch for another strike, Babe then held up two fingers before pointing dramatically toward the center field bleachers—precisely where he deposited Root's next offering.[4]

Whether or not Ruth actually called his shot is still hotly debated, but there's no argument that the Babe's magnificent homer, his last hit in World Series play, turned the contest around. Gehrig followed with another four-bagger, and the Bronx Bombers won the game 7 to 5. The next day, they easily finished off the disheartened Cubs.

Koenig's comeback didn't end with the 1932 season. He stayed in the majors another four years. After spending the 1933 season with the Cubs as a back-up infielder, he played in a career high 151 games for the Cincinnati Reds in 1934. The 1935 season found him in a New York Giants uniform, replacing aging Hughie Critz at second base. The next year, Mark got into a fifth World Series as a Giants reserve. Fittingly, his last big league hit came at Yankee Stadium in a Game 4 pinch-hitting appearance. He returned home the next year to finish his career with the Missions.

In 10 full big league seasons and parts of two others, Mark rang up a .279 career batting mark. Interestingly, his average was actually higher (.283) after his mid-career comeback.

Though seldom the focus of the spotlight, Koenig seemed to have a knack for being close to the action. In addition to Ruth's called shot, he witnessed the Babe's record-setting 60th homer (from third base), Alexander's legendary strikeout of Lazzeri in the 1926 World Series, and Carl Hubbell's 16-game winning streak in 1936. He played on five pennant winning teams with three franchises. He was teammate of no fewer than 25 Hall of Famers during his career, partnering with three of them—Tony Lazzeri, Charlie Gehringer, and Billy Herman—around the keystone sack. In 1929, he played in the first game in which numbers were displayed on the players' back, thus becoming the first player to wear number two by virtue of his position in the second spot in the Yankees batting order. Interestingly, Leo Durocher was the first Yankee to wear the now famous number seven.

In Cincinnati, Koenig was a member of the first team to have its games regularly broadcast by radio. Those 1934 Reds were also the first team to fly commercially as a unit, although Mark and teammate Jim Bottomley passed up the first flight, opting to travel by rail instead.[5]

Finally, Koenig was the last surviving member of the 1927 squad, becoming in his later years the unofficial spokesman for the team many considered the greatest of all time, until his death at age 88 in 1993.

Certainly, there have been more difficult and heroic comebacks than Mark Koenig's, but few have contributed so significantly to baseball lore. Whether Ruth actually pointed to the spot where he proceeded to hammer the next pitch or not (opposing pitcher Charlie Root went to his grave claiming he hadn't), the event became firmly ensconced as baseball's most famous legend when it was depicted in the 1948 Hollywood version of Ruth's life. On the field, Koenig played only a minor role in the drama. In the last inning of the called shot game, he was announced as a pinch-hitter for the Cubs pitcher but gave way to another pinch-hitter when the Yankees changed pitchers. But his mere presence, due to his unlikely comeback, made one of the epic events in baseball history possible.

Mark Koenig

Born: 7/19/1904

Year	Team	Lg	G	HR	RBI	SB	BA	OPS
1921	Moose Jaw	WCAN	84	0	-	-	.202	-
1921	St. Paul	AA	4	0	-	-	.000	-
1922	Jamestown	DAKL	97	2	-	-	.254	-
1922	St. Paul	AA	7	0	-	-	.412	-
1923	Des Moines	WL	156	6	-	6	.288	.690
1924	St. Paul	AA	68	0	-	2	.267	.600
1925	St. Paul	AA	126	11	-	13	.308	.782
	New York	AL	28	0	4	0	.209	.525
1926	New York	AL	147	5	65	4	.271	.682
1927	New York	AL	123	3	62	3	.285	.702
1928	New York	AL	132	4	63	3	.319	.774
1929	New York	AL	116	3	41	1	.292	.751
1930	New York	AL	21	0	9	0	.230	.594
1930	Detroit	AL	76	1	16	2	.240	.595
1931	Detroit	AL	106	1	39	8	.253	.631
1932	Mission	PCL	89	0	-	4	.335	.724
	Chicago	NL	33	3	11	0	.353	.887
1933	Chicago	NL	80	3	25	5	.284	.720
1934	Cincinnati	NL	151	1	67	5	.272	.625
1935	New York	NL	107	3	37	0	.283	.641
1936	New York	NL	42	1	7	0	.276	.770
1937	Mission	PCL	39	0	-	-	.289	.622
12 Yrs	MLB Totals		1162	28	446	31	.279	.683

28

Orlando Hernandez

It was January 2004, and 38-year-old Orlando Hernandez, one-time winner of a record eight straight postseason games for the New York Yankees, was participating in a staged workout for any interested big league organization. Hernandez was out of a job. His last employer, the struggling Montreal Expos organization, for whom he'd pitched a grand total of five minor league innings in 2003, had not been interested in re-signing him.

Different scouts in attendance characterized the event as "a charade... a joke... a waste of time." After Hernandez completed the session, throwing about 35 pitches that topped out around 78 MPH, another scout cracked, "OK, is he done getting loose?"[1]

Six months later, Hernandez was back in harness—back in Yankees pinstripes, as a matter of fact. By September, he was being heralded as a savior in New York. In October, he made his 14th post-season start for the Yankees against the Boston Red Sox in Fenway Park in the American League Championship Series.

It's been said that coming back—returning to the pinnacle of success after falling to the bottom—is harder than the original climb to the top. If this statement is literally true, then Orlando Hernandez's comeback may have been the most difficult in baseball history, because his original scramble to find success in major league baseball was certainly one of the most difficult of all time.

Orlando Hernandez, like his father, Arnando, is a legend in Cuban baseball. He even inherited his father's nickname, "El Duque," which literally translates to "The Duke," although it's been said that it means "The Hurricane" in the case of the Hernandez duo.

Orlando pitched in the Cuban National Series, the top league on the island, reportedly posting a 126–47 won-lost record in ten years with Industriales de Havana. He also represented Havana in the Selective Series, the Cuban version of the postseason, and was a fixture on the Cuban national baseball team, including the 1992 gold-winning Olympic squad. When he left Cuba, he was the island nation's all-time leader in winning percentage.[2]

Due to his baseball celebrity, Hernandez led a life of relative luxury in Havana. The Cuban Sports Ministry provided him with a three-bedroom house and a job, and he had access to the state-run stores that were kept stocked with food and sundries that were not available to the general populace. He was a "niño lindo" of the revolution, one of Castro's favorite sons. Scouts and agents who coveted Cuban stars for American baseball didn't consider him a serious candidate to defect.[3]

All that changed dramatically when his half-brother, Livan Hernandez, defected from the Cuban national team in Monterrey, Mexico, in September 1995. Orlando immediately fell under suspicion.[4] In July 1996, he was detained by Cuban state security and interrogated about a relationship to an American sports agent. He was left off the roster of the national team, although he was permitted to continue playing for Havana. Then in October 1996, shortly before the Industriales were to travel to Mexico for a tournament, Orlando and two teammates were "permanently suspended" from Cuban baseball—banned from setting foot on any official government field, virtually every baseball facility in Cuba.[5]

Of course, Orlando also lost his state-sponsored job, and by the time he fled the island his marriage had ended, and he'd had to move out of his home into a windowless cinder block shack with a corrugated metal roof near the Havana airport. Most of his friends were afraid to be seen with him. If Orlando harbored any remaining doubts about trying to leave Cuba, they were undoubtedly erased when little brother Livan pitched the Florida Marlins to World Series victory in 1997 and became a household name in both Cuba and the United States.

Orlando "El Duque" Hernandez went from refugee to royalty (1999 Topps card).

Hernandez departed Havana for Caibarien, a small city about five hours drive from the Cuban capital, on Christmas Day 1997. Accompanied by his girlfriend, his Cuban catcher who'd also been suspended, his cousin, his best friend, three other refugees, and a three-man crew, they sailed early the next morning on a 30-foot fishing trawler.[6] They were supposed to meet a launch from Miami at Anguilla Cay, a small uninhabited island in the remote southwest Bahamas, that would bring them to Key Biscayne. But the second boat reportedly sank offshore from Miami, so no one was there to meet Orlando's party. The crew had to get back to Cuba, lest their absence be noted, so the refugees were left on the exposed shore to await a boat that would never arrive.[7]

For days they hid from passing planes, subsisting on conchs they peeled off rocks, and sugar, water, and canned meat they'd brought with them. Finally, with their water supply and hopes for rescue dwindling, they hailed a Coast Guard helicopter and a cutter was dispatched to pick them up. Instead of taking them to America, however, the Coast Guard delivered them to Bahamian authorities in Freeport, where they were confined to a crowded, rat-infested detention center for illegal immigrants outside of Nassau. The Bahamian government had a repatriation agreement with Cuba and would normally have deported them back.[8]

Fortunately, the Cuban exile community became aware of the group's plight and exerted tremendous pressure on both U.S. and Bahamian authorities. Eventually the U.S. offered to allow Hernandez to enter the country under a special refugee status, but by that time, he was represented by an agent who'd arranged asylum in Costa Rica. There he would not be subject to baseball's regular draft as he would if he became a U.S. resident, and would be able to negotiate with any organization as a free agent. After two months in Costa Rica, Hernandez entered the U.S. on a visa arranged by the Yankees, with whom he signed a four-year, $6.6 million contract on March 23, 1998.

At the time, the Yankees thought Hernandez was 28 years old—a little long in the tooth for a prospect. Little did they know that they had actually signed a 32-year-old rookie, a fact that would not emerge until the next year, after Orlando had established himself in the major leagues. As of April 2013, the official site of Major League Baseball still lists his birthdate as October 11, 1969, although his passport, his Cuban divorce decree, and even his Cuban baseball card cite his date of birth as October 11, 1965.

Hernandez, who had not pitched competitively in more than a year, began his American baseball career in the Yankees farm system. After posting a 7–1 won-lost record with Tampa of the Florida State League and Columbus of the International League, he debuted with the Yankees on June 3, 1998. Employing a deceptive motion featuring an extremely high leg kick, he was an immediate sensation. Despite missing almost a third of the campaign, he ended up with 12 victories against only four losses along with the top ERA in starting rotation that included Andy Pettitte, David Wells, and David Cone. That fall, he began laying the foundation for his legend by winning 2 games and posting a 0.64 ERA in the postseason. For the 1999 regular season, his 17–9 won-lost record was the best on the staff. In the postseason, he won 3 games without a loss, posted a 1.20 ERA in 30 innings of work, and was selected MVP of the American League Championship Series. His regular season record fell to 12–13 in 2000, but he again starred in the postseason, winning once in the Division Series and twice in the League Championship Series, running his streak to eight postseason victories in a row before losing a start to the New York Mets in the World Series.

Orlando was bothered by elbow troubles early in the 2001 campaign and then sidelined by a toe injury that ultimately required surgery. Going into September he was 0–6 with a 6.00 ERA, but he came back to win 4 of his last 5 decisions and snag a spot in the postseason rotation. He split two decisions and left his World Series start in the seventh with the score tied at one. The subject of constant trade rumors, Hernandez was sidelined for almost two months in 2002, winning only eight games while losing five. He pitched well out of the bullpen but absorbed a loss in the Division Series as the Yankees failed to advance to the World Series for the first time since he joined them.

Before the 2003 season, Hernandez was swapped to the Chicago White Sox, who immediately sent him to Montreal in a deal for Bartolo Colon. In Montreal, he was united with his half-brother Livan, but a sore shoulder kept him from pitching a single inning for the Expos. After a brief minor league rehab stint, he underwent rotator cuff surgery that sidelined him for the year.

Despite his poor showing in the January workout, the Yankees inked Orlando to a $500,000 base contract just prior to the 2004 season. The signing seemed like little more than a public relations stunt. According to general manager Brian Cashman, the club wasn't "particularly enamored" with Hernandez at the time. But, what the heck! It was only half a mil, a gamble the Bombers could readily afford. Furthermore, it kept him away from the Red Sox, who were reported to have some interest.[9]

Hernandez was in no condition to pitch when the season started, but he gradually worked his arm into shape. He made three starts for Tampa and another three for Columbus, retracing the path he took to the majors six years earlier—with much less success this time.

He still hadn't completed his rehabilitation when the Yankees, desperate after a few key starters went down with injuries, called him up. He made his first start on July 11 and won, limiting the Tampa Bay Devil Rays to two runs in five innings. Two months later, following a September 11 victory over the Baltimore Orioles, his won-lost record stood at 8–0 accompanied by a nifty 2.49 ERA. Furthermore, the Yankees had won all but one of his 12 starts—the exception being an August 25 contest he left after six innings with a 3–2 lead. During that period, the club saw its comfortable six-game lead dwindle to two and a half games, with the magnificent pitching of the rejuvenated El Duque the primary reason they managed to keep ahead of the hard-charging Red Sox. In that stretch of 57 games, the club won only 24 of the 45 games Orlando didn't start, a paltry .533 winning percentage compared to an incredible .917 mark when the 38-year-old veteran took the mound.

"You don't lose it here," said manager Joe Torre, tapping his chest. "Knowing that he had done it in New York before, the gamble was certainly worth taking. I knew when we signed him in the spring that if anybody's going to be able to make it back, he's going to do it."[10]

"Even in the spring, when we signed him, we knew it was going to be a long road. And we were racking our brains in the spring: When the time comes when we're going to bring him up, where are we going to fit him in? Now, all of a sudden, he's the guy we need to give the ball to and say, 'Pick us up.'"[11]

Obviously worn out, El Duque failed to get a win for the Yankees in his last three starts of the regular season, suffering two losses while his ERA jumped to 3.30. But he'd managed to get the team over the rough patch, allowing them to cruise to first place in the American League East.

Orlando's late season fade kept him out of the Division Championship Series, but after the Yankees captured the first three games of the League Championship Series against the Red Sox, he was given a chance to close out the Series in Game 4. He managed to handcuff the Boston hitters for four innings before a bout of poor control in the fifth allowed the Sox to score three. He left the game with a 4–3 lead which the Yankees bullpen failed to hold, starting the Red Sox on their skein of four straight backs-to-the-wall wins and eventually their first world championship since 1918.

Before the 2005 season, Hernandez signed as a free agent with the Chicago White Sox and posted a mediocre 9–9 won-lost record for the Central Division champs. But he got another chance to embellish his postseason reputation (as well as exact some revenge on the Red Sox). He didn't get a start but delivered a memorable performance in Game 3 of the Division Series against Boston. Brought on in relief in the bottom of the sixth, with the White Sox clinging to a 4–3 lead, the bases loaded and no outs, he induced two infield pop-ups before striking out Johnny Damon swinging to end the threat. He then held the BoSox scoreless for two more innings as the White Sox went on to win the game, sweeping the Red Sox out of the playoffs. In the World Series against the Houston Astros, he threw a scoreless relief inning as the Sox swept the Series.

After the 2005 season, Hernandez was traded to the Arizona Diamondbacks, then on to the contending Mets in a May 24, 2006, transaction. With the Mets, he went 9–7 with a 4.09 ERA in 20 starts, helping them finish first in the National League East. His stellar pitching in September, going 2–2 with a 2.01 ERA, earned him the nod to start Game 1 of the Division Series. But, he tore a calf muscle running wind sprints the day before the playoffs started and was scratched from the postseason roster. Back with the Mets in 2007, he pitched well when healthy, posting a 9–5 record and 3.72 ERA with 128 strikeouts in 147 innings, but injuries limited him to just 24 starts.

Hernandez underwent surgery on his foot after the 2007 campaign and was not ready to begin the 2008 season with the Mets. During a lengthy minor league rehabilitation program, he suffered an injury to his toe that required more surgery, ending his season before it even got started. He became a free agent and signed a minor league pact with the Texas Rangers in 2009. Despite a good record out of the bullpen for Oklahoma City in the Pacific Coast League, the Rangers let him go in July. A year later, he signed another minor league deal with the Washington Nationals, who already employed his half-brother Livan. He went 2–1 with a 1.72 ERA and 21 strikeouts in 15⅔ innings in the minors before leaving the organization when he was informed him that he was not in line for a September call-up.

Though rumors of another El Duque return continue to surface, he has not pitched professionally since 2010 and, barring a late-forty-something comeback, his career appears to be over. One of the great money pitchers of all time, his career won-lost record of 90–65 and ERA of 4.13 pale in comparison to his 9–3 record and 2.55 ERA in 19 post-season appearances. He pitched all or part of nine major league seasons, with his final campaign the only one in which his team didn't make the post-season.

Orlando Hernandez

Born: 10/11/1965

Year	Team	Lg	G	IP	W	L	ERA	WHIP
1998	*Tampa*	*FLOR*	*2*	*9*	*1*	*1*	*1.00*	*0.67*
	Columbus	*IL*	*7*	*42*	*6*	*0*	*3.83*	*1.37*
	New York	AL	21	141	12	4	3.13	1.17
1999	New York	AL	33	214	17	9	4.12	1.28
2000	New York	AL	29	195	12	13	4.51	1.21
	NYY-ML Rehab	*A*	*1*	*4*	*0*	*0*	*0.00*	*0.50*
2001	*NYY-ML Rehab*	*(var)*	*3*	*13*	*1*	*0*	*0.00*	*0.77*
	New York	AL	17	94	4	7	4.85	1.39
2002	*NYY-ML Rehab*	*AAA*	*1*	*5*	*1*	*0*	*1.59*	*1.41*
	New York	AL	24	146	8	5	3.64	1.14
2003	*MON-Minors*	*A+*	*2*	*5*	*0*	*1*	*10.80*	*1.80*
2004	*NYY-ML Rehab*	*(var)*	*6*	*29*	*3*	*1*	*3.94*	*1.01*
	New York	AL	15	84	8	2	3.30	1.29
2005	Chicago	AL	24	128	9	9	5.12	1.46
	CHW-ML Rehab	*AAA*	*1*	*4*	*0*	*1*	*2.25*	*1.00*
2006	Arizona	NL	9	45	2	4	6.11	1.58
	New York	NL	20	116	9	7	4.09	1.23
2007	New York	NL	27	147	9	5	3.72	1.17
2008	*NYM-ML Rehab*	*(var)*	*4*	*15*	*0*	*1*	*4.02*	*1.09*
2009	*Oklahoma City*	*PCL*	*8*	*11*	*2*	*0*	*2.45*	*0.73*
2010	*Nationals*	*GULF*	*5*	*6*	*1*	*0*	*1.50*	*0.83*
	Harrisburg	*EL*	*6*	*9*	*1*	*1*	*1.86*	*1.03*
9 Yrs	MLB Totals		219	1314	90	65	4.13	1.26

29

Sal Maglie

In baseball, as in real life, true drama often eclipses anything Hollywood writers can imagine. Sal Maglie's 1956 comeback with the Brooklyn Dodgers never made the silver screen, although it moved popular author of juvenile baseball books John R. Tunis to write one last youth novel, *Schoolboy Johnson*, which featured a fictionalized version of Maglie's feat.[1]

For the first half of the 1950s, Maglie was Public Enemy Number 1 in Brooklyn, the most despised man in the borough, with the possible exception of his manager, Leo Durocher.[2] Pitching for the New York Giants from 1950 through 1954, Sal beat the Dodgers 22 times, every one of them a big game (or so it seemed) while coming out on the losing end on only 6 occasions. Even worse, he regularly beat Brooklyn's beloved bums in their own backyard, winning 10 straight games on Ebbets Field turf before he was finally bested late in the 1954 season. And it wasn't just that he beat the Dodgers so regularly. It was the way he beat them.[3]

"He was sinister looking, with dark, hooded eyes, and a heavy beard," wrote Peter Golenbock in *Bums: An Oral History of the Brooklyn Dodgers*. "For years Maglie was a symbol of all that Brooklyn detested about the scurrilous and loathsome Giants."[4]

The Dodgers and Giants had shared a deep-seated mutual hatred of each other for decades. Their relationship was truly unique in that they were the only major league teams to occupy the same city with another team in their own league. According to old-timers, the feud was spawned by a bitter argument between former best-of-friends and long-time Baltimore Oriole teammates John McGraw, manager of the Giants from 1902 to 1932, and Wilbert (Uncle Robbie) Robinson, who skippered the Dodgers from 1914 to 1931. It was nursed along by comments like the one made by former Giants manager Bill Terry, who when asked to comment on the Dodgers' chances for the upcoming 1934 season, responded with his mocking query, "Is Brooklyn still in the League?"

The rivalry peaked in the early 1950s when the Giants, under the leadership of feisty Durocher, and the Dodgers, managed by equally pugnacious Charlie Dressen, were the dominant teams in the National League. Duster wars between the two contenders were ongoing dramas during this era, with Maglie, the bellwether of the Giants staff, usually playing the villain role with relish. Sal had never been hesitant to get a hitter's attention by knocking him on his rear. In fact, he earned his nickname "the Barber" because of the "close shaves" he was known to give opposing batsmen. And Dodgers hitters, for some reason, seemed to be his favorite customers. To Brooklyn players and fans, Maglie was evil incarnate.

The battle began in earnest in 1951 when Jackie Robinson, in retaliation for a couple of those close shaves, dumped a bunt down the first base line and blasted "The Barber" with a football block when he covered first. It reached a crescendo in 1953 when another of Sal's arch enemies, Carl Furillo, touched off a wild melee by losing his bat in the pitcher's direction after a fastball sailed over his head. And feelings hadn't tempered with age. In 1955, Jackie, at age 36, pushed a bunt toward first base with the intention of taking the 38-year-old Maglie out when he covered first. Instead, Giants second baseman Davy Williams, taking the throw at first when Maglie failed to get there, bore the brunt of Robinson's wrath, suffering a back injury that curtailed his career.[5]

To the Dodgers faithful, Maglie donning Brooklyn flannels was outrageous, akin to a Hatfield attending a McCoy family reunion.

Yet on May 24, 1956, Sal Maglie took the mound to face the Philadelphia Phillies wearing the uniform of the Brooklyn Dodgers. At least it was the club's gray road flannels rather than Dodgers blue.

The following quotes from a life-long Dodgers fan are probably typical of the reaction to Maglie's joining the Dodgers: "I hated Maglie.... (He) was our archenemy. And he would constantly shut us out. He would murder our right-handed hitters, absolutely murder them, curveball them to death, brush them back off the plate. He'd make guys like Hodges and Campanella want to cry. A mean pitcher.... And when Maglie came to the Dodgers, I was shocked."[6]

But the Sal Maglie who reported to Brooklyn a month into the 1956 campaign was not the famed Dodgers killer of yore. After winning 59 games against a mere 18 defeats from 1950 through 1952, chronic back problems had limited him to a mediocre 31–22 won-lost record over the next three seasons. In fact, his last victory had come more than 10 months earlier, before the Giants waived the veteran hurler out of the National League to the Cleveland Indians.

The Indians didn't really need Sal. Their rotation already included future Hall of Famers Bob Feller, Bob Lemon, and Early Wynn, as well as veteran Mike Garcia and 1955 Rookie of the Year Herb Score. In the last two months of the campaign, Maglie started twice and relieved eight times for the Indians, incurring two losses without a victory. The suspicion was that the Indians only claimed Sal to keep him out of the hands of the rival New York Yankees. The ploy didn't help the Indians, who finished three lengths behind New York in 1955, but it may have helped the Dodgers capture the world championship that fall by keeping Maglie out of the Yankees' pinstripes.

Maglie swallowed a 20 percent pay cut, the maximum allowed under existing rules, before reporting to the Indians training camp in Phoenix, Arizona, in the spring of 1956, amid low expectations.

Sal Maglie and the Dodgers became strange bedfellows (1957 Topps card).

"Look for Sal Maglie to be a big help to the

Indians during the early spring," wrote *Sporting News* columnist Dick Young. "But when hot weather sets in, I'm afraid the old Barber will have had it."[7]

Sal quickly became the forgotten man on the Indians staff. During the exhibition season, his name came up more often in conjunction with the Giants' efforts to find a Dodgers-killing replacement than any plans Cleveland might have for him.

A month into the 1956 season, Maglie had thrown only five relief innings for the Indians, while the defending world champion Dodgers, with last year's Series star Johnny Podres in the service, were struggling with a rotation comprised of 20-game-winner Don Newcombe, creaky-armed Carl Erskine, flaky Billy Loes, and a bunch of kids with names like Drysdale, Koufax, and Craig. With the trading deadline looming, Cleveland general manager Hank Greenberg offered his Dodgers counterpart, Buzzie Bavasi, a chance to acquire Maglie for a song. Bavasi was intrigued, but leery. He knew the Brooklyn fans would be difficult, but he was more concerned about the players.

A few weeks earlier, pitching the last four innings of an exhibition game between the two clubs in Jersey City, Sal had shut down the Dodgers on one hit. Afterward, veteran shortstop Pee Wee Reese exclaimed, "I'm glad he's in the other league now. He's still tough."[8]

Bavasi consulted with Reese, as well as manager Walt Alston, about picking Maglie up, and both gave their enthusiastic endorsement.[9]

Nevertheless, there was some tension when Maglie walked into the Brooklyn clubhouse for the first time. But it was quickly alleviated when his old adversary, Furillo, met him with a handshake and gruff, "Glad you're here."[10]

Though the social aspect of Maglie's joining the Dodgers went amazingly well, his initial mound efforts were not inspiring. To allow time for Brooklyn fandom to get used to the idea of Maglie on their side, Alston didn't pitch the old warhorse until the club left on an extended road trip. In his initial appearance against the Phils in Philadelphia, he threw two innings in relief of 19-year-old Don Drysdale and yielded two runs on four hits. Sal's first two months with the Dodgers were spotty, although he did pick up his first victory in 11 months with a three-hit shutout of the Milwaukee Braves. On July 24, the Dodgers were languishing in third place, six games behind the pace-setting Braves, when Sal hurled a gritty 13-hit 10 to 5 complete game victory over the Cincinnati Reds. The win evened his Brooklyn won-lost record at 3–3 with a mediocre 4.24 ERA.

From that point on, however, Maglie pitched as well as he ever had in his prime. Over the remainder of the season, he won 10 games, 6 of them route-going efforts, while losing twice. His ERA for the period was an eye-popping 1.79.

Led by the spectacular pitching of Maglie and Newcombe, the Dodgers managed to catch the Braves, pulling even on September 11 thanks to a route-going 4–2 Maglie victory over the Braves' Bob Buhl.

The lead jockeyed back and forth down the stretch. When Maglie took the Ebbets Field mound against the Phillies on September 25, the Dodgers trailed the Braves, who'd won earlier that day, by a game. A win would put them half a game behind the Braves with four games left (only three for the Braves), while a loss would be devastating to their pennant hopes.

Sal not only beat the Phillies 5–0 to further embellish his reputation as one of the great clutch pitchers of his era, he made baseball history by firing a no-hitter. Four days later, he capped off his incredible comeback season with a 6–2 complete game victory over the Pittsburgh Pirates, giving the Dodgers the one-game advantage over the Braves they would finish the season with.

For the year, Maglie won 13 games and lost 5 while posting a 2.87 ERA for the Dodgers. He finished second to 27-game-winner Newcombe in both MVP and Cy Young Award balloting and got the Comeback Player of the Year nomination from the Chicago Chapter of the Baseball Writers Association of America. He finished fourth in the National League in ERA, third in winning percentage, and yielded the fewest hits per nine-innings in the league. The 39-year-old veteran with the bad back threw 3 shutouts to rank among the league leaders and pitched 9 complete games.

But Sal still had one item remaining on his bucket list. His three main goals as a pitcher were to win 20 games—which he'd accomplished in 1951; to pitch a no-hitter—which he'd now done; and to win a World Series game—something he'd failed to accomplish with the Giants. He realized that ambition on October 3, 1956, when he bested Whitey Ford of the Yankees 6–3 in the first game of the World Series. He came back in the fifth game to limit the Bronx Bombers to a meager two runs, but was out-dueled by Don Larsen, who happened to pitch a perfect game that day.

Maglie's career path to major league stardom was incredibly twisted, bordering on the bizarre. He got a late start in pro baseball to begin with. From Niagara Falls, New York, hardly a hotbed of baseball activity, Sal was 21 years old when he pitched his first professional game for the International League Buffalo Bisons in 1938. Three years later, he sported an embarrassing 6–19 career won-lost mark as a pro, and had drifted into the Detroit Tigers farm system. Pitching for Elmira in the Eastern League, he won 20 games in 1941 and was drafted by the Giants. Working primarily in relief, he pitched effectively for Jersey City in 1942 and seemed to be on his way to the Big Time. But World War II intervened and he was forced to put his baseball career on hold while he went to work in a chemical warfare plant for the next two years. With the war winding down, Maglie reported back to Jersey City for the 1945 season. He was promoted to the Giants in late July for his major league debut at the relatively advanced age of 28.[11]

Despite an excellent 2.35 earned run and 7 complete games in 10 starts for the Giants over the last half of the 1945 campaign, Maglie was regarded as little more than a wartime pitcher. With the hostilities ended and veteran players flooding back into the league, he received little attention at the Giants 1946 spring training camp. Meanwhile, the Mexican League, backed by the fabulous Pasquel family fortune, was trying to establish itself as a major league, and its agents were recruiting big leaguers with generous salary offers. Maglie, having no assurances that he would even make the Giants staff, signed on to play south of the border.

Then as now, organized baseball was quick to react to any threat to its monopoly. The Mexican League was declared an outlaw league and jumpers were suspended from organized baseball for five years. The most notable players involved were St. Louis Cardinals hurler Hal Lanier, and catcher Mickey Owen and outfielder Luis Olmo of the Dodgers. The Giants lost a total of twelve players. But an indication of the club's concern over the loss of Maglie and the others can be summed up by the comment of one sportswriter who wrote, "The Giants lost Danny Gardella, Harry Feldman and a couple of guys named Joe."[12]

When the Mexican League venture fell apart after a few years, Maglie eked out a living barnstorming with the other banned jumpers and playing winter ball in Cuba. During the 1948–49 offseason, he returned to Niagara Falls and purchased a gas station. Hours spent lying on a cold, damp floor underneath cars or toiling in the grease pits soon took their toll, and he developed rheumatic pains in his back and shoulders, as well as his right arm. Sal feared he was through in baseball. The ban on the Mexican League jumpers wasn't scheduled to be lifted until 1951, and he knew he wouldn't be able to return to the big leagues if he kept working in the garage. So when the Drummondville team of the independent Canadian Provincial League offered him a job, he jumped at it.

In Canada, Sal often pitched in near freezing temperatures which further aggravated his sore back. But at least he was playing ball. Then in June 1949, it was announced that Major League Baseball was reinstating the Mexican League jumpers in reaction to a suit brought by Maglie's former teammate Danny Gardella.

Since most of the Mexican Leaguer jumpers were fringe players, they weren't exactly welcomed back with open arms. But their former teams were obligated to give them a chance (Gardella's chance would consist of a single at-bat). Most of the reinstated players reported back to their former clubs immediately, but Maglie asked the Giants for permission to finish out the Canadian League season and report the following spring. Sal knew he wasn't in shape to pitch in the big leagues and felt an obligation to the Drummondville club. The Giants were perfectly willing to grant his request. After all, how much could they realistically expect from a 33-year-old wartime pitcher?[13]

But when Maglie reported to the Giants' spring training complex in Phoenix the next spring, he began opening a few eyes. One of the most effective pitchers in camp, he earned a spot in the bullpen. On July 21 he joined the starting rotation. That day he went 11 innings to beat the Cardinals 5–4 and followed that performance with 10 more complete game victories in a row.

Sal finished the 1950 season with 13 victories (12 complete games) in 17 starts and also made 31 relief appearances. Despite being in the rotation less than half the season, he tied for the major league lead in shutouts and finished 10th in MVP voting. His .818 winning percentage based on an overall 18–4 won-lost mark was the highest in the majors, and his 2.71 ERA was the lowest in the both leagues.

In 1951, Maglie enjoyed another magnificent season, posting a 23–6 won-lost mark to lead the Giants to the pennant. He tied teammate Larry Jansen for most victories in the major leagues, finished fourth in MVP voting (highest among pitchers) and was the winning All-Star Game pitcher. Although he didn't get the win, he started and pitched eight tough innings in the memorable Dodgers-Giants playoff game won by Bobby Thomson's dramatic homer, "The Shot Heard Around the World!"

Maglie began the 1952 season with nine straight victories—the ninth, an Ebbets Field shutout on May 27 that lowered his ERA to an incredible 1.12. This made his won-lost record since rejoining the Giants a spectacular 50–10 for what amounted to approximately two full seasons as a starter. But his days as an elite hurler were about to end. His old back problems flared up and he was little more than an average big league hurler from mid–1952 until he joined the Dodgers in 1956.

After his magnificent comeback in 1956, Sal pitched two more seasons in the major leagues. He served as an effective spot starter for the Dodgers in 1957 before being acquired by the Yankees in a September 1 waiver deal to provide pennant insurance. In 6 appearances down the stretch, he won 2 starts and earned 3 saves out of the bullpen. Unfortunately (for the Yankees), he was not eligible to pitch in the Series, which New York lost four games to three. The wily veteran just might have been able to stave off one of Milwaukee's victories. An ineffective 1958 campaign with the Yankees and Cardinals ended Maglie's career. He was released by the Cards prior to the 1959 season, retiring from the active ranks to become a successful pitching coach.

Maglie left the major leagues with 119 victories on the books against only 62 losses, and a lifetime ERA of 3.15 for 1,723 innings of work. He didn't spend a full season in the majors until he was 33 years old, finishing with nine full seasons and half of another for his big league career. Yet, between 1950 and 1956, he placed first, second, and third one time each and sixth twice among National League leaders in winning percentage. In fact his .657 career winning percentage ranks 12th all-time among retired pitchers (at least 100 decisions) who completed most of their career after 1900. Only three current Hall of Famer hurlers—Whitey Ford, Lefty Grove, and Christy Mathewson—outrank him, although Pedro Martinez and Roger Clemens, who will probably enter the Hall eventually, are among the 11 hurlers ahead of him on the list. Among those behind Sal are Sandy Koufax and Dizzy Dean, two Hall of Famers whose abbreviated careers weren't that much longer that his.

As remarkable as Sal's 1956 comeback was, it wasn't his most unlikely success. The fact that Sal Maglie had a successful major league career at all is even more amazing.

Sal Maglie

Born: 4/26/1917

Year	Team	Lg	G	IP	W	L	ERA	WHIP
1938	*Buffalo*	*IL*	5	12	0	1	3.75	1.67
1939	*Buffalo*	*IL*	39	101	3	7	4.99	1.43
1940	*Buffalo*	*IL*	23	54	0	7	7.17	1.93
	N.F./Jamestown	*PONY*	7	56	3	4	2.73	1.23
1941	*Elmira*	*EL*	43	270	20	15	2.67	1.25
1942	*Jersey City*	*IL*	50	165	9	6	2.78	1.31
1943	*Jersey City*	*IL*	(Did not play Organized Baseball)					
1944	*Jersey City*	*IL*	(Did not play Organized Baseball)					
1945	*Jersey City*	*IL*	14	88	3	7	4.09	1.41
1945	New York	NL	13	84	5	4	2.35	1.12
1946	New York	NL	(Suspended—Mexican League)					
1947	New York	NL	(Suspended—Mexican League)					
1948	New York	NL	(Suspended—Mexican League)					
1949	New York	NL	(Suspended—Mexican League)					
1950	New York	NL	47	206	18	4	2.71	1.24
1951	New York	NL	42	298	23	6	2.93	1.14
1952	New York	NL	35	216	18	8	2.92	1.27
1953	New York	NL	27	145	8	9	4.15	1.41
1954	New York	NL	34	218	14	6	3.26	1.34
1955	New York	NL	23	129	9	5	3.75	1.47
	Cleveland	AL	10	25	0	2	3.86	1.29
1956	Cleveland	AL	2	5	0	0	3.60	1.60
	Brooklyn	NL	28	191	13	5	2.87	1.08
1957	Brooklyn	NL	19	101	6	6	2.93	1.18
	New York	AL	6	26	2	0	1.73	1.12
1958	New York	AL	7	23	1	1	4.63	1.54
	St. Louis	NL	10	53	2	6	4.75	1.34
10 Yrs	MLB Totals		303	1723	119	62	3.15	1.25

30

Jimmie Wilson

The 1940 World Series was history, and bedlam reigned in the locker room of the world champion Cincinnati Reds, who had just triumphed over the Detroit Tigers. As the Reds toasted their hard fought seven-game victory, 40-year-old catcher Jimmie Wilson, probably the most unlikely Series hero ever, sat in front of his locker—too sore and tired to move, but grinning from ear to ear.

A few months earlier, Wilson, whose expertise with a cue stick earned him the nickname Ace, didn't figure to ever play another major league game—much less star in a World Series. He'd caught only once in 1938, when he managed the Philadelphia Phillies, and made only one brief appearance behind the plate as a Reds player-coach in 1939. In the spring of 1940, he reported to the Cincinnati training camp solely as a coach, confident he'd never again be strapping on the old "tools of ignorance" in earnest.

But an injury to star catcher Ernie Lombardi and the suicide of backup receiver Willard Hershberger pressed Jimmie into emergency duty behind the plate late in the season. He rose to the occasion like the old pro he was, catching six of the seven Series games and batting a solid .353—second best on the team. Like Sal Maglie's comeback, Wilson's brief comeback was also memorialized by John R. Tunis, in his signature 1940 youth novel, *The Kid from Tomkinsville*.[1]

Wilson's stellar World Series performance wouldn't have been a surprise if not for his age and recent inactivity. In the 1920s and early 1930s, he was one of the top catchers in the game. A native Philadelphian who'd played professional soccer before turning to baseball full-time, Wilson broke in with the Phillies in 1923 and was their regular catcher for five years. His big break came when he was swapped to the pennant bound St. Louis Cardinals early in the 1928 season. Wilson participated in three World Series with the Cards and was their top receiver through the 1933 campaign. That year, he was the National League's starting catcher in the first major league All-Star Game. Considered a fine handler of pitchers and an excellent defensive catcher, he led National League receivers in putouts and double plays three times and in assists twice while with St. Louis. At the plate, he hit for a pretty good average for a backstop, although he didn't have much power.

After the 1933 season, Jimmie got a chance to return to his hometown as player-manager of the Phillies. The Phils of the mid-thirties were one of the worst teams in baseball, consistently in the hunt for occupancy of the National League cellar. In 1933 they'd won only 60 games and finished in seventh place. They failed to improve under Manager Wilson, averaging a meager 56 victories a year from 1934 through 1938, finishing in seventh place twice, and occupying last place the other three seasons. In addition to managing, Jimmy shared the Phillies catching duties through 1936, experiencing more success on the playing field than in command. By 1937, he'd turned the regular catching duties over to younger—though not necessarily more able—men.

After winning a paltry 45 contests in 1938, the Phillies mercifully dismissed Wilson at the end of the season, and he signed on as a player-coach for the Reds under his old Cardinals skipper, Bill McKechnie.

The Reds had the strongest catching corps in the National League when Wilson joined them. Ernie Lombardi, also known as "Schnozz" in honor of his astounding nasal feature, was the number one backstop. The 32-year-old future Hall of Famer was at the peak of a 17-year major league career which would end with a lusty .306 career batting average and the distinction of being the only catcher to win two batting titles. He'd won the National League batting championship in 1938 (he'd win his other title in 1942), as well as league MVP.

Lombardi's understudy, Willard Hershberger, had spent six years stuck in the New York Yankees farm system before being rescued by the Reds in 1938. He hit a solid .276 as a rookie and raised his average to a lofty .345 average and drove in 32 runs in only 63 games in 1939. An exceptional defensive catcher, Hershberger was considered by many to be the best number two backstop in the game.

Though he'd signed on as a player-coach, Wilson was de-activated midway through the 1939 campaign to make room for Dick West, a hard-hitting young catcher who also played the outfield.[2]

The Reds won the 1939 National League pennant but were overpowered by the Yankees in the World Series. Despite rumors linking him to other managerial vacancies, Wilson returned to Cincinnati in 1940 for another season as McKechnie's trusted assistant.

The club got off to a good start, but the surprising Brooklyn Dodgers kept pace until after the All-Star break when the Reds started pulling away from the pack. It looked like they'd waltz to a second straight pennant until their catching situation began to unravel. Lombardi had gone down with an injury on July 23, but Hershberger stepped in and the team continued to win. They were eight games up on July 31 when they dropped a heartbreaker. The New York Giants rallied from a 4–1 deficit to win in the ninth on a dramatic two-strike, two-out homer by catcher Harry Danning. Hershberger was distraught after the game, blaming his pitch selection for the loss. He became even more depressed when the Reds lost a doubleheader two days later.[3]

When the Reds gathered at Braves Field in Boston for a Sunday doubleheader on August 3, 1940, Hershberger was missing. Someone was sent to the hotel and found him dead, having taken his own life by slitting his throat with a straight razor while leaning over the bathtub. He was hitting a solid .309 at the time of his death.[4]

Shortly afterward, the Reds activated Wilson from the coaching lines, but he really didn't figure to see that much action. Lombardi was healthy again, and rookie Bill Baker, who'd hit .338 the previous year for the Reds' top farm club in Indianapolis, was waiting in the wings. In fact, almost two weeks passed before Wilson got into a game as a late-inning substitute for Lombardi, and for the next month he played sparingly as the Reds continued to roll towards the pennant.

Then on September 15, three days before the Reds clinched the flag, Lombardi severely sprained his ankle when he crashed into a wall chasing a foul pop. He was through for the remainder of the regular season. The Reds immediately recalled West from Indianapolis and he began sharing catching duties with Baker and Wilson. At first the combination clicked, but then the Reds began to falter, dropping six of their last eleven contests.

On the eve of the World Series, Lombardi's status was up in the air. He was working out with the team and hoped to be able to catch, so the Reds included him on their World Series roster along with Bill Baker. For the third catching spot, McKechnie elected to go with Wilson over young Dick West. Appearing in 16 games, Wilson had batted .243 for the season, while West hit a robust .393 in seven late-season contests. But McKechnie, aware of the fact that the Reds won 8 (and tied one) of the 10 games Jimmie started, had more faith in the grizzled veteran.

Lombardi wasn't physically able to catch when the Series began, so McKechnie turned to Wilson as his starting catcher. Besides the absence of their star receiver for all but one game, the Reds would also be without sure-handed center fielder Harry Craft and brilliant second baseman Lonny Frey, both relegated to reserve duty with injuries. The banged up Reds had their work cut out for them against a talented Tigers squad that featured Hank Greenberg, Charlie Gehringer, Rudy York, and Barney McCosky in the batting order and Bobo Newsom, Tommy Bridges, and Schoolboy Rowe on the mound.

But Cincinnati aces Bucky Walters and Paul Derringer won two games each, proving too much for the Tigers. And then there was the Reds' secret weapon—Jimmie Wilson. He went the distance behind the plate in all four of their victories and chipped in with several timely hits. As the Series wore on, the grind of catching every day caught up with the 40-year-old gamer. Suffering from charley horses in both legs, he hobbled in pain, his aching thigh muscles, swathed in yards of tape, screaming from the constant squatting, and his glove hand so sore and swollen that he could barely get his mitt on.[5] At times it looked like he would need help from the umpire to get up from his crouch after giving the sign.[6]

Yet, the old-timer fielded his position perfectly. He threw two runners out stealing, preventing the Tigers, who finished second in the American League in stolen bases, from swiping a single sack. In fact, the old warhorse topped the total of the entire Detroit club all by himself when he pulled off a surprise steal of second in the seventh game of the series, the only stolen base of the series by either team.

But Jimmie's greatest contribution to the Cincinnati effort didn't show up in any box score. The experience of the spirited veteran receiver, playing in his fourth World Series, was invaluable as he guided the talented Reds pitching staff with a steady, experienced hand behind the plate.

In fact, his handling of Bucky Walters may have turned the entire series around early in the second game. The Reds began the classic with a discouraging 7–2 loss and sent Walters to the mound to try to even things up in game 2. It looked pretty grim for the Reds, however, when Bucky walked the first two batters of the game and seemed ready to blow sky high.

Jimmie called time and slowly trudged to the mound to calm his rattled hurler. The Walters-Wilson relationship went back a ways. Six years earlier, Wilson, then player-manager of the Philadelphia Phillies, convinced Walters, then a strong-armed light-hitting third baseman, that his future was on the mound. The reluctant Walters agreed to give pitching a try and soon developed into one of the best pitchers in the game.[7]

So Walters was certainly listening when his catcher and former mentor growled, "Just calm down. You're throwing too hard. Just be yourself. Let them hit the ball."[8]

"He was right," Walters later admitted. "I was trying to strike everybody out."[9]

After Wilson's visit, Walters settled down and held the powerful Tigers in check for the rest of the game as the Reds went on to a 5 to 3 victory to even the Series.

Jimmie's gutsy performance was somewhat overshadowed by a touching human interest story involving Tigers ace pitcher Bobo Newsom. Newsom's father suffered a fatal heart attack after watching his son win the first game of the Series. After Bobo shut out the Reds in the fifth game, he tearfully told reporters, "I pitched that one for my Daddy." The stouthearted Newsom returned on two days rest to face the Reds again in the final game, but this time came out on the short end of a classic pitchers duel with Derringer. Wilson rapped out two hits, laid down a key sacrifice bunt, and garnered his previously mentioned stolen base when he caught the defense napping. He also handled Derringer deftly as the Reds prevailed by a 2–1 score.[10]

The veteran receiver was wildly cheered by admiring Reds fans throughout the Series, becoming an instant celebrity with his tremendous clutch performance. His return to the spotlight resulted in another managerial opportunity, this time with the Chicago Cubs. Despite talk of doing some catching for the Cubs, Jimmie never played another game.[11]

In Chicago, Wilson again failed to inspire his troops as a manager. Under his leadership, the Cubs finished in the second division three years in a row. He resigned after ten games in 1944 and rejoined the Reds coaching staff, watching the Cubbies march to the 1945 pennant from that vantage point.

No one knew at the time that Jimmie Wilson's life was almost over. His son, Robert, a promising baseball player before World War II and a decorated pilot, was killed in the closing stages of the conflict. Jimmie never recovered from the shock. When his close friend Bill McKechnie left the Reds after the 1946 season, a despondent Jimmie Wilson retired from baseball. He died in May 1947 at the age of 46.[12]

For his career, Jimmie Wilson hit a respectable .284 in 1,525 major league games spread over 18 seasons. He hit over .300 four times and was named to start two All-Star Games, despite the fact that the games weren't initiated until late in his career.

During the 1940 Series, Jimmie joked about another comeback. He claimed he planned to retire again—until the next fall classic. "At my age," he said, "I can't afford to waste energy in anything short of a World Series."[13]

Jimmie Wilson

Born: 7/23/1900

Year	Team	Lg	G	HR	RBI	SB	BA	OPS
1920	New Haven	EL	36	1	-	-	.306	.694
1921	New Haven	EL	128	2	-	-	.295	.683
1922	New Haven	EL	111	3	-	-	.293	.673
1923	Philadelphia	NL	85	1	25	4	.262	.586
1924	Philadelphia	NL	95	6	39	5	.279	.744
1925	Philadelphia	NL	108	3	54	5	.328	.820
1926	Philadelphia	NL	90	4	32	3	.305	.760
1927	Philadelphia	NL	128	2	45	13	.275	.662
1928	Philadelphia	NL	21	0	13	3	.300	.765
1928	St. Louis	NL	120	2	50	9	.258	.678
1929	St. Louis	NL	120	4	71	4	.325	.859
1930	St. Louis	NL	107	1	58	8	.318	.802
1931	St. Louis	NL	115	0	51	5	.274	.669
1932	St. Louis	NL	92	2	28	9	.248	.633
1933	St. Louis	NL	113	1	45	6	.255	.609
1934	Philadelphia	NL	91	3	35	1	.292	.691

30. Jimmie Wilson

Year	Team	Lg	G	HR	RBI	SB	BA	OPS
1935	Philadelphia	NL	93	1	37	4	.279	.684
1936	Philadelphia	NL	85	1	27	5	.278	.658
1937	Philadelphia	NL	39	1	8	1	.276	.667
1938	Philadelphia	NL	3	0	0	0	.000	.000
1939	Cincinnati	NL	4	0	0	0	.333	.667
1940	Cincinnati	NL	16	0	3	1	.243	.579
18 Yrs	MLB Totals		1525	32	621	86	.284	.707

31

Satchel Paige

Comeback player of the year at 46 years of age? Heck, that's no more absurd than Rookie of the Year at 42. Of course, *The Sporting News* didn't honor a Comeback Player of the Year back in 1952. But if they had, Satchel Paige probably would have won it—just like he won the publication's Rookie of the Year award as a 42-year-old freshman in 1948.

Satchel Paige was one of the biggest names in baseball long before he ever threw a pitch in the major leagues. In his heyday, he was the top pitcher in Negro League baseball, if not the entire world. His was a household name, recognized even by people, black or white, who didn't follow baseball. One of the greatest gate attractions of all time, he shared top billing with the likes of Babe Ruth, Dizzy Dean, Bob Feller, and Joe DiMaggio, eventually attaining the status of an American folk hero.

Pitching year-round in Mexico, Cuba, Puerto Rico, Venezuela, and the Dominican Republic, as well as most of the rest of the North American continent, Satch is estimated to have pitched about 2,500 games for no fewer than 250 different teams in various professional and semipro contests, including exhibition matches in which he was invariably the main attraction.[1] He personally claimed to have thrown around 300 shutouts and 55 no-hitters against all levels of competition.[2]

But Satchel's greatest accomplishment may have been the spectacular comeback he engineered for the St. Louis Browns in 1952. Like virtually every aspect of his legendary career, the resurrection of Paige's major league baseball career is an amazing story, and is one of the few that is thoroughly documented.

After a sensational rookie campaign with the Cleveland Indians, Satch faded from the big league scene following a somewhat disappointing 1949 sophomore season. He spent the next 1½ years on the barnstorming circuit, completely out of organized baseball, before resurfacing with the Browns midway through the 1951 season.

Although Major League Baseball had been integrated since 1947, black players were still a rarity in the early 1950s. Paige was the seventh black major leaguer when he debuted in 1948. When he joined the Browns three years later, only 14 other black players occupied roster spots on the 16 big league teams then in existence. Furthermore, Don Newcombe of the Brooklyn Dodgers was the only black pitcher who had found success in the majors, other than Paige himself. In fact, Satchel was still the only black pitcher to have toed the rubber in the American League. The fact that all major league umpires were white men (their ranks wouldn't be integrated until 1966) probably contributed to the dearth of black pitchers. Hitters could adjust somewhat to a discriminating umpire's strike zone by enlarging their own hitting zones and going after anything close. Pitchers, on the other hand, were much more at the mercy of the man in blue.

Battling both age and racial prejudice, as well as a lack of support from his woefully inept Brownie teammates, Paige won only three games against four losses in the second half of the 1951 season while posting a less-than-scintillating 4.79 ERA. His effort left much doubt as to his whether or not he was still a viable big leaguer hurler at age 45.

Those doubts would be laid to rest in 1952 as old Satch won 12 games and racked up 10 saves for the seventh-place Browns. His combined total of 22 victories and saves gave him a hand in almost 35 percent of his team's 64 wins—the highest percentage in major league baseball that year. Paige's pitching led the Browns to the highest winning percentage (.416) the franchise would post from 1946 through 1955. In addition, he was named to the American League All-Star Team, making him, at age 46, the oldest All-Star in the history of the game. The man who'd faced Babe Ruth in his prime and later frustrated a young Joe DiMaggio would be an All-Star teammate of the latest Yankees great, Mickey Mantle. Although he didn't appear in the contest, Satch was thrilled with the honor, exclaiming, "This completes everything in baseball for me."[3]

That statement certainly covered a lot of ground. By the time Jackie Robinson broke major league baseball's color barrier in 1947, Paige had been pitching professionally for more than 20 years. His success against major leaguers in exhibition contests around the country was legendary, but he was generally considered too old for the big leagues.

Of course, nobody really knew exactly how old "Ole Satch" really was. When Bill Veeck, the maverick owner of the Indians, finally gave him a chance to pitch in the major leagues in 1948, he claimed to be 39 years old. But some skeptics believed that he was actually closer to 50 than 40. An old Negro League contemporary, Ted "Double Duty" Radcliffe, who grew up with Satch in Mobile, maintained he'd been born in 1902 and Satch was two years his senior.[4] To silence the doubts about his age, Satch once offered to pay $500 to anyone who could prove that he'd pitched professionally before 1927. In due time, a photostatic copy of a 1926 box score listing Paige as the pitcher of record for the Chattanooga Black Lookouts in a contest against the Memphis Red Sox was produced, to which Satch responded, "I must have slept a year."[5] Eventually a birth certificate with a July 7, 1906, date became generally accepted as the most credible source for the date of Leroy Robert Paige's entry into the world, despite the fact that the last name was spelled "Page."

Veeck, who a year earlier had made Larry Doby the first black player in the American League, didn't care how old Paige was. His Indians were fighting for the pennant, and they needed another pitcher. And if he happened to put a few more butts in the seats, so much the better.

Most of the baseball world seemed to regard Paige's signing as just another one of Veeck's publicity stunts. Some purists were not amused, however. *The Sporting News* lambasted Veeck in a scathing editorial. "Veeck has gone too far in his quest of publicity and he has done his league's position absolutely no good insofar as public reaction is concerned," the editorial ranted. "To bring in a pitching 'rookie' of Paige's age casts a reflection on the entire scheme of operation in the major leagues," the editors went on to say. "To sign a hurler of Paige's age is to demean the standards of baseball in the big circuits. Further complicating the situation is the suspicion that if Satchel were white, he would not have drawn a second thought from Veeck."[6]

But the ancient rookie proceeded to stifle his critics with a performance that was nothing short of spectacular. In his first weeks with the Indians, he provided the bullpen boost they needed by allowing only 4 earned runs in 18 innings of relief.

Satchel's outstanding work out of the pen earned him his first major league start on August 3 against the visiting Washington Senators. A record-breaking crowd of 72,434 showed up to see the Negro League legend pitch seven strong innings, earning a 5–3 victory. After another win in relief, Paige threw his first major league shutout on August 13, a five-hit masterpiece against the Chicago White Sox in front of a capacity crowd of 51,013 at Comiskey Park. A week later, on the night of August 20, he pitched his greatest game as a big leaguer before a standing-room-only crowd of 78,382 at Cleveland's Municipal Stadium—another new attendance record. With the White Sox again providing the competition, Satch blanked them 1–0 with a brilliant three-hitter for his second straight shutout. The veteran then won his fifth game of the month on August 30, beating the Senators 10–1 with a seven-hit complete game effort.

Though Satchel's effectiveness waned in the closing weeks of the campaign, he finished with a won-lost record of 6–1 along with a glittering 2.48 ERA that was the second best on the Cleveland staff behind league leader Gene Bearden's 2.43 mark. He made seven starts, winning four of them without a loss, and relieved 14 times. With his help, the Indians ended the regular season tied for first place and won the American League in a playoff with the Boston Red Sox. In the World Series against the Boston Braves, he became the first black man to pitch in the fall classic when he relieved in the seventh inning of the fifth game and retired the only two batters he faced.

After the Series, *The Sporting News* ate a substantial helping of crow and named Satchel their 1948 Rookie of the Year, despite the fact that he was only in the league about half of the season.

The 1949 campaign was a disappointment for both the Indians and Paige. The veteran pitcher experienced stomach trouble and wound up with a 4–7 won-lost mark, although his ERA was a fine 3.04. That year he also began having problems getting along with the Indians field management. Satch was used to making his own rules and setting his own schedule. He paid little attention to team rules, a fact that exasperated his manager, Lou Boudreau, as it would subsequent managers he played for. As a Veeck favorite, he was protected, but when Veeck sold the Indians at the end of the 1949 season, the new owners gave Paige his unconditional release.[7]

His major league career apparently over, Satch went back to barnstorming where his big league exposure put him more in demand than ever. He toured the country, often pitching six or seven three-inning stints a week.

Halfway through the 1951 campaign, Veeck got back into baseball, acquiring the lowly Browns and immediately summoning Satch to pitch for his new club. The 45-year-old veteran arrived in St.

Satchel Paige came back with the Browns at age 46 (1953 Topps card).

Louis July 17 and started against Washington the next day. Though he was in no shape to pitch a complete game, he lasted eight innings and yielded four earned runs in a 7–1 St. Louis loss. In his next start, he held the mighty New York Yankees scoreless for five innings before tiring and yielding eight runs in the seventh. Thereafter, he was used out of the bullpen with the exception of one late season start, compiling a mediocre 4.79 ERA for the year.

Satch would complete his comeback in 1952 by putting together what may be the best season a pitcher of his advanced years has ever enjoyed. It was not without a few hitches, however. In the offseason, Veeck hired Rogers Hornsby, one of the greatest hitters the game has even seen, to manage the Browns. Hornsby, a crusty, old-school tyrant, was suspected of not having much use for black players. In fact, the Seattle Rainiers, whom he managed in 1951, were the only segregated team left in the Pacific Coast League. Aware of his reputation, he'd felt compelled to bring it up shortly after being named manager, saying, "If they're good players, they'd be welcome to play for me." Paige, the only black player on the 1952 Browns, would be the only African American that Hornsby would ever find "good enough" to manage in a major or minor league game.[8]

Their relationship got off to a rocky start when Hornsby fined Paige for arriving late for an exhibition game in Corpus Christi, because he couldn't get a cab to venture into the black section of town where he was forced to stay.[9]

But Paige pitched brilliantly for "The Rajah." Used exclusively out of the bullpen, he made 14 appearances, winning 5 games, saving 4, and posting a miserly 1.84 ERA for the first third of the season. He continued his excellent work under Marty Marion, who took over when Hornsby was fired in June. When the All-Star squads were selected, Satch, who sported a 6–3 won-lost record with a 2.19 ERA and was leading the league with nine saves, couldn't be left off.

Shortly before the All-Star contest, Paige pitched 10⅔ innings in relief of Ned Garver in a 19-inning game against Cleveland. This started speculation that maybe old Satch, who'd been bugging Marion for a start, could hold up as a starting pitcher. When he went almost eight innings in relief of Stubby Overmire after the break, the die was cast. On July 28, Satch got his first start of the season against the Senators and pitched into the seventh inning, allowing three earned runs and garnering a win. After two more relief appearances, he got another start on August 9 and threw a 12-inning shutout of the Detroit Tigers to become the oldest pitcher to hurl a shutout in the major leaguers. He started four more games over the remainder of the season, winning two and losing twice. He even pitched another shutout on September 20 against the White Sox. He would hold the distinction of being the oldest to throw a shutout for 33 years until Phil Niekro trumped him on the last day of the 1985 season.

Paige finished the 1952 season with a 4–2 won-lost record as a starter and an 8–8 record in relief. His overall 3.07 ERA in 6 starts and 40 relief appearances was well below the league mark of 3.67 for that year. His 8 relief victories and 35 games finished led the league, while his 10 saves and 46 total appearances were each good for second place. In a retroactive calculation of the popular modern stat, pitcher's WAR (Wins Against Replacement value), he tied for ninth place in the league among all pitchers, with those ahead of him all being starters. In postseason voting, he garnered significant support for the American League MVP, finishing in a 17th place tie for an award that's usually dominated by hitters from contending teams. The 1953 season wasn't quite as successful for Satch, although he was once again selected to the American League All-Star squad. This time he got a chance to take the mound, simultaneously becoming the first black American League pitcher, as well as the oldest player, to appear in the All-Star Game. The 47-year-old workhorse's 57 appearances (including four starts) and 34 games finished were both the fourth highest total in the American League. His won-lost record was only 3–9, but his 3.53 ERA was the second best mark on the woeful last place club. And he was credited with saving 11 of the Browns' paltry total of 54 victories, the fourth highest save total in the league.

Despite the fact that he was still one of the club's top pitchers in 1953, Satch was cut loose after the season when Veeck was forced to sell the Browns. The new owners were moving the franchise to Baltimore and were seeking a fresh start. The official reason they gave for Satch's release was that they wanted to go with younger players, but his reputation for ignoring authority is what convinced the new management to sever ties with the ancient reliever. In this regard, Bill Veeck probably did Paige a disservice by repeatedly allowing the old-timer to disregard the rules and undermining his field manager's efforts to make the veteran hurler toe the line. If Veeck had insisted on treating Paige like any other player and supported Boudreau's initial efforts to reform him, Satch might have lasted longer in the big time ... or he might have walked away earlier.[10]

Satch returned to the barnstorming circuit for the next two years before hooking up with the Miami Marlins of the International League, thanks to Veeck, who had a stake in the new club. From 1956 through 1958, Paige was a mainstay of the Marlins' staff, winning more than 10 games each year for the Triple A club. His first season in Miami, his won-lost record was 11–4 with a brilliant 1.86 ERA. In his final year, he won 10 games at the ripe old age of 52, completing 7 of 15 starts, throwing a shutout, and compiling an excellent 2.95 ERA.

Paige didn't get along too well with the Marlins' management after Veeck moved on following the 1956 season, especially when it came to salary. After the 1958 campaign, he rode off into the sunset—literally. Trying his hand at acting, Satch signed on for a sidekick role in *The Wonderful Country*, a forgettable western starring Robert Mitchum and Julie London.

Following his Hollywood stint, Paige took to the road again. For a while it looked like he might get another chance at the big time when Veeck purchased the White Sox in 1959, but Sox manager Al Lopez refused to go along with the idea. Despite persistent rumors that one major league club or another wanted to sign him, Satch remained a free agent, barnstorming and occasionally touring as a sideshow with the Harlem Globetrotters basketball team. At age 55, he signed with the Pacific Coast League's Portland Beavers for the last month of the 1961 season. He made five starts and posted a 2.88 ERA with 19 strikeouts in 25 innings, but didn't get a decision.[11]

Satch did finally get one last opportunity to strut his stuff on baseball's center stage when Kansas City Athletics owner Charley Finley recruited him to pitch for the A's late in the 1965 season. On September 25, the 59-year-old hurler made his first big-league appearance in 12 years. He started against the Boston Red Sox and shut them out for three innings, striking out a batter, and yielding just one hit—to a rising 26-year-old star named Carl Yastrzemski. No one on either team's roster had been born when Paige began his professional baseball career.

Despite continued rumors of another comeback, Paige's major league career was finally over after his outing against the Red Sox. The next year, he made a start for the Peninsula Grays in the Carolina League, giving up two runs in a two-inning stint in his last appearance in organized baseball. A few years later, the Atlanta Braves gave him a coaching job to enable him to qualify for pension benefits. Inevitably, there was talk of him taking the mound for the Braves, but it never happened.

In semi-retirement, Paige frequently granted interviews and made public appearances, embellishing his baseball legend and reputation as a philosopher. Several minor league teams employed him for promotions, where his duties generally consisted of signing autographs and chatting with fans in the stands during games. In his sixties he'd begun to suffer from emphysema and heart problems, and he died of a heart attack at the age of 75 in his Kansas City home on June 8, 1982.

Even without his 1952 comeback, Satchel Paige's place in baseball history was secure. But that great season led to an article in *Sport* magazine entitled "Let's Get Old Satch into the Hall of Fame" which started the dialog that would eventually result in the institution opening its doors to the stars of the old Negro Leagues. No one was the least bit surprised when Satchel was the first player selected to be enshrined by the newly formed Negro League Committee in 1971.[12]

In addition, Satch's success in the big leagues at such an advanced age erased any doubt that he was among the greatest pitchers of all time, black or white. In their prime, Paige's favorite mound foe on the barnstorming circuit was the great Dizzy Dean, who often praised Paige as the best pitcher he'd ever run up against. Although he was more than three years younger than Paige, Ol' Diz hadn't won a major league game in more than seven years when Satch finally debuted in the big leagues. Joe Cronin, Bill Dickey, Joe Medwick, Ernie Lombardi, Mel Ott, Billy Herman, Lefty Gomez, and Jimmie Foxx were also younger contemporaries of Paige who had already completed their Hall of Fame careers before Satch appeared in his first big league game. Of the 72 pitchers in the Hall of Fame, only knuckleballers Phil Niekro and Hoyt Wilhelm remained active in the major leagues past the 47 years Satch had attained when he appeared in the 1953 All-Star Game.

No Satchel Paige profile would be complete without mention of his personal charisma, the only thing that could overshadow his brilliance on the mound. He was one of baseball's greatest characters. While his accomplishments on the field boosted the credibility of Negro baseball and helped erase doubts about the ability of black players, his keenly developed sense of humor helped defuse prejudice. His oft-repeated maxim, "Don't look back. Something might be gaining on you," is an all-time classic.

When informed that *The Sporting News* had named him Rookie of the Year after his first major league season, the 42-year-old freshman's comment was, "I'm not sure what year they had in mind."[13]

Satchel Paige

Born: 7/7/1906

Year	Team	Lg	G	IP	W	L	ERA	WHIP
1948	Cleveland	AL	21	72	6	1	2.48	1.14
1949	Cleveland	AL	31	83	4	7	3.04	1.24
1950	(Did not play Organized Baseball)							
1951	St. Louis	AL	23	62	3	4	4.79	1.55
1952	St. Louis	AL	46	138	12	10	3.07	1.25
1953	St. Louis	AL	57	117	3	9	3.53	1.30

Year	Team	Lg	G	IP	W	L	ERA	WHIP
1954				(Did not play Organized Baseball)				
1955				(Did not play Organized Baseball)				
1956	*Miami*	*IL*	*37*	*111*	*11*	*4*	*1.86*	*1.16*
1957	*Miami*	*IL*	*40*	*119*	*10*	*8*	*2.42*	*0.92*
1958	*Miami*	*IL*	*28*	*110*	*10*	*10*	*2.95*	*0.99*
1961	*Portland*	*PCL*	*5*	*25*	*0*	*0*	*2.88*	*1.32*
1965	Kansas City	AL	1	3	0	0	0.00	0.33
1966	*Peninsula*	*CARL*	*1*	*2*	*0*	*0*	*9.00*	*2.50*
6 Yrs	MLB Totals		179	476	28	31	3.29	1.28

32

Darryl Strawberry and Dwight "Doc" Gooden

Darryl and Doc—the Mickey and Whitey of the 1980s. Slugging outfielder Darryl Strawberry and strikeout king Dwight "Doc" Gooden were the toast of the baseball world, the self-described "studs" of the swaggering New York Mets squad that captured a world championship in 1986 and shoved the proud cross-town New York Yankees to the back pages of the Big Apple sports sections.[1]

Ten years later, after alcohol and narcotics induced roller coaster rides that sent both plunging to the bottom, the dynamic duo re-emerged as key members of a resurgent Yankees team that captured the storied franchise's first World Series in almost 20 years.

The careers of Strawberry and Gooden so closely paralleled each other, and their fortunes were so tightly intertwined, that it's virtually impossible to cover the exploits of one without the other. They joined the Mets a year apart and rewarded the franchise with back-to-back Rookie of the Year Awards. They were together at their peak, and their glorious careers started to unravel around the same time. Their subsequent comebacks with the Yankees also followed the same path.

Strawberry, a slender 6'6' left-handed hitter with a long looping swing and a perfectly chiseled physique, was the epitome of a power hitter. His homers were magnificent and his frequent strikeouts almost as exciting. After gaining national attention at Crenshaw High School in Los Angeles, he was the first player selected in the 1980 amateur draft. The Mets intended to bring their young prodigy along slowly, but at the age of 21, with less than three years of professional experience under his belt, he forced them to give him an early shot at the big time. Despite spending the first three weeks of the season in the minors, he slammed 26 homers and swiped 19 bases to capture the 1983 National League Rookie of the Year Award. For the next five years, he blended Ruthian power with greyhound speed, belting at least 26 homers and stealing at least 26 bases each year in an era when pitchers ruled.

Gooden, a stylish, hard-throwing right-hander, made an even more impressive debut. The Tampa, Florida, native was also drafted directly out of high school, the fifth player chosen in the 1982 draft. While Strawberry was garnering rookie honors with the parent club, Dwight was striking out 300 batters in only 191 innings and posting a sensational 19–4 won-lost record in his first full professional season in the Mets minor league organization. The next year, at the tender age of 19, he burst upon the major league scene, winning 17 games against 9 losses with a sparkling 2.60 ERA. His incredible 276 strikeouts in 218 innings established a rookie record that is still unmatched and earned him the nickname "Dr. K." A year after Strawberry's runaway Rookie of the Year selection, Gooden also captured the award hands down.

With these two young phenoms, the Mets seemed primed to embark on a dynasty to rival the proud Yankees. After a shocking world championship in 1969 and a surprising National League flag in 1973, both won primarily on the strong right arm of golden boy Tom Seaver, the Mets had fallen on hard times. By 1977 they'd plummeted to the depths of the National League East and had alienated their fans by peddling Seaver to the Cincinnati Reds. The Yankees, meanwhile, had shaken off their late-1960s and early-1970s doldrums to reclaim their spot atop of the baseball standings by besting the Los Angeles Dodgers in the 1977 World Series.

From 1977 through 1982, the Mets finished last in the six team National League Eastern Division four times, managing to wrest fifth place from the hapless Chicago Cubs the other two years. In 1983, they again placed last despite the introduction of Strawberry, the temporary return of Seaver, and the midseason acquisition of All-Star first baseman Keith Hernandez from the St. Louis Cardinals.

But 1984 would be a turnaround year. The Mets jumped from 68 to 90 victories and captured second place in the National League East on the strength of rookie Gooden's strong right arm, second-year-man Strawberry's powerful bat, veteran Hernandez's clutch hitting, and new manager Davey Johnson's brilliant leadership.

They boosted their victory total to 98 in 1985, although they again finished second. Gooden was simply magnificent. As a 20-year-old sophomore, he won 24 games while losing only 4 and recorded a spectacular 1.53 ERA. He led the major leagues in wins, ERA, and

Darryl Strawberry and Dwight Gooden were the Mickey and Whitey of the 1980s (1984 and 1985 Topps cards).

strikeouts while becoming the youngest hurler to ever claim the Cy Young Award. Injuries limited Strawberry to 111 games, undoubtedly costing the Mets the pennant as they finished three games behind the St. Louis Cardinals. Despite missing more than 50 games, Darryl managed to blast 29 homers, drive in 79 runs, and steal 26 bases.

The Mets weren't to be denied in 1986. They won 108 games, finishing 22 lengths ahead of the second place Philadelphia Phillies, before going on to beat the Boston Red Sox in the World Series. Star catcher Gary Carter had been acquired from Montreal before the 1985 season, and the pitching staff was bolstered by the development of starters Ron Darling, Sid Fernandez, and Rick Aguilera, and relievers Roger McDowell and Jesse Orosco. In addition, Wally Backman, Lenny Dykstra, Ray Knight, Howard Johnson, and Kevin Mitchell had also joined the club since 1983. The coup de grace was accomplished with the acquisition of veteran lefthander Bobby Ojeda from the Red Sox before the season.

They were an arrogant, energetic, young team. Like the Mantle-Ford Yankees of the 1950s, their macho credo was to play hard and party hard. Strawberry and Gooden were the heart of the talented squad, although their impressive stats still managed to fall short of the lofty expectations that had been established. In 1986, Strawberry again missed significant time with injuries, but he still led the club in homers with 27 and drove in 93 runs. Gooden won 17 games and lost 6 with a relatively pedestrian 2.84 earned run mark. Both his shutout and strikeout totals dipped significantly, however.

With a world championship under their belt, the Mets seemed poised for a long run at the top. No one could match their overall talent. Their pitching was overpowering and their offense was both versatile and volatile. Strawberry at 25 and Gooden at 22 years of age both seemed a lock for the Hall of Fame. But both the Mets dynasty and the careers of their two young superstars were already beginning to unravel.

The first red flag appeared when Gooden, after a disappointing Series performance, missed the parade to celebrate the Mets victory. That winter, he was arrested in an altercation with Tampa police. The Mets already suspected drug use, so when Gooden signed his 1987 contract, it contained a clause permitting regular drug testing by the club.[2]

Meanwhile, Strawberry was having some problems of his own. In January 1987, his wife, Lisa, filed a petition for legal separation, accusing Darryl of breaking her nose after a game the previous October.[3]

But these were merely the initial storm clouds gathering over the careers of the two young superstars. Unlike Mantle and Ford, the young Mets stars were into more serious transgressions than nightclub brawls and missed curfews.

The drug testing clause in Gooden's new contract came into play almost immediately when he tested positive for cocaine in April 1987. He was admitted to the Smithers Alcoholism and Treatment Center in New York City and missed the first two months of the season. He returned to post a 15–7 won-lost record, but his ERA was an alarmingly mortal 3.21 ERA. Strawberry, on the other hand, picked up his pace. He almost became major league baseball's first 40–40 man, slamming 39 homers and stealing 36 bases to go with 104 runs batted in, 108 runs scored, and a career-best to date .284 batting average. But Whitey Herzog's pesky Cards beat the Mets out again for first place in the National League Eastern Division.[4]

The Mets managed to regain the division championship in 1988 as Strawberry led the league in homers, again blasting 39 circuit shots, and Gooden won 18 games. But they succumbed to the Los Angeles Dodgers in the league championship series.

In 1989, Strawberry and Gooden both endured their first poor seasons as the Mets finished runner-up to the Chicago Cubs in the National League East. Dwight suffered his first serious arm problem—a muscle tear in his shoulder that shut him down in midseason with a 9–4 won-lost record—while Darryl hit a lowly .225 with only 77 RBIs.

Strawberry's year off the field didn't go very well either. In April, he was named in a paternity suit, and a month later Lisa filed for divorce, although they later reconciled—temporarily. Darryl's personal problems continued in the offseason. In January 1990, blood tests revealed that the paternity case was valid.[5] Two days later, he was arrested for assault with a deadly weapon during an altercation with Lisa. February 3, 1990, he entered the Smithers Center for alcohol rehabilitation.[6]

It's a tribute to Darryl's sheer natural talent that he was able to overcome these distractions and post outstanding numbers in 1990, banging 37 homers and driving in a career best 108 runs. Doc rebounded as well, winning 19 games and fanning 223 batters, although his ERA rose to 3.83. But the Mets once again played the National League bridesmaid role, this time to the Pittsburgh Pirates.

Sadly, the 1990 campaign would be Strawberry and Gooden's last hurrah as Mets teammates.

Despite his stellar performance, the Mets were understandably wary of making a long term commitment to Strawberry, and the unstable slugger had become disenchanted with the Mets front office. When the two parties couldn't agree on a new contract, Strawberry became a free agent and signed a five-year, $20 million contract to play for the Los Angeles Dodgers in his hometown.

Even though Strawberry and Gooden were no longer teammates, their careers continued to run on an eerily parallel course. After a decent 1991 campaign in Los Angeles, Strawberry totally flopped. Injuries limited him to a total of 43 games in 1992. He underwent back surgery in the offseason and tried to come back too early, resulting in a horrid .140 batting mark for 32 games in 1993. Back in New York, Gooden also ran into physical problems. He ended the 1991 season on the disabled list after 13 victories and had an operation to repair rotator cuff damage that September. He returned to post losing seasons in 1992 and 1993, winning only 22 games while losing 28 times.

The downward spiral that Darryl and Doc were caught up in really picked up steam in 1994. Both talented, and still relatively young, stars hit rock bottom—and hit it hard! They briefly lost their status as major league ballplayers and were disciplined for substance abuse as their careers and personal lives fell apart.

In September 1993, Strawberry was arrested for allegedly striking Charisse Simons, whom he was living with and would eventually marry (he'd divorced Lisa by then). Subsequently, he became the subject of an I.R.S. investigation for failing to report income from autograph and memorabilia shows while with the Mets. Then on April 3, 1994, he failed to show up for the Dodgers final exhibition game. The next day the Dodgers announced, to no one's surprise, that Strawberry had a substance abuse problem and placed him on the disabled list. This time Darryl tried a 28-day stay at the Betty Ford Center, but his contract was bought out by the Dodgers shortly after he finished his treatment. He signed with the San Francisco Giants, but after playing himself into shape at Phoenix, he hit only .239 in 29 games before the strike prematurely ended the season.[7]

Gooden also went on the disabled list early in the 1994 season after injuring a toe. He worked his way back with minor league rehab appearances but was ineffective when he rejoined the Mets. Doc had been regularly tested for drugs and come up clean since his 1987 problems, but he suffered a relapse and failed a drug test, leading to a suspension for the balance of the season. At the time, his won-lost record stood at 3–4, with a miserable 6.31 ERA for 41 innings of work.[8]

Dwight continued to flunk drug tests during his suspension and eventually had it extended through the entire 1995 season.[9] When Strawberry also tested positive for cocaine in the offseason and drew an automatic 60-day suspension, the Giants cut him loose. His problems were compounded when he was ordered to repay $350,000 in back taxes and penalties to the I.R.S. and sentenced to six months of home confinement.[10]

At the ages of 33 and 30 respectively, Strawberry and Gooden's baseball careers were in serious doubt. Strawberry hadn't played a full season in three years, and hadn't been productive when in the lineup. With his domestic problems, injury history, drug abuse background, and reputation as a negative influence in the clubhouse, it wasn't surprising that no one was willing to take a chance on him. Meanwhile, Gooden was still regularly failing drug tests and seemed to be helplessly hooked. It had been three years since his last winning season, and there was no assurance that his surgically repaired arm was sound.

But once again the paths of the two fallen superstars crossed. To Strawberry's rescue rode renowned do-gooder George Steinbrenner, owner of the New York Yankees. Of course, St. George was primarily interested in Darryl's personal well-being, but the "The Boss" also needed a left-handed power hitter, and Darryl Strawberry was still a big name in New York. The Yankees signed the troubled slugger to a contract which included provisions that allowed the club to hold him under virtual house arrest to assure his complete rehabilitation.

Strawberry's 1995 campaign was not exactly a smashing success, although it certainly surpassed Gooden's year. After completing his suspension and a minor league rehab assignment, the "Straw Man" finally joined the Yankees late in the year, getting into 32 games and hitting .276 with 3 homers. Meanwhile, Gooden sat out the entire season on suspension. But, at least he finally seemed to have kicked his drug habit and starting passing his tests. Although the Mets had been supportive during his rehabilitation, they weren't particularly interested in retaining his services. So he signed with the Yankees in October and pitched winter ball to get his arm back into shape for the 1996 season. Six weeks after signing Doc, the Yankees announced that they would not be picking up Strawberry's 1996 contract. A few days later, Darryl was charged with failing to make child support payments.[11]

Joining the Yankees was a blessing for Gooden. For the first time, he was not expected to be the ace of the staff. Former Mets teammate Dave Cone held that honor. In addition, the staff featured young Andy Pettitte, who would blossom into a 21-game-winner that year; free agent signee Kenny Rogers, who won 17 games the previous year for the Texas Rangers; and veteran Jimmy Key, returning from arm trouble. Gooden was slotted for the bottom of the rotation, which was fortunate since he got off to a terrible start. After four starting assignments, he was 0–3 with an 8.38 ERA when Cone went to the sidelines with an aneurism in his throwing arm. Suddenly, the struggling Gooden was the club's only right-handed starter.

Doc rose to the occasion, pitching well in his next two starts. On May 14, he was slated to pitch against the powerful Seattle Mariners, but his father, who was already on kidney dialysis, was facing life threatening heart surgery, and the hurler was torn between leaving to be by his father's side or staying an extra day to help his team. After asking himself what his father would want him to do, he decided to stay and face Seattle. That fateful decision marked a turning point for the former ace.

Dedicating the game to his dad, the 31-year-old has-been was miraculously transformed back to the Dr. K of old. He fired a dramatic no-hitter against a lineup that featured Ken Griffey, Jr., Alex Rodriguez, Edgar Martinez, and Jay Buhner. The next morning he flew to Tampa and rushed to the hospital to place the game ball in his father's hand. Although heavily medicated, the senior Gooden had followed the game from his hospital bed. His doctors later speculated that the strength and pride that surged through him from his son's accomplishment helped him survive the difficult operation.[12]

The Yankees were two games ahead of the pack when Cone went out, but with Gooden winning 11 of 13 decisions, they'd extended their lead to six lengths. Though his arm wore down and he faltered at the end of the campaign, he finished the season with 11 victories against 7 defeats.

While Gooden was engineering his stirring comeback, his old buddy Strawberry was putting his talents on display for the St. Paul Saints in the independent Northern League. After failing to negotiate a major league contract, Strawberry had signed with the Saints in hopes of attracting the attention of a big league team. He demonstrated that his bat still retained its old quickness by belting 18 homers in 29 games for St. Paul, and on the Fourth of July, the Yankees purchased his contract, reuniting him with Gooden in New York.

Darryl was a big help to the Yankees, blasting 11 homers and driving home 36 runs in 63 games down the stretch. Though Gooden's tired arm kept him out of postseason play, Strawberry blasted 3 homers and hit .417 to lead the Yankees to victory in the League Championship Series.

The Yankees World Series triumph over the Atlanta Braves gave the franchise its first world championship since 1978. Once again, they were the toast of the town and once again, Strawberry and Gooden basked in the limelight. The duo reported to spring training before the 1997 season assured of spots with the Yankees. But success proved difficult to maintain. Gooden went on the disabled list with a sore arm on April 6, and Strawberry followed a day later with a bad knee. Dwight returned after two months and went on to win 9 games against 5 losses and record a quality start in the Division Championship Series, but Darryl missed almost the whole season after undergoing arthroscopic surgery on his left knee. The team didn't make it past the first round of the postseason, losing to the Cleveland Indians in the division championship matchup.[13]

The paths of the two former phenoms diverged again in 1998. Gooden signed with Cleveland as a free agent, while Strawberry enjoyed another remarkable resurgence with the Yankees, slamming 24 homers in only 295 at-bats as their left-handed designated hitter (DH). Just before the start of postseason play, however, he was felled by colon cancer. He underwent surgery on October 3, and a 16-inch portion of his large intestine was removed. The Yankees dedicated their successful postseason drive to their stricken teammate, who was released from the hospital to join his teammates in the victory parade through downtown New York to celebrate another world championship.[14]

Now a sympathetic character due to his cancer, the baseball world was rooting for Strawberry to make yet another comeback in 1999. He'd had to undergo chemotherapy after his surgery when it was found that the cancer had spread to a lymph node. He'd borne up manfully through the ordeal, however, and seemed poised to make a triumphant return. He appeared in exhibition games while still undergoing chemotherapy but was left behind for extended spring training when the regular season got underway.

Then on April 14, 1999, Strawberry again stepped in it—or maybe on it—when he was arrested and charged with possession of cocaine and soliciting a prostitute. According to police reports, Darryl struck a deal with an undercover cop for $50 worth of sex. When subsequently searched, some cocaine was found in his wallet. Major League Baseball suspended him for the bulk of the season after he pleaded no contest to the charges. At age 37, his career appeared to be over, but the Yankees again demonstrated that extraordinary capacity for understanding and forgiveness they reserved for valuable talents.[15]

Strawberry returned from his suspension on September 2 and made another remarkable comeback, hitting .327 in 24 games as the club's lefty DH down the stretch. He then helped the Yankees to their second straight world championship by batting .333 with a pair of homers in post-season play.

As for Gooden, the 33-year-old hurler appeared to be walking into an ideal situation when he joined Cleveland before the 1998 campaign. The Indians were a perennial powerhouse whose only weakness was in the starting rotation. Doc showed flashes of his former brilliance in his first year with the Indians, winning eight games, losing six, and recording a 3.76 ERA, but he pitched poorly in the postseason. He never really got on track in 1999 and was let go by the Tribe after the season.

For the millennium season, Darryl was being counted on to be the Yankees' primary DH. His outstanding performance in the closing weeks of the 1999 season had once again turned public opinion around, and New York fans were solidly behind the tormented slugger—until he blew it again. On February 22, 2000, it was announced that Strawberry had tested positive for cocaine as part of his routine drug testing program. As a three-time loser in major league baseball's drug program, the 38-year-old slugger was immediately suspended for the entire 2000 season. A re-occurrence of cancer necessitated additional surgery while he was under suspension.[16]

Gooden began the 2000 spring training session in the gaudy uniform of the Houston Astros. But like Strawberry almost a decade earlier, he returned to his roots when the Tampa Bay Devil Rays purchased his contract early in the season. As with Darryl, Dwight's homecoming was a disaster. The right-hander lasted less than six weeks in Tampa before drawing his release. He subsequently signed with—who else—the Yankees for the remainder of the 2000 season and performed effectively as a spot starter and long reliever to help them capture a third straight world championship.

Any dreams of another Darryl and Doc comeback reunion in 2001 were squelched when in September Strawberry was arrested and charged with reckless driving in a bizarre incident in Tampa.[17] Six weeks later, he violated his court-ordered house arrest when he left an exclusive treatment facility in Florida to share some drugs with a female friend. At his hearing, he stood in shackles before the judge and calmly stated that he wanted to die. "Life hasn't been worth living for me, that's the honest truth," said the ballplayer who practically owned the city of New York a few short years earlier.[18]

Gooden's big league career ended a few months later when the Yankees released him during spring training, and nobody stepped up to claim him.

Even in retirement, the lives of Strawberry and Gooden paralleled each other, as they both encountered difficulties adapting to life without baseball. Both had additional substance abuse problems, domestic problems that required police intervention, and time in prison.

During their careers, Strawberry had always been perceived as the bad boy, while Doc was the good guy who'd fallen in with the wrong crowd. But surprisingly, it's Strawberry who finally seems to have his act together. He reconciled with the Mets, working as a hitting instructor for the franchise in 2005, and serving as an anchor on the club's pre- and postgame shows before eventually settling into a part-time analyst slot in 2009. His memoir, *Straw: Finding My Way*, was published in 2009 and in August 2010, he opened his own restaurant, Strawberry's Sport Grill, in Queens. He's said to be a generous donor to charitable causes. Along with his third wife, Terry, he founded the Darryl Strawberry Foundation, an organization dedicated to helping children with autism.[19]

Gooden, on the other hand, continues to get his name in the papers for all the wrong reasons. After numerous altercations with police, he left the scene of an accident, apparently in an inebriated condition. Placed on probation, he appeared at a meeting with his probation officer "intoxicated with cocaine," according to officials. Charged with violating probation, he opted for a prison term over extended probation, perhaps in the hope that incarceration would separate him from the temptations of his addiction. He entered prison April 17, 2006, and served through November 9, 2006.[20]

In July 2009, he was hired as a vice president of community relations for the Atlantic League's Newark Bears but lasted only a few months on the job. In March 2010, Gooden was arrested near his New Jersey home after again leaving the scene of a traffic accident. He was found nearby and charged with DWI with a child passenger, leaving the scene of an accident, and other traffic violations. He was also charged with endangering the welfare of a child. He eventually pled guilty to child endangerment, receiving five years probation and an order to undergo outpatient drug treatment.[21]

Darryl Strawberry belted more homers in his first five years with the Mets than Mickey Mantle did in his first five years in the Bronx. He slammed 280 big league homers before his 30th birthday. In comparison, all-time home run king Barry Bonds, only 2½ years younger than Darryl, had only 253 homers when he turned 30. An eight-time All-Star, Strawberry was a National League starter in right field in his first five full big league seasons. At the age of 25 in 1987, he became only the 10th member of the exclusive 30–30 club. The next year, he led the National League in homers, slugging percentage, and on-base plus slugging percentage (OPS) while stealing 29 bases, finishing second to Dodgers star Kirk Gibson in MVP voting, despite overwhelmingly superior stats.

But Darryl's picture perfect swing and unlimited speed and power resulted in an ordinary .259 lifetime batting average for his 17-year career, while his 335 homers and 1000 RBIs place him well behind Dave Kingman on the all-time charts. He was a member of four world championship clubs and played in 10 postseason series, eight times for the winning team.

As a teenage rookie in 1984, Dwight Gooden set a since-broken major league record for most strikeouts per innings pitched, broke Herb Score's 29-year-old rookie strikeout record, and became the youngest player to appear in the All-Star Game, striking out the side in his first all-star inning. The next year, he became the youngest pitcher to start an All-Star Game. By his 25th birthday, he'd already won 100 major league games. A 300-win career seemed assured, but he didn't even make it to the 200-win level, ending his 16-year career with a 194–112 won-lost record, a 3.51 ERA, and 2,293 strikeouts in 2,801 innings. He never won a postseason game while losing 4 times, although his 3.97 post-season ERA for nine starts and three relief appearances isn't too bad.

Though drug abuse is commonly blamed for Gooden's early burnout, his incredible early-career workload, which would make a modern pitching coach cry, may be at least partly to blame. Between the major and minor leagues, he threw 763 innings of professional baseball, striking out 928 batters, before celebrating his 21st birthday. In his historic sophomore season, the 20-year-old pitched 276 innings, a figure that hasn't been reached in the National League since.

The comebacks of Dwight Gooden and Darryl Strawberry did not cap off memorable careers like the late-career resurgences of Ted Williams or Stan Musial. Instead Dwight and Darryl's modest comebacks merely highlighted their tragically wasted careers.

Darryl Strawberry

Born: 3/12/1962

Year	Team	Lg	G	HR	RBI	SB	BA	OPS
1980	*Kingsport*	*Rk*	*44*	*5*	*20*	*5*	*.268*	*.770*
1981	*Lynchburg*	*A*	*123*	*13*	*78*	*31*	*.255*	*.809*
1982	*Jackson*	*AA*	*129*	*34*	*97*	*45*	*.283*	*1.021*
1983	*Tidewater*	*AAA*	*16*	*3*	*13*	*7*	*.333*	*1.061*
	New York	NL	122	26	74	19	.257	.848
1984	New York	NL	147	26	97	27	.251	.810
1985	New York	NL	111	29	79	26	.277	.947
1986	New York	NL	136	27	93	28	.259	.865
1987	New York	NL	154	39	104	36	.284	.981
1988	New York	NL	153	39	101	29	.269	.911
1989	New York	NL	134	29	77	11	.225	.779
1990	New York	NL	152	37	108	15	.277	.879
1991	Los Angeles	NL	139	28	99	10	.265	.852
1992	Los Angeles	NL	43	5	25	3	.237	.707
1993	*LAD-ML Rehab*	*AAA*	*5*	*1*	*2*	*1*	*.316*	*.960*
	Los Angeles	NL	32	5	12	1	.140	.577
1994	*Phoenix*	*AAA*	*3*	*2*	*3*	*0*	*.300*	*1.173*
	San Francisco	NL	29	4	17	0	.239	.787
1995	*St. Paul*	*Ind*	*29*	*18*	*39*	*4*	*.435*	*1.538*
	NYY-ML Rehab	*(var)*	*31*	*8*	*35*	*3*	*.286*	*.983*
	New York	AL	32	3	13	0	.276	.812
1996	*NYY-ML Rehab*	*AAA*	*2*	*3*	*5*	*0*	*.375*	*1.875*
	New York	AL	63	11	36	6	.262	.849
1997	*NYY-ML Rehab*	*(var)*	*16*	*6*	*23*	*0*	*.321*	*1.123*
	New York	AL	11	0	2	0	.103	.325
1998	New York	AL	101	24	57	8	.247	.896
1999	*NYY-ML Rehab*	*AAA*	*21*	*4*	*15*	*1*	*.288*	*.920*
	New York	AL	24	3	6	2	.327	1.112
17 Yrs	MLB Totals		1583	335	1000	221	.259	.862

Dwight "Doc" Gooden

Born: 11/16/1964

Year	Team	Lg	G	IP	W	L	ERA	WHIP
1982	*Kingsport*	*Rk*	*9*	*66*	*5*	*4*	*2.47*	*1.19*
	Little Falls	*A*	*2*	*13*	*0*	*1*	*4.15*	*1.08*
1983	*Lynchburg*	*A*	*27*	*191*	*19*	*4*	*2.50*	*1.22*
1984	New York	NL	31	218	17	9	2.60	1.07
1985	New York	NL	35	277	24	4	1.53	0.97
1986	New York	NL	33	250	17	6	2.84	1.11

Year	Team	Lg	G	IP	W	L	ERA	WHIP
1987	*NYM-ML Rehab*	*(var)*	*5*	*26*	*3*	*0*	*1.73*	*1.27*
	New York	NL	25	180	15	7	3.21	1.20
1988	New York	NL	34	248	18	9	3.19	1.20
1989	New York	NL	19	118	9	4	2.89	1.18
1990	New York	NL	34	233	19	7	3.83	1.29
1991	New York	NL	27	190	13	7	3.60	1.27
1992	New York	NL	31	206	10	13	3.67	1.30
1993	New York	NL	29	209	12	15	3.45	1.19
1994	*NYM-ML Rehab*	*(var)*	*2*	*8*	*1*	*0*	*0.00*	*0.50*
	New York	NL	7	41	3	4	6.31	1.48
1995	New York	NL	(Suspended—Did not play)					
1996	New York	AL	29	171	11	7	5.01	1.51
1997	*NYY-ML Rehab*	*(var)*	*5*	*30*	*4*	*1*	*3.30*	*0.97*
	New York	AL	20	106	9	5	4.91	1.59
1998	*CLE-ML Rehab*	*AAA*	*4*	*16*	*1*	*2*	*9.00*	*1.88*
	Cleveland	AL	23	134	8	6	3.76	1.39
1999	Cleveland	AL	26	115	3	4	6.26	1.69
	CLE-ML Rehab	*(var)*	*2*	*7*	*0*	*1*	*2.70*	*1.95*
2000	Houston	NL	1	4	0	0	9.00	2.25
	Tampa Bay	AL	8	37	2	3	6.63	1.83
	NYY-ML Rehab	*Rk*	*2*	*8*	*0*	*0*	*0.00*	*0.50*
	New York	AL	18	64	4	2	3.36	1.35
16 Yrs			430	2801	194	112	3.51	1.26

33

Dennis Martinez

When the 1987 baseball season opened, Dennis Martinez, the first native of Nicaragua to play major league baseball and winner of 111 major league games, did not have a job with a big league franchise. He was barely hanging on the fringes of organized baseball with the Miami Marlins, an independent Class A minor league team at the time. Considered one of the most talented hurlers in the game a few years earlier, he'd been reduced to competing in the obscurity of the Florida State League with the same team in the same league he began his professional career with 13 years earlier.

Though still a few weeks shy of his 32nd birthday, the veteran hurler seemed to be all done. But it would be more than a decade before he would finally hang up his toe plate for good. After fighting his way back to the big leagues, he would be named to four All-Star squads, pitch a perfect game, set a new all-time record for victories by a Latin American hurler, and earn the honorific nickname "El Presidente" in his native country.

Martinez was a 17-year-old engineering student at the University of Managua when his true calling was discovered. He'd played a lot of baseball, but the skinny third baseman's ability didn't garner much attention until he joined the Granada Tiburones. After watching Martinez snap off a few curves warming up on the sidelines, the Tiburones manager tried him on the mound. A few days later, Dennis held the Nicaraguan National Team to one hit in an exhibition contest and soon found himself heading the national squad's pitching staff.[1]

In 1973, he lost a 1–0, ten-inning heartbreaker to the United States team in the championship game of the amateur World Series. It was the last game Martinez would ever pitch on his home soil for a Nicaraguan team. After the game, he got smashed on a bottle of rum and passed out, the beginning of a drinking problem that would plague him through the first half of his career in professional baseball.[2]

Dennis signed with the Baltimore Orioles shortly thereafter and progressed rapidly through their farm system, winning 45 games while dropping only 19 and posting a cumulative ERA of 2.42 in three season. He debuted with the Orioles late in the 1976 season, becoming the Nicaraguan Jackie Robinson.

In 1977, Martinez compiled a 14–7 won-lost record as a 22-year-old in his first full big league campaign and returned to a hero's welcome in Nicaragua after the season. Thousands greeted him at the airport, and a caravan of cars escorted him past crowds of waving people on his route from Managua to Granada.[3]

The next year, Dennis was 16–11 for the Orioles, pitching 15 complete games and throwing 276 innings. In 1979, he led the American League with 292 innings pitched and 18 complete games, although his won-lost record slipped to 15–16. The Orioles won the

American League Eastern Division, and Martinez pitched well in the League Championship Series. But he got knocked around by the Pittsburgh Pirates in two World Series appearances, including one start. After Baltimore lost the Series four games to three, his drinking started spinning out of control.[4]

"I was young, I had a big contract, and I lost my head," he says. "I thought, now they have to pay me no matter what I do, and I got very cocky. I was getting drunk in front of people, trying to act like a big shot. I always did everything to extremes. If I had one drink, I didn't want to leave until the bar closed."[5]

Given his lifestyle and his extreme workload the previous two years, it's not surprising that the slender 6'1", 160-pounder developed a sore arm and missed much of the 1980 campaign. But he rebounded nicely to tie for the major league lead with 14 victories in the strike-shortened 1981 season.

According to Martinez, his already serious drinking problem worsened after his father died in 1982. He'd never really gotten to know his father, Edmundo, who'd separated from his mother when Dennis was young. "Every time I saw him he was drunk," he remembered. "When he was drinking, he would sell our pigs to get money for liquor."[6]

Nevertheless, Dennis returned to Granada for the funeral. Though he'd vowed to himself that he would never be like his father, Edmundo's death seemed to have the opposite effect.

"From that point on, I went even deeper [into drinking]," Dennis admitted later. "Maybe I was trying to take his place."[7]

By this time, Dennis's thirst had begun to control him. "I never drank the night before I pitched," he said, "and I thought it didn't affect me. But, I had trouble going to sleep those nights, and it didn't occur to me until much later that it was because I had no alcohol in my system. And during the game I was already thinking, 'Tonight I'm going to drink two or three beers.'"[8]

Dennis Martinez graduated from alcoholic to "El Presidente." (1979 Topps card).

Though he won 16 games against 12 losses in 1982, his ERA jumped to 4.21, his worst to date. He started 39 games and pitched 252 innings that year. In 1983, the Orioles captured the world championship. But instead of being their ace, Martinez was a liability. His won-lost record was a miserable 7–16 and his 5.53 ERA was two runs per game more than the rest of the staff averaged. The 28-year-old former ace lost his spot in the starting rotation and didn't throw a pitch in the postseason as the Orioles beat the Chicago White Sox for the League Championship and triumphed over the Philadelphia Phillies in the World Series.

The demotion hastened his decline. "That was the killing point," he says. "Now I didn't have to worry about pitching, so I drank every night."[9]

In the offseason, he was arrested for drunken driving and was admitted to Sheppard Pratt Hospital for treatment of his alcoholism. He spent two months drying out in the hospital and joined Alcoholics Anonymous upon his release.[10]

Though Martinez said he'd stopped drinking, sobering up didn't seem to do much for his pitching as he posted an ERA of 5.02 in 1984 while compiling a 6–9 won-lost mark.

"The first year I was concentrating more on my recovery than baseball," he recalled. "That was the number one thing in my life. I knew everybody thought I was washed-up."[11]

The next year, he got back in the starting rotation, winning 13 while losing 11, but his ERA remained elevated at 5.16. He had acquired a reputation as a chronic under-achiever, and the Orioles had become fed up with his attitude and disputes with management and teammates. In 1986, he relieved four times for Baltimore before being demoted to the minors, where a 6.05 ERA in 4 starts failed to impress. Finally, in mid–June, the Orioles essentially gave Martinez to the Montreal Expos, trading him and a "player to be named later" for another "player to be named later." Inserted in the Expos rotation, Martinez showed little improvement, winning 3 of 9 decisions and recording a 4.59 ERA in his first National League exposure. In the offseason, he was granted free agency.

Nineteen eighty-seven was one of the years that major league owners were eventually found guilty of collusion, and Martinez was one of the players who was compensated. He'd refused the Expos offer of a steep salary reduction, but no other offer was forthcoming, and he was ultimately forced to re-sign on their terms. Furthermore, he had to complete a minor league assignment with their Indianapolis farm club before reporting to Montreal.

Martinez made his first start of the 1987 season for the Expos on June 10, against Pittsburgh. He yielded only two runs on three hits in seven innings, but didn't get the decision. Five days later, he shut out the New York Mets on three hits and his comeback was officially underway. His pitching helped the Expos climb into contention for the National League Eastern Division Championship before they faded back to third place. He wound up with an 11–4 won-lost mark and 3.30 ERA.

But the fun was just beginning.

Over the next six years, Dennis was the ace of the Expos staff, averaging more than 14 wins a season for the perennial also-rans with an ERA below 3.00. Often the victim of non-support, he was bidding for the Cy Young Award in 1988 when the Montreal bats seem to go silent every time he pitched. He lost 6 of his last 8 starts, 3 by shutouts. In 1990, his won-lost record was only 10–11 despite a 2.95 ERA. The Expos scored only 16 runs in his 11 losses.[12]

On July 28, 1991, the 36-year-old Expos ace pitched the game of his life, a perfect game against the Los Angeles Dodgers at Dodger Stadium.

Following the 1993 season, Martinez joined the free agent exodus out of Montreal, inking a three-year contract with the powerful Cleveland Indians. At 39 years of age, he was expected to lead the Indians staff. And he did, providing needed stability and a veteran presence. After being the opening day starter for the Expos from 1988 through 1993, he was extended the same honor by the Indians the next three seasons. In total, he posted a 32–17 won-lost record for the Indians, helping them reach the World Series in 1995. After missing much of the last half of the 1996 season with arm trouble, he departed Cleveland as a free agent to sign with the Seattle Mariners. Two months into the 1997 season, he was released by the Mariners after winning only one of nine starts. Shortly thereafter, he announced his retirement when no other team offered him a contract. His 241 major league victories left him two behind the record for a Latin pitcher held by Dominican Hall of Famer Juan Marichal.

But like many of the great ones, Martinez still had another comeback left in him. After sitting out the last two-thirds of the 1997 season, he signed with the Atlanta Braves for the 1998 campaign. Working primarily out of the bullpen, he won his 242nd game in relief and then tied Marichal on June 2 with a 12-hit shutout of the hard-hitting Milwaukee Brewers in a rare spot start. The tie-breaker came more than two months later, when he entered a tie game and was the beneficiary of a two-run Braves ninth. Dennis finished out his career with four scoreless relief appearances in the National League Championship Series that fall, which the Braves lost.

Dennis Martinez ended up winning 245 games while losing 193 and posting a 3.70 ERA in a major league career that lasted 23 seasons. During his career, he led or tied for the league lead in wins, ERA, complete games, innings pitched, and shutouts. He is one of only nine pitchers to win 100 games in both the American and National Leagues and has the most career victories of any pitcher who never won 20 games in a season.

In many respects, his early career presaged that of Dwight Gooden. Both found tremendous success at an early age, only to crash before celebrating their 30th birthday. But Gooden never completely overcame his personal demons, winning only 37 games, while Martinez actually became a better pitcher. His won-lost record was 108–93 with a 4.15 ERA for the first part of his career in Baltimore and 137–100 with a 3.34 ERA after his comeback in Montreal.

Despite winning more games than Juan Marichal, who was voted into the Hall of Fame his third time on the ballot, Martinez has never received serious consideration from the electorate. In fact, he only appeared on the ballot one time, failing to garner the required 20 percent to remain eligible, although his career numbers compared favorably with several pitchers whose plaques hang in Cooperstown.

But his comeback was certainly Hall of Fame caliber, and his 1991 perfect game put an exclamation point on it. Nicaragua's state-run television interrupted regular programming to show the final innings, and President Chamorro later declared the date a national sports day in Martinez's honor.[13]

During a celebration with friends and several teammates later that night, Dennis was toasted with champagne. He raised his glass with the others, then set it back down without a sip. "Right then I thought about where I had come from and everything I've been through," he said later. "People thought I was washed-up. Now look at this."[14]

Dennis Martinez

Born: 5/14/1954

Year	Team	Lg	G	IP	W	L	ERA	WHIP
1974	*Miami*	*FLOR*	25	179	15	6	2.06	0.99
1975	*Miami*	*FLOR*	20	145	12	4	2.61	1.10
	Asheville	*SOUL*	6	45	4	1	2.60	1.27
	Rochester	*IL*	2	5	0	0	5.40	1.80
1976	*Rochester*	*IL*	25	180	14	8	2.50	1.10
	Baltimore	AL	4	27	1	2	2.60	1.12
1977	Baltimore	AL	42	166	14	7	4.10	1.33
1978	Baltimore	AL	40	276	16	11	3.52	1.27
1979	Baltimore	AL	40	292	15	16	3.66	1.22
1980	Baltimore	AL	25	99	6	4	3.97	1.48
	BAL-ML Rehab	*A*	*2*	*12*	*0*	*0*	*0.00*	*0.67*
1981	Baltimore	AL	25	179	14	5	3.32	1.31
1982	Baltimore	AL	40	252	16	12	4.21	1.39

33. Dennis Martinez

Year	Team	Lg	G	IP	W	L	ERA	WHIP
1983	Baltimore	AL	32	153	7	16	5.53	1.66
1984	Baltimore	AL	34	141	6	9	5.02	1.29
1985	Baltimore	AL	33	180	13	11	5.15	1.48
1986	*BAL-Minors*	*AAA*	*4*	*19*	*2*	*1*	*6.05*	*1.40*
1986	Baltimore	AL	4	6	0	0	6.75	1.95
	Rochester	*IL*	*4*	*19*	*2*	*1*	*6.05*	*1.40*
	Montreal	NL	19	98	3	6	4.59	1.34
1987	*Miami*	*FLOR*	*3*	*19*	*1*	*1*	*6.16*	*1.26*
	Indianapolis	*AA*	*7*	*38*	*3*	*2*	*4.46*	*1.17*
	Montreal	NL	22	144	11	4	3.30	1.20
1988	Montreal	NL	34	235	15	13	2.72	1.15
1989	Montreal	NL	34	232	16	7	3.18	1.19
1990	Montreal	NL	32	226	10	11	2.95	1.06
1991	Montreal	NL	31	222	14	11	2.39	1.12
1992	Montreal	NL	32	226	16	11	2.47	1.03
1993	Montreal	NL	35	224	15	9	3.85	1.22
1994	Cleveland	AL	24	176	11	6	3.52	1.19
1995	Cleveland	AL	28	187	12	5	3.08	1.18
1996	Cleveland	AL	20	112	9	6	4.50	1.42
1997	Seattle	AL	9	49	1	5	7.71	1.92
1998	Atlanta	NL	53	91	4	6	4.45	1.41
23 Yrs	MLB Totals		692	3999	245	193	3.70	1.27

34

Fernando Valenzuela

The announcement out of the Los Angeles Dodgers 1991 spring camp jolted baseball fans all over the nation. The Dodgers had unconditionally released their 30-year-old former ace, Fernando Valenzuela. One of the most celebrated players in the game since taking baseball by storm a decade ago, Valenzuela was a cultural icon, easily the most prominent native of Mexico to play in the big leagues.

Upon his release, Dodgers club owner Peter O'Malley gratuitously threw a shovelful of dirt on Valenzuela's magnificent career, intoning: "All great careers must come to an end." His observation seemed most prophetic when Valenzuela flopped dismally in a brief stint with the California Angels and returned to Mexico.[1]

Five years later, Valenzuela would not only be back in the big leagues, he would have the honor of hurling the first regular season major league game played outside of the United States and Canada. Pitching for the Western Division Championship bound San Diego Padres, he went six innings to beat the New York Mets in Monterrey, Mexico's Estadio de Beisbol. It was the 35-year-old veteran's 10th victory of the season, tying him for the team lead and keeping the Padres even with the Dodgers in the race for first place.

No one ever broke in quite like Fernando Valenzuela. He won his first ten major league decisions after joining the Dodgers in mid–September 1980, a little more than a year after Los Angeles purchased his contract from the Yucatan Lions of the Mexican League. In the midst of a pressure-packed 1980 division championship race, the pudgy, 19-year-old lefthander pitched eighteen scoreless innings out of the bullpen, winning two games as the Dodgers finished a game behind the Houston Astros in the National League Western Division race.

But Fernando was just warming up. He got the 1981 Opening Day start as an emergency replacement for Jerry Ruess and began the season with a five-hit shutout of the Astros. He then proceeded to win seven more in a row and record an astonishing ERA of 0.50 for his first 8 major league starts. Those first 8 outings included 7 complete games, 5 shutouts, and a 36-inning scoreless streak.

En route to being named the 1981 *Sporting News* Player of the Year and becoming the first rookie to win the Cy Young Award, Valenzuela gave Los Angeles a long-sought sports hero for the local Mexican population. "Fernandomania," a cult-like craze that dominated the sports pages for most of the 1981 season was born, and Dodger Stadium became the site of a Mexican fiesta on the days he pitched.[2]

The 1981 campaign was interrupted by baseball's first prolonged player strike, which shortened the Dodgers schedule to 110 games. For the abbreviated season, Fernando won 13 games and lost 7, with an excellent 2.48 ERA. His 8 shutouts led the majors as did his

180 strikeouts in 192 innings. He also led the National League in innings pitched and complete games, tied for second in victories, and finished third in fewest hits allowed per game.

The labor strike split the season in two and necessitated a special best-of-five playoff for the division championship between the winners of each half. Los Angeles won the first half, thanks largely to Fernando's heroics. They bested Houston, winner of the second half, in the playoff series, with Valenzuela winning the deciding game. He also won a start in the League Championship Series and went the distance to win the third game of the World Series as the Dodgers triumphed over the New York Yankees in six games.

Fernando was a slam dunk for the National League Rookie of the Year Award, the third of four Dodgers rookies to garner the honor in consecutive seasons. Despite the fact that the strike shortened his rookie season by more than 50 games, Valenzuela's eight shutouts tied the all-time rookie record set by Reb Russell of the Chicago White Sox in 1913. In addition, he was one of a select few rookie pitchers to rate an All-Star Game start.

Fernando Valenzuela came back to pitch the first major league baseball game in Mexico (1988 Topps card).

But, Valenzuela's accomplishments on the field were only part of the Fernandomania phenomenon. He was a naturally colorful character. With a huge torso perched atop skinny legs, he looked like a bull standing on its hind legs and was christened with the nickname "Toro" in Mexico. As he delivered the ball to the plate, he would roll his eyes skyward—a disconcerting sight from the batters box.[3] Even his devastating screwball had a name of its own, "Fernando's Fadeaway."[4]

A definite air of mystery surrounded Valenzuela. The youngest of twelve children from a poor Mexican farm family, he entertained fans with profound observations made through an interpreter. The husky, moon-faced lefthander stood 5'11", and his weight was listed at 180 pounds—an obvious lie. Although he steadfastly insisted that he'd been born on November 1, 1960, there were doubts about the accuracy of that claim as well. Fernando not only looked at least ten years older, he was rumored to have already been an established Mexican League veteran when he was acquired by the Dodgers from the Yucatan club in 1979.[5]

Though Valenzuela couldn't possibly maintain the dominance he showed in the first half of his rookie reason, he won 19 games as a sophomore and became the first player to be awarded $1 million in arbitration the next year. He was the ace of the Dodgers staff for most of the decade of the 1980s, averaging 16 wins a season from 1981 through 1987. In 1986, he set a major league record by throwing 44⅓ consecutive innings without allowing an earned run to start the season. That season was Fernando's only 20-victory campaign, but he missed becoming the first Mexican-born twenty game winner in the major leagues when Teddy Higuera of the Milwaukee Brewers beat him out by a matter of days. He also narrowly lost out to the Astros' Mike Scott in balloting for the National League Cy Young Award.

Fernando seemed to be blessed with a rubber arm and was always ready to pitch. Beginning with his Opening Day heroics in 1981, he made 255 consecutive starts through July 1988 without missing a turn. He topped the majors with 20 complete games in 1986 and tied for the league lead with 12 the following year, giving him a total of 96 route-going performances in seven seasons as a starter. Inevitably, the massive workload took its toll. A stretched anterior capsule in his pitching shoulder disabled him midway through the 1988 season. But, he returned to the rotation in 1989, working 196 innings and winning 10 games with an encouraging 3.43 ERA.[6]

The following year, Valenzuela's innings-pitched total was back over 200 for the seventh time in ten major league seasons. He made 33 starts and threw his first major league no-hitter against the St. Louis Cardinals on July 29, yet there were indications that he might be nearing the end of the line as an effective starter. He won 13 decisions against the same number of losses, but his ERA jumped to 4.59, an increase of more than a run per game. In addition, he gave up 223 hits in 204 innings, an unacceptable stat for a front-line hurler.

In the offseason, the Dodgers acquired lefty starter Bobby Ojeda from the Mets, making the fading Valenzuela and his large contract expendable. The Dodgers let him go near the end of spring training, convinced he was through—that his once seemingly indestructible left arm was simply worn out. And no wonder! As was the custom of the day, Dodgers manager Tommy Lasorda shamefully abused Valenzuela's arm. From 1982, his first full season, through 1987, he threw an average of more than 265 innings a season before blowing out his arm in 1988. Then Lasorda proceeded to work him almost 200 innings when he came back in 1989.

Fernando's release also gave new life to the suspicion he was much older than his official baseball age of 30. Consequentially, no other major league team leapt at the chance to sign the veteran southpaw.

Eventually, the California Angels, understandably anxious to stick it to the neighboring Dodgers, signed Valenzuela. After two terrible starts, an examination revealed that the blood flow around Fernando's heart was restricted. It was determined that he suffered from a rare heart ailment that could be controlled through medication. He missed a few weeks before consenting to an unsuccessful minor league rehab assignment. He was subsequently released late in the season.[7]

Fernando signed with the Detroit Tigers in the spring of 1992, but he never played for them, spending the season pitching and playing first base for the Jalisco Charros of the Mexican League. He lost his first five decisions, but his arm finally came around after the horrible start. He finished the season with a 10–9 won-lost mark and managed to wangle a spring training invitation from the Baltimore Orioles after a strong performance in the Mexican Winter League.[8]

Valenzuela was the sensation of the Orioles 1993 camp, earning a spot in the starting rotation. He started the regular season slowly before catching fire in late June and reeling off a string of 25 consecutive scoreless innings. For the month of July, Fernando won three games without a loss and was named American League Pitcher of the Month. But his year-round pitching regimen took its toll in the second half of the season. He finished the season with an 8–10 won-lost mark and 4.94 ERA, again drawing his release at the end of the campaign.[9]

Returning to Jalisco for the 1994 season, Valenzuela went 10–3 with a 2.67 ERA to earn a midseason shot with the Philadelphia Phillies. In nine appearances (eight starts) he posted a nice 3.00 ERA. He really seemed to have found himself when he held the Mets to one run and four hits in eight innings, striking out seven on August 11. But, as with his rookie season, Fernando's comeback would be interrupted by a strike. Major League Baseball shut down for the season the next day.

In 1995, the Padres decided to take a flyer on the (supposedly) 34-year-old veteran, inviting him to spring training. Actually, the Padres had been interested in Fernando three years earlier. With San Diego's proximity to the border and large Mexican population, the Padres figured Valenzuela would be a tremendous gate attraction, if he had anything left. They dispatched a scout to look him over in the Mexican League, but passed on him when the scouting report concluded that he was washed-up.[10]

Ironically, Fernando's main competition for a spot on the Padres staff was expected to come from fellow countryman Teddy Higuera, who probably owed his original big league opportunity to Fernando. Thanks to Valenzuela's success, major league teams began more actively recruiting Mexican League talent. Higuera, who looked and pitched like a slightly smaller version of Fernando, was almost 26 years old when the Brewers purchased his contract from Ciudad Juarez in 1983. He averaged more than 17 wins a year for his first four seasons in the majors. Unfortunately, like Fernando, he was overworked and developed arm trouble. At the age of 36, he was attempting a comeback with the Padres after winning only five games in his four previous years with the Brewers.

Neither Valenzuela and Higuera were impressive in spring training, but the Padres were so thin in left-handed pitching that Fernando was given a spot on the roster. He began the season in the starting rotation, but was soon relegated to bullpen work with an occasional spot start. After eight starts and 14 relief appearances, his won-lost record was 3–3 with a bloated 5.46 ERA. Then in late August, he was given another starting opportunity and held the Mets to one earned run in six innings. Starting regularly through the remainder of the season, he won four more games without a loss to finish with an 8–3 record.

Many considered Valenzuela's whirlwind finish a fluke, but the next year the 35-year-old southpaw confounded the experts by completing his comeback to become a key figure in the Padres starting rotation the next season. "Fernandomania II" was born when he reeled off seven straight victories in the second half of the campaign to help the Padres beat out the Dodgers for the 1996 Western Division Championship. Though the second coming of Fernando wasn't quite as glorious as the original, it was a reasonable facsimile. In fact, Fernando finished his comeback season with a 13–8 won-lost record, compared to his 13–7 rookie mark fifteen years prior.

The high point of Fernando's comeback occurred on August 16, 1996, when he pitched and won the first major league game ever played on Mexican soil. After a hero's welcome from the Monterrey fans, he held the Mets scoreless into the seventh inning before leaving with a huge lead.[11]

Fernando reported to the Padres spring training base in 1997, assured of a roster spot for the first time in years. But a combination of hard luck and ineffectiveness resulted in only two wins in ten decisions before he was dealt to the pennant-contending St. Louis Cardinals. The Cards hoped that Valenzuela could regain his magic and help them down the stretch, but he couldn't get back on track, and he was released in July with an overall 2–12 won-lost mark. Fernandomania II was officially over when no other team was interested in signing him.

Valenzuela posted a won-lost record of 173–153, accompanied by a 3.54 ERA for a career that spanned 18 years. He ranked in the top four in the National League in strikeouts each year from 1981 through 1986, was the league's winningest pitcher in 1986, and led in complete games in 1986 and 1987. In addition to his 1981 Cy Young Award, he finished among the top five in the voting three other times. Always a great money pitcher, he won three of four decisions and posted a 1.95 ERA in three League Championship Series, and won his only World Series start. He made the All-Star Team in each of his first six full seasons, striking out nine without yielding an earned run in strikeouts in 7⅔ innings. In the 1986 All-Star Classic, he tied Carl Hubbell's All-Star Game record by fanning five straight American League All-Star hitters.

Despite his chunky physique, Fernando was a good all-around athlete. He slammed ten homers in his career and was occasionally used as a pinch-hitter. He also made emergency appearances in the outfield and at first base. He was awarded the Silver Bat as the best hitting pitcher in the league in 1981 and 1983, and in 1986 he captured a Gold Glove Award.

Like Dennis Martinez, Valenzuela was a trailblazer. He wasn't the first Mexican to make the major leagues. In fact, Veracruz native Bobby Avila won the American League batting title six years before Fernando was born. But Valenzuela certainly kindled an interest in Mexican League players, especially pitchers. In addition to Higuera, Salome Barojas, Houston Jimenez, and Vincente Palacios were other successful Mexican hurlers signed in Valenzuela's wake.

After leaving the majors for good, Valenzuela continued to pitch in Mexico. The Dodgers even offered him an invitation to spring training in 1999, but he turned them down.[12] Limiting himself to Winter League ball, he led the Hermosillo Orange Growers to Mexico's 2000–2001 Pacific Coast League title. Thousands cheered him as he sat on the back of a flat-bed truck for a victory parade through the streets of town. It was his fourth year with the Orange Growers and his best yet.[13]

Fernando became a Spanish language color commentator for the Dodgers in 2003 and was inducted into the Hispanic Heritage Baseball Museum Hall of Fame in a pre-game ceremony at Dodger Stadium that season. He also continued to pitch in the Winter League through the 2005–2006 season when he was (at least) 44 years old. One of his teammates that year was his son, Fernando Jr., a first baseman who'd played in the San Diego organization. The senior Valenzuela retired as an active player after that season ... well, maybe not completely.[14]

In March 2011, shortly before showing fine form in tossing out the ceremonial first pitch to open the Dodgers 2011 season in Los Angeles, Fernando made an appearance on the mound in a Mexican League All-Star contest. According to a Yucatan newspaper, the 50-year-old southpaw entered the game to face his 28-year-old son, then starring for the same Yucatan Lions franchise his father pitched for more than three decades earlier. Fernando Sr. departed to a thunderous ovation after inducing Fernando Jr. to ground out.[15]

Who knows? Fernandomania III could be on the horizon.

Fernando Valenzuela

Born: 11/1/1960

Year	Team	Lg	G	IP	W	L	ERA	WHIP
1978	Guanajuato	Mex	16	93	5	6	2.23	-
1979	Yucatan	Mex	26	181	10	12	2.49	-
	Lodi	CALL	3	24	1	2	1.12	1.42

Year	Team	Lg	G	IP	W	L	ERA	WHIP
1980	*San Antonio*	*TL*	*27*	*174*	*13*	*9*	*3.10*	*1.30*
	Los Angeles	NL	10	17	2	0	0.00	0.74
1981	Los Angeles	NL	25	192	13	7	2.48	1.05
1982	Los Angeles	NL	37	285	19	13	2.87	1.16
1983	Los Angeles	NL	35	257	15	10	3.75	1.34
1984	Los Angeles	NL	34	261	12	17	3.03	1.24
1985	Los Angeles	NL	35	272	17	10	2.45	1.15
1986	Los Angeles	NL	34	269	21	11	3.14	1.16
1987	Los Angeles	NL	34	251	14	14	3.98	1.51
1988	Los Angeles	NL	23	142	5	8	4.24	1.53
1989	Los Angeles	NL	31	196	10	13	3.43	1.44
1990	Los Angeles	NL	33	204	13	13	4.59	1.47
1991	California	AL	2	6	0	2	12.15	2.55
	CAL-ML Rehab	*(var)*	*12*	*63*	*6*	*4*	*4.81*	*1.51*
1992			(Mexican League)					
1993	Baltimore	AL	32	178	8	10	4.94	1.44
	BAL-ML Rehab	*(var)*	*2*	*9*	*0*	*1*	*4.82*	*1.39*
1994	Philadelphia	NL	8	45	1	2	3.00	1.09
1995	San Diego	NL	29	90	8	3	4.98	1.49
1996	San Diego	NL	33	171	13	8	3.62	1.42
1997	San Diego	NL	13	66	2	8	4.75	1.75
	St. Louis	NL	5	22	0	4	5.56	1.59
17 Yrs	MLB Totals		453	2930	173	153	3.54	1.32

35

Julio Franco

At the age of 41 in 2000, three-time big league All-Star and former American League batting king Julio Franco was playing first base for the Samsung Lions of the Korean Baseball Organization—about as far away from Major League Baseball as a professional ball player can get.

Six years later, at age 47, he became the oldest player ever to hit a major league home run, a record he would officially extend to 48 years 254 days when he smacked his last big-time homer on May 4, 2007.

In a unique professional baseball career that spanned 31 years, Franco spent 20 seasons and parts of three others playing for nine different teams in the major leagues, including a pair of return engagements. He also spent five seasons in the Philadelphia Phillies minor league system at the beginning of his career, three years in the Mexican League, and two seasons in the Japan Pacific League, in addition to the aforementioned campaign in Korea.

Franco grew up in the Dominican Republic province of San Pedro de Macoris, the aptly named "Cradle of Shortstops." Franco himself was a shortstop for the first third of his career, although he was a distinct departure from the normal slick-fielding, light-hitting model. In fact, he is one of the most prolific hitters to emerge from the Caribbean nation that shares the island of Hispaniola with Haiti, but he was never considered a strong defender of the area around the keystone sack.

Signed by the Phillies at the age of 19, the error-prone young shortstop worked his way up the ladder before getting a late season trial with the Phils in 1982. That offseason, he was swapped to the Cleveland Indians as a key component of the infamous trade in which Franco, All-Star second baseman Manny Trillo, and three other players were traded for Von Hayes, an outfielder who never fulfilled the lofty expectations set for him.

Franco immediately took over as the Indians shortstop and finished second to Chicago White Sox outfielder Ron Kittle in the 1983 American League Rookie of the Year voting. He developed into one of the best offensive middle infielders of the 1980s, hitting .295 and averaging over 22 stolen bases a year in six seasons with the Indians. However, he led American League shortstops in errors in 1984 and 1985, and after resisting several attempts to shift him to second base, he finally moved over to the other side of the keystone sack in 1988.

Traded to the Texas Rangers before the 1989 campaign, Franco emerged as a team leader. His first season in a Texas uniform, he hit .316 with 92 RBIs and stole 21 bases in 24 attempts. In 1991 he enjoyed a career year, hitting a league-leading .341, banging out 201 hits, scoring 108 runs, stealing 36 bases, and smacking 15 homers. He also captured his fourth straight Silver Slugger award as a second sacker, an honor he never received as a shortstop due to the presence of Cal Ripken and Alan Trammell.

The following year, a knee injury limited him to 35 games, and he never fully regained his speed thereafter. He was used as a designated hitter in 1993, hitting .289, which was well below his standards. In 1994, he joined the Chicago White Sox as a free agent and, at age 35, was on pace for a great offensive year. He was batting .319 and had already reached career highs with 20 homers and 98 RBIs in 112 games when the strike brought the season to a close in mid–August. That year, he finished eighth in American League MVP balloting, the highest ranking of his career.[1]

When the work stoppage threatened to drag on into 1995, Julio's former Texas manager, Bobby Valentine, recruited him to play for the Chiba Lotte Marines in Japan. The next year he was back in the States, signing on for another tour of duty in Cleveland. He enjoyed a productive 1996 campaign, but his numbers dropped in 1997 and he was released in August. The Milwaukee Brewers immediately

Julio Franco returned to the big leagues at age 43 (1988 Topps card).

picked him up, and he finished the year with them before heading off to Japan for another stint with Chiba Lotte.

Julio attempted a big league comeback with the Tampa Bay Devil Rays in 1999, but got only a single at-bat. He spent most of the season with the Mexico City Tigers, where he hit .423 in 93 games. While Franco was toiling south of the border, fellow countryman Tony Fernandez overtook him to become the new all-time Dominican major league hits leader.

After spending the 2000 season in Korea, the 42-year-old Franco returned to Mexico City in 2001 to lead the Mexican League in batting with an amazing .437 average in 110 games. On August 31, the Atlanta Braves acquired him for the stretch run. Taking over the Braves' troubled first base spot, he batted .300 with three home runs and 11 RBIs in 25 games. Frank Wren, then the Braves' assistant general manager, said, "Our offense started coming around, getting some clutch hits, around the start of September, about the time we signed Franco."[2]

When Julio was inserted into the lineup on September 1, the Braves were tied with the Phillies for first place. They promptly won six of eight with the veteran manning first base to open up a 3.5 game lead that they never relinquished. In fact, they reversed their 12–16 August won-lost record, winning 16 while losing 12 through the remainder of the regular season. Franco started all eight post-season games for Atlanta, delivering a pair of homers as the Braves swept the Division Series before falling to the Arizona Diamondbacks in the League Championship Series.

Spending the next four seasons platooning at first base in Atlanta and hitting a solid .291, Franco became a big fan favorite. During the 2002 campaign, he caught up with the retired Tony Fernandez, regaining the top spot in big league hits among Dominicans. After a 2005 season in which he slammed nine homers and hit a creditable .275 platooning with Adam LaRoche at first base, Julio left the Braves for a two-year contract with the New York Mets.

On April 20, 2006, the 47-year-old veteran banged his history-making home run, passing hurler Jack Quinn who held the distinction of being the oldest man to homer in a major league game for more than 75 years. The two-run, eighth inning pinch shot, which put the Mets ahead by a run, proved to be the game-winner.

Franco hit .273 with two home runs and swiped six bases as a pinch-hitter and back-up first baseman for the 2006 Eastern Division Champion Mets. He was back with the Mets to start the 2007 season and slammed his final home run, a two-run shot to deep left-center field, off hard-throwing Arizona Diamondback Randy Johnson on May 4 to seal a 5–3 Mets victory. The matchup with the 43-year-old Johnson was thought to represent the oldest hitter-pitcher duel in baseball history since 37-year-old Rube Walberg retired 57-year-old Nick Altrock on the last day of the 1933 season.

Unfortunately, such heroics had become too infrequent. Hitting only .200, Julio was released on July 16, 2007. He re-upped with Atlanta a few days later, but was unable to work his magic one more time. The Braves ended up third in the National League East, breaking Julio's string of six straight post-season appearances.

One of Franco's goals was to collect both a paycheck and a pension check from Major League Baseball at the same time; in other words, play until age 50. But the Braves dropped him after the 2007 season, and no other big league team made him an offer. Shooting for another comeback to draw those dual benefits, Julio signed with the Mexican League's Quinta Roo (Cancun) Tigers for the 2008 season, but packed it in after hitting only .250 in 36 games.[3]

Julio Franco retired with 2,586 major league hits, the most by a Dominican player until Vladimir Guerrero surpassed him during the 2011 season. Franco also rapped out 626 hits in the American Minor Leagues, 348 in Mexican baseball, 286 in Japan, and 156 in the Korean Baseball Association for a remarkable total of 4,002 safeties as a professional baseball player, a total that doesn't even include Winter League play. Although he hit a solid .285 after returning to the big leagues at the age of 43 in 2001, it dropped his lifetime batting mark below the charmed .300 level to .298. But his after-40-something comeback created a plethora of fascinating seniority records.

From 2001 to 2003, Franco was the oldest position player in the majors, and from 2004 until 2007 he was the oldest player—period. With the Braves in 2005, he became the oldest player to appear in 100 games in a season, and with the Mets in 2006, he became the oldest player to appear in a postseason game. In 2007, he appeared in 55 games for the Mets and Braves, making him the oldest (49 years of age when he made his last appearance on September 17) regular position player to perform in the major leagues. In fact, only nine players in history have made a major league appearance at a more advanced age. Satchel Paige, Charley O'Leary, Nick Altrock, Jimmy O'Rourke, Minnie Minoso, Hughie Jennings, and Arlie Latham made only token appearances at age 49 or older. Jack Quinn was a regular pitcher until he was 50. And Jamie Moyer pitched at age 49 in 2012 to become the most recent addition to the club, and he might not be through yet. The intrepid Moyer already stole one distinction from Franco in 2012, replacing him as the oldest hitter to drive in a run.

Hitting from a distinctive knock-kneed stance, with his bat wrapped high behind his ear, Franco was still a physical marvel in his late 40s. In major league history, only 25 homers have been belted by players 45 years of age or older. The previously mentioned John Quinn hit one, as did Hall of Famer Carlton Fisk, and all-time great Cap Anson hit three. The other 20 were struck by Franco—which is what makes Julio Franco's magnificent comeback as unique as the rest of his extraordinary career.[4]

Julio Franco

Born: 8/23/1958

Year	Team	Lg	G	HR	RBI	SB	BA	OPS
1978	Butte	PION	47	3	28	4	.305	.814
1979	Central Oregon	NORW	71	10	45	22	.328	.893
1980	Peninsula	CARL	140	11	99	44	.321	.808
1981	Reading	EL	139	8	74	27	.301	.754
1982	Oklahoma City	AA	120	21	66	33	.300	.856
	Philadelphia	NL	16	0	3	0	.276	.633
1983	Cleveland	AL	149	8	80	32	.273	.693
1984	Cleveland	AL	160	3	79	19	.286	.679
1985	Cleveland	AL	160	6	90	13	.288	.723
1986	Cleveland	AL	149	10	74	10	.306	.760
1987	Cleveland	AL	128	8	52	32	.319	.818
1988	Cleveland	AL	152	10	54	25	.303	.771
1989	Texas	AL	150	13	92	21	.316	.848
1990	Texas	AL	157	11	69	31	.296	.785
1991	Texas	AL	146	15	78	36	.341	.882
1992	Texas	AL	35	2	8	1	.234	.683
1993	Texas	AL	144	14	84	9	.289	.798
1994	Chicago	AL	112	20	98	8	.319	.916
1995	Chiba Lotte	Japan	127	10	58	11	.306	-
1996	Cleveland	AL	112	14	76	8	.322	.877
1997	Cleveland	AL	78	3	25	8	.284	.734
	Milwaukee	AL	42	4	19	7	.241	.720
1998	Chiba Lotte	Japan	131	18	77	7	.290	-
1999	Tampa Bay	AL	1	0	0	0	.000	.000
1999	Mexico City	Mex	93	14	77	9	.423	-
2000	Samsung	Korea	-	-	-	-	-	-
2001	Mexico City	Mex	110	18	90	15	.437	1.175
	Atlanta	NL	25	3	11	0	.300	.821
2002	Atlanta	NL	125	6	30	5	.284	.739
2003	Atlanta	NL	103	5	31	0	.294	.824
2004	Atlanta	NL	125	6	57	4	.309	.818
2005	Atlanta	NL	108	9	42	4	.275	.799
2006	New York	NL	95	2	26	6	.273	.699
2007	New York	NL	40	1	8	2	.200	.588
2007	ATL-ML Rehab	(var)	8	0	3	1	.296	.721
2007	Atlanta	NL	15	0	8	0	.250	.636
2008	Quintana Roo	Mex	36	1	15	3	.250	.692
23 Yrs	MLB Totals		2527	173	1194	281	.298	.782

36

Johnny Lindell

Johnny Lindell is a rare example of a good hitter who made a successful comeback as a pitcher after his batting and fielding skills diminished. But what really sets Lindell's efforts apart from other players who have made the conversion is that he'd already made the reverse transformation earlier in his big league career.

In 1941, the 24-year-old Lindell was named the Minor League Player of the Year after winning 23 games for the International League Newark Bears. In 1952, he won 24 games for the Hollywood Stars to capture Pacific Coast League MVP honors. In between, he was a solid major league outfielder for eight seasons, an important part of three world champion teams.

The conversion from pitcher to productive position player is certainly no piece of cake. But, successfully making the reverse transformation is infinitely more difficult, judging from the scarcity of players who have accomplished the feat.

Several weak-hitting infielders and outfielders have become top pitchers. Most notable are Bob Lemon, Bucky Walters, Bob Smith, and Jack Harshman, who forfeited their careers as marginal batsmen to join the ranks of top flight-hurlers. Much more plentiful, however, are the soft-hitting position players who made the transition to hard-hit pitchers. Mel Queen, Jr., Danny Murphy, and twin brothers Johnny and Eddie O'Brien are a few of the "big names" who fall into this category. The king of this group is Hal Jeffcoat, who spent the first six years of his career as a mediocre back-up outfielder (.248 career batting average) before seamlessly making the conversion to second-line pitcher, where he put in another six years (39–37 career won-lost record).

A few aging hitting stars made brief comebacks, of sorts, as pitchers in their declining years. Former New York Yankees star Ben Chapman began taking the mound while managing in the minors after his career as a big league outfielder ended. He was successful enough that the Brooklyn Dodgers brought him up in 1944 to bolster their wartime-depleted staff. A 5–3 won-lost record earned him a return engagement in 1945, which he managed to parlay into a big league managerial job after a midseason trade to the Philadelphia Phillies. Ben enjoyed little success as a pitcher, or as a manager, in Philadelphia, but he apparently inspired future Hall of Fame slugger Jimmie Foxx to give pitching a shot. Foxx actually did pretty well on the mound, posting an excellent 1.59 ERA in nine appearances. But that was as far as it went, because old "Double X" retired at the end of the season.

Yet another Phillie, long-time 1950s shortstop Granny Hamner, made a serious attempt to re-invent himself as a knuckleball pitcher after his bat and legs slowed. The Topps Gum Company was even persuaded to list him as a pitcher on his 1957 baseball card! The experiment was shelved after one appearance, and he was forced to return his aching knees and .220 bat back to the infield, where he was still better than anyone else the feeble Phillies had to offer. Granny's major league career seemed over when he was released after the 1959 season, but the pitching dream lived on. After serving two years in the minors as an infielder and part-time hurler, he posted an impressive 10–4 record with Binghamton in 1962 and returned to the majors with the Kansas City Athletics late that year for a short-lived comeback attempt as a knuckleballing relief pitcher.

None of the aforementioned players, however, had what amounted to three separate careers as Lindell did.

Lindell, a strapping 6'4", 217-pounder, was a well-rounded athlete. In addition to baseball, he played football and basketball and ran track in high school, winning 15 letters and a scholarship to play football and run track for the University of Southern California, where he attended a few months before signing with the New York Yankees in 1936. Like many talented youngsters, the right-handed hitter and thrower starred at the plate and on the mound in amateur ball.[1]

Johnny Lindell converted from pitcher to outfielder and back (1954 Bowman card).

The Yankees recruited him to pitch, however, and he posted a 17–8 won-lost record for the Joplin Miners in the Class C Western Association in 1936 as a 19-year-old freshman. Progressing through the talent-laden Yankees chain, he made stops at Binghamton, Oakland, and Kansas City, generally pitching impressively while occasionally pinch-hitting and helping out in the outfield.

After tying for the American Association lead with 18 wins for Kansas City in 1940, Lindell began the 1941 campaign with the Yankees. But he made only one appearance (as a pinch-hitter) before being sent down to Newark, the Yankees' top farm club. With Newark, he posted a gaudy 23–4 won-lost mark with a league-leading 2.05 ERA and also hit .298 to lead the Bears in a waltz to the International League pennant.

Despite his big year at Newark, Lindell spent the 1942 season buried in the Yankees bullpen. Evidently, Yankees manager Joe McCarthy didn't think Johnny's fastball was big league caliber. He posted a 2–1 record with a 3.76 ERA in 23 games and also went two-for-five as a pinch-hitter. He didn't make an appearance in the Yankees' World Series loss to the St. Louis Cardinals that fall.[2]

Before the 1943 season, the Yankees lost center fielder Joe DiMaggio and right fielder Tommy Henrich to Uncle Sam, so McCarthy decided to try Lindell in the outfield. He performed so well in spring training that he was in right field on Opening Day, slotted eighth in the batting order. The first half of the season was like something out of an old Lester Chadwick *Baseball Joe* novel. In early June, he was batting .322 when he was elevated to DiMaggio's old cleanup spot in the batting order, and shortly thereafter, he was shifted to center field, the Yankee Clipper's old job. He was even selected to the American League All-Star squad, although he didn't get in the game.

Johnny tailed off badly in the second half of the season, finishing the year with a lowly .245 batting average and only four homers in 122 games. He did, however, demonstrate a nice blend of speed and power, tying Wally Moses for the American League lead in triples.

With a year of experience in the outfield under his belt, Lindell assaulted wartime pitching for a .300 average in 1944, while slamming 18 home runs and driving in 103 runs. He finished ninth in the league in batting, third in homers, RBIs, and slugging, and fifth in on-base plus slugging percentage (OPS), while again tying for the league in triples. His 67 extra base hits led all American League hitters.

Now an established center fielder and one of the top hitters in the game, the 28-year-old star's pitching days were only a memory. Before the 1945 season, manager McCarthy observed, "With (Dick) Wakefield and Stan (Musial) in the service, Lindell could be the greatest outfielder in baseball." But six weeks into the campaign, the Navy beckoned, and Lindell reported for duty after appearing in 41 games.[3]

With DiMaggio, Henrich, and Charlie Keller returning from military service to reclaim their former jobs, there was no regular position for Lindell in the post-war 1946 Yankees lineup. In fact, he never played regularly again, though he proved to be an invaluable fourth outfielder. In the 1947 World Series, he batted .500 and led the team with seven RBIs in six games, and in 1948, he hit .317 with 13 homers as a part-timer during the regular season. His clutch homer on the next-to-last day of the 1949 season clinched the first pennant of the Casey Stengel era for New York. But a .242 average that year and the emergence of young flychasers Gene Woodling and Hank Bauer spelled the end of his Yankees career. The 33-year-old veteran was sold to the St. Louis Cardinals early in the 1950 season.

Johnny never got going with the Cards, hitting .186 in 36 games before being demoted to Columbus in the American Association and subsequently swapped to the Brooklyn Dodgers in July. The Dodgers assigned him to the Pacific Coast League Hollywood Stars, where he batted only .247. Johnny Lindell's career as a major leaguer appeared to be history.

Late in the 1950 campaign, Hollywood manager Fred Haney advised Lindell that his future as an outfielder looked bleak and suggested that he concentrate on a return to pitching. Johnny pitched in a couple of games near season's end with encouraging results, so the Hollywood franchise held onto his contract when it entered into a new working agreement with the Pittsburgh Pirates in the offseason.[4]

Over the years Lindell had developed a pretty good knuckleball, a pitch that would be easy on his 34-year-old arm. Taking a regular turn in the Stars rotation in 1951, he went 12–9 with a tidy 3.03 ERA and also contributed as a part-time outfielder and first baseman, hitting .292 with nine homers in 179 at-bats. The next year, Johnny was the sensation of the Pacific Coast League, posting a 24–9 record with a 2.52 ERA and leading the Stars to the pennant. Late in the season there was much speculation about Lindell being picked up by a contender for the stretch run, but Haney had other plans for his star hurler.

The 1953 campaign saw both Lindell and Haney back in the major leagues, the 36-year-old Lindell as a starter on the woeful Pirates pitching staff, and Haney as the club's new manager. The Stars' veteran catcher, Mike Sandlock, was also brought to Pittsburgh to handle Johnny's fluttery knuckleball.

The Pirates lost 104 games in 1953, an improvement over their 112 defeats the previous year, but still the worst record in either league. It's safe to say that none of the Pittsburgh hurlers received good support, but Johnny's was particularly bad. After completing five of his first six starts, he sported a dandy 2.76 ERA, but had only two victories against four defeats. He would go on to post a 5–16 won-lost record for the Pirates, his teammates backing him with a paltry 36 runs in his 16 losses, while permitting 14 unearned runs. In addition, before the advent of a mitt customized for the knuckler, Lindell's "personal catcher," Sandlock, led the league in passed balls. Though his winning percentage was actually worse than the overall team's, Johnny's 4.71 ERA was significantly better than the 5.29 average his mound mates posted that year. He also led the staff in strikeouts and complete games, finishing 13 of his 23 starts. In addition, he was the club's top pinch-hitter and played a couple of games at first base.

On August 31, the Philadelphia Phillies acquired Lindell for a reported $25,000. The deal was more than a late-season pennant race purchase, since the Phils were pretty much out of contention. Clearly, they were interested in the veteran knuckleballer for the future. Johnny pitched well for his new club, completing two of three starts and posting a 1–1 record with a 4.24 ERA in five appearances, but the Phils' offensively-oriented catching platoon of Smoky Burgess and Stan Lopata had trouble corralling his elusive knuckleball.

Before the 1954 season, the Phillies got Sandlock from the Pirates to once again serve as Lindell's personal catcher. Manager Steve O'Neil predicted 15 wins for the veteran knuckleballer, but Johnny reported with a sore arm from pitching in the California winter league. Although he pinch-hit seven times, he never got to pitch for the Phillies before he and Sandlock were released at the deadline for reducing the roster.[5]

Shortly thereafter, it was announced that Johnny had succeeded Babe Herman as youth director of the Seven-up Foundation in Los Angeles, a position he would hold for many years.

For his career, Lindell batted .273 in 854 games and hit .324 in three World Series with the Yankees. Though his won-lost record at the big league level was only 8–18 in two seasons (a dozen years apart), he enjoyed extraordinary success in the minors. In total, he won 117 games against only 60 losses in eight full minor league seasons as a pitcher.

Johnny Lindell's comeback to become a respectable pitcher after a fine career as an established big league hitter is a rare accomplishment. Classifying him as a star might be a stretch, but he was a fine outfielder for the winningest team of the era and ranked among the league leaders in several offensive categories during his career. Classifying his comeback as a success requires even more flexibility, since he did lose 17 games in his only full season as a major league hurler. But, despite pitching for a horrible team, he finished sixth in the National League in complete games and finished among the top ten in fewest hits yielded and most strikeouts per nine innings in 1953.

What really distinguishes Lindell's comeback, however, is that he is the only well-known player to return to his pitching roots after earlier turning his back on a pitching career.

As his old Yankees manager Casey Stengel observed when Lindell took the mound for the Pirates, "That fella doesn't know what it means to feel sorry for himself or quit. He came up as a pitcher, switched to the outfield, and now he's back in the big leagues again as a pitcher—because he didn't fold up."[6]

Johnny Lindell

Born: 8/30/1916

Hitting

Year	Team	Lg	G	HR	RBI	SB	BA	OPS
1936	Joplin	WA	42	0	23	1	.325	.675
1937	Binghamton	NYPL	32	0	8	0	.317	.794
1938	Newark	IL	4	0	0	0	.000	.000
	Oakland	PCL	60	4	27	2	.368	.893
1939	Kansas City	AA	40	1	8	0	.185	.407
1940	Kansas City	AA	41	1	11	1	.273	.625
1941	New York	AL	1	0	0	0	.000	.000
	Newark	IL	51	0	9	0	.298	.652
1942	New York	AL	27	0	4	0	.250	.542
1943	New York	AL	122	4	51	2	.245	.694
1944	New York	AL	149	18	103	5	.300	.851
1945	New York	AL	41	1	20	2	.283	.740
1946	New York	AL	102	10	40	4	.259	.738
1947	New York	AL	127	11	67	1	.275	.734
1948	New York	AL	88	13	55	0	.317	.898
1949	New York	AL	78	6	27	3	.242	.724
1950	New York	AL	7	0	2	0	.190	.510
	St. Louis	NL	36	5	16	0	.186	.685
	Columbus	AA	5	-	-	-	.200	-
	Hollywood	PCL	35	4	8	0	.247	.760
1951	Hollywood	PCL	75	9	31	0	.292	.876
1952	Hollywood	PCL	74	8	25	1	.213	.679
1953	Pittsburgh	NL	58	4	15	0	.286	.909
	Philadelphia	NL	11	0	2	0	.389	.986
1954	Philadelphia	NL	7	0	2	0	.200	.629
12 Yrs	MLB Totals		854	72	404	17	.273	.773

Pitching

Year	Team	Lg	G	IP	W	L	ERA	WHIP
1936	Joplin	WA	29	212	17	8	4.03	1.46
1937	Binghamton	NYPL	20	102	5	8	2.74	1.45
1938	Oakland	PCL	33	166	9	8	3.42	1.53
	Newark	IL	4	17	1	1	-	1.47
1939	Kansas City	AA	23	131	8	5	4.40	1.44
1940	Kansas City	AA	31	203	18	7	2.70	1.22
1941	Newark	IL	31	228	23	4	2.05	1.16
1942	New York	AL	23	52	2	1	3.76	1.41
(MLB outfielder 1943–1950)								
1950	Hollywood	PCL	2	7	0	1	0.00	1.14
1951	Hollywood	PCL	26	190	12	9	3.03	1.45
1952	Hollywood	PCL	37	282	24	9	2.52	1.17
1953	Pittsburgh	NL	27	175	5	16	4.71	1.65
	Philadelphia	NL	5	23	1	1	4.24	1.93
2 Yrs	MLB Totals		55	251	8	18	4.47	1.62

37

Fred Mitchell

Like Johnny Lindell, Fred Mitchell is *not* included in these pages because his comeback was so statistically impressive or historically significant. He's included because his feat was unique, which could reasonably be attributed to the difficulty factor.

Mitchell started his big league career at age 23 as a pitcher and concluded it 10 years later at the polar opposite end of the baseball spectrum—as a catcher.

The catcher's position is generally regarded as the most physically demanding in baseball. It's also the least like any of the other defensive positions. The catcher is the only one who wears full body armor. He's also the only one who plays facing his teammates rather than the opposition. He spends most of his time playing in foul territory, only occasionally venturing out on the diamond to chase a ball in front of the plate. He even wears a glove that's different from anyone else's and is the only player who wears his cap backwards.

Hard-hitting catchers, like Joe Torre, are often shifted to other positions to keep their bats in the lineup. Even Johnny Bench and Yogi Berra, considered by many to be the greatest receivers of all time, spent considerable time at other positions. Two of today's top catchers, Buster Posey and Joe Mauer, are already being discussed as candidates to be moved to another position to extend their careers. But, other than the occasional utilityman learning to fill in behind the plate to extend his career, it's extremely rare for another position player to take up catching.

And even rarer is the case of a pitcher making the transformation to catcher.

After all, pitcher is the position that rivals catcher in distinctiveness. In fact, the two positions essentially form a team within a team and even have a name for their exclusive relationship—the battery. More often than not, they are the only players to touch the ball on a given play.

Yet the two positions couldn't be more different in terms of physical and psychological requirements. Pitchers are a breed of their own. They're baseball's prima donnas. Many of them, the starters, work only about once a week, while the others, the relievers, never do a full day's work. American League pitchers don't even have to bat, while in the senior circuit they're not really expected to hit. On defense, the pitcher is the center of attention, regally standing up on a hill specifically built for him, dictating when play can begin. Meanwhile, his gritty battery mate wallows in the dirt some 60 feet away, ready to accept anything the pitcher decides to hurl his way. In fact, the catcher's protective equipment has long been known as "the tools of ignorance."

For the reasons outlined above, the otherwise mediocre career of Fred Mitchell is most noteworthy. Mitchell was a regular big league pitcher for five years, followed by another three years of toiling on minor league mounds. Then, at the age of 31, he decided to become a catcher, despite an absence of professional experience at the position. The next year, he was catching regularly for a pennant contender in the major leagues.

No other big league pitcher is known to have made a successful mid- or late-career conversion to catcher. True, Hall of Fame receiver Roger Bresnahan started his big league career on the mound, but by the time he reached his 21st birthday, he'd traded in his toeplate for a chest protector (he hadn't invented shin guards yet). And old Negro League star Ted Radcliffe acquired the nickname "Double Duty" because he would often pitch the first game of a doubleheader and catch the second—but that wasn't the major leagues. Mike Ryba, a former minor league catcher, occasionally caught after he made the big leagues as a pitcher, but only on a fill-in basis. Current Los Angeles Dodgers closer Kenley Jansen spent five years as a weak-hitting catcher in their minor league system, but it's hard to imagine him going behind the plate again given his success out of the bullpen.

Born Frederick Francis Yapp, Mitchell changed his name for obvious reasons. He began his career in organized baseball with the Boston Americans in 1901, the first year of the American League's existence as a recognized major league. He'd been playing semi-pro ball around the Boston area when manager Hugh Duffy signed him to pitch for the newly-minted Americans, who would soon become known as the Red Sox. Mitchell, in fact, pitched in the franchise's very first game, an exhibition contest in Charlottesville, Virginia.[1]

The rookie pitcher appeared in Boston's second regular season game, in relief of Cy Young. He made his first start a few days later earning the victory in a 10–5 win over the Chicago White Sox. After a won-lost record of 6–6, accompanied by an ordinary 3.81 ERA for the second place Americans, Fred was swapped to the Philadelphia Athletics early the next season. The A's won the American League pennant that year with Rube Waddell and Eddie Plank heading the pitching staff. Mitchell started 14 games for the Athletics, going 5–8 for them after losing his only decision for Boston.

The next spring, Mitchell jumped to the Philadelphia Phillies in the National League when Connie Mack refused his request for a raise. Reportedly he won the first game of an inter-city pre-season exhibition series 1–0 against Plank and then beat Waddell 2–0 in the fourth contest.[2]

For the 1903 season, Mitchell won 11 games for the seventh-place Phils, while losing 16 times. His .407 winning percentage was much better than the club's .363 overall mark, and he completed 24 of 28 starts, working 227 innings. But, he hurt his arm the next season, and the Phillies shipped him to the Brooklyn Superbas late in the campaign. For the 1904 season, his record was only 6–12. When his arm failed to come around, and he recorded a 3–7 record in 1905, the 27-year-old Mitchell's days as a big league hurler were over.

The husky 5'10", 185-pound right-hander was signed by manager Ed Barrow of the Eastern League Toronto Maple Leafs in 1906 and toiled on the mound for them through 1908. He only won 23 games while losing 28 during that three-year period, but he pitched better than his record indicates and even threw a no-hitter against Montreal in 1908.[3]

When the 1909 season rolled around and another big league opportunity hadn't presented itself, Fred decided a drastic move was in order. "I'm going to be a catcher," he told Toronto manager Joe Kelley, "or else I'm going home."[4]

At the time, no evidence existed that Fred possessed the ability to become a big league catcher at the age of 31. Although he'd filled in a few games at other positions, mostly first base, he'd never gone behind the plate in a major league game. Furthermore, he'd displayed

Fred Mitchell made the rare transformation from pitcher to catcher (Bain Collection, Library of Congress).

little talent with the bat. In his five major league seasons, he'd hit .198 without a single homer, and in three campaigns with Toronto, he'd hit minor league pitching at a .209 rate. In fact, he'd hit a woeful .143 for the Maple Leafs in 1908, although he did manage his first professional home run that year.

Nevertheless, he worked his way into the club's first-string catcher job and hit a solid .295 while appearing in 109 games during the 1909 season. This performance earned the former hurler a trip back to the major leagues when his contract was purchased by the New York Highlanders of the American League. Playing for legendary manager George Stallings, he appeared in 68 games, sharing the regular job with Jeff Sweeney. Fred hit only .230, but it was better than Sweeney's .200. Yet, it was Sweeney who stayed with New York. In the off-season, the Highlanders sold Mitchell to the Rochester Broncos in the Eastern League, retaining Sweeney despite his lesser performance.

Apparently, the infamously crooked Hal Chase had something to do with Mitchell's departure from New York. Late in the season, manager Stallings accused Chase of throwing games and said he wouldn't manage the team as long as Chase was on it. Highlanders owner Frank Farrell, a well-known gambling figure himself, ended up dismissing Stallings and installing Chase as manager. Mitchell had supported Stallings in the matter, so Chase got rid of him as soon as he could.[5]

Mitchell hit .292 in 88 games for Rochester in 1911 and moved to Buffalo for the 1912 season to once again play for George Stallings, who'd taken over the Bisons after leaving the Highlanders. Serving as Stallings' unofficial coach and assistant manager, Fred's average fell to .232 in 82 games.

The next year, Stallings was hired to manage the Boston Braves and brought Mitchell along with him "as instructor and trainer of his young catchers and pitchers." Fred did get to the plate four times as a pinch-hitter that year to conclude his playing career.[6]

In 1914, Mitchell, in effect, served as the pitching coach for the famous "Miracle Braves," who won 27 of their last 33 games to capture the National League pennant before sweeping the heavily favored Athletics in the World Series. He was on the roster as a catcher, but according to the *Washington Post*: "He [Mitchell] never plays, his duty being to warm up and instruct the young pitchers."[7]

Before the Series, Stallings said: "The fans do not appreciate the work Mitchell is called upon to do.... He is the hardest worker on the team." Referring to the club's three top starters, 26-game-winners Bill James and Dick Rudolph, and 16-game-winner Lefty Tyler, Stallings wrote, "Mitchell, almost single-handed, is responsible for their remarkable showing this year. Mitchell has worked with the catchers with equal care and has made [Hank] Gowdy, once turned back by McGraw, one of the best backstops in the league."[8]

After another season coaching under Stallings, Mitchell was appointed coach of the Harvard baseball team. But he returned to the Braves when Harvard wasn't able to field a team in 1917. Before the season, however, the Chicago Cubs recruited him to replace Joe Tinker as manager. Outfielder Joe Kelly and cash were sent to Boston for Mitchell's rights, and the Cubs signed him to a two-year contract.

The Cubs had finished a distant fifth in 1916, but by 1918 Mitchell had built them into a pennant winner. He lasted in Chicago through 1920 and then moved over to manage the Braves, replacing his old mentor, Stallings. After the 1923 season, he left the dugout to become the club's business manager. He remained in the Braves' front office and also coached at Harvard until he retired in 1938. He was inducted into Harvard's Hall of Fame in 1958.[9]

Fred Mitchell's major-league playing career ran from 1901 to 1913. He appeared in 97 games and posted a 31–50 won-lost record with a 4.10 ERA as a pitcher. At the plate, he was a .210 hitter in 572 at-bats spread across 202 games. He played every infield and outfield position, as well as pitching and catching at the major league level.

Years later, renowned sportswriter Frederick Lieb wrote that the 1914 Miracle Braves' success "would not have been possible without battery coach, Fred Mitchell ... one of the few men who ever played in the majors on both ends of the battery."[10]

Fred Mitchell's one-of-a-kind comeback resulted in one-of-a-kind career.

Fred Mitchell

Born: 6/5/1887

Pitching

Year	Team	Lg	G	IP	W	L	ERA	WHIP
1901	Boston	AL	17	108	6	6	3.81	1.53
1902	Boston	AL	1	4	0	1	11.25	3.25
	Philadelphia	AL	18	107	5	8	3.59	1.66
1903	Philadelphia	NL	28	227	11	16	4.48	1.55
1904	Philadelphia	NL	13	108	4	7	3.40	1.45
	Brooklyn	NL	8	66	2	5	3.82	1.46
1905	Brooklyn	NL	12	96	3	7	4.76	1.51
1906	*Toronto*	*EL*	*29*	*239*	*11*	*15*	*-*	*1.18*
1907	*Toronto*	*EL*	*14*	*100*	*6*	*3*	*-*	*1.10*
1908	*Toronto*	*EL*	*21*	*166*	*6*	*10*	*-*	*1.14*
5 Yrs	MLB Totals		97	718	31	50	4.10	1.54

Hitting

YEAR	Team	Lg	G	HR	RBI	SB	BA	OPS
1901	Boston	AL	20	0	4	0	.159	.446
1902	Boston	AL	1	0	0	0	.000	.000
	Philadelphia	AL	20	0	3	1	.188	.454
1903	Philadelphia	NL	29	0	10	0	.200	.442
1904	Philadelphia	NL	25	0	3	1	.207	.521
	Brooklyn	NL	8	0	6	0	.292	.763
1905	Brooklyn	NL	27	0	8	0	.190	.428
1906	*Toronto*	*EL*	*39*	*0*	*-*	*-*	*.218*	*.487*
1907	*Toronto*	*EL*	*44*	*0*	*-*	*-*	*.256*	*.560*
1908	*Toronto*	*EL*	*35*	*1*	*-*	*-*	*.143*	*.333*
1909	*Toronto*	*EL*	*109*	*1*	*-*	*-*	*.295*	*.670*
1910	New York	AL	68	0	18	6	.230	.560
1911	*Rochester*	*EL*	*88*	*0*	*-*	*-*	*.292*	*.629*
1912	*Buffalo*	*IL*	*82*	*0*	*-*	*-*	*.232*	*.494*
1913	Boston	NL	4	0	0	0	.333	.667
7 Yrs	MLB Totals		202	0	52	8	.210	.508

38

Tony Cuccinello

Tony Cuccinello, or "Cooch," thought his days as a major league performer were over after he hit a woeful .226 for the 1940 New York Giants. The former National League All-Star had suffered a leg injury the previous season that surgery failed to repair. After the season, the 32-year-old veteran accepted an offer to manage the American Association Jersey City Giants.[1]

Five years later, Cuccinello rang up the second highest batting average in the American League—a scratch hit away from becoming the oldest batting champ in major league history.

Tony was signed off the sandlots of Long Island and eventually gravitated to Branch Rickey's extensive St. Louis Cardinals' farm system. At 5'7" and 160 pounds, he hit with surprising power for a little guy. In 1929, playing second base for the Columbus Senators, he hit .357 with 20 homers and 111 RBIs. After the season he was traded to the Cincinnati Reds.

Spending most of his time at third base, Tony hit .312 as a Reds rookie in 1930, with 10 homers and 78 RBIs in 125 games. The next year, he shifted to second base and raised his average to .315 with 93 RBIs, while appearing in every game.

A salary squabble led to Cuccinello's trade to the Brooklyn Dodgers in the spring of 1932, a deal that sent veteran slugger Babe Herman and young catcher Ernie Lombardi to the Reds.[2]

From 1932 through 1935, Cooch manned second base for Brooklyn with occasional forays to third. Even with Herman and long-time manager Wilbert "Uncle Robbie" Robinson gone, the Dodgers still retained the "Daffiness Boys" image with the likes of Dazzy Vance, Boom-Boom Beck, Hack Wilson, Lefty O'Doul, Jack Quinn, and Van Lingle Mungo on the roster. Though his batting average didn't reach the levels he attained with the Reds, he played in the first major league All-Star Game in 1933 and reached career highs with 14 homers and 94 RBIs in 1934. In Brooklyn, he also became fast friends with a young catcher by the name of Al Lopez, a long-lasting relationship that would prove mutually beneficial to both.

Before the 1936 season, Tony was traded to the Boston Bees along with Lopez, and enjoyed one of his finest seasons, hitting .308 with 86 RBIs. After two more solid, if unspectacular, years, he was headed toward another banner season when he was cut down by a Rowdy Dick Bartell slide in early May. He ended up hitting .313 for the year, but the injury limited him to only 81 games.[3]

Despite surgery, Tony's leg would never be the same. With his diminished range in the field, the Bees shifted him to third base in 1940, then dealt him to the New York Giants on the June 15 trade deadline. The Giants were only two games behind the Dodgers at the time, and the addition of the two-time All-Star to their infield was expected to provide a big boost. But Cooch, who was out of the lineup with leg problems when the trade was made, was a bust in New York. Shifting between second and third, he hit only .208 in a Giants uniform.

"Tony Cuccinello has turned out to be a little slower than had been feared.... It was known that the veteran had lost some of his zip and dispatch, but it was not realized how much he had slipped until Billy Jurges [was injured] and Tony had to step into a regular job," wrote Dan Daniel in *The Sporting News*.[4]

A few weeks later Daniel opined, "It looks as if [Giants manager Bill] Terry received something of a disappointment in the acquisition of Tony Cuccinello from the Bees. Tony looks terribly tired. Nobody around here ever suspected Tony had slowed up so much."[5]

Shortly after the end of the season, it was announced that Cuccinello was taking over the reins of the Giants American Association farm club in Jersey City in 1941. Of course, Cooch didn't throw out his spikes and glove. Filling in at second and third base, he hit a workman-like .277 in 86 contests, a mark that didn't exactly elicit dreams of a return to big league stardom for the 33-year-old veteran.

After Jersey City finished fifth in Cooch's first year at the helm, he was set to try managing again in 1942, until Casey Stengel asked him to rejoin the Boston franchise as a player-coach. Cuccinello, who suffered from chronic laryngitis which made him unfit for military duty, coached third base, pinch-hit, and filled in around the infield for the team until he drew his release midway through the 1943 campaign. Tony promptly signed on with the Chicago White Sox, managed by Jimmy Dykes. Despite a roster that had been ravished by Uncle Sam, the Sox called Cooch off the bench only 72 times in the last half of 1943 and all of the 1944 campaign combined.[6]

Cooch didn't even make the 1945 edition of *Who's Who in Baseball*. But when Ralph Hodgin, Chicago's regular third baseman and leading hitter the previous campaign, was inducted into the army, it left the hot corner in the hands of the gimpy 37-year-old-veteran.

The 1945 White Sox tipped off the season with an Opening Day lineup that averaged almost 33 years of age. Long-time Sox southpaw Thornton Lee, age 38, was on the mound with 31-year-old ironman Mike Tresh behind the plate. The only other established big leaguer listed was 34-year-old Wally Moses, who patrolled right field. Long-time minor leaguers Roy Schalk, Johnny Dickshot, and Bill Nagel manned second base, right field, and first base respectively, at ages 36, 35, and 29. Wartime recruit Oris Hockett, age 35, was in center field. On the left side of the infield, Cuccinello manned third, while 19-year-old shortstop Cass Michaels brought the average age down a few notches.

Amazingly, the geriatric southsiders burst out of the gate to win their first five contests, occupying first place until May 24, with Cuccinello's .366 average leading the way.

Before the season, the White Sox held spring training camp in French Lick, Indiana (later to gain fame as Larry Bird's birthplace), where Cuccinello enjoyed a mineral bath every day, followed by a rubdown and a nap. He entered the campaign feeling the best he'd felt in years.[7]

Starting 81 of the club's first 89 games at third base, Tony was leading the league with a .331 average at the end of July. Though Dykes usually gave him the second game of doubleheaders off and often pulled him in the late innings, Cooch's weary legs were beginning to give out. He missed 13 of the next 15 games, but the surprising Sox managed to stay in the pennant race. He returned to the lineup with a well-rested bat and immediately drove his average up to .339 by August 18. That day, after a 16 to 1 thrashing of the Boston Red Sox, the Pale Hose found themselves in third place with a 58–51 won-lost record, only 4½ games behind the front-running Detroit Tigers.

Unfortunately, age caught up with the ancient White Sox warriors all at once. Over the last five weeks of the season, they won only 13 times while dropping 27 contests to fall out of the pennant race. Meanwhile, Cuccinello's batting average dropped more than 30 points, although he still clung to the league lead. By September 16, his average was down to .305, and several American Leaguer batsmen, including teammates Johnny Dickshot and Wally Moses, were nipping at his heels. The long season had taken a toll on Cooch's aching legs, but he needed a minimum of 400 at-bats to qualify for the batting title and couldn't afford to take much time off to rest.

On September 17, Tony rapped out five hits in eight at-bats in a doubleheader against the Red Sox to lift his average to .311. With only five games left on the White Sox schedule, he looked like the favorite to win for the batting crown. Dickshot's average stood at .304, while Moses and Washington Senators outfielder George Case, who'd been dogging Cooch for months, had slumped below .300. But a newcomer had joined the hunt. George "Snuffy" Stirnweiss, the New York Yankees' second baseman, had been on a tear. His average stood at .298, but the Yankees had ten games left to play.

Cuccinello played only two more games. After going 0-for-4 against the Cleveland Indians on September 22, he still led the league but was still a single at-bat shy of qualifying for the batting title. He rested the next day with Bob Feller on the mound for the Indians, but he was back in the lineup two days later when the Sox opened a season-ending three-game series with the Browns in St. Louis. He knocked out a single in three at-bats to keep his season average at .308 with two games left on the schedule. But the weatherman didn't cooperate. The Sox' last two games of the season in St. Louis were rained out and finally cancelled.

Meanwhile, the Yankees kept playing, and Stirnweiss kept hitting, setting a torrid .475 pace in New York's last 10 games. In the Yankees season finale against the Boston Red Sox, five days after the White Sox wrapped up their season, Stirnweiss hit a sharp grounder that was initially ruled an error on the Boston third baseman. Subsequently, the official scorer, who happened to be a reporter for the *Bronx Home News*, changed his decision, awarding Stirnweiss a single.

In the tightest batting title race in major league baseball history, Stirnweiss edged Cuccinello out by less than one-hundredth of a point, .30854 to .30846. The tainted base hit given Stirnweiss in the Yankees' last game of the season was the difference, robbing Cooch of the batting title after he held the top spot for five months.[8] It probably didn't make Cuccinello feel any better five years later, when Stirnweiss confirmed that something had been amiss. "He (the scorer) gave it to me," he confided to Tony after they became teammates in Cleveland, Cuccinello a coach and Stirnweiss a utility infielder.[9]

In retrospect, the White Sox 1945 season was a minor miracle. Expected to contend for the American League cellar, the financially strapped club was in the fight for the pennant until the last weeks of the campaign. Incredibly, the aging club used only 27 players all season, the 25 guys they started with and late season additions Luke Appling and Bill Mueller, who joined the club after being discharged from military duty. Yet the Sox ended up with four of the top ten hitters in American League: Cuccinello, Dickshot, Moses and Oris Hockett. Ironically, only Moses would ever play major league baseball again.

The 1946 season would be Cuccinello's only year out of professional baseball between

1926 and 1969. It's unclear whether Cuccinello's departure from the White Sox was totally voluntary. In Rich Westcott's *Diamond Greats*, he's quoted as saying: "I wasn't going to play anymore [after 1945].... Before the season ended, I already had my release in my pocket."[10] *The Biographical History of Baseball* says that two days before the end of the 1945 season, he was told he would not be invited back because of the younger players expected to be released from the military.[11] But, according to *Baseball Reference*, the Sox didn't release him until December 8, 1945, and *The Ballplayers: Baseball's Ultimate Biographical Reference* quotes him as saying, "I'm the most surprised guy in baseball," upon his release.[12]

In 1947, Cooch was back on the field, managing the Tampa Smokers of the Florida International League. He led the club to 104 wins and a second-place finish and even played a few games. He signed on as a coach for the American Association Indianapolis Indians under his old buddy Al Lopez in 1948. From 1949 through 1951, he served a three-year stint as a coach with his first big league team, the Reds. Then Al Lopez recruited him to join his coaching staff in Cleveland in 1952. He followed Lopez to Chicago in 1957, where he served as his lieutenant through 1965 when Lopez retired. After a year under Eddie Stanky, Cooch joined the Tigers coaching staff, where in 1968 he became a member of a world championship team for the first time. He left Detroit for Chicago when Lopez was lured out of retirement to return to the manager's seat in 1969. But Al stepped down after only 17 games and Cuccinello retired to Tampa where he would work as a Yankees scout in the area until retiring from baseball completely in 1985.[13]

Cuccinello ended his major league career with a .280 lifetime batting average. He batted over .300 five times, and hit more than 10 homers and drove in more than 80 runs four times—pretty good numbers for a second baseman of that era. In fact, his 93 RBIs in 1931 established a Cincinnati Reds record for second basemen that held up until Joe Morgan broke it in 1975.

According to his good friend Al Lopez, "[Cuccinello] didn't have a real good arm and he had bad legs and wasn't real fast. But he could field the ball and knew how to handle himself out there."[14] In fact, he led National League second basemen in assists and double plays three times each.

It was in Chicago, where he'd enjoyed his last glory as a player, that the limelight again found Cuccinello, 14 years after his playing days ended. Coaching third base for the White Sox in the second game of the 1959 World Series, he sent lead-footed catcher Sherm Lollar home from first base on a double with no outs, only to have him cut down at the plate by a good margin. Many felt the controversial play was the turning point of the Series, which the Sox went on to lose in six games, and placed the goat horns squarely on Cuccinello's head. A quarter of a century later, the play was included in a summary of the worst coaching blunders in *The Baseball Hall of Shame*, written by Bruce Nash and Allan Zullo.[15]

Fortunately, that's not the only comeback Cooch is remembered for.

Tony Cuccinello

Born: 11/8/1907

Year	Team	Lg	G	HR	RBI	SB	BA	OPS
1926	Lawrence	NENL	36	2	-	-	.283	.718
	Syracuse	IL	4	0	-	-	.750	-

Year	Team	Lg	G	HR	RBI	SB	BA	OPS
1927	Lawrence	NENL	91	8	-	-	.310	.793
1928	Danville	IIIL	127	11	-	-	.310	.820
	Columbus	AA	14	1	-	-	.396	-
1929	Columbus	AA	162	20	-	-	.357	.929
1930	Cincinnati	NL	125	10	78	5	.312	.832
1931	Cincinnati	NL	154	2	93	1	.315	.805
1932	Brooklyn	NL	154	12	77	5	.281	.752
1933	Brooklyn	NL	134	9	65	4	.252	.704
1934	Brooklyn	NL	140	14	94	0	.261	.734
1935	Brooklyn	NL	102	8	53	3	.292	.796
1936	Boston	NL	150	7	86	1	.308	.776
1937	Boston	NL	152	11	80	2	.271	.746
1938	Boston	NL	147	9	76	4	.265	.697
1939	Boston	NL	81	2	40	5	.306	.747
1940	Boston	NL	34	0	19	1	.270	.660
	New York	NL	88	5	36	1	.208	.547
1941	Jersey City	IL	86	2	33	1	.277	.758
1942	Boston	NL	40	1	8	1	.202	.525
1943	Boston	NL	13	0	2	0	.000	.136
	Chicago	AL	34	2	11	3	.272	.732
1944	Chicago	AL	38	0	17	0	.262	.589
1945	Chicago	AL	118	2	49	6	.308	.780
1946			(Did not play Organized Baseball)					
1947	Tampa	FLIN	7	0	-	-	.067	-
15 Yrs	MLB Totals		1704	94	884	42	.280	.737

39

Van Lingle Mungo

Tony Cuccinello wasn't the only Dodger of the "Daffiness" era to make a surprising comeback during World War II. One of the daffiest of the bunch, Van Lingle Mungo, also returned from a seven-year stretch in baseball oblivion to temporarily regain his standing as one of the top pitchers in the National League.

With the manpower demands of the United States military taking precedence, major league baseball found itself severely strapped for legitimate professional ballplayers during World War II. An assortment of teenagers, old-timers, and handicapped performers were recruited to fill out big-league rosters, and 4-F's became an extremely valuable commodity.

Lefty Joe Nuxhall took the mound for the Cincinnati Reds at the tender age of 15, and Carl Scheib toiled on the hill for the Philadelphia Athletics at age 16. Another 16-year-old, Tommy Brown, handled shortstop for the Brooklyn Dodgers. At the other end of the spectrum, 40-year-old semi-pro star Chuck Hostetler was signed off the sandlots to patrol the outfield for the Detroit Tigers. And 35-year-old Roy Schalk was rewarded for his many years of minor league service with the Chicago White Sox regular second base job. The St. Louis Browns employed one-armed center fielder Pete Gray, and the Reds used Dick Sipek, who was deaf, as a pinch-hitter and spare outfielder. The Washington Senators even signed combat-wounded veteran Bert Shepard to pitch with a wooden leg.

Another intriguing source of wartime baseball talent was former star players who could be persuaded to oil up the old glove, loosen up the old arm, and once again listen to the roar of the crowd. Their efforts were sometimes successful, sometimes unfortunate, but always entertaining.

Forty-six-year-old Hod Lisenbee, who had won 18 games for Washington and served up Babe Ruth's 58th homer in 1927, pitched in 31 games for Cincinnati in 1945. He'd been out of the majors for nine years. After a two-year absence from the majors, 40-year-old Pepper Martin, charter member of the old Gashouse Gang, reported to the 1944 edition of the St. Louis Cardinals and hit a credible .279 as a part-time outfielder. Future Hall of Famer Jimmie Foxx left the coaching ranks of the Woman's Professional Baseball League to sign on with the Philadelphia Phillies for the 1945 season. At the time, old "Double X" was second on the all-time career home run list to the Babe, but sinus problems had forced him into early retirement. His seven homers as a 37-year-old part-timer tied for the second highest on the team, and he even helped out on the mound.

As a coach with the Athletics, former slugger and future Hall of Fame inductee Al Simmons had been a vociferous critic of young Boston Red Sox star Ted Williams. When Williams joined the Navy in 1943, the 41-year-old Simmons charged out of retirement to take over Ted's left field spot and show the Fenway fans what a real ballplayer could do. Sadly, it was a meager .203 batting average in 40 games before the chagrined veteran returned to the coaching lines. But Al wasn't giving up that easy. The next year, the Athletics briefly activated him again, and he batted .500 in six plate appearances.

Leo "the Lip" Durocher, Brooklyn's manager during the war, made two ill-fated attempts to return to active duty as a player. Leo had surrendered the regular shortstop job to young Pee Wee Reese in 1941 and managed strictly from the bench in 1942. With Reese in the service as the 1943 season rolled around, Dodgers president Larry MacPhail offered Leo a bonus if he would take over his old shortstop post. The 37-year-old veteran jumped at the extra money, but his aging legs gave out after only six games. Two years later, Leo became frustrated watching his young middle infielders butcher double plays and installed himself at second base. This time he lasted only two games before breaking a finger on a mishandled double play attempt.

One of the most memorable wartime comebacks was the return of old Brooklyn favorite Babe Herman to his old stomping grounds during the 1945 season. Babe's original stint with the Dodgers had ended after the 1931 season, and his last appearance in the big leagues had been with Detroit in 1937. But the Dodgers implored him to return to Brooklyn as a pinch-hitter. The 42-year-old Herman, one of baseball's greatest characters, had been active in the minors through the previous season but wasn't doing much at the time, so he agreed to report. The Brooklyn faithful, remembering the Babe's exploits from more than a decade earlier, greeted him enthusiastically on his first trip to the plate and he promptly lined a solid single to center field. With the cheers echoing in his ears, he cruised majestically down the baseline, and proceeded to fall flat on his face when he encountered an uncooperative first base bag. The fans roared in appreciation. After 14 years—nothing had changed.

Herman was actually a fairly productive player in his wartime comeback, hitting a respectable .265 in 37 games. But it was Mungo, Babe's successor as Brooklyn's favorite bum, who engineered the more successful wartime comeback.

Mungo joined the Dodgers late in the 1931 season, Herman's last year with the club. From 1932 through 1936, he rivaled Dizzy Dean of the St. Louis Cardinals as the premier fireballer, as well as the greatest managerial challenge, in the National League. Despite pitching for one of the more hapless teams in the league, Van won 81 games during that period, an average of more than 16 a year. In 1936, at the age of 25, he led the league in strikeouts and won 18 games for a Brooklyn squad that finished seventh in fielding and hitting, as well as seventh in the standings.

He was setting a similar pace in 1937, until he hurt his arm in the All-Star Game. Afterward, he was a mere shadow of his former self, winning only 13 major league games over the next 6½ years before joining the army in February 1944.[1]

But only a year after entering the service as a baseball has-been, the former strikeout king was a National League All-Star once again, a 14-game-winner for the New York Giants in 1945. In deference to the war effort, the All-Star game wasn't played that year, but Mungo was selected to represent the National League in a series of exhibition games against service teams made up of enlisted major league stars.

Van Lingle Mungo was a strapping 6'2" country boy who weighed in around 200 pounds. He was an intense competitor with a blazing fastball and a temper to match. Few hitters dug in on the high-kicking right-hander who often placed among the league leaders in walks issued, wild pitches, and hit batsmen. He had an overly combative personality, as well as a penchant for partying a bit too heartily that cost him dearly throughout his career. Dizzy Dean, a friend and kindred spirit, once described Mungo as being "outright mean."[2] He gained as many headlines from hotel-room brawls and bar fights as from his exploits on the field and claimed to have paid more than $15,000 in fines during his career—roughly equal to his highest yearly compensation.[3]

Mungo hated to lose and eventually became so frustrated with the play of his Dodgers teammates that he quit the club and demanded to be traded during the 1936 campaign. Fortunately, he calmed down and rejoined the team after a few days when the club elected to fine him rather than accede to his trade demand.[4] Later, after a particularly difficult loss when journeyman outfielder Tom Winsett muffed an easy fly ball, he fired off a memorable telegram to his wife that said, in effect: "Join me in Chicago. Good chance for you to get job in Dodgers outfield because you can play better than Tom Winsett."[5]

In retrospect, having Ms. Mungo on the team may not have been such a bad idea, although it's doubtful that Van would have been happy with the arrangement. A *New York Post* article, written years after his death, identified Mungo as among the greatest Lotharios in all of baseball. In one account, his long-suffering wife was grilling him about steamy love letters that had been arriving regularly at the Mungo homestead. "Must be some other Van Lingle Mungo," reasoned the star hurler with stunning aplomb. In fact, it was Mungo's overactive libido and fondness for drink, as much as an arm injury, that would eventually lead to the close of his career in Brooklyn.[6]

Mungo was born June 8, 1911, in Pageland, South Carolina, and made the small southern town his home for the rest of his life. Van's father was a respected merchant and a pretty good athlete, rumored to have once pitched in the South Atlantic (Sally) League.[7]

Signed by former Dodgers pitching great Nap Rucker, Mungo made an auspicious major league debut late in the 1931 season by throwing a three-hit, 12-strikeout shutout against the Boston Braves and knocking in both Brooklyn runs. The youngest player in the league, he was promptly tabbed as the successor to Dazzy Vance, another colorful power pitcher who was wrapping up his Hall of Fame career with the Dodgers at the time.

From 1932 through 1936, Mungo posted an 81–71 won-lost record for the Dodgers and established himself as one of the finest pitchers in the National League. A workhorse, he started the most games in the National League in 1934 and 1936 and also led in innings pitched in 1934. After finishing second in strikeouts in 1934 and third in 1935, he broke Dizzy Dean's four-year reign as the league's strikeout king with 238 in 1936 and tied Dazzy Vance's National League record by fanning seven straight hitters.[8]

Mungo, however, had become a huge pain in the managerial posterior. He was constantly at odds with Casey Stengel, the Brooklyn manager from 1934 through 1936. He was often rumored to be on the trading block, with a trade for Dean, who was causing a few headaches himself in St. Louis, being the juiciest and most persistent gossip tidbit.[9]

In 1937, the Dodgers replaced Stengel with Burleigh Grimes, but the former pitching star didn't have any better luck with the Brooklyn problem child than Casey had. In late May, Mungo conducted a 4:00 a.m. invasion of teammate Jimmy Bucher's hotel room. An argument ensued which quickly expanded to involve other players, hotel staff, and the local police. The next day, Mungo showed up with a bandaged face and was presented with a $1,500 repair bill by the hotel.[10]

Nevertheless, Mungo pitched magnificently the first half of the season and made the National League All-Star Team for the third time in his brief career. But he'd strained his back shortly before the big game, and Grimes instructed him not to pitch against the American Leaguers if it still bothered him. When word got out that Mungo might not pitch, he was accused of ducking the game. His pride tweaked, the macho hurler told All-Star manager Bill Terry that he was okay to take the mound.[11]

The 1937 All-Star Game would become infamous for the hot line drive off the bat of Earl Averill that broke Dizzy Dean's toe. The injury led to the ruination of the Cardinals star's spectacular career when, returning to action too soon, he adjusted his delivery to favor the injured foot and hurt his arm. Dizzy's, however, was not the only outstanding pitching career ruined that day. Throwing with a cramped motion because of his sore back, Mungo also hurt his arm in two ineffective innings of relief. Thus, in one meaningless exhibition game, major league baseball saw the careers of two wildly popular, 26-year-old pitching aces go down in flames.[12]

Like Dean, Mungo was pressed back into service too soon and further damaged his valuable arm. His won-lost record going into the All-Star break game was 9–6, but he didn't win another game that season. Mungo and the Dodgers tried everything—except rest. The club decided that the pitcher's tonsils were the source of the problem and pressured him into having them removed.[13] The operation didn't help. Mungo lost more than 20 pounds and returned to the mound using an unnatural sidearm delivery. In September he refused to take prescribed diathermic treatments and was suspended for "failing to do his utmost to get into shape to pitch."[14] In the offseason, Mungo swore he wouldn't pitch for Grimes again, because the manager doubted that his arm was really sore.[15] *The Sporting News* rated Van's chances of staying in Brooklyn as remote as that of "Hitler and Stalin operating together on a WMCA debating team."[16]

But when a trade failed to materialize, Van found himself back in Brooklyn, promising to be a model citizen and claiming, "I haven't had as much as a glass of beer in three months." Interestingly, he didn't mention whiskey.[17]

Sadly, the "reformed" Mungo could not recapture his fearsome velocity. In 1938 he posted a dismal 4–11 won-lost mark and walked as many batters as he struck out. In the offseason, he further incurred the wrath of the Dodgers front office by resisting a 66 percent salary cut and blaming the club for mishandling his injury. Things were finally patched up with Van vowing to "pitch back into big money." But he won only four games against five losses in 1939. A fast man for his size and a decent hitter, Mungo toyed with converting to first base or the outfield. In fact, he finished the first game of a July 16 doubleheader in left field and started the second contest on the mound. Shortly thereafter, he broke his foot trying to break up a double play in a pinch-running assignment and was finished for the year. In 1940, he underwent surgery on his arm and missed most of that season.[18]

Meanwhile, the Dodgers had begun a determined rise from the doldrums of the National League. Leo Durocher took over as manager in 1939 and led the club to a surprising third place finish, and the next year they climbed to second place. The Bums figured to be a contender in 1941, but their pitching was suspect. They were fervently hoping for a return to form by Mungo to solidify the staff.

But, while the onetime ace of the Dodgers staff had fallen on bad times in the pitching department, he was still the "King of the Hill" when it came to raising hell. Before the team traveled to Havana, Cuba, during spring training, the veteran hurler was already on probation for excessive drinking and carousing. Of course, he solemnly pledged to mend his ways and did behave himself for a few weeks. It even began to look like he might be able to help the club. Havana, however, simply offered too many temptations for the lusty-living hurler. After the Dodgers demolished the visiting Cleveland Indians in a Friday afternoon exhibition contest, Mungo celebrated a little too enthusiastically. When Saturday's game was rained out, it gave him a head start on Saturday night, which is when things really got complicated. After disappearing for most of the day, Mungo showed up at the hotel that evening, feeling no pain—until he ran into Durocher.[19]

Leo sent his troublesome pitcher staggering back to his room. But shortly thereafter, Mungo sneaked out of the hotel, accompanied by a club singer named Lady Vine, as well as the female half of a Latin dance team also entertaining at the hotel. He failed to return from this intriguing tryst until the wee hours of the morning, causing Durocher to become incensed—and possibly a little envious. The Dodgers manager promptly reported the situation to owner Larry MacPhail, the recipient of Mungo's latest promise to reform. MacPhail responded with an angry letter to the pitcher, informing him that he was fined and suspended. He was to leave for Macon, Georgia, the site of their Montreal farm team's training camp, that very evening.[20]

When the note was delivered to him at the ballpark before Sunday's game, Mungo, still probably under the influence, threatened to flatten Durocher. Somehow a fight was averted, and Mungo exited the premises.[21]

Mungo was supposed to be on the boat that took the Indians team back to the mainland, but he didn't quite make the final "all aboard" call. Apparently Van resumed his alcohol consumption after stomping out of the ballpark and ended up in bed with both the mysterious Lady Vine *and* the female dancer. Inevitably, the dancer's husband, reportedly a former bullfighter, got wind of the shenanigans and went looking for Mungo, brandishing a carving knife. In an escape worthy of Indiana Jones, the Dodgers managed to get Mungo out of the hotel and onto a plane while the knife-wielding husband searched in vain for the errant American pitcher.[22]

While the Dodgers marched to the National League pennant without his help, Mungo spent most of the 1941 season in Montreal. He was involved in only four decisions on the mound, and was traded to the Minneapolis Millers, the top farm team of the New York Giants, shortly after the conclusion of the season.

With Minneapolis in 1942, Mungo posted an impressive record of 11 wins against only 3 losses to earn a late season shot with the Giants. He stuck with the parent club in 1943, but won only three times while chalking up seven losses pitching mostly in relief.

Mungo's major league career appeared at an end when he joined the army, but pitching for Uncle Sam actually rejuvenated his career. He reportedly won 18 and lost 3 starring for the Camp Atterbury Army Air Force Base team before receiving a medical discharge.[23]

Van returned to the Giants for the 1945 season and surprised everyone by grabbing a job in the starting rotation. In fact, he became the ace of the staff. Despite missing the last month of the season with a dislocated left arm, he posted a 14–7 won-lost record along with a fine 3.20 ERA. Even though his fastball was gone, he fanned 101 batters in 183 innings, the fourth highest strikeout total and the second best strikeout-to-innings-pitched ratio in the league that year.

There were suspicions surrounding Mungo's remarkable comeback, however. Like some modern stars, players of yesteryear also were known to employ certain performance enhancing substances, although in those days the substance was usually applied to the ball rather than ingested. In Van's case, the substance was rumored to be slippery elm—a moist, gum-like resin that would make a pitch do wondrous things when properly applied to the sphere. The old high hard one had become a distant memory, so his self-christened "slippery ball" (some might call it a spitter) had became his new "out pitch." By Mungo's own admission, he kept some of the resin on his inner sock and would reach down for a fresh supply when all eyes were diverted by a foul ball or a play in the field.[24]

Alas, it shouldn't be surprising that Mungo's comeback was short-lived. He reported to the Giants for the 1946 campaign, expected to anchor the pitching staff. But Van's big league career came to a sudden end when manager Mel Ott arrived early for an exhibition game in Richmond and found him in no condition to pitch. The veteran pitcher had already broken training several times that spring and was rumored to be among those negotiating with the Mexican League. The Giants had had enough and gave him his unconditional release.[25]

When no major league team would touch him, Mungo returned to his South Carolina home. But, he was not quite finished with professional baseball. He was persuaded to manage the nearby Clinton team in the Tobacco State League and frequently played first base or the outfield, batting .471. Naturally, controversy continued to plague him. An August 1946 Tobacco State League game between Wilmington and Clinton turned into a riot when fans spilled onto the field and beat up the umpire. Both Mungo and the Wilmington manager were suspended for the balance of the season for their roles in inciting the crowd.[26]

Reinstated in 1947, Van hit .362 before retiring and eventually maturing into one of Pageland's town leaders and most prosperous businessman. His son Ernest, an outfielder, played in the Washington Senators organization in the early 1960s.

In 1970, the magical sounding name of Van Lingle Mungo became known to a whole new generation as the title and chorus of a bossa nova style recording. The lyrics of the popular ballad consisted entirely of the names of old baseball players strung together. A quarter of a century after disappearing from the limelight, Mungo had made another comeback.[27]

Van Lingle Mungo

Born: 6/8/1911

Year	Team	Lg	G	IP	W	L	ERA	WHIP
1929	Fayetteville	ECAR	24	159	10	9	3.11	1.26
	Charlotte	SALL	1	4	0	0	6.75	2.50
1930	Winston-Salem	PIED	32	212	11	11	5.26	1.51
	Charlotte	SALL	1	5	0	0	10.80	2.60
1931	Hartford	EL	28	191	15	5	2.12	1.24
	Brooklyn	NL	5	31	3	1	2.32	1.29
1932	Brooklyn	NL	39	223	13	11	4.43	1.52
1933	Brooklyn	NL	41	248	16	15	2.72	1.24
1934	Brooklyn	NL	45	315	18	16	3.37	1.28
1935	Brooklyn	NL	37	214	16	10	3.65	1.38
1936	Brooklyn	NL	45	311	18	19	3.35	1.26
1937	Brooklyn	NL	25	161	9	11	2.91	1.19
1938	Brooklyn	NL	24	133	4	11	3.92	1.54
1939	Brooklyn	NL	14	77	4	5	3.26	1.33
1940	Brooklyn	NL	7	22	1	0	2.45	1.55
1941	Montreal	IL	10	45	3	1	4.00	1.36
	Brooklyn	NL	2	2	0	0	4.50	1.50
1942	Minneapolis	AA	24	124	11	3	4.57	1.44

Year	Team	Lg	G	IP	W	L	ERA	WHIP
	New York	NL	9	36	1	2	5.94	1.62
1943	New York	NL	45	154	3	7	3.91	1.42
1944	New York	(Military service—Did not play)						
1945	New York	NL	26	183	14	7	3.20	1.27
1946	*Clinton*	*TOBS*	*5*	*18*	*1*	*1*	*3.50*	*1.06*
14 Yrs	MLB Totals		364	2113	120	115	3.47	1.34

Appendix: Comeback Player of the Year Award

The Associated Press (unofficial)

American League

Year	Player	Age
1950	??	
1951	??	
1952	??	
1953	Virgil Trucks	36
1954	Joe Coleman	31
1955	Tommy Byrne	35
1956	Vic Wertz	32
1957	Bobby Shantz	31
1958	Pete Runnels	30
1959	Early Wynn	39
1960	Ted Williams	41
1961	Al Kaline	26
1962	Robin Roberts	35
1963	Dick Stuart	30
1964	Jimmy Piersall	34
1965	Frank Howard	28
1966	Boog Powell	24
1967	Dean Chance	26

National League

Year	Player	Age
1950	*Eddie Waitkus*	30
1951	??	
1952	Enos Slaughter	36
1953	Carl Furillo	31
1954	??	
1955	??	
1956	*Sal Maglie*	39
1957	Hank Sauer	40
1958	Robin Roberts	31
1959	Gene Conley	28
1960	Stan Musial or	39
	Curt Simmons	31
1961	??	
1962	Stan Musial	41
1963	Dick Ellsworth	23
1964	Jim Bunning	32
1965	Vern Law	35
1966	Orlando Cepeda	28
1967	Mike McCormick	28

The Sporting News

American League

Year	Player	Age
1965	Norm Cash (1)	30
1966	Boog Powell (1)	24
1967	Dean Chance	26
1968	Ken Harrelson	26
1969	*Tony Conigliaro*	24
1970	Clyde Wright	29
1971	Norm Cash (2)	36

National League

Year	Player	Age
1965	Vern Law	35
1966	Phil Regan	29
1967	Mike McCormick	28
1968	Alex Johnson	25
1969	Tommie Agee	26
1970	Jim Hickman	33
1971	Al Downing	30

Year	Player	Age	Player	Age
1972	*Luis Tiant*	31	Bobby Tolan	26
1973	*John Hiller*	30	Davey Johnson	30
1974	Ferguson Jenkins	31	Jimmy Wynn	32
1975	Boog Powell (2)	33	Randy Jones	25
1976	Dock Ellis	31	*Tommy John*	33
1977	Eric Soderholm	28	*Willie McCovey*	39
1978	Mike Caldwell	29	Willie Stargell	38
1979	Willie Horton	36	Lou Brock	40
1980	Matt Keough	24	Jerry Reuss	31
1981	Richie Zisk	32	Bob Knepper	27
1982	Andre Thornton	32	Joe Morgan	38
1983	Alan Trammell	25	John Denny	30
1984	Dave Kingman	35	Joaquín Andújar	31
1985	Gorman Thomas	34	Rick Reuschel	36
1986	John Candelaria	32	Ray Knight	33
1987	Bret Saberhagen (1)	23	Rick Sutcliffe (1)	31
1988	Storm Davis	26	Tim Leary	29
1989	Bert Blyleven	38	Lonnie Smith	33
1990	Dave Winfield	38	John Tudor	36
1991	José Guzmán	28	Terry Pendleton	30
1992	Rick Sutcliffe (2)	36	Gary Sheffield	23
1993	*Bo Jackson*	30	*Andrés Galarraga (1)*	32
1994	José Canseco	29	Tim Wallach	36
1995	Tim Wakefield	28	Ron Gant	30
1996	Kevin Elster	31	*Eric Davis*	34
1997	David Justice	31	Darren Daulton	35
1998	Bret Saberhagen (2)	34	Greg Vaughn	32
1999	John Jaha	33	Rickey Henderson	40
2000	Frank Thomas	32	*Andrés Galarraga (2)*	39
2001	Rubén Sierra	35	Matt Morris	26
2002	Tim Salmon	33	Mike Lieberthal	30
2003	Gil Meche	24	Javy López	32
2004	Paul Konerko	28	Chris Carpenter (1)	29
2005	Jason Giambi	34	Ken Griffey, Jr.	35
2006	Jim Thome	35	Nomar Garciaparra	32
2007	Carlos Peña	29	Dmitri Young	33
2008	Cliff Lee	29	Fernando Tatis	33
2009	Aaron Hill	27	Chris Carpenter (2)	34
2010	Vladimir Guerrero	35	Tim Hudson	34
2011	Jacoby Ellsbury	27	Lance Berkman	35
2012	Adam Dunn	32	Buster Posey	25

Major League Baseball

	American League		*National League*	
Year	Player	Age	Player	Age
2005	Jason Giambi	34	Ken Griffey, Jr.	35
2006	Jim Thome	35	Nomar Garciaparra	32
2007	Carlos Pena	29	Dmitri Young	33
2008	Cliff Lee	29	Brad Lidge	31
2009	Aaron Hill	27	Chris Carpenter	34
2010	Francisco Liriano	26	Tim Hudson	34
2011	Jacob Ellsbury	27	Lance Berkman	35
2012	Fernando Rodney	35	Buster Posey	25

Chapter Notes

1. Tommy John

1. Tommy John with Dan Valenci, *T.J., My 26 Years in Baseball* (New York: Bantam, 1991), p. 146.
2. John, *T.J., My 26 Years in Baseball*, p. 143.
3. John, *T.J., My 26 Years in Baseball*, p. 143.
4. John, *T.J., My 26 Years in Baseball*, p. 146.
5. John, *T.J., My 26 Years in Baseball*, p. 147.
6. John, *T.J., My 26 Years in Baseball*, p. 148.
7. John, *T.J., My 26 Years in Baseball*, p. 150.
8. Seth Livingstone, "The Top 100 Things That Impacted Baseball in the 20th Century," *USA Today Baseball Weekly*, 5–11 Jan. 2000, p. 17.

2. Hank Greenberg

1. Mike Shatzkin and Jim Charlton, *The Ballplayers: Baseball's Ultimate Biographical Reference* (New York: Arbor House, 1990), p. 410.
2. Ralph Berger, "Hank Greenberg," SABR Baseball Biography Project (http://sabr.org/bioproj/person/64198864).
3. Robert Creamer, *Baseball in 1941* (New York: Penguin, 1991), pp. 126–127.
4. Creamer, *Baseball in 1941*, p. 142.
5. Creamer, *Baseball in 1941*, pp. 125–130.
6. Creamer, *Baseball in 1941*, pp. 129–131.
7. Creamer, *Baseball in 1941*, p. 134.
8. Creamer, *Baseball in 1941*, p. 136.
9. Creamer, *Baseball in 1941*, p. 136.
10. Creamer, *Baseball in 1941*, p. 127.
11. Creamer, *Baseball in 1941*, p. 136.
12. Hank Greenberg with Ira Berkow, *Hank Greenberg: The Story of My Life* (Chicago: Triumph Books, 2001), p. 142.
13. Greenberg, *Hank Greenberg: The Story of My Life*, p. 145 ref *The Sporting News* 1945.
14. Greenberg, *Hank Greenberg: The Story of My Life*, p. 145 ref Whitney Martin, Associated Press, June 22, 1945.
15. Ibid.
16. Greenberg, *Hank Greenberg: The Story of My Life*, p. 168.
17. Greenberg, *Hank Greenberg: The Story of My Life*, pp. 172–185.

3. Smoky Joe Wood

1. Wil A. Linkugel and Edward J. Pappas, *They Tasted Glory* (Jefferson, NC: McFarland, 1998), p. 12.
2. Lawrence S. Ritter, *The Glory of Their Times* (New York: Quill, 1966), p. 157.
3. Ritter, *The Glory of Their Times*, p. 13.
4. Ritter, *The Glory of Their Times*, p. 154.
5. Ritter, *The Glory of Their Times*, p. 166.
6. Ritter, *The Glory of Their Times*, p. 166.
7. Ritter, *The Glory of Their Times*, p. 167.
8. Linkugel and Pappas, *They Tasted Glory*, p. 20.
9. Ritter, *The Glory of Their Times*, pp. 168–169.
10. James Costello and Michael Santa Maria, *In the Shadows of the Diamond* (Dubuque, IA: Elysian Fields Press), p. 199.
11. Mike Sowell, *The Pitch That Killed* (New York: Macmillan, 1989) p. 207.
12. Ritter, *The Glory of Their Times*, pp. 166.
13. Tim Horgan, "Let's Clear the Air About Smoky Joe," *Boston Herald American*, Apr. 25, 1982, p. 69.
14. Tim Horgan, "Let's Clear the Air About Smoky Joe," *Boston Herald American*, Apr. 25, 1982, p. 69.

4. Monty Stratton

1. "The Stratton Story," Wikipedia. http://en.wikipedia.org/wiki/The_Stratton_Story.
2. "The Stratton Story," Wikipedia. http://en.wikipedia.org/wiki/The_Stratton_Story.
3. Costello and Santa Maria, *In the Shadows of the Diamond*, p. 222.
4. Linkugel and Pappas, *They Tasted Glory*, p. 228.
5. John Carmichael, "The Chicago White Sox," in *The American League*, edited by Ed Fitzgerald (New York: Grosset & Dunlap, 1959), p. 55.
6. Linkugel and Pappas, *They Tasted Glory*, p. 228.
7. Richard Lindberg, *Who's on Third?* (South Bend, IN: Icarus Press, 1983), p. 57.
8. *The Stratton Story*, film production by Metro-Goldwyn-Mayer, 1949.
9. Costello and Santa Maria, *In the Shadows of the Diamond*, p. 224.
10. *The Sporting News*, 7 Aug. 1946, p. 31.

11. *The Sporting News*, 7 Aug. 1946, p. 31.
12. *The Sporting News*, 21 Aug. 1946, p. 13.
13. *The Sporting News*, 15 Sep. 1954, p. 9.
14. *The Sporting News*, 16 Jun. 1953, p. 34.

5. Bo Jackson

1. "Bo Jackson." Wikipedia. http://en.wikipedia.org/wiki/Bo_Jackson.
2. Frank Cooney, "With 40-yd Dash Times, Nothing's Quite Official," Special to *USA Today*, 24 Feb. 2008, http://usatoday30.usatoday.com/sports/football/nfl/2008-02-22-40-yard-dash_N.htm.
3. *You Don't Know Bo*, ESPN special, aired 8 Dec. 2012.
4. Bo Jackson and Dick Schaap, *Bo Knows Bo* (New York: Bantam, 1990), pp. 126–128.
5. Bo Jackson and Dick Schaap, *Bo Knows Bo* (New York: Bantam, 1990), pp. 126–128.
6. Bo Jackson and Dick Schaap, *Bo Knows Bo* (New York: Bantam, 1990), pp. 126–128.
7. *You Don't Know Bo*, ESPN special, aired 8 Dec. 2012.
8. Dave Anderson, "What Bo Didn't Want to Know," *The New York Times*, 1 Mar. 1992.
9. Maurice Weaver, "Pain and Glory," *Ebony*, Aug. 1993.
10. Maurice Weaver, "Pain and Glory," *Ebony*, Aug. 1993.
11. Maurice Weaver, "Pain and Glory," *Ebony*, Aug. 1993.
12. Jackson and Schaap, *Bo Knows Bo*, p. 1.
13. Peggy Beck, "Replacement Joints Not for Elite Athletes," Health and Wellness, http://www4.xpresssites.com/waf.srv/buffalo/buffalo/hw.
14. Peggy Beck, "Replacement Joints Not for Elite Athletes," Health and Wellness, http://www4.xpresssites.com/waf.srv/buffalo/buffalo/hw.

6. Eric Davis

1. Eric Davis with Ralph Wiley, *Born to Play* (New York: Penguin Putnam, 1999), p. 124.
2. Davis, *Born to Play*, p. 192.
3. Davis, *Born to Play*, pp. 194–196.
4. Davis, *Born to Play*, p. 213.
5. Murray Chass, "Ex-A's Employee Cites Schott Racial Remark," *The New York Times*, 26 Nov. 1992.
6. Davis, *Born to Play*, pp. 191–192.
7. Davis, *Born to Play*, p. 224.
8. Davis, *Born to Play*, pp. 228–230.
9. Davis, *Born to Play*, pp. 72–73.
10. Davis, *Born to Play*, pp. 77–89.
11. Davis, *Born to Play*, p. 277.
12. Davis, *Born to Play*, p. 123.

7. Andres Galarraga

1. Richard Justice, "Andres Galarraga Called Best in National League," *Washington Post*, 3 Jul. 1988, http://articles.latimes.com/1988-07-03/sports/sp-8740_1_national-league-leaders.
2. Anthony McCarron, "Putting Up a Brave Front," *New York Daily News*, 12 Oct. 1999, http://articles.nydailynews.com/1999-10-12/news/18115437_1_spring-training-braves-team-national-league-championship-series.
3. Anthony McCarron, "Putting Up a Brave Front," *New York Daily News*, 12 Oct. 1999.
4. Anthony McCarron, "Putting Up a Brave Front," *New York Daily News*, 12 Oct. 1999.
5. Jesse Sanchez, "Andres Galarraga: The Big Cat," MLB.com, 6 Mar. 2005, http://www.serendipityrancher.com/bb-galarraga.htm.
6. Paul Newberry, "Galarraga: Take That," *Tallahassee Democrat*, 23 Apr. 2000.

8. Ted Williams

1. Ted Williams as told to John Underwood, *My Turn at Bat* (New York: Simon & Shuster, 1970), p. 182.
2. Williams, *My Turn at Bat*, p. 182.
3. Williams, *My Turn at Bat*, p. 38.
4. Williams, *My Turn at Bat*, p. 184.
5. Tom Meany, *Baseball's Greatest Players* (New York: Grossett & Dunlap, 1953), p. 280.
6. *The Sporting News*, 14 May 1952, p. 15.
7. *The Sporting News*, 2 Apr. 1952, p. 4.
8. Williams, *My Turn at Bat*, p. 155.
9. Williams, *My Turn at Bat*, p. 161.
10. Williams, *My Turn at Bat*, p. 163.
11. Williams, *My Turn at Bat*, p. 174.
12. Williams, *My Turn at Bat*, p. 181.
13. Williams, *My Turn at Bat*, p. 190.

9. Stan Musial

1. Brad Snyder, *A Well-Paid Slave*, (New York: Viking Press, 2006), p. 53.
2. Peter Golenbock, *The Spirit of St. Louis* (New York: HarperCollins, 2000), p. 432.
3. Stanley Musial and Bob Broeg, *Stan Musial: The Man's Own Story* (New York: Doubleday, 1964), p. 207.
4. Musial and Broeg, *Stan Musial: The Man's Own Story*, p. 212.
5. *The Sporting News*, 1 June 1960, p. 15.
6. *The Sporting News*, 8 June 1960, p. 8.
7. Musial and Broeg, *Stan Musial: The Man's Own Story*, pp. 211–214.
8. Musial and Broeg, *Stan Musial: The Man's Own Story*, pp. 215–216.
9. *The Sporting News*, 22 June 1960, p. 1.
10. Musial and Broeg, *Stan Musial: The Man's Own Story*, p. 221.
11. Musial and Broeg, *Stan Musial: The Man's Own Story*, pp. 222–223.

12. Musial and Broeg, *Stan Musial: The Man's Own Story*, p. 233.
13. Musial and Broeg, *Stan Musial: The Man's Own Story*, p. 233.

10. Grover Cleveland "Pete" Alexander

1. *The Winning Team*, film production by Warner Bros., 1952.
2. *The Sporting News*, 24 June 1926, p. 4.
3. *The Sporting News*, 24 June 1926, p. 4.
4. Meany, *Baseball's Greatest Players*, p. 1.
5. Meany, *Baseball's Greatest Players*, p. 1.
6. Meany, *Baseball's Greatest Players*, p. 1.
7. Meany, *Baseball's Greatest Players*, p. 6.
8. Martin Appel and Burt Goldblatt, *Baseball's Best: The Hall of Fame Gallery* (New York: McGraw-Hill, 1977), pp. 8–10.
9. Fred Lieb, *Baseball As I Have Known It* (New York: Grosset & Dunlap, 1977), pp. 219–221.
10. Meany, *Baseball's Greatest Players*, p. 3.
11. Appel and Goldblatt, *Baseball's Best: The Hall of Fame Gallery*, pp. 8–10.
12. Lieb, *Baseball As I Have Known It*, p. 216.

11. Rabbit Maranville

1. Appel and Goldblatt, *Baseball's Best: The Hall of Fame Gallery*, p. 278.
2. Jack Orr, "Some Bad Boys Who Were Good for the Game," *Baseball Digest*, Jan. 1965, pp. 35–40.
3. *The Sporting News*, 1 July 1926, p. 3.

12. Willie McCovey

1. Mark Armour, "Willie McCovey," SABR Baseball Biography Project, http://sabr.org/bioproj/person/2a692514.
2. *The Sporting News*, 15 Oct. 1977, p. 6.
3. *The Sporting News*, 29 Jan. 1977, p. 41.
4. *The Sporting News*, 20 Jan. 1986, p. 42.

13. Eddie Waitkus

1. Dan Gutman, *Baseball Babylon* (New York: Viking Penguin, 1992), p. 28.
2. Danny Peary, *Cult Baseball Players* (New York: Simon & Schuster, 1990), p. 189.
3. Gutman, *Baseball Babylon*, p. 28.
4. Gutman, *Baseball Babylon*, p. 28.
5. Gutman, *Baseball Babylon*, p. 28.
6. Danny Peary, *We Played the Game* (New York: Hyperion, 1994), p. 94.
7. *The Sporting News*, 29 June 1949, p. 2.
8. *The Sporting News*, 29 June 1949, p. 20.
9. William Marshall, *Baseball's Pivotal Era: 1945–1951* (Lexington: University Press of Kentucky, 1999), p. 366.
10. *The Sporting News*, 13 July 1949, p. 7.
11. "Waitkus, Who Beat Death Rap, Comeback King," *Ellensberg Daily Record*, 10 Nov. 1950, p. 3.
12. John Theodore, *Baseball's Natural* (Carbondale: Southern Illinois University Press, 2002), pp. 73, 108.
13. Peary, *Cult Baseball Players*, p. 189.
14. Peary, *We Played the Game*, p. 273.
15. *The Sporting News*, 22 June 1949, p. 2.
16. *The Sporting News*, 23 Nov. 1949, p. 26.
17. Theodore, *Baseball's Natural*, pp. 73.
18. Peary, *Cult Baseball Players*, p. 190.
19. Theodore, *Baseball's Natural*, p. 90.
20. Peary, *Cult Baseball Players*, p. 190.
21. Peary, *Cult Baseball Players*, p. 190.

14. Tony Conigliaro

1. Robert Rubin, *Up From Despair* (New York: Putnam's, 1971), pp. 59–60.
2. Linkugel and Pappas, *They Tasted Glory*, p. 160.
3. Tim Wendel, "An Ill-Fated Night," *USA Today Baseball Weekly*, Aug 13–19, 1997, pp. 8–11.
4. Wendel, "An Ill-Fated Night," *USA Today Baseball Weekly*, Aug 13–19, 1997, pp. 8–11.
5. Tony Conigliaro with Jack Zanger, *Seeing It Through* (Toronto, ON: Macmillan, 1970), p. 10.
6. Conigliaro, *Seeing It Through*, p. 18.
7. Wendel, "An Ill-Fated Night," *USA Today Baseball Weekly*, pp. 8–11.
8. Conigliaro, *Seeing It Through*, pp. 29, 56.
9. Wendel, "An Ill-Fated Night," *USA Today Baseball Weekly*, pp. 8–11.
10. Conigliaro, *Seeing It Through*, p. 104.
11. Wendel, "An Ill-Fated Night," *USA Today Baseball Weekly*, pp. 8–11.
12. Wendel, "An Ill-Fated Night," *USA Today Baseball Weekly*, pp. 8–11.
13. *The Sporting News*, 31 July 1971, p. 23.
14. *The Sporting News*, 7 Dec. 1974, p. 52.
15. Wendel, "An Ill-Fated Night," *USA Today Baseball Weekly*, pp. 8–11.
16. Wendel, "An Ill-Fated Night," *USA Today Baseball Weekly*, pp. 8–11.

15. Charley Gelbert

1. *Ripley's Believe It or Not*, first series, 26 Mar. 1941.
2. Roy Stockton, "The Cardinals' Forgotten Man," *St. Louis Post Dispatch*, 1935, p. 346.
3. Stockton, "The Cardinals' Forgotten Man," p. 346.
4. *The Sporting News*, 22 Dec. 1932, p. 1.
5. *The Sporting News*, 2 Feb. 1933, p. 1.
6. *The Sporting News*, 6 Apr. 1933, p. 5.
7. Stockton, "The Cardinals' Forgotten Man," p. 346.
8. *The Sporting News*, 30 Nov. 1933, p. 5.

9. *The Sporting News*, 4 Jan. 1934, p. 2.
10. *The Sporting News*, 12 Apr. 1934, p. 3.
11. *The Sporting News*, 10 May 1934, p. 4.
12. *The Sporting News*, 7 June 1934, p. 4.
13. Stockton, "The Cardinals' Forgotten Man," p. 346.

16. Dennis Eckersley

1. *The Sporting News*, 6 Apr. 1987, p. 21.
2. *The Sporting News*, 20 Apr. 1987, p. 16.
3. Terry Pluto, *The Curse of Rocky Colavito* (Cleveland: Gray, 1994), pp. 159–160.
4. Pluto, *The Curse of Rocky Colavito*, p. 166.
5. Pluto, *The Curse of Rocky Colavito*, pp. 165–168.
6. Joe Wancho, "Dennis Eckersley," SABR Baseball Biography Project, http://sabr.org/bioproj/person/98aaf620.
7. Wancho, "Dennis Eckersley."
8. Wancho, "Dennis Eckersley."
9. Wancho, "Dennis Eckersley."
10. Pluto, *The Curse of Rocky Colavito*, pp. 173–174.
11. *The Sporting News*, 6 Apr. 1987, p. 21, and 20 Apr. 1987, p. 16.
12. Mike Puma, "Saving the Best for Last," ESPN Classic, http://www.espn.go.com/classic/biography/s/Eckersley_Dennis.html.
13. *The Sporting News*, 1 June 1987, p. 21.
14. Wancho, "Dennis Eckersley."
15. Dennis Eckersley, "Lives Changed Forever," Boston Health Care for the Homeless Program, http://bhchp.org/documents/Eckersley.pdf.
16. Wancho, "Dennis Eckersley."
17. Wancho, "Dennis Eckersley."
18. Wancho, "Dennis Eckersley."
19. *The Sporting News*, 23 May 1988, p. 9.

17. Red Schoendienst

1. Al Hirshberg, *The Man Who Fought Back* (New York: Julian Messner, 1961), pp. 30–31.
2. Hirshberg, *The Man Who Fought Back*, pp. 32–33.
3. Hirshberg, *The Man Who Fought Back*, pp. 124–126.
4. Hirshberg, *The Man Who Fought Back*, pp. 141–144.
5. Hirshberg, *The Man Who Fought Back*, pp. 145–146.
6. Hirshberg, *The Man Who Fought Back*, p. 174.
7. Hirshberg, *The Man Who Fought Back*, p. 175.
8. Hirshberg, *The Man Who Fought Back*, pp. 181–182.
9. Hirshberg, *The Man Who Fought Back*, p. 168.

18. Rico Carty

1. *The Sporting News*, 6 June 1964, p. 11.
2. *The Sporting News*, 6 June 1964, p. 11.

3. *The Sporting News*, 1 July 1967, p. 12.
4. *The Sporting News*, 24 Feb. 1968, p. 28.
5. *The Sporting News*, 13 Apr. 1968, p. 38.
6. *The Sporting News*, 20 Apr. 1968, p. 15.
7. *The Sporting News*, 26 Dec. 1970, p. 41.
8. *The Sporting News*, 11 Aug. 1973, p. 18.
9. *The Sporting News*, 23 Feb. 1980, p. 34.
10. *The Sporting News*, 19 Apr. 1980, p. 33.

19. Dave Dravecky

1. Dave Dravecky with Tim Stafford, *Comeback* (San Francisco: Zondervan Books, 1990), pp. 97–98.
2. Dravecky, *Comeback*, pp. 34–36.
3. Dravecky, *Comeback*, pp. 46–48.
4. Dravecky, *Comeback*, pp. 55–60.
5. Dravecky, *Comeback*, pp. 93–97.
6. Dravecky, *Comeback*, pp. 93–97.
7. Dravecky, *Comeback*, p. 111.
8. Dravecky, *Comeback*, pp. 137–138.
9. Dravecky, *Comeback*, p. 141.
10. Dravecky, *Comeback*, p. 181.
11. Dravecky, *Comeback*, p. 183.
12. Dravecky, *Comeback*, p. 197.
13. Dravecky, *Comeback*, p. 248.
14. Dravecky, *Comeback*, p. 248.

20. Jack Quinn

1. *The Sporting News*, 12 Dec. 1912, p. 3.
2. *The Sporting News*, 15 Nov. 1928, p. 3.
3. Charles F. Faber, "Jack Quinn," SABR Baseball Biography Project, http://sabr.org/bioproj/person/cf88d73c.
4. *The Sporting News*, 15 Jan. 1931, p. 7.
5. Faber, "Jack Quinn," SABR Baseball Biography Project.
6. *The Sporting News*, 25 Apr. 1946, p. 20.
7. H.G. Salinger, "John Picus Quinn, the Perennial Spitballer," (The Umpire-HOF file fragment).
8. "The Oldest Veteran in the Major Leagues," *Baseball Magazine*, Sep. 1930, http://www.stevesteinberg.net/baseball_history/baseball_personalities/JohnPicusQuinn_OldestVeteran.asp.
9. HOF file press release document, 24 Feb. 1929.
10. Jonathan Frazier Light, *The Cultural Encyclopedia of Baseball* (Jefferson, NC: McFarland, 1997), p. 539.
11. *The Sporting News*, 17 May 1934, p. 1.
12. *The Sporting News*, 4 Apr. 1935, p. 3.
13. *The Sporting News*, 15 Feb. 1950, p. 5.

21. John Hiller

1. *The Sporting News*, 6 Mar. 1971, pp. 31–32.
2. Joe Falls, "John Hiller's Heart is in the Right Place," *Sport*, Apr. 1974, pp. 109–114.
3. Joe Falls, "John Hiller's Heart is in the Right Place," *Sport*, Apr. 1974, pp. 109–114.

4. Gene Shalit, "Hiller's Heart," *Sport*, Sep. 1973, pp. 10–12.
5. *The Sporting News*, 6 Mar. 1971, pp. 31–32.
6. *The Sporting News*, 24 Apr. 1971, p. 27.
7. *The Sporting News*, 22 May 1971, p. 9.
8. Shalit, "Hiller's Heart," *Sport*, pp. 10–12.
9. Falls, "John Hiller's Heart Is in the Right Place," *Sport*, pp. 109–114.
10. Falls, "John Hiller's Heart Is in the Right Place," *Sport*, pp. 109–114.
11. Shalit, "Hiller's Heart," *Sport*, pp. 10–12.

22. Steve Howe

1. Gutman, *Baseball Babylon*, p. 118.
2. Steve Howe with Jim Greenfield, *Between the Lines* (Grand Rapids, MI: Masters Press, 1989), pp. 23–28, 38–41.
3. Howe, *Between the Lines*, pp. 128–129.
4. Howe, *Between the Lines*, pp. 130–131.
5. Howe, *Between the Lines*, pp. 153–157.
6. Howe, *Between the Lines*, p. 11.
7. Howe, *Between the Lines*, p. 176.
8. Howe, *Between the Lines*, p. 184.
9. Howe, *Between the Lines*, p. 192.
10. Howe, *Between the Lines*, pp. 219–220.
11. John Dewan and Don Zminda, *The Scouting Report: 1994* (New York: HarperPerennial, 1994), p. 252.
12. "Total Baseball," Associated Press, 10 Dec. 1999, http:www.totalbaseball.com/team/news/991209.991209.0467.html.
13. "Steve Howe Had Drugs in His System When He Died," Yahoo! Sports, 28 June 2006, http://sports.yahoo.com/mlb/news?slug=howetoxicology.
14. Kevin Nelson, *Baseball's Even Greater Insults* (New York: Fireside Books, 1993), p. 22.
15. Howe, *Between the Lines*, p. 65.

23. George McQuinn

1. *The Sporting News*, 22 Jan. 1947, p. 10.
2. George Vass, "Seven Comeback Candidates for 1975," *Baseball Digest*, Jan. 1975, p. 42.
3. George Vass, "Seven Comeback Candidates for 1975," *Baseball Digest*, Jan. 1975, p. 42.
4. *The Sporting News*, 11 June 1947, p. 5.
5. Arthur O.W. Anderson, "Another Veteran Rookie—George McQuinn," *Baseball Magazine*, July 1938, p. 357.
6. Ronald A. Mayer, *1937 Newark Bears* (East Hanover, NJ: Vintage Press, 1985), p. 172.
7. *The Sporting News*, 23 Apr. 1947, p. 6.
8. *The Sporting News*, 23 Apr. 1947, p. 6.
9. *The Sporting News*, 23 Apr. 1947, p. 6.
10. *The Sporting News*, 1 Oct. 1952, p. 60.

24. Luis Tiant

1. Luis Tiant and Joe Fitzgerald, *El Tiant* (New York: Doubleday, 1976), p. 109.
2. Tiant and Fitzgerald, *El Tiant*, pp. 70–72.
3. Tiant and Fitzgerald, *El Tiant*, pp. 78–82.
4. Tiant and Fitzgerald, *El Tiant*, pp. 88–91.
5. Tiant and Fitzgerald, *El Tiant*, p. 113.
6. *The Lost Son of Havana* (5-Hole Productions, Hock Films, NY, 2009).
7. Peary, *Cult Baseball Players*, p. 285
8. Tiant and Fitzgerald, *El Tiant*, p. 198.

25. Robin Roberts

1. Bob Stewart, "The Comebacks—Robin Roberts and Stan Musial," *Baseball's Greatest Players Today* (New York: Franklin Watts, 1963), p. 144.
2. *The Sporting News*, 21 July 1962, pp. 5–6.
3. Stewart, "The Comebacks—Robin Roberts and Stan Musial," *Baseball's Greatest Players Today*, pp. 144–145.
4. Donald Honig, *Baseball Between the Lines* (Lincoln: University of Nebraska Press, 1976), pp. 242–246.
5. *The Sporting News*, 21 July 1962, pp. 5–6.
6. *The Sporting News*, 21 July 1962, pp. 5–6.
7. *The Sporting News*, 21 July 1962, pp. 5–6.
8. *The Sporting News*, 21 July 1962, pp. 5–6.
9. Honig, *Baseball Between the Lines*, p. 245.

26. Babe Adams

1. Pete Cava and Paul Sandin, "The First Babe," *Sports Collectors Digest*, 7 Apr. 1995, pp. 167–168.
2. *The Sporting News*, 10 Aug. 1916, p. 3.
3. Brian Stevens, "Babe Adams," SABR Baseball Biography Project, http://sabr.org/bioproj/person/617bd0ad.
4. Harry Grayson, *They Played the Game* (New York: Barnes, 1945), p. 101.
5. Cava and Sandin, "The First Babe," *Sports Collectors Digest*, pp. 167–168.
6. David Pietrusza, Matthew Silverman, and Michael Gershman, *Baseball: The Biographical Encyclopedia* (New York: Sports Illustrated, 2000), p. 5.
7. *The Sporting News*, 23 July 1914, p. 3.
8. *The Sporting News*, 10 Aug. 1916, p. 3.
9. Cava and Sandin, "The First Babe," *Sports Collectors Digest*, pp. 167–168.
10. Cava and Sandin, "The First Babe," *Sports Collectors Digest*, pp. 167–168.
11. Cava and Sandin, "The First Babe," *Sports Collectors Digest*, pp. 167–168.
12. Cava and Sandin, "The First Babe," *Sports Collectors Digest*, pp. 167–168.
13. Cava and Sandin, "The First Babe," *Sports Collectors Digest*, pp. 167–168.
14. Pietrusza, Silverman, and Gershman, *Baseball: The Biographical Encyclopedia*, p. 6.

15. Cava and Sandin, "The First Babe," *Sports Collectors Digest*, pp. 167–168.
16. Cava and Sandin, "The First Babe," *Sports Collectors Digest*, pp. 167–168.
17. Pietrusza, Silverman, and Gershman, *Baseball: The Biographical Encyclopedia*, p. 6.

27. Mark Koenig

1. Charles C. Alexander, *Rogers Hornsby* (New York: Holt, 1995), p. 176.
2. Charles C. Alexander, *Rogers Hornsby* (New York: Holt, 1995), p. 176.
3. Daniel Okrent and Steve Wulf, *Baseball Anecdotes* (New York: Oxford University Press, 1989), p. 125.
4. Joe Reichler, and Ben Olan, *Baseball's Unforgettable Games* (New York: Ronald Press, 1960), p. 70.
5. Light, *The Cultural Encyclopedia of Baseball*, p. 8.

28. Orlando Hernandez

1. *The Sporting News*, 27 Sep. 2004, p. 26.
2. Baseball Reference.com, "Orlando Hernandez," http://www.baseball-reference.com/bullpen/Orlando_Hernandez.
3. Steve Fainaru and Ray Sanchez, *The Duke of Havana* (New York: Villard Books, 2001), pp. xx, 4.
4. Fainaru and Sanchez, *The Duke of Havana*, p. xxiii.
5. Fainaru and Sanchez, *The Duke of Havana*, pp. 155–159.
6. Fainaru and Sanchez, *The Duke of Havana*, p. xxiii.
7. Fainaru and Sanchez, *The Duke of Havana*, pp. 206–207.
8. Fainaru and Sanchez, *The Duke of Havana*, pp. 206–207.
9. *The Sporting News*, 27 Sep. 2004, p. 26.
10. Seth Livingstone, "Hernandez Energizes Weary Yanks," *USA Today Sports Weekly*, Sep. 15–21, 2004, pp. 31–32.
11. Seth Livingstone, "Hernandez Energizes Weary Yanks," *USA Today Sports Weekly*, Sep. 15–21, 2004, pp. 31–32.

29. Sal Maglie

1. John R. Tunis, *Schoolboy Johnson* (New York: Morrow, 1958).
2. "Maglie, Ex-Nemesis of Dodgers, Bought by Brooks from Indians," *The New York Times*, 16 May 1956, p. 4.
3. Milton J. Shapiro, *The Sal Maglie Story* (New York: Messner, 1957), pp. 165–166.
4. Peter Golenbock, *Bums* (New York: Putnam's, 1984), p. 411.
5. *The Sporting News*, 1 Feb. 1956, p. 10.
6. Golenbock, *Bums*, pp. 411–415.
7. *The Sporting News*, 22 Feb. 1956, p. 9.
8. *The Sporting News*, 16 May 1956, p. 12.
9. Golenbock, *Bums*, p. 411.
10. Golenbock, *Bums*, p. 415.
11. Shapiro, *The Sal Maglie Story*, p. 44.
12. Shapiro, *The Sal Maglie Story*, p. 58.
13. Shapiro, *The Sal Maglie Story*, pp. 68–70.

30. Jimmie Wilson

1. John R. Tunis, *The Kid from Tomkinsville* (New York: Harcourt, Brace, 1940).
2. *The Sporting News*, 17 Aug. 1939, p. 1.
3. Reichler and Olan, *Baseball's Unforgettable Games*, pp. 124–127.
4. William Nack, "The Razor's Edge," *Sports Illustrated*, May 6, 1991, pp. 55–58.
5. *The Sporting News*, 17 Oct. 1940, p. 1.
6. John Kieran, "Red Is the Winning Color," *The New York Times*, 9 Oct. 1940.
7. Donald Honig, *Baseball When the Grass Was Real* (Lincoln: University of Nebraska Press, 1975), p. 97.
8. Donald Honig, *Baseball When the Grass Was Real* (Lincoln: University of Nebraska Press, 1975), p. 97.
9. Donald Honig, *Baseball When the Grass Was Real* (Lincoln: University of Nebraska Press, 1975), p. 97.
10. John Durant, *Highlights of the World Series* (New York: Hastings House, 1971), p. 101.
11. Henry McLemore, "Jimmy Wilson" *Sports Illustrated*, Feb. 1941, p. 149.
12. Red Smith, *To Absent Friends* (New York: Atheneum, 1982), pp. 101–103.
13. Kieran, "Red Is the Winning Color," *The New York Times*, 9 Oct. 1940.

31. Satchel Paige

1. Donald Dewey and Nicholas Acocella, *The Biographical History of Baseball* (Chicago: Triumph Books, 2002), p. 320.
2. James A. Riley, *The Biographical History of the Negro Leagues* (New York: Carroll & Graf, 1994), p. 600.
3. *The Sporting News*, 9 July 1952, p. 25.
4. Shatzkin and Charlton, *The Ballplayers*, p. 840.
5. A.S. "Doc" Young, *Great Negro Baseball Stars* (New York: Barnes, 1953), p. 78.
6. *The Sporting News*, 14 July 1948, p. 8.
7. LeRoy "Satchel" Paige as told to David Lipman, *Maybe I'll Pitch Forever* (Lincoln: University of Nebraska Press, 1993), pp. 229–230.
8. Alexander, *Rogers Hornsby*, p. 258.
9. Alexander, *Rogers Hornsby*, p. 261.
10. Paige, *Maybe I'll Pitch Forever*, p. 264.
11. Bill Veeck and Ed Linn, *Veeck—as in Wreck* (New York: Bantam Books, 1962), pp. 350–351.

12. Young, *Great Negro Baseball Stars*, p. 90.
13. David Gallen, *The Baseball Chronicles* (New York: Carroll & Graf, 1991), p. 225.

32. Darryl Strawberry and Dwight "Doc" Gooden

1. "A Sad Chapter for Strawberry," *Los Angeles Times*, 5 Feb. 1990, http://articles.latimes.com/1990-02-05/sports/sp-185_1_strawberry.-home.
2. Bob Klapisch, *High and Tight* (New York: Villard Books, 1996), p. 89.
3. Darryl Strawberry Chronology," CBS SportsLine, 2 Mar. 2000, wysiwyg://75/http://cbs.sportsline ... ll/bol/news/mar00/straw030200.html.
4. Klapisch, *High and Tight*, pp. 104–108.
5. "Darryl Strawberry Chronology," CBS Sports-Line.
6. "A Sad Chapter for Strawberry," *Los Angeles Times*, 5 Feb. 1990.
7. "Darryl Strawberry Chronology," CBS Sports-Line.
8. Klapisch, *High and Tight*, pp. 132–133.
9. Klapisch, *High and Tight*, pp. 132–133.
10. "Darryl Strawberry Chronology," CBS Sports-Line.
11. "Darryl Strawberry Chronology," CBS Sports-Line.
12. Bob Klapisch, *Doc Was Simply Masterful*, ESPN Special, 31 Dec. 1999, http://espn.go.com/mlb/columns/klapisch_bob/254403.html.
13. "Darryl Strawberry Chronology," CBS Sports-Line
14. "Darryl Strawberry Chronology," CBS Sports-Line.
15. "Darryl Strawberry Chronology," CBS Sports-Line.
16. "Darryl Strawberry Chronology," CBS Sports-Line.
17. *The Sporting News*, 11 Sep. 2000, http://www.sportingnews.com/baseball/articles/20000911/258178.html.
18. Vickie Charachere, "Strawberry Tells Court of Death Wish," TotalSports.net, 3 Nov. 2000, wysiwyg://8/http://www.totalbaseball.com/news/20001103/bbo/001103.2043.html.
19. Wikipedia, "Darryl Strawberry," http://en.wikipedia.org/wiki/Darryl_Strawberry.
20. Wikipedia, "Dwight Gooden," http://en.wikipedia.org/wiki/Dwight_Gooden.
21. Wikipedia, "Dwight Gooden," http://en.wikipedia.org/wiki/Dwight_Gooden.

33. Dennis Martinez

1. Bruce Newman, "Return of the Native," *Sports Illustrated*, 30 Dec. 1991, http://sportsillustrated.cnn.com/vault/article/magazine/MAG1140050/index.htm.
2. Newman, "Return of the Native," *Sports Illustrated*.
3. Newman, "Return of the Native," *Sports Illustrated*.
4. Newman, "Return of the Native," *Sports Illustrated*.
5. Newman, "Return of the Native," *Sports Illustrated*.
6. Newman, "Return of the Native," *Sports Illustrated*.
7. Newman, "Return of the Native," *Sports Illustrated*.
8. Newman, "Return of the Native," *Sports Illustrated*.
9. Newman, "Return of the Native," *Sports Illustrated*.
10. Newman, "Return of the Native," *Sports Illustrated*.
11. Newman, "Return of the Native," *Sports Illustrated*.
12. Newman, "Return of the Native," *Sports Illustrated*.
13. Newman, "Return of the Native," *Sports Illustrated*.
14. Newman, "Return of the Native," *Sports Illustrated*.

34. Fernando Valenzuela

1. *The Sporting News*, 8 Apr. 1991, p. 18.
2. Shatzkin and Charlton, *The Ballplayers*, p. 1112.
3. Pietrusza, Silverman, and Gershman, *Baseball: The Biographical Encyclopedia*, pp. 1156–1157.
4. Shatzkin and Charlton, *The Ballplayers*, p. 1112.
5. Pietrusza, Silverman, and Gershman, *Baseball: The Biographical Encyclopedia*, pp. 1156–1157.
6. Pietrusza, Silverman, and Gershman, *Baseball: The Biographical Encyclopedia*, pp. 1156–1157.
7. *The Sporting News*, 24 June 1991, p. 20; 1 July 1991, p. 19.
8. Baseball-Refernce.com, "Fernando Valenzuela" http://www.baseball-reference.com/bullpen/Fernando_Valenzuela.
9. Dewan and Zminda, *The Scouting Report: 1994*, p. 41.
10. Tom Pedulla, "Valenzuela Rights Career: Lefthanders Firm Faith Still Reaps Rewards," *USA Today*, 5 Sep. 1996, http://pqasb.pqarchiver.com/USAToday/main ... le-002%261D%3dUSAT%26FMT%3dFT%26FMTS%3dFT.
11. Tom Pedulla, "Valenzuela Rights Career: Lefthanders Firm Faith Still Reaps Rewards" *USA Today*, 5 Sep. 1996, http://pqasb.pqarchiver.com/USAToday/main ... le-002%261D%3dUSAT%26FMT%3dFT%26FMTS%3dFT.
12. *The Sporting News*, 15, Feb. 1999; 24 June 1991, p. 20
13. Eloy O. Aguilar, "Valenzuela Makes His Pitch in Mexico" *USA Today*, 5 Feb. 2001, wysiwyg://3http://www.usatoday.co.../stories/2001–02–03-valenzuela.htm.
14. "Valenzuela, Son to Play Together in Mexican Pacific League" CBS SportsLine.com, 17 Oct. 2006, http://www.cbssports.com/mlb/story/9735881/valenzuela-son-to-play-together-in-mexican-pacific-league.
15. "Fernando Valenzuela Pitching in Mexico" Vin Scully Is My Homeboy, http://www.vinscullyismyhomeboy.com/2011/03/fernando-valenzuela-pitching-in-mexico.html.

35. Julio Franco

1. Pietrusza, Silverman, and Gershman, *Baseball: The Biographical Encyclopedia*, p. 379.
2. *The Sporting News*, 22, Oct. 2001, p. 9.
3. Baseball-Refernce.com, "Julio Franco," http://www.baseball-reference.com/bullpen/Julio_Franco.
4. Baseball-Refernce.com, "Julio Franco," http://www.baseball-reference.com/bullpen/Julio_Franco.

36. Johnny Lindell

1. Gene Karst and Martin J. Jones, Jr., *Who's Who in Professional Baseball* (New York: Arlington House, 1973), p. 563–564.
2. Shatzkin and Charlton, *The Ballplayers*, p. 623.
3. *The Sporting News*, 5 Apr. 1945, p. 8.
4. *The Sporting News*, 15 Apr. 1953, p. 8.
5. *The Sporting News*, 19 May 1954, p. 11.
6. *The Sporting News*, 15 Apr. 1953, p. 8.

37. Fred Mitchell

1. Bill Nowlin, "Fred Mitchell," SABR Baseball Biography Project, http://sabr.org/bioproj/person/67676a31.
2. Bill Nowlin, "Fred Mitchell," SABR Baseball Biography Project.
3. Bill Nowlin, "Fred Mitchell," SABR Baseball Biography Project.
4. Bill Nowlin, "Fred Mitchell," SABR Baseball Biography Project.
5. Bill Nowlin, "Fred Mitchell," SABR Baseball Biography Project.
6. Bill Nowlin, "Fred Mitchell," SABR Baseball Biography Project.
7. Bill Nowlin, "Fred Mitchell," SABR Baseball Biography Project.
8. Bill Nowlin, "Fred Mitchell," SABR Baseball Biography Project.
9. Bill Nowlin, "Fred Mitchell," SABR Baseball Biography Project.
10. *The Sporting News*, 6 Oct. 1948, p. 5.

38. Tony Cuccinello

1. Rich Wescott, *Diamond Greats* (Westport, CT: Meckler, 1988), pp. 97–98.
2. Wescott, *Diamond Greats*, p. 96.
3. Wescott, *Diamond Greats*, pp. 97–98.
4. *The Sporting News*, 18 July 1940, pp. 1–2.
5. *The Sporting News*, 8 Aug. 1940, p. 1.
6. Barb Mantegani, "Tony Cuccinello," SABR Baseball Biography Project, http://sabr.org/bioproj/person/be5d770b.
7. Barb Mantegani, "Tony Cuccinello," SABR Baseball Biography Project.
8. B. Chastain, "This Was the Closest Race Ever for a Batting Title," *Baseball Digest* 52 (Dec. 1993), p. 63.
9. B. Chastain, "This Was the Closest Race Ever for a Batting Title," *Baseball Digest* 52 (Dec. 1993), p. 63.
10. Wescott, *Diamond Greats*, p. 98.
11. Dewey and Acocella, *The Biographical History of Baseball*, p. 89.
12. Shatzkin and Charlton, *The Ballplayers*, p. 241.
13. Mantegani, "Tony Cuccinello," SABR Baseball Biography Project.
14. Baseball-Refernce.com, "Tony Cuccinello," http://www.baseball-reference.com/bullpen/Tony_Cuccinello.
15. Bruce Nash and Allan Zullo, *The Baseball Hall of Shame* (New York: Pocket Books, 1985), pp. 134–135.

39. Van Lingle Mungo

1. *The Sporting News*, 3 Feb. 1944, p. 1.
2. Herman Helms, "The Mungo-Hemingway Duel," *The State*, July 29, 1973.
3. Robert McG. Thomas, Jr., "Van Lingle Mungo, 73, Dies; Colorful Pitcher for Dodgers," *The New York Times*, 14 Feb. 1985.
4. *The Sporting News*, 18 June 1936, p. 4.
5. Ira Smith, *Baseball's Famous Pitchers* (New York: Barnes, 1954), p. 242.
6. Pete Coutros, "Greatest Lovers in All Baseball," *New York Post*, 27 July 1990, p. 60.
7. *The Sporting News*, 26 Oct., 1944, p. 14.
8. *The Sporting News*, 26 Oct., 1944, p. 14.
9. *The Sporting News*, 8 Oct. 1936, p. 7.
10. *The Sporting News*, 29 May 1937, p. 1.
11. *The Sporting News*, 22 July 1937, p. 3.
12. *The Sporting News*, 22 July 1937, p. 3.
13. *The Sporting News*, 29 July 1937, p. 2.
14. *The Sporting News*, 2 Sep. 1937, p. 1.
15. *The Sporting News*, 25 Nov. 1937, p. 1.
16. *The Sporting News*, 21 Oct. 1937, p. 7.
17. *The Sporting News*, 3 Feb. 1938, p. 1.
18. *The Sporting News*, 23 Nov. 1939, p. 3.
19. Creamer, *Baseball in 1941*, pp. 113–115.
20. Creamer, *Baseball in 1941*, pp. 113–115.
21. Creamer, *Baseball in 1941*, pp. 113–115.
22. Creamer, *Baseball in 1941*, pp. 113–115.
23. *The Sporting News*, 26 Oct. 1944, p. 14.
24. "Van Lingle Mungo, Pitcher in '30s–'40s," *Philadelphia Inquirer*, 14 Feb. 1985, p. 3-C.
25. *The Sporting News*, 18 Apr. 1946, p. 11.
26. *The Sporting News*, 4 Sep. 1946, p. 33.
27. David Frishberg, "Van Lingle Mungo," song, published 1970.

Bibliography

Books

Alexander, Charles C. *Rogers Hornsby*. New York: Holt, 1995.

Appel, Martin, and Burt Goldblatt. *Baseball's Best: The Hall of Fame Gallery*. New York: McGraw-Hill, 1977.

Boswell, Thomas. *The Heart of the Order*. New York: Viking Penguin, 1989.

Carmichael, John. "The Chicago White Sox." In *The American League*, edited by Ed Fitzgerald. New York: Grosset & Dunlap, 1959.

Conigliaro, Tony, with Jack Zanger. *Seeing It Through*. Toronto, ON: Macmillan, 1970.

Conner, Floyd. *Baseball's Most Wanted*. Washington, DC: Brassey's, 2000.

Costello, James, and Michael Santa Maria. *In the Shadows of the Diamond*. Dubuque, IA: Elysian Fields Press.

Creamer, Robert. *Baseball in 1941*. New York: Penguin, 1991.

Davis, Eric, with Ralph Wiley. *Born to Play*. New York: Penguin Putnam, 1999.

Dewan, John, and Don Zminda. *The Scouting Report: 1994*. New York: HarperPerennial, 1994.

Dewey, Donald, and Nicholas Acocella. *The Biographical History of Baseball*. Chicago: Triumph Books, 2002.

Dravecky, Dave, with Tim Stafford. *Comeback*. San Francisco: Zondervan Books, 1990.

Durant, John. *Highlights of the World Series*. New York: Hastings House, 1971.

Fainaru, Steve, and Ray Sanchez. *The Duke of Havana*. New York: Villard Books, 2001.

Gallen, David. *The Baseball Chronicles*. New York: Carroll & Graf, 1991.

Gilbert, Bill. *They Also Served*. New York: Crown, 1992.

Goldstein, Richard. *Spartan Seasons*. New York: Macmillan, 1980.

Golenbock, Peter. *Bums*. New York: Putnam's, 1984.

_____. *The Spirit of St. Louis*. New York: HarperCollins, 2000.

Grayson, Harry. *They Played the Game*. New York: A.S. Barnes, 1945, p. 101.

Greenberg, Hank, with Ira Berkow. *Hank Greenberg: The Story of My Life*. Chicago: Triumph Books, 2001.

Gutman, Dan. *Baseball Babylon*. New York: Viking Penguin, 1992.

Hirshberg, Al. *The Man Who Fought Back*. New York: Messner, 1961.

Hodges, Russ. *Baseball Complete*. New York: Grosset & Dunlap, 1952.

Honig, Donald. *Baseball America*. New York: Barnes & Noble Books, 1997.

_____. *Baseball Between the Lines*. Lincoln: University of Nebraska Press, 1976.

_____. *Baseball When the Grass was Real*. Lincoln: University of Nebraska Press, 1975.

Howe, Steve, with Jim Greenfield. *Between the Lines*. Grand Rapids, MI: Masters Press, 1989.

Ivor-Campbell, Fredrick. *Baseball's First Stars*. Cleveland: SABR, 1996.

Jackson, Bo, and Dick Schaap. *Bo Knows Bo*. New York: Bantam, 1990.

James, Bill. *Historical Baseball Abstract*. New York: Villiard Books, 1988.

_____. *The New Bill James Historical Baseball Abstract*. New York: Simon & Schuster, 2001.

_____. *1984 Bill James Baseball Abstract*. New York: Ballantine Books, 1984.

John, Tommy, with Dan Valencia. *T. J.: My 26 Years in Baseball*. New York: Bantam, 1991.

Karst, Gene, and Martin J. Jones, Jr. *Who's Who in Professional Baseball*. New York: Arlington House, 1973.

Klapisch, Bob. *High and Tight*. New York: Villard Books, 1996.

Lieb, Fred. *Baseball As I Have Known It*. New York: Grosset & Dunlap, 1977.

Light, Jonathan Frazier. *The Cultural Encyclopedia of Baseball*. Jefferson, NC: McFarland, 1997.

Lindberg, Richard. *Who's on Third?* South Bend, IN: Icarus Press, 1983.

Linkugel, Wil A., and Edward J. Pappas. *They Tasted Glory*. Jefferson, NC: McFarland, 1998.

Marshall, William. *Baseball's Pivotal Era: 1945–1951*. Lexington: University Press of Kentucky, 1999.

Mayer, Ronald A. *1937 Newark Bears*. East Hanover, NJ: Vintage Press, 1985.

Mead, William B. *The 10 Worst Years of Baseball*. New York: Van Nostrand, Reinhold, 1978.

Meany, Tom. *Baseball's Greatest Players*. New York: Grosset & Dunlap, 1953.

Murdock, Eugene. *Baseball Players and Their Times*. Westport, CT: Meckler, 1991.

Musial, Stanley, and Bob Broeg. *Stan Musial: The Man's Own Story*. New York: Doubleday, 1964.

Nash, Bruce, and Allan Zullo. *The Baseball Hall of Shame*. New York: Pocket Books, 1985.

Nelson, Kevin. *Baseball's Even Greater Insults*. New York: Fireside Books, 1993.

Okrent, Daniel, and Steve Wulf. *Baseball Anecdotes*. New York: Oxford University Press, 1989.

Paige, LeRoy "Satchel," as told to David Lipman. *Maybe I'll Pitch Forever*. Lincoln: University of Nebraska Press, 1993.

Peary, Danny. *Cult Baseball Players*. New York: Simon & Schuster, 1990.

_____. *We Played the Game*. New York: Hyperion, 1994.

Pietrusza, David, Matthew Silverman, and Michael Gershman. *Baseball: The Biographical Encyclopedia*. New York: Sports Illustrated, 2000.

Pluto, Terry. *The Curse of Rocky Colavito*. Cleveland: Gray, 1994.

Reichler, Joe, and Ben Olan. *Baseball's Unforgettable Games*. New York: Ronald Press, 1960.

Riley, James A. *The Biographical History of the Negro Leagues*. New York: Carroll & Graf, 1994.

Ritter, Lawrence S. *The Glory of Their Times*. New York: Quill, William Morrow, 1966.

Rubin, Robert. *Up from Despair*. New York: Putnam's, 1971.

Salin, Tony. *Baseball's Forgotten Heroes*. New York: Masters Press, 1999.

Shapiro, Milton J. *The Sal Maglie Story*. New York: Messner, 1957.

Shatzkin, Mike, and Jim Charlton. *The Ballplayers: Baseball's Ultimate Biographical Reference*. New York: Arbor House, 1990.

Smith, Ira. *Baseball's Famous Pitchers*. New York: Barnes, 1954.

Smith, Red. *To Absent Friends*. New York: Atheneum, 1982.

Snyder, Brad. *A Well-Paid Slave*. New York: Viking Press, 2006.

Sowell, Mike. *The Pitch That Killed*. New York: Macmillan, 1989.

Theodore, John. *Baseball's Natural*. Carbondale: Southern Illinois University Press, 2002.

Tiant, Luis, and Joe Fitzgerald. *El Tiant*. New York: Doubleday, 1976.

Tunis, John R. *The Kid from Tomkinsville*. New York: Harcourt, Brace, 1940.

Veeck, Bill, and Ed Linn. *Veeck—as in Wreck*. New York: Bantam Books, 1962.

Wescott, Rich. *Diamond Greats*. Westport, CT: Meckler, 1988.

Wilbert, Warren N. *Rookies Rated*. Jefferson, NC: McFarland, 2000.

Williams, Ted, as told to John Underwood. *My Turn at Bat*. New York: Simon & Shuster, 1970.

Young, A.S. "Doc." *Great Negro Baseball Stars*. New York: Barnes, 1953.

Articles, Credited

Aguilar, Eloy O. "Valenzuela Makes His Pitch in Mexico." *USA Today*, 5 Feb. 2001, wysiwyg://3http://www.usatoday.co.../stories/2001-02-03-valenzuela.htm.

Anderson, Arthur O.W. "Another Veteran Rookie—George McQuinn." *Baseball Magazine*, July 1938, p. 357.

Anderson, Dave. "What Bo Didn't Want to Know." *The New York Times*, 1 Mar. 1992.

Beck, Peggy. "Replacement Joints Not for Elite Athletes." Health and Wellness, http://www4.xpresssites.com/waf.srv/buffalo/buffalo/hw.

Cava, Pete, and Paul Sandin. "The First Babe." *Sports Collectors Digest*, 7 Apr. 1995.

Charachere, Vickie. "Strawberry Tells Court of Death Wish." TOTALSPORTS.NET, 3 Nov. 2000, wysiwyg://8/http://www.totalbaseball.com/news/20001103/bbo/001103.2043.html.

Chass, Murray. "Ex-A's Employee Cites Schott Racial Remark." *The New York Times*, 26 Nov. 1992.

Chastain, B. "This Was the Closest Race Ever for a Batting Title." *Baseball Digest* 52 (Dec. 1993), p. 63.

Cooney, Frank. "With 40-Yd Dash Times, Nothing's Quite Official." Special to *USA Today*, 24 Feb. 2008, http://usatoday30.usatoday.com/sports/football/nfl/2008-02-22-40-yard-dash_N.htm.

Coutros, Pete. "Greatest Lovers in All Baseball." *New York Post*, 27 July 1990, p. 60.

Eckersley, Dennis. "Lives Changed Forever." Boston Health Care for the Homeless Program, http://bhchp.org/documents/Eckersley.pdf.

Falls, Joe. "John Hiller's Heart Is in the Right Place." *Sport*, Apr. 1974, pp. 109–114.

Helms, Herman. "The Mungo-Hemingway Duel." *The State*, July 29, 1973.

Horgan, Tim. "Let's Clear the Air About Smoky Joe." *Boston Herald American*, 25 Apr. 1982, p. 69.

Justice, Richard. "Andres Galarraga Called Best in National League." *Washington Post*, 3 Jul. 1988, http://articles.latimes.com/1988-07-03/sports/sp-8740_1_national-league-leaders.

Klapisch, Bob. "Doc Was Simply Masterful." ESPN Special, 31 Dec. 1999, http://espn.go.com/mlb/columns/klapisch_bob/254403.html.

Kieran, John. "Red Is the Winning Color." *The New York Times*, 9 Oct. 1940.
Livingstone, Seth. "Hernandez Energizes Weary Yanks." *USA Today Sports Weekly*, 15–21 Sep. 2004, pp. 31–32.
_____. "The Top 100 Things That Impacted Baseball in the 20th Century." *USA Today Baseball Weekly*, 5–11 Jan. 2000.
McCarron, Anthony. "Putting Up a Brave Front." *New York Daily News*, 12 Oct. 1999, http://articles.nydailynews.com/1999-10-12/news/18115437_1_spring-training-braves-team-national-league-championship-series.
McLemore, Henry. "Jimmy Wilson." *Sports Illustrated*, Feb. 1941, p. 149.
Nack, William. "The Razor's Edge." *Sports Illustrated*, May 6, 1991, pp. 55–58.
Newberry, Paul. "Galarraga: Take That." *Tallahassee Democrat*, 23 Apr. 2000.
Newman, Bruce. "Return of the Native." *Sports Illustrated*, 30 Dec. 1991, http://sportsillustrated.cnn.com/vault/article/magazine/MAG1140050/index.htm.
Orr, Jack. "Some Bad Boys Who Were Good for the Game." *Baseball Digest*, Jan. 1965, pp. 35–40.
Pedulla, Tom. "Valenzuela Rights Career: Lefthanders Firm Faith Still Reaps Rewards." *USA Today*, 5 Sep. 1996, http://pqasb.pqarchiver.com/USAToday/main ... le-002%261D%3dUSAT%26FMT%3dFT%26FMTS%3dFT.
Puma, Mike. "Saving the Best for Last." ESPN Classic, http://wwww.espn.go.com/classic/biography/s/Eckersley_Dennis.html.
Salinger, H.G. "John Picus Quinn, the Perennial Spitballer." Hall of Fame file fragment, from "The Umpire," *Detroit News*, April 21, 1937, p. 25.
Sanchez, Jesse. "Andres Galarraga: The Big Cat." MLB.com, 6 Mar. 2005, http://www.serendipityrancher.com/bb-galarraga.htm.
Shalit, Gene. "Hiller's Heart." *Sport*, Sep. 1973, pp. 10–12.
Stewart, Bob. "The Comebacks—Robin Roberts and Stan Musial." In *Baseball's Greatest Players Today*, by Jack Orr. New York: Watts, 1963, p. 144.
Stockton, Roy. "The Cardinals' Forgotten Man." *St. Louis Post Dispatch*, 1935, p. 346.
Thomas, Robert McG., Jr. "Van Lingle Mungo, 73, Dies; Colorful Pitcher for Dodgers." *The New York Times*, 14 Feb. 1985.
Vass, George. "Seven Comeback Candidates for 1975." *Baseball Digest*, Jan. 1975, p. 42.
Weaver, Maurice. "Pain and Glory." *Ebony*, Aug. 1993
Wendel, Tim. "An Ill-Fated Night." *USA Today Baseball Weekly*, 13–19 Aug. 1997, pp. 8–11.

Newspapers and Periodicals, Staff Articles

HOF file press release document, 24 Feb. 1929
"Maglie, Ex-Nemesis of Dodgers, Bought by Brooks from Indians." *The New York Times*, 16 May 1956, p. 4.
"The Oldest Veteran in the Major Leagues." *Baseball Magazine*, Sep. 1930, http://www.stevesteinberg.net/baseball_history/baseball_personalities/JohnPicusQuinn_OldestVeteran.asp.
The Sporting News. numerous articles.
"Steve Howe Had Drugs in His System When He Died." Yahoo! Sports, 28 June 2006, http://sports.yahoo.com/mlb/news?slug=howetoxicology.
"Van Lingle Mungo, Pitcher in '30s-'40s." *Philadelphia Inquirer*, 14 Feb. 1985, p. 3-C.
"Waitkus, Who Beat Death Rap, Comeback King." *Ellensberg Daily Record*, 10 Nov. 1950, p. 3.

Other Media

The Lost Son of Havana. 5-Hole Productions, Hock Films, NY, 2009.
The Stratton Story. film production by Metro-Goldwyn-Mayer, 1949.
"Van Lingle Mungo." Song, by David Frishberg, published 1970.
The Winning Team. film production by Warner Bros., 1952.
You Don't Know Bo. ESPN special, aired 8 Dec. 2012.

SABR Biography Project

Armour, Mark. "Willie McCovey." SABR Baseball Biography Project, http://sabr.org/bioproj/person/2a692514.
Berger, Ralph. "Hank Greenberg." SABR Baseball Biography Project. http://sabr.org/bioproj/person/64198864.
Faber, Charles F. "Jack Quinn." SABR Baseball Biography Project, http://sabr.org/bioproj/person/cf88d73c.
Mantegani, Barb. "Tony Cuccinello." SABR Baseball Biography Project, http://sabr.org/bioproj/person/be5d770b.
Nowlin, Bill. "Fred Mitchell." SABR Baseball Biography Project, http://sabr.org/bioproj/person/67676a31.
Stevens, Brian. "Babe Adams." SABR Baseball Biography Project, http://sabr.org/bioproj/person/617bd0ad.
Wancho, Joe. "Dennis Eckersley." SABR Baseball Biography Project, http://sabr.org/bioproj/person/98aaf620.

Websites

Baseball-Reference.com, http://www.baseball-reference.com/bullpen/[Player].

"Darryl Strawberry Chronology." CBS SportsLine, 2 Mar. 2000, wysiwyg://75/http://cbs.sportsline ... ll/bol/news/mar00/straw030200.html.

"Fernando Valenzuela Pitching in Mexico." Vin Scully Is My Homeboy, http://www.vinscullyismyhomeboy.com/2011/03/fernando-valenzuela-pitching-in-mexico.html.

"A Sad Chapter for Strawberry." *Los Angeles Times*, 5 Feb. 1990, http://articles.latimes.com/1990-02-05/sports/sp-185_1_strawberry.-home.

"Total Baseball." *Associated Press*, 10 Dec. 1999, http:www.totalbaseball.com/team/news/991209.991209.0467.html.

"Valenzuela, Son to Play Together in Mexican Pacific League." CBS SportsLine.com, 17 Oct. 2006, http://www.cbssports.com/mlb/story/9735881/valenzuela-son-to-play-together-in-mexican-pacific-league.

Statistical References

Baseball Almanac. http://www.baseball-almanac.com/.

The Baseball Encyclopedia, 10th ed. New York: Macmillan, 1996.

Baseball-Reference.com. http://www.baseball-reference.com/.

Carter, Craig. *Daguerreotypes 8th Edition*. St. Louis: Sporting News, 1990.

Deane, Bill. *Award Voting*. Cleveland: SABR, 1988.

Minor League Baseball Stars, Vol. 2. Cleveland: SABR, 1985.

Minor League Baseball Stars, Vol. 3. Cleveland: SABR, 1992.

The Minor League Register. Durham, NC: Baseball America, 1994.

Obojski, Robert. *Bush League*. New York: Macmillan, 1975.

Roberts, Brendan. *2000 Official Major League Fact Book*. St. Louis: Sporting News, 2000.

Solomon, Burt. *The Baseball Timeline*. New York: DK, 2001.

Spatz, Lyle. *The SABR Baseball List and Record Book*. New York: Scribner, 2007.

The Sporting News Baseball Register. St. Louis: Sporting News, annual.

Thorn, John, Pete Palmer, Michael Gershman, and David Pietrusza. *Total Baseball*. New York: Total Sports, 1999.

Who's Who in Baseball. New York: *Who's Who in Baseball* Magazine, annual.

Index

Aaron, Hank 14, 45, 52, 67, 68, 92, 97–99, 137
Adams, Babe: profile 139–145; record 145
Adams, Sparky 80
Agee, Tommie 5, 99, 221
Aguilera, Rick 175
Alexander, Aimee 54
Alexander, Dale 124
Alexander, Grover Cleveland 22, 60, 61, 122; profile 54–58; record 58–59
Allen, Dick 5, 98
Allyson, June 21
Alou, Felipe 36, 98
Alou, Matty 98, 100
Alston, Walt 157
Altman, George 52
Altrock, Nick 196
Anson, Cap 197
Appling, Luke 210
Arroyo, Luis 135
Ashburn, Richie 48, 137
Averill, Earl 216
Avila, Bobby 192

Backman, Wally 175
Bailey, Bob 6
Baker, Bill 162, 163
Baker, Del 11
Baker, Dusty 34
Baker, Home Run 3
Banks, Ernie 68
Barber, Steve 136
Barojas, Salome 192
Barrow, Ed 204
Bartell, Dick 208
Baseball Joe 199
Bauer, Hank 200
Bavasi, Buzzie 157
Baylor, Don 37
Bearden, Gene 168
Beazley, Johnny 10
Beck, Boom Boom 208
Belushi, John 122
Bench, Johnny 203
Berra, Yogi 6, 134, 203

Bigbee, Carson 144
Bird, Larry 209
Black, Joe 137
Blair, Paul 74
Blanchard, Johnny 134
Blasingame, Don 92
Blyleven, Bert 130
Bonds, Barry 14, 37, 180
Borowy, Hank 70
Boswell, Thomas 26
Bosworth, Brian 26
Bottomley, Jim 80, 148
Boudreau, Lou 168
Bouton, Jim 135
Boyer, Clete 99, 134
Branca, Ralph 87, 88
Breeden, Hal 6
Bresnahan, Roger 16, 204
Brett, George 27, 28, 34
Bridges, Tommy 163
Briggs, Walter 13
Brock, Lou 52
Broeg, Bob 50
Broglio, Ernie 52
Brown, Chris 103
Brown, Jim 27
Brown, Mordecai, "Three Finger" 144
Brown, Tommy 213
Brumley, Mike 86
Bruton, Bill 137
Bucher, Jimmy 215
Buckner, Billy 86
Buhl, Bob 157
Buhner, Jay 178
Bunning, Jim 132
Burgess, Smoky 201
Burkett, Jesse 16
Burnes, Bob 50
Busch, Gussie 48, 49, 52, 92
Bush, Joe 110
Butler, Brett 34
Butler, Johnny 62
Buzhardt, Johnny 134

Caldwell, Mike 68
Camitz, Howie 141

Campanella, Roy 137, 156
Campbell, Bill 116
Campbell, Jim 115
Canseco, Jose 26, 30, 87
Carey, Max 144
Carpenter, Chris 8
Carter, Gary 175
Carty, Rico 95; profile 97–102; record 102
Case, George 210
Casey, Ben 28
Cash, Norm 2
Cashman, Brian 152
Cater, Danny 131
Cepeda, Orlando 49, 66–68
Chadwick, Lester 199
Chalmers Award 60, 63
Chance, Dean 130
Chance, Frank 60
Chandler, Happy 125
Chandler, Spud 124
Chapman, Ben 41, 198
Chapman, Ray 19
Chase, Hal 206
Church, Bubba 137
Clarke, Fred 141–144
Clemens, Roger 160
Clemente, Roberto 97, 98
Clemente Award 33
Cobb, Ty 52, 139, 141, 142
Cochrane, Mickey 74
Colavito, Rocky 5
Colbert, Nate 68
Collins, Ripper 80
Colon, Bartolo 152
Combs, Earle 56
Comeback Player of the Year Award 2, 30, 33, 36, 37, 40, 51, 52, 66, 72, 77, 99, 101, 116, 131, 158, 166
Comiskey, Charles 110
Cone, David 152, 177, 178
Conigliaro, Billy 75
Conigliaro, Tony 98; profile 74–78; record 78
Conigliaro, Vinnie 74
Cottier, Chuck 94

Index

Covington, Wes 137
Cox, Ted 85
Craft, Harry 163
Craig, Roger 105, 157
Cramer, Roger 41
Crandall, Del 98
Crawford, Sam 141
Critz, Hughie 148
Cronin, Joe 171
Crowe, George 49
Cuccinello, Tony 213; profile 208–211; record 211–212
Culp, Ray 130
Cunningham, Joe 49–51

Dahlgren, Babe 123, 124
Damon, Johnny 153
Daniel, Dan 209
Danning, Harry 162
Dark, Alvin 67, 92, 129, 130, 132
Darling, Ron 175
Davis, Eric: profile 30–34; record 34–35
Davis, Mark 103
Davis, Mike 87
Davis, Stinky 124
Davis, Tommy 51
Davis, Willie 6
Day, Doris 54
Dean, Dizzy 80, 129, 160, 166, 171, 214–216
DeLancey, Bill 91
Dent, Bucky 85
Derringer, Paul 163, 164
Devine, Bing 50
Diaz, Bo 85
Dickey, Bill 10, 171
Dickshot, Johnny 209, 210
DiMaggio, Joe 10, 14, 37, 42, 99, 125, 126, 166, 167, 199, 200
Doby, Larry 167
Donald, Atley 124
Dravecky, Dave: profile 103–106; record 106–107
Dravecky, Janice 104
Dressen, Charlie 94, 155
Drew, J.D. 34
Drysdale, Don 132, 157
Dubiel, Monk 70
Duffy, Hugh 204
Duncan, Dave 89
Durocher, Leo 80, 81, 146–148, 155, 214, 216, 217
Dykes, Jimmy 21, 209
Dykstra, Lenny 175

Eckersley, Dennis: profile 84–89; record 90
Eckersley, Nancy 86
Eckersley, Wally 86, 88
Edmonds, Jim 28
Edwards, Vince 28
Ellsworth, Dick 130
English, Woody 146, 147

Ennis, Del 70, 71, 137
Erskine, Carl 157
Estrada, Chuck 136
Etten, Nick 123, 125
Evers, Johnny 60

Face, Roy 116
Fain, Ferris 126
Farrell, Frank 206
Feldman, Harry 158
Feller, Bob 10, 156, 166, 210
Fernandez, Sid 175
Fernandez, Tony 195
Fingers, Rollie 89
Finley, Charlie 170
Finn, Huck 91
Fisher, Jack 45, 136
Fisk, Carlton 197
Flood, Curt 50
Ford, Whitey 19, 134, 135, 158, 160, 100, 000
Fournier, Jacques 62
Foxx, Jimmie 14, 41, 45, 125, 171, 198, 213
Franco, Julio 112; profile 194–197; record 197
Freehan, Bill 116
Freese, Gene 49
Frey, Lonny 163
Fridley, Jim 72
Frisch, Frank 80–82
Furillo, Carl 50, 95, 156, 157

Galarraga, Andres 99, 105; profile 36–39; record 39
Gamble, Oscar 100, 101
Gammons, Peter 131
Garber, Gene 116
Garcia, Mike 156
Gardella, Danny 158, 159
Garr, Ralph 100
Garver, Ned 169
Gehrig, Lou 10, 14, 41, 56, 57, 68, 123–126, 148
Gehringer, Charlie 148, 163
Gelbert, Charley 63; profile 79–83; record 83
Gelbert, Jerry 79
Gibson, Bob 76
Gibson, Kirk 87, 88, 180
Gilliam, Jim 95, 137
Gold Glove Award 34, 36, 98, 192
Golenbock, Peter 49, 155
Gomez, Lefty 171
Gomez, Ruben 137
Gooden, Dwight: profile 173–181; record 181–182
Gordon, Joe 42, 123–125
Gossage, Goose 89
Gowdy, Hank 206
Graney, Jack 18
Gray, Dolly 142
Gray, Pete 213

Green, Dallas 134
Greenberg, Hank 42, 125, 157, 163; profile 10–14; record 14–15
Grey, Zane 109
Griffey, Ken, Jr. 178
Griffin, Merv 77
Grimes, Burleigh 62, 112, 215, 216
Grimm, Charlie 22, 147
Groat, Dick 52
Grove, Lefty 19, 160
Guerrero, Vladimir 38, 96
Gutman, Dan 118
Gwynn, Tony 39

Hack, Stan 48, 147
Haines, Jesse 56, 57
Hamilton, Jack 74–76
Hamner, Granny 137, 198
Haney, Fred 200
Hanssen, Arlen 29
Harrelson, Ken 2, 76
Harris, Bucky 123, 126
Harshman, Jack 198
Hart, Jim Ray 98
Hassett, Buddy 123
Hayes, Von 194
Helton, Todd 139
Hemus, Solly 48–50
Henderson, Dave 88
Henderson, Rickey 30, 87
Henrich, Tommy 123–126, 199, 200
Herman, Babe 62, 201, 208, 214
Herman, Billy 146, 171
Hernandez, Aranado 150
Hernandez, Keith 174
Hernandez, Livan 150–152, 154
Hernandez, Orlando: profile 150–154; record 154
Hershberger, Willard 161, 162
Herzog, Whitey 36
Heydler, John 142, 144
Higuera, Teddy 189, 191, 192
Hill, Ken 36
Hiller, John: profile 114–117; record 117
Hirshberg, Al 91
Hitler, Adolf 32, 216
Hobbs, Roy 70, 73
Hockett, Oris 209, 210
Hodges, Gil 36, 50, 156
Hodgin, Ralph 209
Hoffman, Trevor 89
Hollocher, Charlie 61
Hornsby, Rogers 14, 56, 57, 80, 92, 146, 147, 169
Horton, Willie 101
Hostetler, Chuck 213
Houk, Ralph 134
Howard, Elston 134
Howard, Frank 45
Howe, Steve: profile 118–122; record 122

Index

Howell, Jay 87
Hoyt, Waite 147
Hubbell, Carl 148, 192
Hudson, Tim 8
Hughes, Chuck 115
Hunter, Jim, "Catfish" 132
Hutchinson, Fred 48
Hutchinson Memorial Award 33
Hyland, Robert 80

Irvin, Monte 137
Isringhausen, Jason 9
Ivie, Mike 68

Jackson, Bo: profile 25–29; record 29
Jackson, "Shoeless Joe" 121
James, Bill 206
Jansen, Kenley 204
Jansen, Larry 159
Javier, Julian 50
Jeffcoat, Hal 198
Jennings, Hughie 196
Jeter, Derek 139
Jethroe, Sam 137
Jimenez, Houston 192
Jimenez, Jose 34
Jobe, Frank 5, 6, 7
John, Sally 6, 7
John, Tommy 144; profile 5–9; record 9
Johnson, Alex 2, 99, 100
Johnson, Ban 10
Johnson, Billy 125
Johnson, Darrell 75, 128, 130, 136
Johnson, Davey 174
Johnson, Howard 175
Johnson, Randy 196
Johnson, Walter 17, 19, 128, 144
Jones, Andruw 38
Jones, Sad Sam 110
Jones, Sam, "Toothpick" 49
Jones, Willie 137
Joss, Addie 19, 144
Joyner, Wally 38
Jurges, Billy 41, 146, 147, 209

Kasko, Eddie 130, 131
Keane, Cliff 131
Keane, Johnny 51
Keeler, Wee Willie 91
Keller, Charlie, "King Kong" 124–126, 200
Kelley, Joe 204
Kelly, Joe 206
Kendall, Fred 85
Keough, Matt 2
Kerr, Dickey 47, 110
Key, Jimmy 177
Kilkenny, Mike 115
Killefer, Bill 61, 62
Kiner, Ralph 13, 48

Kingman, Dave 68, 180
Kittle, Ron 194
Klein, Lou 92
Klesko, Ryan 38
Knight, Ray 32, 175
Koenig, Mark: profile 146–149; record 149
Konstanty, Jim 135, 137
Koufax, Sandy 157, 160
Kroc, Ray 68
Kubek, Tony 134
Kuenn, Harvey 66, 67
Kuhn, Bowie 119
Kurowski, Whitey 92

Lane, Frank 92
Lanier, Max 158
Lardner, Ring 91
LaRoche, Adam 196
Larsen, Don 158
LaRussa, Tony 84, 87–89
Lasorda, Tommy 118, 190
Latham, Arlie 196
Lazzeri, Tony 54, 56, 57, 148
Lee, Thornton 209
Leever, Sam 141
Lefferts, Craig 103
Leifield, Lefty 141, 142
Lemon, Bob 156, 198
Leonard, Dutch 70
Levy, Ed 123
Lewis, Allen 43
Lewis, Buddy 11
Lieb, Fred 58, 207
Lindell, Johnny 123, 125, 126, 203; profile 198–201; record 202
Lisenbee, Hod 213
Loes, Billy 157
Lolich, Mickey 114, 115
Lollar, Sherm 211
Lombardi, Ernie 161–163, 171, 208
Lonborg, Jim 75
London, Julie 170
Long, Howie 26
Lopata, Stan 137, 201
Lopez, Al 170, 208, 211
Lowrey, Peanuts 72
Lurie, Bob 66
Lyle, Sparky 131
Lynn, Fred 77
Lyons, Ted 10

Mack, Connie 11, 126, 204
MacPhail, Larry 214, 217
MacPhail, Lee 135
Maddox, Nick 141, 142
Maglie, Sal: profile 155–160; record 160
Mahaffey, Art 134
Malamud, Bernard 70
Manning, Rick 85
Mantilla, Felix 94

Mantle, Mickey 134, 167, 173, 175, 180
Maranville, Rabbit 56, 80; profile 60–64; record 64
Marichal, Juan 68, 185, 186
Marion, Marty 92, 169
Maris, Roger 41, 134
Marquard, Rube 139, 142
Martin, Billy 116
Martin, Pepper 80–82, 213
Martinez, Dennis 192; profile 183–186; record 186–187
Martinez, Edgar 178
Martinez, Edmundo 184
Mathews, Eddie 68, 92, 93
Mathewson, Christy 17, 57, 58, 93, 141, 144, 160
Mauer, Joe 203
Maye, Lee 98
Mays, Willie 14, 34, 48, 66, 68, 97, 137
McCarthy, Joe 54, 56, 199, 200
McCosky, Barney 163
McCovey, Willie: profile 65–69; record 69
McCoy, Benny 156
McDowell, Roger 175
McDowell, Sam 129
McGraw, John 10, 155, 206
McGuire, Deacon 8
McGwire, Mark 87
McKechnie, Bill 57, 58, 143, 144, 162–164
McLain, Denny 114, 129
McQuinn, George 135; profile 123–127; record 127
Meany, Tom 43
Medwick, Joe 74, 80, 171
Meyer, Russ 72, 137
Michaels, Cass 74, 209
Miller, Big Ed 18
Miller, Bob 137
Miller, Dick 177
Minoso, Minnie 51, 196
Mitchell, Clarence 111
Mitchell, Fred: profile 203–207; record 207
Mitchell, Kevin 103, 105, 175
Mitchum, Robert 170
Mize, Johnny 10, 48, 70, 135
Moore, Donnie 88
Morgan, Joe 211
Morris, Matt 8
Moses, Wally 200, 209, 210
Most Valuable Player Award (MVP) 10, 11, 14, 42, 43, 47, 48, 51, 60, 63, 65, 67, 87, 88, 92, 98, 100, 111, 116, 125, 126, 137, 138, 152, 158, 159, 162, 169, 180, 195, 198
Moyer, Jamie 8, 112, 192, 196
Mueller, Bill 210
Mulcahy, Hugh 11, 12
Mullin, George 141

Mungo, Ernest 218
Mungo, Van Lingle 208; profile 213–218; record 218–219
Murphy, Danny 198
Murray, Eddie 34
Musial, Stan 14, 68, 92, 181, 200, profile 47–53; record 53
Myers, Billy 82

Nagel, Bill 209
Nash, Bruce 211
National League Top Player Award 163
Nettles, Graig 130
Neun, Johnny 124
Newcombe, Don 137, 157, 158, 166
Newsom, Bobo 135, 163, 164
Nichols, Kid 3
Niekro, Phil 169, 171
Nieman, Bob 49
Norris, Mike 120
Nuxhall, Joe 213

O'Brien, Eddie 198
O'Brien, Johnny 198
O'Connell, Dick 77
O'Doul, Lefty 16, 208
Ojeda, Bobby 175, 190
O'Leary, Charley 196
Oliva, Tony 98, 99
Olmo, Luis 58
O'Malley, Peter 188
O'Malley, Walter 7
O'Neill, Steve 201
Onslow, Eddie 18
Orosco, Jesse 75
O'Rourke, Jimmy 196
Orsatti, Ernie 62
Ott, Mel 41, 68, 78, 171, 218
Overmire, Stubby 169
Owen, Mickey 158

Paige, Satchel: profile 166–171; record 171–172
Palacios, Vincente 192
Palmer, Jim 77, 136
Pappas, Milt 136
Parker, Dave 32
Pascual, Camilo 41
Paxton, Mike 85
Pena, Carlos 3
Perkins, Cy 135
Perranoski, Ron 122
Peters, Gary 130
Pettitte, Andy 152, 177
Petty, Jess 62
Phillippe, Deacon 141
Phillips, Jack 125
Plank, Eddie 204
Podes, Johnny 157
Posey, Buster 2, 3, 203
Powell, Boog 101
Priddy, Gerry 123
Pujols, Albert 13, 14

Queen, Mel, Jr. 198
Quinn, Jack 196, 197, 208; profile 108–112; record 112–113
Quisenberry, Dan 87

Radcliffe, Ted, "Double Duty" 167, 204
Raines, Tim 34, 105
Ramos, Pedro 75
Reagan, Ronald 21, 54
Redford, Robert 70
Reese, Pee Wee 10, 157, 214
Reiser, Pete 34
Reitz, Ken 120
Rice, Jim 77
Rice, Sam 16
Richardson, Bobby 67, 134
Rickey, Branch 54, 56, 62, 81, 91
Righetti, Dave 87
Rigney, Bill 66, 76
Ripken, Cal, Jr. 139, 195
Rivera, Mariano 89, 139
Rizzuto, Phil 10, 11, 125
Roach, Mel 94
Roberts, Robin 66; profile 134–138; record 138
Robinson, Frank 51, 84, 99, 100
Robinson, Jackie 137, 155, 167, 183
Robinson, Wilbert 62, 111, 155, 208
Rodgers, Kenny 8
Rodriguez, Alex 14, 178
Rogell, Billy 147
Romano, John 5
Rookie of the Year Award 3, 26, 65, 66, 70, 118, 156, 166–168, 171, 173, 174, 189, 194
Root, Charlie 148
Rose, Pete 105
Roseboro, John 68
Roth, Bobby, "Braggo" 18
Rowe, Schoolboy 163
Rudolph, Dick 206
Ruess, Jerry 188
Ruffing, Red 10, 19
Runnels, Pete 41, 44
Russell, Reb 189
Ruth, Babe 14, 16, 18, 19, 41, 45, 56, 57, 63, 77, 148, 166, 167
Ryan, Nolan 8
Ryba, Mike 204

Sadecki, Ray 67
Sain, Johnny 135
Sandberg, Ryne 3, 30
Sandlock, Mike 200, 201
Sauer, Hank 138
Schalk, Roy 209, 213
Schang, Wally 112
Scheib, Carl 213
Schoendienst, Red 99; profile 91–95; record 95–96
Schott, Marge 31, 32

Sconiers, Daryl 120
Score, Herb 156
Scott, Everett 110
Scott, Michael D. 108
Scott, Mike 189
Seaver, Tom 174
Seminick, Andy 71, 72, 137
Shantz, Bobby 135
Sheffield, Gary 2
Sheldon, Rollie 134
Shepard, Bert 22, 23, 213
Short, Chris 134
Silver Slugger Award 36, 37, 39, 195
Simmons, Al 213
Simmons, Curt 137
Sipek, Dick 213
Sisler, Dick 72, 137
Sisler, George 16, 72
Skowron, Bill, "Moose" 134
Slade, Gordon 80
Slaughter, Enos 10, 135
Smith, Bob 198
Smith, Frank 110
Smith, Ozzie 693
Smoltz, John 8, 89
Snider, Duke 50
Snow, J.T. 38
Souchock, Bud 123, 125
Spahn, Warren 50, 92
Speaker, Tris 18, 19
Spikes, Charlie 101
Stafford, Bill 134
Stalin, Joseph 216
Stallings, George 60, 62, 206
Stanky, Eddie 211
Steinbrenner, George 120, 121, 177
Steinhagen, Ruth Ann 71, 73
Stengel, Casey 200, 201, 209, 215
Stewart, Dave 87
Stewart, Jimmy 21
Stirnweiss, George, "Snuffy" 14, 210
Strasburg, Stephen 8
Stratton, Ethel 21, 22
Stratton, Monty 54; profile 21–23; record 24–25
Strawberry, Charisse Simmons 176
Strawberry, Darryl 31, 32, 34, 121; profile 173–181; record 180–181
Strawberry, Lisa 175, 176
Strawberry, Terry 180
Suggs, George 110
Summers, Ed 141
Sweeney, Jeff 206

Tabor, Jim 82
Terry, Bill 155, 209, 216
Terry, Ralph 134
Thevenow, Tommy 62
Thomas, Derrell 120
Thompson, Hank 137

Thompson, Sam 14
Thomson, Bobby 67, 88, 159
Tiant, Luis 85; profile 128–132; record 133
Tiant, Luis, Sr. 132
Tinker, Joe 60, 206
Torgeson, Earl 72
Torre, Joe 98, 99, 153, 203
Trammell, Alan 195
Travis, Cecil 10, 11, 42
Tresh, Mike 209
Trillo, Manny 194
Trout, Dizzy 43
Tunis, John R. 155, 161
Tyler, Lefty 206

Ueberroth, Peter 120
Uecker, Bob 98

Valentine, Bobby 195
Valentine, Ellis 74
Valenzuela, Fernando, Jr. 192
Valenzuela, Fernando, Sr.: profile 188–192; record 192–193
Valli, Violet 146
Vance, Dazzy 62, 208, 215
Van Doren, Mamie 77
Veeck, Bill, Jr. 167–170
Veeck, Bill, Sr. 62
Verban, Emil 92
Vernon, Mickey 126
Vine, Lady 217
Vosmik, Joe 41

Waddell, Rube 93, 204
Wagner, Billy 8
Wagner, Honus 141, 142
Wagner, Leon 49, 50
Waitkus, Eddie 2, 137, 146; profile 70–73; record 73
Waitkus, Edward, "Ted" 73
Wakefield, Dick 42, 200
Walberg, Rube 196
Wallace, Bobby 116
Walsh, Ed 19, 144
Walters, Bucky 163, 198
Wambsganss, Bill 18
Warwick, Dionne 77
Weiss, George 124
Welch, Bob 87
Wells, David 8, 152
West, Dick 162, 163
Westcott, Rich 211
Wetteland, John 121
White, Bill 49
Wilhelm, Hoyt 89, 136, 171
Wilhelm, Kaiser 110
Willett, Ed 141
Williams, Cy 97
Williams, Davy 156
Williams, Dick 75
Williams, Ted 10, 14, 48, 50, 68, 73, 97, 126, 181, 213; profile 40–45; record 46
Willis, Vic 141, 142
Wilson, C.J. 8
Wilson, Hack 208

Wilson, Jimmie: profile 161–164; record 164–165
Wilson, Robert 164
Winfield, Dave 34
Winsett, Tom 215
Wise, Rick 85
Wolfe, Thomas 65
Wolgast, Al 81
Wood, Joe, "Smoky Joe" 223; profile 16–19; record 20
Wood, Kerry 8
Woodling, Gene 200
Wren, Frank 195
Wright, Glenn 61
Wynn, Early 50, 156

Yastrzemski, Carl 75, 76, 132, 139, 170
Yawkey, Tom 40
York, Rudy 11, 13, 126, 163
Yost, Eddie 41
Young, Cy 19, 85, 204
Young, Dick 157
Young Award 8, 16, 87–89, 103, 116, 129, 130, 131, 138, 158, 175, 185, 188, 189, 192
Yount, Robin 139

Zullo, Allan 211

www.ingramcontent.com/pod-product-compliance
Lightning Source LLC
Chambersburg PA
CBHW060259240426
43661CB00060B/2839